Connecting Microsoft® Exchange Server

Connecting Microsoft® Exchange Server

Kieran McCorry

Digital Press

Boston • Oxford • Auckland • Johannesburg • Melbourne • New Delhi

Digital Press™ is an imprint of Butterworth–Heinemann

Library of Congress Cataloging-in-Publication Data

McCorry, Kieran, 1968–
     Connecting Microsoft Exchange Server / Kieran McCorry
        p.   cm.
     Includes index.
     ISBN 1-55558-204-4 (alk. paper)
        1. Microsoft Exchange server.   2. Client/server computing.
     I. Title.
     QA76.9.C55M46 1999
     005.7 '13769—dc21   99-35808
                                                                              CIP

British Library Cataloguing-in-Publication Data
A catalogue record for this book is available from the British Library.

The publisher offers special discounts on bulk orders of this book.
For information, please contact:

     Manager of Special Sales
     Butterworth–Heinemann
     225 Wildwood Avenue
     Woburn, MA 01801–2041
     Tel: 781-904-2500
     Fax: 781-904-2620

For information on all Digital Press publications available, contact our World Wide Web home page at: http://www.bh.com/digitalpress

10 9 8 7 6 5 4 3 2 1

Designed and composed by ReadyText, Bath, UK
Printed in the United States of America

Dedication

This book is dedicated to the memory of my dad, Brendan. While he saw me start to write this book, it is with my deepest regret that he never saw me complete it.

Contents

List of Figures

Chapter 1

Chapter 2

Chapter 3

Chapter 4

Chapter 5

Chapter 6

Chapter 7

Chapter 8

Chapter 9

Foreword

Electronic mail has existed for over twenty years and has become as ubiquitous as electricity in today's world. People all over the planet use electronic mail for virtually every aspect of their lives. They expect their mail to work simply and reliably, and do not want to be bothered with the details of the transmission process in either case. They need fast, reliable, and accurate delivery of services.

It seems that every week we are given amazing statistics about the growth of all things Internet. Some of these statistics are probably even close to being accurate. Sadly, it seems that most people use statistics in the same way a drunk uses a lamppost—support rather than illumination. Worse yet, the IT industry is populated by "experts" who are paid to develop statistics that reflect the expectations of their clientele rather than providing a fuller truth. The full truth about electronic mail is that it continues to grow and become more widely used.

There is no doubt that humanity is more connected electronically every day. Electronic mail may not have the panache and hype given to the World Wide Web, but it provides a mission-critical utility for business. If you doubt this assertion, then try shutting down access for a few hours.

This book is based on the hard knowledge gained in the real world that requires that disparate mail systems be connected smoothly and reliably. Electronic mail is all about connecting people to other people. This is grand and wonderful as long as the people communicating are connected to the same system. In the real world, people have the need to communicate with other people who have the gall to be using a different mail system.

Microsoft Exchange Server is arguably the best enterprise oriented electronic mail system on the market today. It is fast, efficient, easy to manage, and largely based on industry standards today. Depending upon whom you believe, Exchange is being deployed faster than any other mail system. Basing your enterprise electronic mail system on Microsoft Exchange is a safe decision today. It is a very rare enterprise that does not have business requirements for connecting multiple electronic mail systems together. Virtually no enterprise today could consider going without a connection to the Internet.

This book provides the practical information necessary to successfully integrate Exchange Server with the other mail systems. The decisions in setting up any system involve making trade-offs, often comparing apples against oranges. With this invaluable book, designers and implementers can make the best decisions for their enterprise. The information contained herein provides insights into the factors and approaches involved in connecting Exchange Server to external systems.

The most vital factors in your enterprise are its business goals and the way the people in it use the systems. This may add another dimension of complexity in your decision process, but it is a dimension that is vital to your success.

Don Vickers
Compaq Computer Corporation

Preface

The Shorter Oxford English Dictionary Volume I contains the following definition:

> **Integrate**, *v.* 1638. [*-integrat-*, pa. ppl. Stem of L. *integrare*, f. *integer*; see INTEGER, -ATE³.]
>
> **1.** *trans.* To render entire or complete; to make up (a whole); said of the parts or elements. ?*Obs.***b.** To complete (what is imperfect) by the addition of the necessary parts 1675. **2.** To combine (parts or elements) into a whole 1802.

So too is the challenge for the messaging integrator to make complete that which is partial and to bring together that which is disjointed. In sizable organizations it's rare to find just one messaging system. And for those organizations that have set out on the road to messaging Nirvana, with their sights set firmly on a single homogeneous view of the messaging world, there are many hurdles before such perfection can be achieved.

What Is This Book About?

I often think back to the first time, many years ago, that I experienced the thrill that's associated with connecting different messaging systems together and seeing a message transferred from one system to another. The environment was set up for a customer demonstration and there were several systems networked together using X.400 as the backbone technology. I'll scarcely forget my excitement at the first time I actually heard a message (well, heard the disks rattling!) as it struggled from one system, then on to another, then another, and so on, until eventually it ended up where it should have been. Every link in the chain was a different messaging system, yet it hardly mattered as the message hopped from one box to the next.

But messaging integration is also about insulating the user, irrespective of their own messaging platform, from all of the bumps in the road as a message leaves one system and travels to another. As a message is sent, the sender shouldn't know that it's going to another messaging system, and when it is received, there should be no clue to the recipient that it's come from somewhere else. All of the journeying, conversions, and translations that the message may have experienced should be transparent to both sender and recipient alike.

There is little doubt that Microsoft Exchange is one of the top-selling messaging solutions in the marketplace today, and more and more companies are striving to implement their complete messaging environments around Exchange. But this book isn't just about Exchange. Exchange is one of many messaging technologies, and as long as other messaging systems exist so to will the need for messaging integration.

Intended Audience

If you flip through this book expecting to see page after page of technical detail about Microsoft Exchange Server, then you may be in for a shock. Exchange takes a high profile in this book, in relation to its unquestionable popularity, but many other pages are dedicated to discussion of other messaging systems. My experience of the messaging world has been forged on very many different messaging technologies, of which Exchange is but one, and I've attempted to share some of that knowledge in the following chapters.

In writing this book, I haven't explored every aspect of Exchange connectivity. Many other books admirably describe Exchange connectivity to Microsoft Mail, cc:Mail, Lotus Notes, etc., but this book focuses on Exchange connectivity to industrial strength backbones. It has been crafted from many experiences in customer environments where the real challenge has been to completely integrate Exchange into heterogeneous messaging and directory backbones. And in doing so, I've tried to accurately convey the challenge from the consultant's perspective: outlining the options that are available and tips and techniques that work in the real world. Not all of this book may be relevant to you, but hopefully some parts of it will be invaluable.

If you've been working with Exchange and need to completely understand its full potential as a messaging integration platform then you'll find this book useful. Similarly, if you are soon to set out on an integration project which involves Exchange, then I hope that you'll appreciate the perspective that I've used to describe how best to move forward.

A Note on Structure and Naming

This book was written over many months during a period when Digital Equipment Corporation became Compaq Computer Corporation. As such, many of the illustrations and examples in this text are mixed between the two company names.

> If you've any comments or questions on the material in this book, I'd be happy to hear from you. You can contact me at:
>
> Kieran.McCorry@compaq.com

Acknowledgments

Writing is an intensive, time-consuming, yet immensely satisfying pastime. I've thoroughly enjoyed setting down many of my thoughts on the pages that follow, yet none of this would have been possible without the selfless help and sacrifice of a great number of other people. In listing the names of individuals, one always runs the risk of omitting someone. If I have done so, please accept my apologies and know that in any event I am very grateful for your help.

During the many months that I took to write this book, I had lots of questions for many people. In this respect, I'd like to extend my sincere thanks to Jens Trier Rasmussen, Pierre Bijaoui, Derek Flint, Maria Balsamo, Geoff Robb, Barry Hughes, Emer Fitzpatrick, Jacqueline Dean, Michael McKenna, Ian Burgess, Ben Harvey Ellison, Philip Sloan, Ken Tweedie, Paul Herbert, Jane Cherry, Alison Groves, Stuart Hatto, William C. Minor, Roger White, and Glenn Schmid. All of them have helped or contributed in one way or another to the final form of this book. I'd also like to thank Chris Brownstone, Wook Lee, Stan Foster, and Warren Cooley; all from Compaq who answered a number of specific questions that I had on Compaq's own integrated messaging environment, and made sure to point me in the right direction on numerous technical matters. Special thanks are also deserved for Ned Freed, Jeff Allison, and Kristin Hubner from Innosoft; all of them answered the many questions I had about how best to use the wealth of features in PMDF.

Frank Clonan and Tommy Byrne are both worthy of a special mention. During my recent years in Compaq, I've been managed by Frank and Tommy, and both have encouraged and indulged me in writing this book as much as any employee could wish for.

Don Vickers, Don Livengood, Clarissa Carreon, Gary Adams, and Luis Galarza all deserve thanks for reviewing the manuscript and contributing to the book in a number of ways. My special thanks go to Don Vickers for so kindly writing the Foreword to this text.

I must also extend my particular thanks to Tony Redmond. Tony encouraged, although some might say harassed, me into writing this book and there's little doubt that without his help and endless guidance, it would not have been completed.

Before closing, I need to say how much I appreciate the efforts of the people at Digital Press, especially Liz McCarthy, Mike Cash, Pam Chester, and Phil Sutherland. All of them helped me enormously during the writing of the book, and their patience, understanding, and constructiveness as I struggled to complete the text was inspirational.

And finally, I must thank Michele, whose patience, strength, encouragement, love, and support has helped me from the day that I sat down to write the first page.

1

Servers, Sites, and Organizations

1.1   Introduction

Any implementation of Exchange must conform to a certain structure. Exchange employs the concepts of the Server, the Site, and ultimately the Organization to realize an order and a hierarchy. At its simplest level, an entire Exchange implementation for a company may consist of one Organization, one Site, and one Server. Or, at the other end of the spectrum, a company may implement numerous Organizations, Sites, and Servers. There are an infinite number of possibilities for how you might go about implementing Exchange.

In this chapter we'll look inside each of these concepts and outline how they are related. Not least, we'll discuss how best to use them in a real implementation.

1.2   The Exchange Server Model

The smallest main unit in the Exchange hierarchy is the *server*. It may be obvious, but any Exchange implementation must have at least one server. Exchange runs as a server application on a Windows NT Server computer, and you should note that it will not run on Windows NT Workstation. The server has a number of functions to perform: to act as a repository for user mailboxes, to hold public folders, or to act as a dedicated connection server to other services. The functions aren't mutually exclusive and there's nothing to stop you using a single server for all of these tasks. Alternatively, you might delegate the responsibility to dedicated servers, each performing only one of the functions listed above.

It's the Exchange Server software running on your Windows NT Server that provides mailboxes for users, allows sharing of information between different users, and allows e-mail users to communicate with each other. There are a number of core components in Exchange Server:

- The System Attendant;

- The Information Store;

- The Message Transfer Agent; and

- The Directory.

Each of these components run as Windows NT services. You can gain access to many of their properties and characteristics by using the Exchange Administrator program (see Figure 1–1). The Exchange Administrator utility is a Windows NT graphical user interface (GUI) that allows management of all aspects of Exchange Server. This includes the core components I've mentioned above, connectors, and user mailboxes.

FIGURE 1–1
View from the
Exchange
Administrator
Program

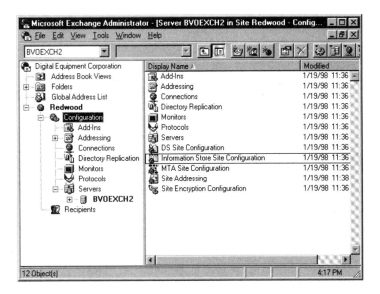

1.2.1   The System Attendant

Perhaps the most crucial of all of the Exchange components is the System Attendant (SA). Without it you won't be able to use your Exchange server for very much. The SA runs as a Windows NT service (like many of the other components) and its main function in life is to oversee the operation of

Exchange. The tasks to which it dedicates itself are listed in Table 1–1. Don't be alarmed by the many new terms that I've introduced here. We'll cover many of them in detail later in this book.

TABLE 1–1 System Attendant Tasks and Descriptions

TASK	DESCRIPTION
Information Gathering	SAs on all servers communicate with each other and share local information, such as what links or connectors are available on their respective servers.
Monitoring	The SA monitors connections between Exchange servers. This means that at any given time it can tell which servers are able to send messages to other servers. The servers may be located in one site or between sites. It also detects alerts generated from Server Monitor or Link Monitor.
Routing	Using data collected from its Information Gathering and Monitoring roles, the SA maintains a Routing Table that is shared amongst all other Exchange servers.
Address Management	When new mailboxes are created on the server, the SA generates e-mail addresses for them.
Tracking Log Maintenance	If Message Tracking has been enabled, then the SA will also maintain log files that contain information about sent messages.
Key Management	If Key Management is running in your Exchange implementation, then the SA manages communication with the Key Management Service.

The SA is crucial to the operation of most other Exchange services. Most of these services require that the SA be running before they can operate properly. If you shut down the SA service from the Windows NT Control Panel, then all of the other Exchange services are shutdown automatically as well.

1.2.2 The Information Store

The Information Store (IS) is actually two Information Stores: a Private Information Store and a Public Information Store. These locations essentially are large container files that exist on your Windows NT file system. (Actually they're database files not very dissimilar from Microsoft Access databases, but they are optimized for use by Exchange.) From the Windows

NT Explorer you can see them as PRIV.EDB and PUB.EDB respectively. They'll be located in the \EXCHSRVR\MDBDATA directory on one of your disk volumes.

The Private IS holds user mailboxes. It contains e-mail messages sent between users or any other documents, including Word documents, Lotus 1-2-3 spreadsheets, executable binaries, etc. These documents are held within folders in the mailbox. Mailboxes held in the Private IS are generally only available to the owner of the mailbox (typically a specific Windows NT account holder) or to another user with delegated mailbox access. (The dedicated mailbox situation is best described using the manager/secretary analogy, where managers give access to their mailboxes so that their secretaries can screen their messages or send mail on their behalf.) The bottom line here is that information in a mailbox in the Private IS is usually available to only one user.

The Public IS, on the other hand, serves a different purpose. Information in this store is meant for sharing. The Public IS logically contains a number of folders that are available to be shared (with appropriate access restrictions). Documents in each public folder can be shared between all users on a server, or indeed between mailboxes located on any Exchange server in your Exchange network.

Clearly the IS is fundamental to Exchange's operation. Given the importance of the information that it contains, it's not surprising that access to it is controlled. The IS Service regulates access to the databases, and it too is a Windows NT service.

The IS Service can accept messages from the Message Transfer Agent. Ultimately it's the last component to help a message on its way as it gets delivered into a recipient's mailbox.

Some of the IS Service's tasks are shown in Table 1–2.

TABLE 1–2   Information Store Service Tasks and Descriptions

TASK	DESCRIPTION
Deal with Local Messages	If a message is sent from one user to another and both user mailboxes are on the same Exchange server, then both mailboxes are in the same Private IS. In this case the IS Service merely moves pointers to messages from one part of the database to another.

continued ▸

TABLE 1–2 Information Store Service Tasks and Descriptions (continued)

TASK	DESCRIPTION
Deal with Remote Messages	If a message is sent to a user on another Exchange server, then the IS Service must hand the message off to another component (the MTA) that can get it to its destination. Similarly, when a message arrives from another server, the MTA will pass the Message to the IS Service, which will place it in the Private IS.
Deal with Clients	Any operation from an Exchange client, such as creating a new message, reading a message, or moving a document to an Exchange folder, is handled by the IS Service.

1.2.3 The Message Transfer Agent

The term *Message Transfer Agent* (MTA) is shared with many other e-mail systems, including Microsoft Mail, SMTP (Internet) mail, and X.400 mail. It is a common component, yet certainly an important one.

When a message is sent outside of the local Private IS, the MTA is responsible for ensuring its delivery. Maybe the message is to go to another Exchange server, or it may even have to leave the Exchange network entirely through a connector and be transferred to the Internet. In any event, the IS Service cannot communicate directly with other servers or connectors.

The MTA receives messages from the IS and can perform a number of functions. These are outlined in Table 1–3.

TABLE 1–3 Message Transfer Agent Tasks

TASK	DESCRIPTION
Message Transfer	If the recipient of the message is on another Exchange server, the MTA will accept the message from the IS Service and transfer it to the MTA on the destination server.
Message Delivery	When the destination MTA receives the message, it is responsible for handing it off to the IS Service.

continued ▸

TABLE 1–3   Message Transfer Agent Tasks (continued)

TASK	DESCRIPTION
Connector Transfer	If the MTA on the server where the recipient is located can't be contacted directly, then the MTA will pass the message to a connector that will help route it to its destination. Also, if the intended recipient is on a foreign messaging system, then the MTA will pass the message off to the connector.
Message Conversion	When a message is destined for transfer through a connector, the MTA may be required to convert the content of the message to another format.

1.2.4   The Directory Service

The Directory Service (DS) stores all of the information about the Exchange environment that's available to be stored. A few configuration details are stored in the Windows NT registry, but the majority of the configuration information is kept in the DIR.EDB file—the Exchange Directory Service database. It too runs as a Windows NT service. The DS controls access to the following information:

- information about the Exchange Organization;

- details of user mailboxes (but not contents);

- e-mail addresses of all users in the Exchange Organization;

- information about any Distribution Lists which might exist;

- information on Public Folders; and

- configuration information about sites and servers.

The information about user mailboxes, addresses, and distribution lists is exposed by the DS as the Global Address List (GAL). The GAL is a complete directory of all users and other objects with e-mail addresses anywhere in the Exchange network. By sharing their local mailbox and address information with each other, all the DSs in the network work together to offer one homogeneous view of the user environment.

Information in the DS store is structured along the lines of the International Telecommunication Union (ITU)[*] Recommendations for X.500

---

[*]   The ITU branch that is concerned with standards for telecommunication was formerly known as the Comité Consultatif International Télégraphique et Téléphonic (CCITT).

Directory Services. These recommendations define, amongst other things, a rigorous syntax for naming objects in a directory. Although the Exchange engineers designed the internals of the DS store in line with these recommendations, other protocols of X.500 that deal mostly with access from external search agents and replication of information to other X.500 directories are not implemented.

As its name suggests, the DIR.EDB file is a database file much like the PRIV.EDB and PUB.EDB files that we met earlier. It's located in \EXCHSRVR\ DSADATA. The DS is responsible for replicating information stored in the directory to other Exchange servers in the organization. When this replication has taken place, we can be confident that there is a uniform and even distribution of important information to all Exchange servers that need to have such details. We'll talk more about directory replication later.

It's clear that the DS has a number of roles that it must perform to ensure the smooth operation of the Exchange server; these roles are detailed in Table 1–4.

TABLE 1–4 Directory Service Tasks

TASK	DESCRIPTION
Information Storage	Store information about objects (mailboxes, distribution lists, servers, sites, etc.)
Replication	The DS can talk directly to another DS in order to replicate information, or it can use the MTA to help it replicate information to a more distant server.
Lookup Services	The information held in the DS store is made available to both users (when you type in a person's name and get their e-mail address) and to other Exchange components, such as the MTA (when it has an address and requires routing and address mapping information for the recipients).

1.2.5 Exchange Server Components Working Together

We've just reviewed the individual components that offer the basic functionality of an Exchange server. This functionality can be summarized into:

- maintaining and updating Exchange server status information (the SA);
- storing messages and documents on behalf of users (the IS);
- exchanging messages between different servers (the MTA); and

■ storing and maintaining naming and address information (the DS).

The absence of any one of these facilities will seriously affect the service an Exchange server can offer. From Figure 1–2 you can see that the IS communicates with the MTA to exchange messages and sends signals to the SA to log message transfers, as does the MTA when it transfers messages. Both the IS and the MTA also make queries to the DS every time a message is to be delivered to retrieve the address of the intended recipient. The DS improves the performance of such queries by maintaining a cache so that subsequent lookups are serviced faster. The SA uses the DS to build routing and address information.

FIGURE 1–2
Exchange Core
Component
Relationships

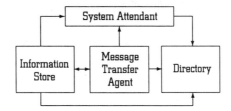

1.2.6 Exchange Connectors

The core components are sufficient for storing and sending e-mail messages between users on a server, or as we'll see in Section 1.3, for exchanging messages between servers in a site. However, most implementations of Exchange have a requirement to trade messages with other messaging systems. Exchange Server uses what's called a *connector* to offer connectivity to these other systems. Some connectors are needed just for external connectivity, but in most circumstances they are used within the Exchange organization to connect a number of Exchange servers together.

The common connectors that are part of Exchange are listed in Table 1–5.

TABLE 1–5   Exchange Built-In Connectors

CONNECTOR	DESCRIPTION
Site Connector	Used to connect separate Exchange sites together.
X.400 Connector	Can be used to connect separate Exchange sites together or to provide connectivity to external X.400 messaging systems.
Internet Mail Service	Used for connection to Internet-style messaging systems.

continued ▶

TABLE 1–5 Exchange Built-In Connectors (continued)

CONNECTOR	DESCRIPTION
Microsoft Mail Connector	Provides connectivity to Microsoft Mail Post Office–based messaging systems.
cc:Mail Connector	Provides connectivity to Lotus cc:Mail Post Office–based messaging systems.
Lotus Notes Connector	Used to connect to Lotus Notes messaging systems.
SNADS Connector	Used to connect to SNADS-based mail systems.
PROFS Connector	Used to connect to IBM PROFS mail systems.

Some connectors do more than just provide e-mail links. Microsoft defines a connector as offering both message transfer capability and additional functionality, which typically is directory synchronization services between Exchange and the messaging system you're using the connector to link to. The Microsoft Mail Connector, the cc:Mail Connector, and the Lotus Notes Connector all offer the ability to provide directory synchronization services. The SNADS and PROFS connector don't have this synchronization built in, so external directory synchronization services must be supplied.

1.3 The Exchange Site Concept

One or more Exchange servers can be grouped together into a *Site*. An Exchange site is a logical collection of servers that share information closely and work together tightly. Although all Exchange servers have great abilities to share information, some special characteristics are associated with grouping servers into a site.

1.3.1 How Servers Work Together in a Site

Within a Site all servers are equal partners. Communication takes place using Remote Procedure Calls (RPCs) and all servers have direct connections to each other. This is illustrated in Figure 1–3. The RPC mechanism is detailed in Section 2.2.3. You can see that as the number of servers in a site increases, the number of connections between them rises quite dramatically. We'll return to this point later in Chapter 2.

FIGURE 1–3 Server
Communications
within a Site

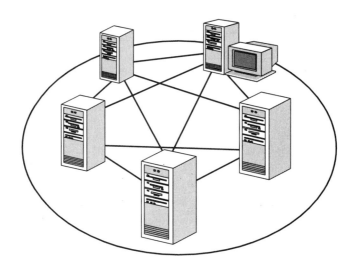

1.3.2 Centralized Management

It is critical to understand that Servers in a Site are managed as a single unit. From time to time you may have to change a site-wide property, such as *Site Addressing*. Changing values for the site addressing property means that you'll be changing the structure of an address. Let's say that you've a number of users that have an Internet address of the form:

    @customercontact.acme.com,

but you want to change the address to:

    @sales.acme.com.

If you change the Site Addressing property to reflect this change for your users, the users on a particular server are not the only ones to have their addresses changed, but users on all the servers that make up that site are affected. The Site Addressing property spans all servers in a site.

This makes management of a group of servers quite easy. You don't need to connect to each individual server in order to manage them. Of course, some aspects of management are server-specific. Setting properties on the Information Store, for example, is a server-specific task because when you make changes there you'll only want them to take effect on that server alone, not all the servers in the site.

1.3.3 Automatic Communication between Servers

Servers that are grouped together in a site share a close relationship with each other. We've seen that each individual server has a number of core components that provide messaging services to clients, but the guiding principle for messaging is *exchange* of information. (I wonder where Microsoft Exchange got its name!) Servers bundled together in a site work together to make information exchange easier. For example, in an Exchange site all of the DSs communicate with each other directly to share and replicate directory information automatically. If the servers aren't grouped into a site this replication can still take place, but it has to be manually configured.

It's not just the Directory Service communication that works seamlessly within a site. Since the servers have detailed knowledge about each other automatically, the transfer of messages between servers takes place quickly and smoothly. When you send a message to a user on another server in the same site, the MTA on the sending server transfers the message directly to the MTA on the receiving system without the least amount of fuss. There's no conversion or tampering to be done with the format of the message. This isn't to say that messages to servers in other sites can't be sent. Of course, they can, but the MTA sometimes has a little bit more work to do in cases like that.

1.3.4 User Management

One of the site's most important features is that users can be moved between servers with great ease. Let's say that you have an Exchange site currently with just one Exchange server in it and that you have one thousand user mailboxes on that one server. Maybe you're beginning to run out of space on that single server and you decide that it's time to buy another server and move some of the users onto it. If you've installed the new server into the same site, then this task is straightforward. It's merely a matter of using the Exchange Administrator program to select the mailboxes of some of the users on the old server and move them to the new server by modifying their Home-Server attribute. You might select five hundred of the users and migrate them to the new server. After performing this operation you'll have five hundred users left on your old server and five hundred users on new server. What could be simpler? If your company is one with a lot of user movement between different locations (for example, people assigned to different cities for six months at a time) and you have an Exchange site that spans the country with servers in each major city, then this site model will work well for you.

1.3.5 When One Site Isn't Enough

Like most aspects of messaging, there are trade-offs to be made between the benefits of grouping servers into a site and factors related to network bandwidth, Windows NT infrastructure, user population, administration, and traffic patterns. The costs of server-to-server links, your DNS and SMTP strategy, and your requirements for security and encryption are also factors that should influence these decisions. We'll look at these factors in Chapter 2 when we lay out guidelines for good site design, but for now let us say that it is not always possible to group all of our servers into a single site.

In such a case we end up with a number of different sites that are connected together. The connections between different sites are made using *site connectors*. One can take a number of different approaches to connecting sites together, but the two main methods are to use the *Site Connector* or the *X.400 Connector*. Don't be misled by the name "Site Connector."[*] It doesn't mean that it's the only mechanism for connecting sites together. Although this is a very efficient connector for use between sites, it has its advantages and disadvantages, just like the X.400 Connector, which is more appropriate in certain circumstances.

1.4   The Exchange Organization

In much the same way as Exchange servers are grouped together to form an Exchange site, sites are grouped together to form *the* Exchange Organization. I very purposefully used the definite article when I introduced *the* Exchange Organization. While you might have many servers and many sites in your Exchange implementation, there should be only one Organization. It's the largest administrative unit in Exchange, and all servers fall into line underneath the umbrella of the Organization.

It's possible to have just one server, in one site, forming one Organization, but it's more likely that you'll have a number of sites, connected via site connectors that make up the Organization. (See Figure 1–4.)

---

[*] In the remainder of this book I'll use the term *site connector* (all lower case) to refer to a generic connection between sites, and *Site Connector* (upper case first letters) to refer to the specific connector dedicated to linking sites together.

FIGURE 1–4
Exchange Servers
and Sites Form the
Exchange
Organization

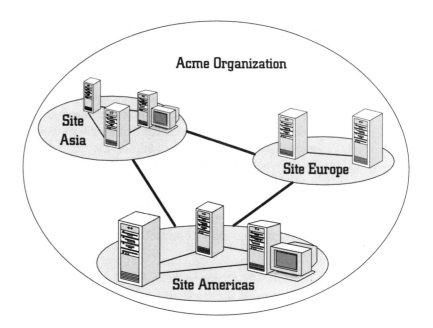

1.4.1 Implications of Organization Name

When you install the first Exchange server in your company you'll be asked to supply an Organization name and a Site name. You might choose *ACME Corporation* for the Organization name, but whatever you choose you must stick with it. It's not easy to change your Exchange Organization name later. When you install a subsequent server it can join the same site, in which case it inherits the Organization name, or you can make it part of a new site, in which case you need to type in the Organization Name manually. If you choose the latter option, you must give the new server the same Organization name; otherwise it's effectively not part of the existing Exchange organization. Having a server segregated in a separate Organization means several things:

- Directory Replication will not work between organizations, so there's no single Global Address List that will span the organizations;

- Public Folders are not accessible across organizations; and

- Key Management Services, the ability to encrypt messages using an Exchange server as the Key Management Server will not work between organizations.

Basically this means that you've got two different Exchange implementations to manage.

Of course, in a large corporation it's not uncommon to find different parts of the corporation (perhaps in different countries) starting their own implementations of Exchange at different times. This can give rise to a segregated Exchange implementation if those responsible for planning and design haven't put a coherent and all-inclusive design in place. A new utility made available in Exchange V5.5 Service Pack 2 allows you to deal with situations like this. The *Move Server Wizard* can perform open heart surgery on all objects in the Exchange Directory and allow you to change the Organization name to a different value. Using the Move Server Wizard is straightforward but it requires careful planning and execution. Life is much simpler if everyone agrees on a common Organization name upfront and just sticks with it!

But it's not the end of the road if you find yourself with segregated Exchange organizations. It is possible to get a reasonable level of mail interoperability between two separate Exchange implementations. Using one of the Exchange connectors (such as the Internet connector or the X.400 connector), you can establish an e-mail link between the two organizations just as if you were connecting an Exchange organization to an external messaging system. The only issue that's not resolved by this solution is a common Global Address List, but you can use directory synchronization techniques (see Chapter 9) to bridge this gap. Unfortunately, nothing can be done to sort out the problems of Public Folder access and Key Management Services at the moment. However, for some companies, this level of interoperability is all that is required.

2

Exchange Site Design

2.1 Introduction

Large-scale deployments of Exchange present a number of challenges to the Exchange architecture designer. Such challenges originate from two sources: the restrictions presented by the environment into which Exchange is to be installed and the requirements of Exchange Server itself. The designer must carefully assess all of the characteristics of the deployment site and deliver a solution that balances the supply of resources from the environment with the demand for resources from Exchange.

This is no easy task by any means. Given an unlimited budget for resources such as server hardware, network bandwidth, and management staff, one can implement an Exchange network with truly supersonic performance and impressive reliability. Very rarely will you find yourself with this kind of blank check for resources and a carte blanche for reengineering existing environments. Once again the notion of trade-off rears its head and we're confronted with the prospect of rolling out an Exchange network that will meet reasonable performance and reliability levels with a less than ideal infrastructure. But even to get this far, we need to have a firm understanding of exactly what demands Exchange will place on an environment and how best to satisfy them.

The recommendations offered in this chapter are based on my experiences with a number of large Exchange deployment projects. They may differ from the clinical figures that you can read in other sources, but more often than not, such figures are obtained from lab-based performance and sizing exercises. While there is nothing contemptible about such sources, I prefer to work with information from real-life situations that can be pretty difficult to simulate in an isolated lab or a test facility. In any event, these recommendations are for purposes of guidance only. Every situation is different and the best we can hope to achieve is to build an Exchange environment that is tolerant of the local circumstances.

The factors that tend to influence the architecture for Exchange are:

- the underlying physical network;
- the Windows NT Domain infrastructure;
- user concentration;
- likely traffic patterns;
- server sizing; and
- management and administration requirements.

An understanding of these requirements and knowledge of the way in which Exchange sends messages from one server to another should be enough to equip the Exchange design architect with the necessary tools for any implementation project.

2.2   Making Design Decisions

We've discussed the three primary concepts of the Exchange model: the Server, the Site, and the Organization. Each one must be addressed when we begin to outline an architecture for Exchange.

2.2.1   Deciding on the Organization Name

The first design decision that you need to make is to choose the name that you'll attribute to the Organization. Of the three concepts, the design decision for the Organization Name *should* be the most straightforward, as it is independent of many of the physical factors (network bandwidth, Windows NT Domain design, etc.). However, from the *political* angle it can be a particularly sticky problem to address, and it requires the agreement of senior decision makers. The issue of deciding on an Organization name is most problematic when the organization wishing to implement Exchange is composed of a number of independent operating companies, each with their own strong identities.

For example, consider the fictional multinational corporation *Worldwide Fruit Trading Inc.* Let's assume that this is an umbrella company for *Florida Orange Growers Corp.* and *Irish Apple Picking Ltd.* Assuming that these are two long-established companies, each with a strong identity, it can be difficult to get them both to agree to a single name for the Organization.

The obvious Organization name suggests itself: *Worldwide Fruit Trading Inc.*, but too many customer experiences reveal that this is not likely to be easily agreed upon, because it excludes any exposure of the individual company name. Maintaining an identity and brand recognition is obviously very important, especially in local markets. The name of the Exchange Organization is very often seen to be directly related to this branding.

Even on a smaller scale, individual departments within a company—each with their own IT groups—will often find it difficult to agree on an Organization Name that can be used across all departments. All too often, this is due to the competitive nature (and large egos) of the IT groups that *know* that their Organization Name is best. Compromise is the essential quality to get a situation like this resolved. However, many companies are now taking a pragmatic approach to naming their organization. Instead of debating the merits of one organization name or another, choosing an arbitrary organization name causes little friction. To this end, it's now common to see a value such as "MAIL" or "MESSAGING" being chosen. It's simple and it offends few.

2.2.2   The Exchange Server

Approaching from the other end of the Exchange architecture model, decisions relating to the sizing of Exchange servers will influence the design of the overall topology.

The ever increasing popularity and constantly improving maturity of Windows NT and PC hardware technology have secured for this operating system a position for itself as a mainstream server platform. IT professionals are confident of building NT server systems that are capable of supporting large numbers of users. The new features of Exchange Server V5.5, which provide the unlimited Information Store and support for clustering technology, has also inspired us to build Exchange systems that are configured for many hundreds, even thousands of users. Some recent benchmarks from Compaq Computer Corporation illustrate the capabilities of Compaq's Alpha AXP-based servers to support up to 11,500 users and Compaq's Intel-based systems to support up to 10,000 users on a single server. While I'm pleased to be able to write about such high performance figures from the company that pays my salary every month, I'm also wary of the fact that by the time this book goes to press these numbers will have been superseded by figures even more impressive!

So what does all of this mean? Well, from an Exchange network design perspective, larger servers mean fewer servers. IT staff, and especially their management, like this approach because fewer servers mean reduced management costs. One of the trends that we see today is centralization of servers into the datacenter where a single team of skilled people can manage Exchange for thousands of users scattered across the country or even a continent. There are many important factors to consider when designing servers that will handle this type of user load. In brief they are:

1. **CPU.** A sufficiently powerful CPU to handle not just the average workload imposed by the users but the peak levels as well. You should make sure that the CPU utilization levels that you see have enough headroom to allow expansion and increased user loads. Saturation of the CPU resource is generally accepted to occur when the utilization level is at 75 percent or above, so whatever platform you decide on, be sure to select one where the benchmarks show utilization at significantly less than this level.

2. **Disk I/O Subsystem.** The disk I/O subsystem has the heaviest workload on an active Exchange system. The nature of electronic mail implies that information is read from and written to disk with intense frequency. Exchange is no different, although the in-memory buffers do their best to smooth the regularity of disk writes. Nevertheless, selecting the right hardware for the I/O subsystem is critical. Make sure that you've got enough disk space for user mailboxes and public folder information. It's not uncommon to allocate around 50MB of disk space to each mailbox, so even for 500 users this equates to around 26GB of required storage. But remember that you'll need to leave room for growth, and if you intend to run the Information Store compression tool (ESEUTIL) you'll need at least another 26GB to hold the temporary database! It's not just the capacity of the disks that is important, but the number of disk spindles that the I/O workload is distributed across. My advice is to choose a RAID* subsystem and use a number of small capacity disk volumes. You'll get better performance if you choose seven 4GB drives to provide 24GB of storage (one disk is used for parity) rather than four 9GB drives offering 27GB of storage.

---

* RAID is an acronym for *Redundant Arrays of Independent Disks*. It's a mechanism for bundling a number of separate physical disk volumes together into one logical volume for improved performance and reliability.

3.   **RAM.** The third important hardware factor to take into account is memory. Operating observations suggest that while memory is an important resource for Exchange servers, there's little point in using vast quantities of it. In my experience 256MB of memory is sufficient for about 500 users on an Intel server. Unless you're using your Exchange server for other applications, this should be sufficient. Surprisingly, memory is one of the areas where more is not always better. Too much memory being available to Exchange can lead to vast quantities of information being cached in the in-memory buffer, especially on a very busy system. Periodically, Exchange flushes the transactions in this buffer to the Information Store databases, which can result in substantial I/O operations that can have an adverse effect on the disk subsystem. Using less memory for the buffers smoothes this flushing process. You have been warned!

4.   **Network connection.** Supporting huge numbers of users on a single server can also impose heavy demands on the network card in your server. It's good practice to assume that every connected user will consume about 5Kb/s of network bandwidth. Irrespective of where your users are located and how distributed they might be across your network, the fact is that all of the traffic from the client to the server will eventually end up at the network card on your Exchange server. If you've got an old 10Mb/s network card and you're supporting 2,000 users, the assumed load on the network card will be 10Mb/s. This is very high, even for 2,000 users, and considerably more dangerous for even higher user levels. Fast network cards of 100Mb/s and switched Ethernet connections of 100Mb/s are the order of the day. If you've got it, a direct connection to an FDDI (Fiber Distributed Data Interface) ring is even better.

I've just scratched the surface of the factors that you need to take into consideration when deciding on the configuration of your Exchange server. A more comprehensive discussion falls beyond the scope of this book,[*] but you will find a wealth of useful sizing information available today from most of the major PC hardware vendors. I suggest that you study it carefully before making any purchasing decisions.

---

[*]   For a comprehensive discussion on performance-related factors of Exchange, I'd suggest that you take a look at *Microsoft Exchange Server Scalability* by Pierre Bijaoui (Digital Press).

2.2.3 How Servers Communicate within a Site

Remote Procedure Call (RPC) communication is the glue that binds
Exchange servers together within the site. In this case, all Exchange servers
use RPCs to talk to each other, and some other components use the RPC
mechanism as well. The Exchange Administrator program, ADMIN.EXE,
communicates with the servers that it manages using RPCs too, as do the clients that connect to the Exchange servers. The majority of the RPC architecture definition was put forward some years ago in work done by the Open
Software Foundation's (OSF) Distributed Computing Environment (DCE).
Since then, RPCs have become a very desirable solution to the problems of
communication between cooperating processes.

The words *Procedure* and *Call* in RPC are the tell-tale sign that helps
illustrate how RPCs work. As in any piece of software, code modules usually
have a requirement to have specific operations or functions performed and
to exchange data with other modules. Within a program, one piece of the
code will usually invoke another module by making a *procedure call*. When
the procedure call is to another module either in the same program or in a
run-time library on the same computer, then we can say that this procedure
call is *local*.

The DCE architecture takes this scenario one step further by allowing a
software component on one computer (we'll call it the "source computer")
to call a module or a procedure on another computer (which we'll call the
"target computer") as if the called module were actually on the source computer. The software component on the source computer is known as the
client, while the procedure on the target computer is the *server*. As far as the
client application is concerned, it thinks it's calling its own subroutines. The
connection between the RPC client and server is catered for by the RPC stub
API (Application Programming Interface). On Windows NT, where the
RPC service is built into the operating system, this stub communicates with
a runtime library called RPCRT4.DLL. When the client makes a call to an RPC,
the RPC stub picks up this call and passes it to RPCRT4.DLL, and it becomes
responsible for contacting the RPC server on the target computer. When
this is done, the server routine performs the requested function and returns
any results back to the calling client. RPCRT4.DLL acts as the intermediary
between the RPC stub and the network transport that is responsible for
making the connection to the RPC server.

For Exchange servers within a site, the components that interact over
RPCs are the Exchange MTA and the Directory Service. They communicate

in a Point-to-Point and fully meshed fashion. This means that every server in a site will communicate with every other server, so for n servers in the site, there will be $n(n-1)$ links between the servers. (See Figure 1–3.) When a message is sent to a user who isn't located on the same server, the Information Store will pass the message to the MTA. It is then up to the MTA to contact the MTA on the server on which the user's mailbox resides. When it makes contact, the sending MTA will pass the message to the MTA on the receiving MTA. Although we'll deal with the subject of Directory Replication later in this book, you should know that the Directory Service communicates with other Directory Services on other Exchange servers to share information. If the Directory Service is running on another computer within the same Exchange site, then the two Directory Services will communicate with each other directly. Both these conversations require the use of RPCs, and communication takes place over a network connection. This relationship between communicating Exchange services is shown in Figure 2–1.

FIGURE 2–1
Network Nature of
Remote Procedure
Calls

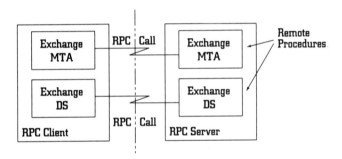

Windows NT provides a rich set of network transports that are available for communication between the processes, and in the case of RPC communication, any one of the transports may be used to ferry RPC traffic. The transports available on Windows NT are local RPCs, TCP/IP, SPX, named pipes, and NetBIOS (as well as a number of others). Local RPCs may only be used if the RPC client and server are colocated on the same computer, but in the case of Exchange server-to-server communication, this is obviously not appropriate. Exchange Server has a natural preference for trying TCP/IP first, then SPX, and finally Banyan Vines transport when it needs to communicate with an RPC partner. The order in which an RPC client (e.g., the Exchange MTA) tries these transports is governed by the value of the registry entry as shown below:

```
Rpc_Svr_Binding_Order=ncacn_ip_tcp,ncacn_spx,ncacn_vns_spp
```

which can be found in:

```
HKEY_LOCAL_MACHINE\SOFTWARE\Microsoft\Exchange\Exchange Provider
```

The network transports that are available and may be defined in the binding order are shown in Table 2–1. ("NCA" stands for "Network Computing Architecture.") You can change the value of this registry entry for testing purposes (e.g., problems with a Site Connector) so that it will use one of the other transports below, but you should not keep these transports active when you've finished the testing since they don't all support the full range of RPC functionality or may introduce security risks.

TABLE 2–1   RPC Transport Providers

TRANSPORT	DESCRIPTION
Ncalrpc	Local RPC, i.e., no network connectivity
ncacn_ip_tcp	TCP/IP transport
ncacn_spx	SPX transport
ncacn_np	Named Pipes
Netbios	NetBIOS transport
ncacn_vns_spp	Banyan Vines IP transport
ncacn_nb_nb	NetBEUI transport

Because the exceptionally flexible RPC mechanism can use almost any network transport you care to throw at it, this makes it well suited to the Exchange environment where many different messaging systems (and sometimes many different network protocols) may already be in use. Much of this is likely to change in the next version of Exchange (currently code-named Platinum). Microsoft's strong leaning toward open protocols for communication is likely to mean the introduction of an SMTP-based mechanism for inter-server communication.

2.2.4   Authenticated RPC Connections

In the real world, when you drop a letter to your friend into the mailbox, you know that for it to get to the address on the front of the envelope, someone from the Postal Service has to collect the message from the mailbox and carry it to a sorting office, and then someone else will actually deliver it to your friend's house. You would not have any confidence in the security of the process if you thought that just anyone could open up the mailbox and take your letter. You probably feel some comfort from the fact that the mail carrier needs a key to open up the mailbox. In a sense, this key *authenticates* the carrier to the mailbox; without a key, he cannot get access to the letters inside.

The problem of sending messages in a secure fashion extends to Exchange, too. When a message is sent from one server to another, you must be confident that no intruder is trying to access the information. Rather than expose Exchange to the risk of someone writing some code and making an RPC call to one of the Exchange components (thus gaining access), the Exchange engineers use the concept of *Authenticated RPCs* to help identify the validity of the component accessing Exchange. Authenticated RPCs are transport independent and currently use the Windows NT Security Service for authentication purposes.

It works like this: When the Exchange Directory Service on server *STARSKY* wants to send some information to the Directory Service on server *HUTCH*, it observes an authentication handshake protocol. *STARSKY* will place its identification information as a parameter in the RPC call. This identification consists of the Domain Name, Username, and Password of the Exchange Service account. When *HUTCH* receives the RPC it extracts the authentication information out of the RPC structure and verifies that the information that has been sent is actually correct. When *HUTCH* goes to send information back to *STARSKY*, it too bundles its identification information into the RPC packet, and then *STARSKY* has to verify that the information that it has received from *HUTCH* is valid. It is, of course, slightly more complex than this, but the general principal is more as less as described above.

For either the RPC client or the RPC server to authenticate each other, they must both be able to access a Windows NT Domain Controller that has knowledge of the domains that are quoted in the respective RPC authentication packets. This means of authenticated communication between Exchange servers has a significant impact on the types of Windows NT Domain models that must be used to allow Exchange to operate correctly.

2.2.5 Encrypted RPC Connections

In addition to using authentication techniques for RPC communication between servers, Exchange encrypts all information that gets transferred between the servers when RPCs are used. This encryption takes place irrespective of whether you've decided to implement Key Management (encryption) within your Exchange organization on a user by user basis. The technology used for RPC communication encryption is a 40-bit CAST (a proprietary encryption technique) algorithm.

This means that all communication between Exchange servers in a site makes use of this encryption technique and the communication across sites using the Site Connector (which also uses RPCs) is encrypted as well. There's no default encryption for information transferred between sites when an inter-site mechanism other than the Site Connector is used, although encryption on SMTP messages can be used when the IMS is performing as a site connector.

2.2.6 Windows NT Domains

Before we proceed to talk about the implications of the Windows NT design on the architecture of your Exchange organization, it's worthwhile to reacquaint ourselves with the fundamentals of NT domains.

Without domains, life on a network would be fairly painful. Here's why. Windows NT servers control access to resources (file shares, printers, applications, etc.) by requiring that users identify themselves by means of a username and a password (logon information) when they try to access the resource. When you specify your logon information, the NT server authenticates the information that you've entered against its accounts database, the Security Accounts Manager (or "SAM"), and decides whether it will grant you access. If every Windows NT server on your network operated in isolation without knowledge of information held on the other servers, then you would require an account on every server to which you needed access. Even in the simplest of cases—if, say, you used one server for your Exchange account, another server for your printer services, and another server for some file shares—you'd have three different sets of usernames and passwords to remember. What's worse is that the System Management people that look after all of the servers would have a huge headache trying to manage different sets of accounts for hundreds or thousands of users on lots of servers.

The simple answer to this problem is to share one common SAM across all of the servers. Therefore, you only need one account for access to all servers, not one for every server. When a user wants to access resources on a particular server, the server in question authenticates the user's logon information by consulting the shared SAM. In essence, this is a Windows NT Domain.

Thus, a domain is essentially a collection of Windows NT computers that share logon information. However, rather than have the SAM database replicated across every server, with each server holding its own local copy of the accounts information, NT uses a special computer known as the *Primary Domain Controller* (PDC) to hold just a single copy of the SAM, which is accessed by the other computers. When any other computer in the domain wants to authenticate user information, it contacts the PDC and asks it to check the SAM. This eliminates the maintenance and update problems associated with replicating the SAM to every server in the domain.

As you might expect, since there can be only one PDC in the domain, the workload on this server can become quite substantial, especially at peak times (such as between 8:00 a.m. and 9:00 a.m. when all the users will be trying to log on). This problem is reduced by using slaves called *Backup Domain Controllers* (BDCs) that maintain a read-only copy of the SAM and can authenticate user logon information when requested by other servers. BDCs tend to be used to provide local authentication at locations where there are lots of users or the connection back to PDC is over the wide area network (Figure 2–2).

FIGURE 2–2
PDC and BDC Authentication across Locations, but within the Same Domain

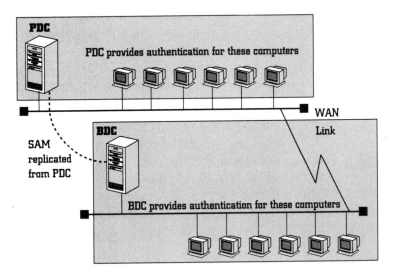

2.2.7   Why Have Multiple Domains?

Domain management would be a breeze if we only ever implemented a single NT domain within an organization. There'd be one SAM shared between all computers and we could use BDCs at sizeable user offices and at remote locations for local authentication. Unfortunately, it's rare to find an organization where this *single domain model* can be easily implemented. In general, the ease of your life as a system or messaging administrator is directly proportional to the number of NT domains that exist in your company. The fewer NT domains that you have, the easier it is to administer and manage that environment.

There are many reasons why multiple domains might exist (or be about to exist) in your company. Regular communication takes place between servers in an NT domain, particularly between the PDC, BDCs, and Browse Masters (those systems that maintain information about other computers available in the domain). They tend to send replication messages to each other with a frequency of generally less than 15 minutes, and servers themselves will update the Browse Master every so often to let it know that they are still alive. If you want to cut down on the amount of this kind of traffic across your network, you should segment it into a number of separate domains where traffic can be contained. I'm not suggesting that you partition every office into a separate NT domain, but it is common to find domain boundaries in large organizations in alignment with national or even continental boundaries, providing that you've got network links to support the connections within those boundaries.

But for less physical reasons, although every bit as compelling, you might have a domain infrastructure based on spheres of management. Again, in larger organizations where there are separate IT groups for separate parts of the company, such as an IT support team for the Sales unit and another one for the Engineering unit, neither IT group may wish to have anything to do with the other. In this case they'll probably establish their own domains and keep their environment well outside the reach of the other lot.

The size of the SAM database is yet another influence on the number of domains that you might have. In addition to user accounts, the SAM also keeps a record for individual machine accounts. If you've decided to deploy Windows NT Workstation as your desktop operating system of choice, you'll find that there are roughly as many entries in the SAM for machine accounts as there are for user accounts. Note that Windows 95, Windows 3.1, Windows for Workgroups 3.11, and good old DOS machines don't have a machine account in the SAM. Windows NT Domain Controllers (DCs) load the SAM into memory at system boot time. If the SAM is very large, there can be a considerable delay in system startup as the SAM gets loaded, and, of course, you must have sufficient RAM on the DC to hold the database in memory. Typically a SAM for 40,000 users in an environment with very few machine accounts would be roughly 40MB in size (the Microsoft stated maximum size). So for these reasons, dependent on how you configure your PDCs and BDCs, you might partition your NT network in manageable domain chunks.

The experience gained from visiting many different customers over the years leads me to believe that one of the most common reasons for seeing multiple domains is mere whim: people just create them. Although a company may impose a policy for the NT structure within, there's little to stop individuals from building their own NT systems and creating their own domains, especially in technology companies, where IT staff huddle in corners surrounded by mountains of expensive computer toys, erm, I mean, "equipment," where there's a natural tendency when building systems for test or evaluation purposes to create yet another domain. Of course this is good practice, since there's no interaction with the production environment, but these servers do get seen on the network and can all too often become systems that provide essential services to your company because they just grew out of a pilot that never really ended. It won't be too long before the whole organization is littered with domains here, there, and everywhere. You can usually spot them straightaway since the domains and servers have strange or obscure names like *STREETFIGHTER* or *DEATH-STAR*. My own favorite, which I chanced across on the Compaq network one day, was obviously a domain created by someone with a name like Charlie O'Neill: it was called *CONDOM*!

Although there can sometimes be strong reasons for establishing multiple domains, as we've seen, it's best to try to avoid the scenario. Managing multiple domains is quite cumbersome, error prone, and leads to confusion. The Domain model is all set for a complete overhaul with Windows 2000, when the Active Directory will be used to store all sorts of directory information including the Domain databases and information about user and computer accounts. So we might expect Windows 2000 to simplify the management of multiple domains, but it's still a little bit too early to tell. One thing's for sure: If you've only got a single domain today, it will be a lot easier to migrate it to Windows 2000 than it will be to migrate a thousand domains.

2.2.8 Trust Relationships

If you've got a network with multiple domains, you've got at least two separate SAMs. Let's say that you need access to resources in each one. Perhaps your user account is in the domain called *EUROPE* but you need to access a file-share that is located on an NT server in the domain *NORTHAMERICA*. If the share you want to access in *NORTHAMERICA* isn't set up to allow guest access and you don't have a valid user account in that domain, you'll have trouble trying to access the file-share.

The answer to this problem is to create a *trust relationship* between the domains *NORTHAMERICA* and *EUROPE* so that *NORTHAMERICA* trusts *EUROPE*. The net result of this is that when you try to access the file-share in domain *NORTHAMERICA*, although the DC in *NORTHAMERICA* has no knowledge itself of who you are (i.e., there's no user account for you in the *NORTHAMERICA* SAM), it trusts domain *EUROPE* and it knows that you do have a valid user account in the SAM in the *EUROPE* domain. The order of trust is important here: The trust relationship that's established is not bidirectional. Although *NORTHAMERICA* trusts *EUROPE*, *EUROPE* does not trust *NORTHAMERICA*, so you would need to establish a separate trust relationship so that *EUROPE* can trust *NORTHAMERICA*. Figure 2–3 shows this relationship.

FIGURE 2–3
Accessing
Resources in
Another Domain
Using a Trust
Relationship

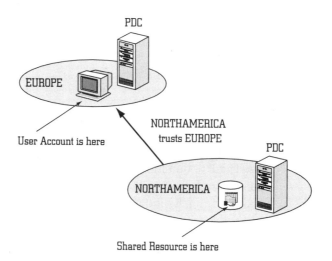

The number of trust relationships that you have will increase quite dramatically if you want every domain in your network to trust every other domain. With two domains you need two trust relationships, for three domains you need six trust relationships, for four domains you need twelve trust relationships, and so on. Get the picture? The mathematics tell us that for n domains, you'll need $n(n-1)$ trust relationships. So for an environment with 15 domains you'd have to set up and manage 210 trust relationships.

2.2.9 Domain Models

There are four basic approaches that can be taken to build an organizational Windows NT Domain network: single domain, master/resource domain, multiple master/resource domains, and complete trust model.

The Single Domain

This is the simplest of all the domain models. There are no relationships to any other domains to be concerned with and you need only administer just the one domain. This may not be appropriate for any reasonably large organization due to (1) organizational/management reasons where individual groups have IT management autonomy, (2) infrastructure reasons where your network may not be able to cope with a single domain spanning wide area links, or (3) the sheer size of your organization.

The Master/Resource Domain

Master/resource domains are typified by having all of the user accounts in one domain (the master) and having all of the server and workstation accounts that offer the resources in the other domains. There should be trust relationships between the domains such that the resource domains trust the master domain, but there's no need for the resource domains to trust each other. Figure 2–3 effectively illustrates this model where *EUROPE* is the master domain and *NORTHAMERICA* is the resource domain. You may of course have more than one resource domain, and it's common to find separate resource domains for file-shares, printers, or Exchange services. The user logs on to the master domain and has access to all resources in the each of the resource domains.

The Multiple Master/Resource Domain

This model should only be used if you have too many users to fit into a single master domain or if your major user population centers are characterized into a small number of large clumps. It's a sort of way station between the Master/Resource Domain model and the Complete Trust model.

Instead of having just one master domain, you'll have several, and you build two-way trust between each master domain. You then build a one-way trust relationship for each resource domain such that it trusts each master domain. For example, if you had two master domains and five resource domains, you'd end up with two trust relationships between the master domains and ten trust relationships so that each of the resource domains trust each master domain (one trust relationship between each resource domain to each master), giving you twelve trust relationships in total. It's important to understand that trust relationships are not transitive. If you've got three master domains (A, B, and C) and you've got bidirectional trust relationships between A and B and between B and C, this doesn't mean that there's any relationship between A and C. To get A to trust C (and vice versa) you'll need to explicitly set up a trust relationship between those two domains.

The Complete Trust

This is just as flexible as the Single Domain model such that there is complete trust between each and every domain, but the drawbacks to this approach lie in the management of it. As mentioned above, for n domains you'll need $n(n-1)$ trust relationships, so to establish complete trust between the seven domains we mentioned when discussing the multiple master/resource domain model, you'll need to maintain 42 trust relationships. When you come to add another domain to this model, you're likely to forget to add a trust relationship somewhere along the way. The real challenge would be in analyzing what's gone wrong and trying to figure out which trust relationship you've missed!

2.2.10 Defining Exchange Site Boundaries

Deciding on how best to partition your Exchange network into a number of sites is no easy task. There are a number of infrastructure scenarios that will critically impact the site design that you choose. It's important to analyze the implications of each one and determine just how big an impact they might have on your site design, but in addition to looking at each factor individually, you must also treat them collectively. Based on the overall picture that they form you must then decide how best to connect your Exchange servers.

The approach that I like to take is to analyze each factor independently and, based on the impact, "trace" my Exchange site design onto an imaginary sheet of acetate. Then I repeat this for each of the other factors, until finally I end up with a thick stack of imaginary acetate sheets. Then I take all the sheets, line them up, and place them up to my imaginary light. The site design that I end up with is the line of best fit between all of the independent designs.

A guiding principle in site design should be to keep the number of sites to the absolute minimum. If you examine all of the factors that influence the make-up of your site design and you can get away with just the one site, then go for it. But ensure that there's room for growth with all of the factors. If you just manage to squeeze a single site design into play, but your network is at the limit for supporting it, then you'll have bigger troubles about six months after implementation as usage of the system increases and you find that your network is no longer able to cope with the demand. Make sure that you leave sufficient room for expansion when you consider each of the design factors, or else you'll be like many others and find yourself with plenty of redesign work looming.

The design considerations that I've listed in the following sections are not strictly in order of importance, but I've tried to group the most important items towards the top of the list.

Network Topology

Unless you can provide a quality network service between your Exchange servers, you shouldn't consider grouping them together into a site. If network quality is poor, but you expect it to improve later, you can define multiple sites now and use the Move Server Wizard to consolidate them in the future. Exchange server-to-server communications within a site demand a permanently connected network link. A LAN-based environment is ideal for intra-site connections, but if your LANs are huge and cobbled together with lots of bridges and routers you might think twice before deciding to implement a single site there. Remember that RPCs are used to provide the link between communicating Exchange services. Although RPCs are reasonably robust, they can be sensitive to the network layer over which they function. If there are significant delays when one service calls another using an RPC, then the RPC may well timeout and the communication will fail. Although the server components will of course retry the communication it's important to note that repeated RPC timeouts will eventually cause a breakdown in the connectivity between the servers in your site.

It is, of course, best to standardize on just one protocol and make sure that your Exchange servers aren't running any others. TCP/IP is certainly the *de facto* standard for network connectivity, but many LANs use additional protocols such as NetBEUI[*] or IPX/SPX. Exchange is quite happy to dispatch RPCs across many of these transports, so for the transport that you intend to employ make sure that all of the bridges and routers are capable of dealing with the protocols that you will use. If you standardize, you'll know that you're using just that one enabled protocol and that there's no risk that Exchange has sneakily decided to use something that you weren't expecting. This eliminates that horrible prospect of moving an Exchange server from one floor in your building to another and suddenly finding that the server can't communicate with its former colleagues because it is using an unexpected protocol that is not enabled on the bridge. (I've seen it happen!)

You should have a rough idea of what the network utilization is like on your LAN. Typically for Ethernet-based networks, sustained utilization levels of over 40 percent is considered to be excessive and a good indication that your LAN is saturated. If this is the case then you might have to start segregating your LAN into discrete segments using active networking equipment. Partitioning the LAN like this will cut down on the number of broadcasts that flood the network cables—they'll get filtered out at the bridges or routers. Most existing LANs will offer speeds of around 10Mb/s, which is shared by all of the network devices connected to any particular LAN segment. In the case of more modern switched LANs, it's a delight to find that you don't have to share a segment with anyone else, but instead you are furnished with a direct connection all to yourself back to the nearest network hub. In this configuration your Exchange server may well have a dedicated 10Mb/s straight to the hub. If you plan to support thousands of users on a server, you'll probably want to make sure that you've got sufficient bandwidth to support the concurrent connections. For cases like this, 100Mb/s switched connections or direct FDDI connections are your best bet. Figure on about 5Kb/s per connected user, so for 2,000 users that's a bandwidth requirement to the server of about 10Mb/s.

Apart from the pure bandwidth that's available on your LAN, you might also be concerned with latency introduced by some of the bridges and routers that sit between one server and another. The more hops that there are between Exchange servers, the greater the likelihood that delays may get introduced into the communications. In general LAN, connectivity usually indicates that it's okay to put all your Exchange servers into one site. If you have to consider putting a site together which spans a number of LANs and

---

[*]   NetBEUI (NetBIOS Extended User Interface) is primarily a LAN-based protocol and cannot be routed from one segment to another. However, it can be bridged.

uses the WAN, then the issues associated with network delay become increasingly important.

Figure 2–4 shows the number of hops between two servers that I use in Compaq, sable.bvo.dec.com, and reoexc2.reo.dec.com. Note that there's only about 4 hops and the ping time between the computers is relatively small (about 30ms, give or take the odd peak).

FIGURE 2–4

Network Delay between Closely Located Servers on the WAN

```
traceroute to reoexc2.reo.dec.com (16.27.32.90), 30 hops max, 40
byte packets
1    bvort1 (16.183.112.34)  7 ms  6 ms  7 ms
2    16.245.24.1 (16.245.24.1)  20 ms  20 ms  21 ms
3    16.250.23.1 (16.250.23.1)  30 ms  33 ms  30 ms
4    reoexc2.reo.dec.com (16.27.32.90)  27 ms  24 ms  24 ms

PING reoexc2.reo.dec.com (16.27.32.90): 56 data bytes
64 bytes from 16.27.32.90: icmp_seq=0 ttl=124 time=36 ms
64 bytes from 16.27.32.90: icmp_seq=1 ttl=125 time=25 ms
64 bytes from 16.27.32.90: icmp_seq=2 ttl=125 time=277 ms
64 bytes from 16.27.32.90: icmp_seq=3 ttl=125 time=79 ms
64 bytes from 16.27.32.90: icmp_seq=4 ttl=125 time=25 ms
64 bytes from 16.27.32.90: icmp_seq=5 ttl=125 time=29 ms
64 bytes from 16.27.32.90: icmp_seq=6 ttl=125 time=22 ms
64 bytes from 16.27.32.90: icmp_seq=7 ttl=125 time=29 ms

----reoexc2.reo.dec.com PING Statistics----
9 packets transmitted, 8 packets received, 11% packet loss
round-trip (ms)  min/avg/max = 22/65/277 ms
```

Compare that with the corresponding figures between sable.bvo.dec.com and dbo-exchangeist.dbo.dec.com in Figure 2–5. You'll see that there's significantly more hops (nine) and correspondingly significantly more delay. I happen to know that there's roughly the same speed of network link between all of the hops shown in both Figure 2–4 and Figure 2–5, so the increased delay is due to the fact that there's more network to traverse.

FIGURE 2–5

Network Delay
between Remotely
Located Servers on
the WAN

```
traceroute to dbo-exchangeist.dbo.dec.com (16.209.80.124), 30
hops max, 40 byte packets
1   bvort1 (16.183.121.34)  6 ms  7 ms  6 ms
2   16.254.24.1 (16.254.24.1)  20 ms  20 ms  22 ms
3   16.205.23.1 (16.205.23.1)  38 ms 16.254.28.1 (16.254.28.1)
    46 ms 16.205.23.1 (16.205.23.1)  45 ms
4   a41rt5.reo.dec.com (16.36.32.122)  61 ms a44rt2.reo.dec.com
    (16.36.32.2)  60 ms a41rt5.reo.dec.com (16.36.32.122)  65 ms
5   16.254.230.1 (16.254.230.1)  46 ms 16.254.233.1
    (16.254.233.1)  39 ms 16.254.230.1 (16.254.230.1)  142 ms
6   16.40.0.1 (16.40.0.1)  27 ms  41 ms  40 ms
7   16.254.234.2 (16.254.234.2)  66 ms  79 ms  56 ms
8   16.254.0.2 (16.254.0.2)  73 ms  93 ms  112 ms
9   16.209.80.142 (16.209.80.124)  114 ms  86 ms  110 ms

PING dbo-exchangeist.dbo.dec.com (16.209.80.124): 56 data bytes
64 bytes from 16.209.80.124: icmp_seq=0 ttl=120 time=92 ms
64 bytes from 16.209.80.124: icmp_seq=1 ttl=120 time=74 ms
64 bytes from 16.209.80.124: icmp_seq=2 ttl=120 time=92 ms
64 bytes from 16.209.80.124: icmp_seq=3 ttl=120 time=81 ms
64 bytes from 16.209.80.124: icmp_seq=4 ttl=120 time=81 ms
64 bytes from 16.209.80.124: icmp_seq=5 ttl=120 time=116 ms
64 bytes from 16.209.80.124: icmp_seq=6 ttl=120 time=186 ms
64 bytes from 16.209.80.124: icmp_seq=7 ttl=120 time=114 ms
64 bytes from 16.209.80.124: icmp_seq=8 ttl=120 time=97 ms

----dbo-exchangeist.dbo.dec.com PING Statistics----
9 packets transmitted, 9 packets received, 0% packet loss
round-trip (ms)  min/avg/max = 74/103/186 ms
```

Provided that there's a high-speed network connection between two LANs, it's generally alright for sites to span across the WAN as well. Microsoft suggests that if a dedicated 56Kb/s link is available between the two servers then it's okay to have the site span that link; for anything less than 56Kb/s Microsoft recommends that servers should be placed in separate sites. Note that the recommendation states a *dedicated* 56Kb/s link. This means that a single 56Kb/s link that you might use for other traffic is not enough. I'd tend to argue that a 56Kb/s link is a bit close to the edge to span a site across. Experience from a number of real-life environments encourages me to look for at least a dedicated 256Kb/s link to be really happy that I'd have no troubles. If you can accommodate this within your budget then do it. Otherwise, you'll probably be safe enough with anything around 128Kb/s. If your network links aren't up to par then you'll have to upgrade them (bandwidth is becoming cheaper all the time) or split your Exchange network into separate sites.

Servers within a site expect *permanent* connectivity, not *scheduled* connectivity. Some time ago, a friend of mine had a bad experience with an ISDN link between two different locations. Although the ISDN line was only scheduled to come up from time to time, Exchange's craving to communicate with its peers kept bringing the line up all of the time. (This should have been overridden on the networking equipment, but it wasn't.) My colleague didn't realize this until a few months later when a huge bill landed on his desk for the ISDN call charges for two months. The charges were so high that it would have paid for a permanently connected high-speed line for a whole year!

Windows NT Infrastructure

Exchange depends on the Windows NT domain implementation in a number of ways:

- for authenticated RPC communication between servers;
- for access to server management from the Exchange Administration program;
- for access to message tracking logs; and
- to allow access to user mailboxes from clients.

Since the communication between Exchange servers in a site uses authenticated RPCs, the server partners in the RPC dialog need to be able to validate the authentication information that each one sends to the other. The servers need to get access to the SAM that holds the record for the quoted NT account and password.

Let's assume that we have a server called *SERVERA* and another server called *SERVERB* both in domain *DOMAINA*. Since both servers are in the same site then there is no problem for *SERVERB* to check with the domain controller to validate the RPC authentication information that it has just received from *SERVERA*. But now let's assume that *SERVERB* isn't in *DOMAINA* but is instead in *DOMAINB*. Since the servers are now in different sites, *SERVERB* will have no way of getting *SERVERA*'s authentication information validated because *SERVERB*'s domain controller will have no knowledge *SERVERA*. (This is a simplified example, as it is the Exchange Service account information that's used for RPC authentication, not the machine account of the server.)

Trust relationships are the answer here. If *DOMAINB* trusted *DOMAINA*, then *SERVERB* would be able to validate the authentication information presented by *SERVERA* and it would happily accept the RPCs. *DOMAINA* would need to trust *DOMAINB* as well for RPCs in the opposite direction to work successfully. Having a single NT domain or a number of NT domains with trust relationships established between them means that we have a *common security context,* which is critical for intra-site communication. In small environments, it's reasonably normal to have just a single domain model so that all of your user accounts, machine accounts, and Exchange servers are in the same domain. If you can live with this configuration and you've got the same people managing user accounts and Exchange servers, then this is the simplest approach to adopt. But in larger environments, it's common to use a more sophisticated form of the master domain/resource domain mode, keeping user accounts in the master domain and having Exchange servers in the resource domains with trust relationships between each of the resource domains.

If you decide to layer your Exchange implementation on top of the existing Windows NT implementation, then depending on the NT domain topology that exists, you may find you need an awful lot of trust relationships. Earlier we noted that it's desirable to have as few trust relationships as possible, but you might need them if you wish to implement a single Exchange site across all of the existing domains. You might question why you have so many domains in the first place. If you think it's possible to implement a single Exchange site across that part of the organization, then why isn't it possible to use just one Windows NT domain? If it is possible to use just the one domain, then consider scrapping the domains that are already in place and starting over. (This is guaranteed to make you a very unpopular person.)

Alternatively, you could approach this matter slightly more delicately by using a dedicated resource domain for all of the Exchange servers and using trust relationships between the resource domain and each of the existing domains. If you can rationalize the existing domains at all, it would be wise to try to move the user accounts into a domain of their own, thus just leaving machine accounts in those domains. If you did this, you could then get away with just a single trust relationship between the new account domain and the Exchange resource domain. For example, if you had ten domains in existence today, each with some user accounts and machine accounts, and you layered Exchange on top of this as a single site with servers in each domain, you'd need 90 trust relationships, according to the formula. This would be pretty difficult to manage! If you created a new resource domain for

Exchange and put all of the Exchange servers into it, then you'd only need ten trust relationships (one trust relationship from the resource domain to each of the existing domains). If you went the extra mile and moved the user accounts into their own domain, then you'd only need the one trust relationship between the accounts domain and the Exchange domain. (There might be a sprinkling of trust relationships required between the other domains, but in general this approach is much cleaner.)

Figure 2–6 shows what an existing infrastructure might look like. You would need to link each of those Existing Domains (EDs) with trust relationships if you wanted to build a single Exchange site, while Figure 2–7 shows that you can still keep the EDs but use a dedicated Accounts Domain and an ED for your Exchange infrastructure.

FIGURE 2–6
Ten Existing NT Domains Implemented across a Geography

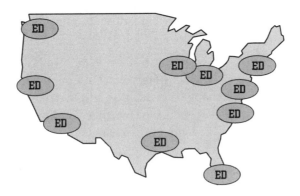

FIGURE 2–7
Existing Domains Remain in Place, but Only New Domains Require Trust Relationships

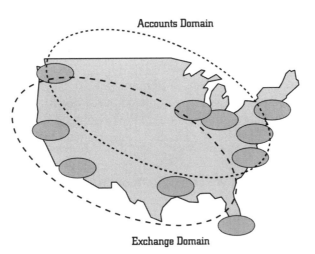

Authenticated RPCs aren't there for exclusive use by intra-site communication. When the Administrator program makes a connection to a server, it uses RPCs too. Therefore, the same rules that apply for Windows NT domain relationships between servers apply to connections between servers and the Administrator program. If you want to connect to an Exchange server using the Administrator program, then you must make sure that the computer on which you're running the Administrator program is in the same domain as the remote server or that there's a trust relationship between them.

If you use the Administrator function of Message Tracking in your Exchange network to record the movements of messages, the tracking log files will be maintained on NT shares. To be able to get access to the log files on each server, again you need to make sure that the servers are in the same domain or that trust relationships exist between the domains that the servers live on and the domain that you're running the Administrator program from.

In figuring out how best to map Windows NT domains to Exchange sites, there are no hard-and-fast rules, but a good rule of thumb is that if you wish to group Exchange servers into a site, then you must have a unified NT security context. The choice of whether you have a single NT domain or multiple trusting NT domains for a single Exchange site will depend on the infrastructure that's already in place. It goes without saying that the fewer NT domains that you have, the better off you are.

User Concentration and Movement

The decision of where to put an Exchange server is usually determined by locating where users are concentrated. If you find an office where hundreds of people are located, it's reasonable to consider putting a server there for those users. It's not very wise to put that server at a location far away from the users so that they'll have to use the WAN to get to their mail, unless you know that you've got lots of network bandwidth available for these connections.

Every company is different in one respect or another, but companies commonly have a lot of staff movement. If your company's users move from location to location every few months or so, then you'll want to try to keep those users all within the same site. Moving users from one server to another within the same site is pretty painless. From the Administrator program, it's more or less a matter of highlighting that user with the mouse and then just modifying the *Home-Server* attribute to point to the new server. After you've done this, all of the user's mail messages and documents are moved from the Private Information Store on the old server to the Private Information Store on the new server. When the user next tries to log on to their mailbox, the old server intercepts the connection attempt and sends a message to the client to let it know that the mailbox actually resides on another server now. (It knows which server the user is now located on because the Home Server attribute in the user's entry in the Directory will have been updated to reflect the new server name. You can see this in Figure 2–8.)

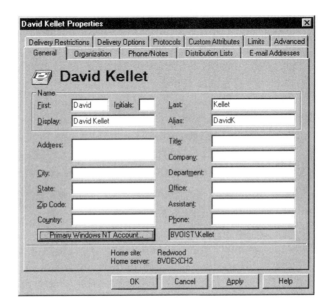

But if you hadn't got the servers in the same site, then I'm afraid life is slightly more difficult when it comes to moving users. Apart from using the EXMERGE tool, there's no easy way to move a user mailbox from a server in one site to a server in another site other than first exporting the user's mailbox to a PST file, and then importing the messages from the PST into the new mailbox on the other server. This isn't altogether impossible, but it is rather cumbersome and can make the process of moving users a time-consuming task.

Traffic Patterns and Collaborative Working

Apart from just identifying users that happen to be based at the same location, it's prudent to look deeper into the working environment to determine how these users might work together. Groups of users, particularly departments or project teams, tend to exchange mail mostly between themselves, while a lesser percentage of their mail is sent outside of the group. Having recognized this, it not only makes sense to try to group those users into the same site, but also onto the same Exchange server.

This is most apparent in the case of a project team that may use public folders to share information. If the members of the project team are split across different sites, then public folder information may have to be replicated across those sites. This inflates network traffic for public folder replication and can also lead to occasional synchronization anomalies (e.g., where one copy of the public folder information is more recent than the other). Hosting users on a single server also takes up less disk space, since Exchange stores only one copy of a message that's sent to a group of recipients and shares it between them. All of the users on a single server share the same Private Information Store. Otherwise, if a mail is sent to users on different servers employing multiple Private Information Stores, then more disk space is required to store the same amount of information.

Organizational and Management Issues

In much the same way as separate NT domains can be viewed as separate units of management, Exchange sites can be viewed as separate management entities as well. Many of the object properties that can be defined apply not just to a single server in a site but to all of the servers in the site. The Site Addressing properties and Information Store Site Configuration are examples of site-wide properties. If you set these properties on one server in the site, their values are set for all servers in that site. For this reason, you might want to compartmentalize groups of servers that will be managed by specific IT groups into sites. If you do this you can be sure that any changes that one IT group makes will not affect the settings on another group.

Directory Replication

The Exchange directory is maintained in a multi-master fashion within a site. This means that every Directory Service process has as much right to perform changes to the Directory as any other Directory Service process. Because changes can be made to the directory on any server, it's important that modifications be communicated to other servers on a regular basis.

Within a site, every server will communicate directly with every other server to request updates and to issue new and updated information. The default directory replication interval within a site is five minutes. If you've got a lot of servers in the site, then there's a good chance that directory replication will be going on at any given time, and if you make lots of changes to the directory on a regular basis, then the amount of network traffic can be significant. Because each server communicates directly with each other server, a lot of update information gets repeated every time another server is being updated. If you split the servers into a number of different sites, you can have more control over the way that directory replication takes place. Directory Replication between sites consumes less network bandwidth since only one copy of the directory information is exchanged between designated servers (called bridgehead servers) and the replication information is then fanned out to all the other servers in the site.

It's also interesting to note that when directory replication takes place within a site there's no compression applied to the replication packets. Exchange assumes that there is sufficient bandwidth to replicate directory information in its native format since you've grouped all of the servers into one site. However, when replication traffic is inter-site, then the DS compresses the packets before they are submitted to the MTA if the total amount of data to be replicated exceeds 50KB. Under this limit the DS doesn't compress replication traffic since the overhead to run the compression algorithm at each end is deemed to exceed the overhead to transmit such a relatively small amount of information over the network. This means that for any given network connection between two servers, less bandwidth is generally consumed by directory replication traffic if the servers are in different sites and you have frequent updates to the directory.

If you suspect that directory replication traffic will be considerable and you've got a number of servers at the far end of relatively slow network links, then you may not wish to group all of your servers into one site. Splitting the servers into separate sites may make more sense in this case.

2.3   Connecting Exchange Sites Together

Having decided that you need to split your Exchange organization into a number of different sites, the next problem you'll be faced with is how to connect the sites together. You need to have some form of site connection so that messaging routing, directory replication, and public folder access can be accommodated within the Exchange environment. Basically there are four different connectors which you can use for linking sites together:

- the Site Connector

- the Dynamic RAS Connector
- the X.400 Connector
- the Internet Mail Service Connector

Depending on which connector you use there are a variety of options available for controlling the flow of information between sites. Information flow between sites takes the form of messages, where all sorts of information is packaged up as a mail message and sent from the MTA on a server in one site to the MTA on a server in the other site. The MTA, like most Exchange components, has a variety of e-mail addresses, so there's little problem in mailing Exchange information from one MTA to another over any type of mail transport.

I'll discuss the Site Connector in some detail here since it's arguably the most common connector in use for linking sites. Apart from that, some of the following chapters will deal explicitly with the X.400 Connector and the Internet Mail Service Connector.

2.3.1   The Site Connector

The Site Connector is the preferred connector for inter-site communication because it is the most efficient and the easiest to set up, but it does require high quality bandwidth. The Site Connector links sites together using RPCs in much the same as servers within a site communicate.

Think of the Site Connector as a tunnel between the two sites. When you configure the connector, you have to set it up at both ends, so you'll have to create and configure the connector at one site, and then do the same at the other site. When you configure the first part of the Site Connector at your local site, you'll be automatically prompted if you wish to set up the other end of the connector in the remote site. If you're setting up the local Site Connector from an NT account that has administrative rights in the other site, then you can proceed to set up this other half of the configuration. Otherwise, you'll have to go and set up the other end manually. When you try to set up the Site Connector you are prompted for a server in the remote site. You can enter the name of any server in the remote site here, because the server name that you enter will not become responsible for hosting the far side of the Site Connector—it is just used to start off communications to allow the rest of the configuration to proceed. Okay, so that's how the Site Connector configured. Here's how it works:

When a server in one site wants to send a message to a server in another site, it can either make the delivery directly to the remote server that hosts the recipient's mailbox or it may employ some intermediate servers to route the message to the remote site. The route that the message takes depends on which of two ways you have decided to configure the connector.

When you first configure the connector, there's an option on the *General* tab that allows you to define a specific server in the local site to act as a bridgehead server or to allow you to use any server in the local site to send messages to the remote site. If you don't select a *Specific server* but decide to use *Any server* (the default setting), then when you send a message to a mailbox in the remote site, the message goes straight to that server from the server that you sent it from. If you select a specific server, then any messages for a server in the remote site will always get routed to this bridgehead server first. When the bridgehead server gets the message, it then becomes responsible for transferring the message to the server in the remote site that hosts the recipient's mailbox. But specifying a bridgehead server in your local site doesn't mean that there's a bridgehead server in the remote site. Figure 2–9 shows how communication takes place between two sites when you select *Any server* as the bridgehead, so that all servers make direct connections to servers in the other site, and Figure 2–10 shows the communication flow when you select a specific one for the local bridgehead.

FIGURE 2–9 All Servers in Local Site (Americas) Act as Bridgeheads and Talk Directly to Servers in Remote Site (Europe)

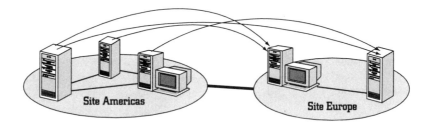

FIGURE 2–10 Bridgehead Server in Local Site (Americas) Handles Communication Directly to Servers in Remote Site (Europe)

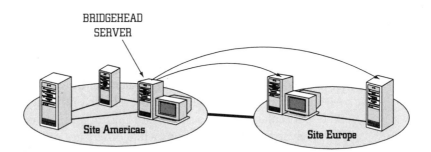

You can take this one step further by specifying particular servers in the remote site that you only ever want to receive messages from the local site. In a sense these could be the communication partners for your local bridgehead servers. When you select these partners, or *target servers,* they become responsible for receiving the messages from the local site and subsequently transferring messages to the destination servers in the remote site. You can select which servers in the remote site are to be target servers using the *Target servers* tab on the *Site Connector* property page. The servers that you list in the *Target servers* box in this tab will be the only ones capable of directly receiving mail from the bridgehead servers in the other site. This doesn't mean that other servers in the remote site are cut off. The upshot of this configuration is such that servers in the remote site that aren't listed as target servers have their messages relayed to them by the target servers, thus introducing an extra hop. Figure 2–11 shows how this works. All mail between servers in the two sites passes through the local bridgehead server and the remote target server. For example, a message sent from *SERVERA* would first go to the *BRIDGEHEAD SERVER,* then to the *TARGET SERVER* and finally to *SERVERE.*

FIGURE 2–11

Bridgehead Server in Local Site (Americas) Handles Communication Directly to Target Server in Remote Site (Europe)

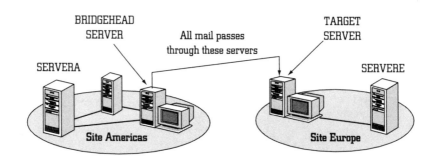

When you set up target servers, you can assign a *cost value* to each one. Assigning costs to individual servers allows you to control which servers in the target site are more likely to receive messages. Exchange uses the cost values that you define to "load balance," by means of a weighted average algorithm, across the servers in the remote site. Assigning a low cost value to a particular server doesn't mean that this server is used exclusively as a receiver for site connections while others are only used should there be a problem with the low cost one. The truth is that the low cost server will be used more often than the others; everyone gets their turn.

Remember that however you set up one side of the Site Connector the configuration only applies to messages that *leave* that site. So in the example that I've described in Figure 2–11, the channel that the message takes between the bridgehead and target servers is only valid for messages from *AMERICAS* to *EUROPE*. If you wanted to have the same kind of routing topology for the opposite direction then you'd have to have a similar configuration on the *EUROPE* side of the Site Connector.

Think carefully before you use the Site Connector to link your sites together. If you want to be sure of the path that messages will take when they transit from one site to another, then you'd be well advised to configure bridgehead servers and target servers as I've described above. Adopting this approach means that you can use dedicated servers for connecting sites together. The downside of strict message routing like this is that you introduce some criticality into the message path. If you select a specific server to be the bridgehead server, then you must be confident that the bridgehead server will be available, or else message delivery between the sites will stop. While you can select a number of specific target servers in the remote site to improve resilience, you may only specify one local bridgehead server, not a specific group of servers. (It sure would be nice if the Site Connector allowed you to specify a subset of the local servers to act as bridgehead servers, rather than the all-or-nothing approach that exists today.) You may only have one Site Connector configured between two sites, otherwise you could configure two, each one with a different local bridgehead server. If you do want to have message routing using bridgeheads and have some resilience, then you could use one Site Connector and perhaps another backup connector (X.400) for linking the sites together.

If you just accept the default settings when you configure the Site Connector, you'll get the greatest resilience for inter-site message transfer at the expense of not knowing exactly what route your messages will take.

Like intra-site communications, Site Connectors require permanent connections offering high bandwidth. You'll probably want to have a network connection of the same type you would use for intra-site communications, although you can probably get away with a little less bandwidth. Since the link across a Site Connector is sometimes only between two Exchange servers, depending on how you've configured it, with each one hosting one end of the Site Connector, there are fewer links than what you'll get with intra-site communication where all servers will have links with each other. Again your experiences with bandwidth requirements may vary from mine, but link speeds in the range of 64Kb/s to 128Kb/s are reasonable minimums with which to work.

Much like the RPC communication that takes place within a site, authenticated RPCs are used by the Site Connector as well, so you must ensure that the two sites you'll be linking together with the Site Connector share the same NT security context (same domain or different domains with trust relationships). There's also little in the way of "throttle control" with the Site Connector: It's an eager beast and as soon as it receives messages to be sent across it to the other site it will dutifully try to send them. That's why a permanent link is required; the Site Connector is not particularly suitable for scheduled connections.

You may well say that there doesn't appear to be a great difference in requirements between intra-site communication and inter-site communication using the Site Connector. And you'd be quite right. If you can use the Site Connector to link sites together, then there's probably little reason why you can't put all the servers into the same site in the first place. The only valid reason that I can come up with for building multiple sites and connecting them with a Site Connector is that you might want to partition your Exchange network into separate management domains. Otherwise I wouldn't be bothered with the trouble and I'd have all my servers in one big happy site. Table 2–2 lists the advantages and disadvantages of the Site Connector.

TABLE 2–2   Site Connector Advantages and Disadvantages

ADVANTAGES	DISADVANTAGES
▪ Easy to configure because it does not require configuration of a network transport (uses RPCs over available transport). ▪ Most efficient because there is no message translation. ▪ Well integrated into Exchange MTA and useful for failover/resilience when multiple connectors defined.	▪ Requires permanent high bandwidth connections. ▪ Requires single NT domain or trust relationships between domains. ▪ Cannot control message size sent through the site connector. ▪ Cannot schedule when connections are to be made.

2.3.2   The Dynamic RAS Connector

RAS is an acronym for Remote Access Services. The Dynamic RAS Connector is designed especially for connecting sites where a permanent connection is not available but there is a facility for using normal telephone connections to provide dial-up access from one server to another. This type of connection isn't optimal for large corporate environments or for connecting servers that will generate large amounts of traffic. However, if you need to connect a handful of people on a single server in a remote location, and reliable permanent links are either prohibitively expensive or hard to come by, then this is a good answer.

For the RAS Connector to work you'll need a modem on each of your servers at either end of the RAS connection, and you'll have to install and configure the Windows NT RAS Service on both servers. If you go to the *Control Panel* on your Windows NT server, select *Network,* and then click on the *Add* button within the *Services* tab, you'll be able to install the RAS service. I've always found modems to be rather tricky to install and get working (apart from on Windows 95!), but the RAS Service Installer and the Modem Installer seem to help you through the process pretty smoothly. Many other books go into good detail for configuring RAS, so I'm not going to belabor the point here. Once you've installed and configured the RAS Service in NT on both servers it might be a good idea to test it by making a dial-up connection from a remote PC just to check that the service is functioning properly and is capable of accepting connections.

That's only half the work done. Now you have to install the RAS Transport Stack from the Exchange Administrator's *File/New Other/MTA Transport Stack* menu item. There isn't much to configure here, but the important thing that you might want to set up is the *MTA callback number*. It's an optional parameter, so you don't need to give it a value. This number should be the telephone number of your local RAS server, i.e., the server that you're currently setting up the transport stack on. When you use the RAS connector to establish a session with another server, your local server first gives the callback number (if it exists) to the remote server. The session is then terminated and the remote server calls the local server back. This is a kind of authentication check (because you can check where the call went to), but it can also save on phone bills for the initiating server. (I use this from my Exchange server at home to dial back to the office.) With the transport stack configured you then need to set up the Dynamic RAS Connector itself from the *File/New Other/Dynamic RAS Connector* menu item, again from the Exchange Administrator Program. You can see how you might set this up in Figure 2–12.

FIGURE 2–12
RAS Transport
Stack Properties

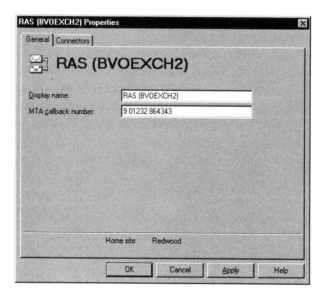

On the RAS connector property pages there are a number of settings you may want to adjust. Given that the connector is commonly used for slow telephone lines, you might want put some limits on the size of the messages that you'll be prepared to send over this connector. Sending huge files over a slow modem line could take a significant amount of time, so a limit of perhaps 2MB (set it on the *General* page) on the size of file that you'll accept is not unreasonable. Take a look at the *General* property page of the RAS connector in Figure 2–13.

FIGURE 2–13
RAS Connector
General Property
Page

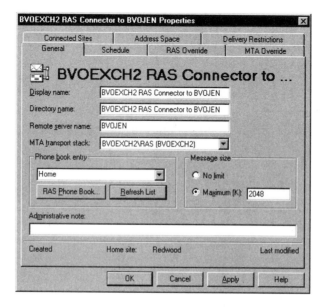

There's also a way to override some of the default MTA parameters. Exchange expects to use permanent, relatively high-speed network connections for sending messages from one server to another so the MTA parameters are defined with this view of the connected world in mind. Over a RAS connection, we should be more forgiving of network delays and other glitches. On the *MTA Override* page set higher values for *Transfer timeouts* to take the slow line speed into account, and lower values for *Association parameters* so that the link doesn't stay open for too long after the last message is transferred. Leaving the other settings for *RTS* and *Connection retry values* at their normal levels is adequate.

You'll need to set up the other property pages (Connected Sites, etc.) as you would for any other of the connectors. We'll discuss such connectors in detail later. The dial-up mechanism need not only be the normal telephone network: RAS connectors are happy to work over telephone line modems, ISDN modems, or X.25 modems. Table 2–3 lists the advantages and disadvantages of Dynamic RAS Connectors.

TABLE 2–3 Dynamic RAS Connector Advantages and Disadvantages

ADVANTAGES	DISADVANTAGES
■ Controlled/scheduled dial-up connections. ■ Useful over slow links or when reliable, permanent connectivity is hard to come by.	■ Complex to configure. ■ Information exchange is dependent on link speed and can be very slow. ■ Not useful when public folder replication is important.

2.3.3 The X.400 Connector

People tend to cringe at the prospect of having to implement X.400 just to get messaging working between Exchange sites. In reality, setting up X.400 Connectors for inter-site messaging is not the painful experience you might imagine. It is actually quite a flexible little devil that can run across a number of different transports and can be used to connect to external messaging systems as well as just other Exchange servers. We'll talk more about the X.400 Connector in a later chapter, but for the time being it's worth noting that this connector provides a very real alternative to the Site Connector for linking sites together.

The only two connectors that we've talked about so far have been the Site Connector and the RAS Connector. While each are certainly useful in their own way, you'll remember that the Site Connector uses RPCs between sites and has a significant bandwidth requirement of at least 64Kb/s or even higher. And the RAS Connector is typically only used when there's no permanent network connectivity at all. But in between these two levels of networking availability, we might just have a requirement for a connector to function over a permanent link that doesn't just have the dedicated 64Kb/s bandwidth available. Rather than take a risk with the Site Connector, you might decide to use the X.400 Connector.

The X.400 Connector does not use RPCs to transfer information between sites. (Remember that the information to be transferred can be interpersonal mail messages, public folder replication messages, or directory replication information.) Instead of sending the information in RPCs, the X.400 connector wraps up the information into special mail messages that it sends to the X.400 Connector on the target server. Sending messages over the X.400 transport is much less sensitive to the idiosyncrasies of the network transport, unlike the RPC mechanism, so there's less chance of the communication getting into trouble. This means that you can use the X.400 Connector over network lines where bandwidth may be questionable.

FIGURE 2–14
Using X.400
Connectors to
Connect Sites

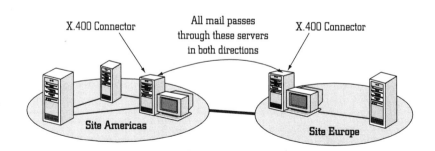

Using X.400 Connectors provides an implicit routing for messages between different sites. In Figure 2–14, you can be certain that mail sent between any server in one site to a server in the other site will always pass through both the X.400 Connectors. This routing is not dissimilar to the Bridgehead concept that is used by Site Connectors, but the message flow is much more rigid. Site Connectors offer some degree of resilience for inter-site traffic because of the many-to-many relationship between servers in different sites which eliminates a single point of failure. But we've introduced a single point of failure for inter-site traffic using X.400 Connectors as shown in Figure 2–14. In this environment, if any of the X.400 Connectors is unavailable, then all message transfer between the sites comes to a halt. This, of course, is not good, and could be considered to be major drawback for using X.400 Connectors. The only solution is to use a backup X.400 Connector between two other servers, so that should the primary connector route become unavailable, an alternative route is available for message transfer between the two sites.

FIGURE 2–15
Backup X.400
Connectors
Eliminate Single
Point of Failure

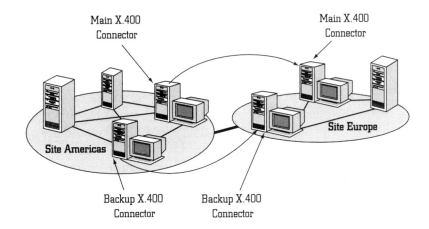

Figure 2–15 shows how you might use dedicated systems to provide a backup to the main X.400 inter-site connection. Typically you'd set the cost on this backup connector route to be higher than the cost for the main connection. Setting the costs like this means that messages will always be routed across the main link unless that link becomes unavailable for some reason (say a hardware fault on one of the systems). When a failure on the main link occurs, all inter-site traffic then takes place across the backup link. There's no interruption to service and users will never notice that the main link has been out of action. When the main link becomes available again, all inter-site traffic returns to it, and the backup link becomes dormant again. I have a particular preference for X.400 Connectors because the route that messages will take is always well defined. Unlike the free-will that's afforded to Site Connector-based traffic, where almost any server in a site can talk directly to any server in the other site, the X.400 connector ensures that messages always follow a known path. This can be of great help to support people when a user rings up to complain that their messages aren't getting delivered to their colleague that works in another country. Knowledge of the route that messages will definitely take will allow staff to quickly identify (and hopefully fix) the server that's causing the problems.

It may not be within your budget to have two servers dedicated to just sitting around waiting to spring into action should disaster strike your main X.400 site link. But there's no real need to have separate systems perform this function. Most messaging system administrators would probably set up the backup connectors on existing mailbox servers. There should be little impact on the mailbox servers during normal operation and you can still be assured that there's a route for the messages to take in the event of an emergency.

Flexibility is another key attribute of the X.400 Connector that can make it, at least to some people, pretty desirable. The Site Connector assumes that you've got lots of bandwidth to play with, whereas the X.400 Connector assumes very little. There are a number of options on the property pages of the X.400 Connector that allow you to put restrictions on how messages are sent. For example, you can put a limit on the size of messages that will be processed, you can schedule when you want mail to be sent across the link and you can even put restrictions on authorized users of the link thus allowing only certain people to send mail across the connector. This connector is also capable of running over a wide variety of network transports: TCP/IP, OSI TP4, X.25, and RAS, so it's happy to work with whatever network you might have and can link sites across a number of different transport types.

Now we must return to the concept of balance. There is a price to be paid for all of this flexibility, but it's not too high. The following factors need to be considered before you decide to implement the X.400 Connector:

- The X.400 Connector requires more setup effort because you have to configure transport stacks on both systems at either end of the connector and then you have to set up some parameters on the connector itself.

- Using X.400 as the connection between sites adds a little bit of overhead to the operation of the server because at the very least the header of an Exchange message must be converted to an X.400 format. (Depending on the configuration of the X.400 Connector, the whole message may need to be converted to X.400 but this should not be the case for inter-site connections.)

- There's no default encryption that's applied to messages in the same way that Site Connector traffic is encrypted.

We'll cover a lot more material about the X.400 Connector later, but in this section we've outlined how you can use it for linking sites together. Table 2–4 lists the basic advantages and disadvantages associated with the X.400 Connector in its role as a site connector.

TABLE 2–4 Advantages and Disadvantages for the X.400 Connector

ADVANTAGES	DISADVANTAGES
■ Controlled/scheduled connections between sites. ■ Offers restrictions on message size. ■ Good connector choice when inter-site available bandwidth is low, or network unreliable. ■ Provides well-defined path for message routing.	■ More complex to configure than the Site Connector. ■ Slight overhead when used for inter-site connections.

2.3.4 The IMS (SMTP) Connector

There is little doubt that the IMS (Internet Mail Service) Connector is the most popular means of connecting Exchange networks to external systems or to the Internet. While it's certainly well suited to this task given the growing popularity of the Internet—even my teenage nephew has an Internet address now—it's not the best connector to use for linking Exchange sites together.

This is not to say that you can't use it for this purpose, because indeed you can. But it should really only be used as a last resort. Of all the connector types that are available, this connector is the least efficient for inter-site messaging because all messages must get converted to SMTP/MIME* format before they travel across it. The size of the message after conversion is typically larger than the message in its native Exchange format so the impact that this message size will have on the network link should be carefully weighed up too. The conversion from native Exchange format to SMTP/MIME and vice versa is a processor intensive task and, of course, it needs to be performed twice: once at the sending system and then again at the receiving system. Irrespective of what conditions might exist on your network (bandwidth problems, unreliability, etc.) there's usually nothing that would prevent use of the X.400 as a viable alternative to the Site Connector, so you shouldn't really find yourself in the position where the IMS is the only connector that you can use.

Having said that, there is one special circumstance where using the IMS to connect sites is an appropriate measure to take. Let's say that you've got

---

* We'll learn more about SMTP/MIME in Chapter 6.

remote sites located in various parts of the world and you don't have an internal network infrastructure within your company that reaches those remote locations, but you do have the ability to send Internet mail from each location. At first sight, it seems that there's no way that you can create Exchange sites at these places and have them participate in the same Exchange organization. Site Connectors and X.400 Connectors are surely not appropriate because there's no permanent network connection, so you might be tempted to use the Dynamic RAS connector. The problem here is that the RAS connectors only provide very limited bandwidth for inter-site traffic, so it would be good if we could avoid using them at all. If there's local Internet connectivity available at each location, it's possible that you could manage to get a high-speed connection to the local Internet Service Provider (ISP). Using the IMS, you can link sites together by the Internet to backbone e-mail messages from one MTA to the other.

FIGURE 2–16
Backboning
Exchange across
the Internet

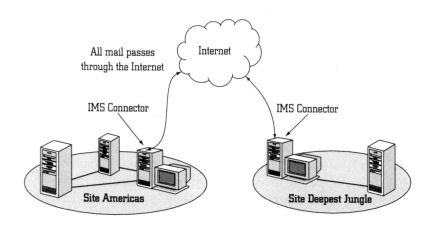

Take Figure 2–16 as an example. If you imagine *Site Deepest Jungle* to be located somewhere that a high-speed connection to an ISP can be provided, then a site connector can easily be established to link both *Deepest Jungle* and *Americas* together. If you do decide to backbone across the Internet, then you should be careful with replicating directory information and public folder information between sites. If you set the replication intervals to be very frequent then a lot of mail messages will be generated between the two sites, and this can all too easily clog up the Internet gateways.

When I use the words *high* speed for connection to the local ISP, I'm using it as a relative term. If the fastest ISP connection you can get is about 33Kb/s then there's not much in it between using the IMS and the RAS connectors for inter-site traffic. But it is less expensive to invest in a high-speed (let's say at least 64Kb/s) link to an ISP, rather than an international link between two different sites at the same speed to facilitate use of the X.400 Connector.

With this in mind, the IMS provides a reasonable solution for linking sites together in the face of a lack of connectivity options. However, if you have confidential information that you will be regularly sending between Exchange users, or if you will be replicating public folder information, then you might have cause to be concerned. The fact that you will have to send this sensitive information across the Internet, where any unscrupulous fellow may be able to intercept your information, may be a major risk but it should be possible to minimize the exposure of using the Internet for this mechanism. Using encryption techniques, either Exchange's built-in Key Management Service, or specialized encryption software at your Internet mail gateways, you could encrypt the inter-site traffic as it journeys across the Internet. This should serve to offer some protection.

In summary, Table 2–5 suggests not to use the IMS as a site connector unless you can possibly avoid it.

TABLE 2–5   Advantages and Disadvantages for the IMS as a Site Connector

ADVANTAGES	DISADVANTAGES
▪ Can use the Internet to backbone inter-site traffic.	▪ Conversion required (twice) for all messages that pass across the connector. ▪ Uses more bandwidth for inter-site traffic. ▪ No scheduling for connections available. ▪ When used across Internet, may expose sensitive information.

3

Message Routing and the Message Transfer Agent

3.1   Introduction

The Message Transfer Agent (MTA) is a critical component in an Exchange network if you've got anything more than one Exchange server. If you only have the one server in your whole network then you'll never be sending mail to a user that's located on a different server. The MTA is only used to transfer messages to mailboxes on other servers or to recipients on external messaging systems. So, with just the one server and no external connection requirements, then the MTA is pretty useless. If this is the kind of Exchange topology that you're likely to have then you can probably close this book now, and throw it away. This chapter won't be of much interest to you, and the rest of the book will be more or less useless as well.

Fortunately, the make-up of most corporate messaging environments is a little bit more complex than a single isolated server. That's good for me since I probably keep your attention for a little while longer!

We've already mentioned the MTA to some extent (see Section 1.2.3), but that was more or less just a general description of its role. In this section, we'll explore exactly how the MTA functions and what parameters and values affect its operation.

3.2   MTA Responsibilities

Apart from just transferring messages between systems, the MTA performs a number of other essential functions. Most of the MTA's functions are listed in Table 3–1, but we'll expand upon many of them in later sections.

TABLE 3-1 Important MTA Functions

FUNCTION	DESCRIPTION
Message Route Selection	This is the primary MTA responsibility. When messages are to be transferred between servers or foreign systems, the MTA determines which connectors provide a route to the destination server.
Connector Selection	After determining the route a message should take, the MTA must select a connector to route the message through.
Fan-Out	When a message arrives at an MTA and there are multiple recipients to the message, if this is not its final destination, the local MTA may have to route the message to a number of other MTAs or connectors. It's up to the MTA to recognize this situation and split the message into a number of separate instances, each one going to a separate MTA.
Conversion	When a message is transferred from one server to another some conversion on the contents might need to be applied. For example, messages will be stored in their native content type (say an SMTP/MIME message) unless instructed otherwise (*Convert incoming messages to MS Exchange contents* option on the *MTA* properties page). The MTA is responsible for performing this conversion.
Loop Detection	The MTA uses standard X.400 loop detection and trace information. As messages pass through MTAs, the loop trace fields in the messages are checked and if a loop is detected corrective action is taken.
Distribution List Expansion	Distribution Lists can be expanded on the local (any) server from which the message has originated, or it may be forwarded to the Exchange server that owns the Distribution List for expansion to take place there. The MTA determines if expansion is done locally or not, but is ultimately responsible for the expansion.
Report Handling	If a message has a report request associated with it, for example a delivery notification, it is the responsibility of the MTA to generate and then deliver this report to the originator of the message.

3.3   **Message Transfer on the Same Server**

Sending a message to another user on the same server is a pretty routine task for the Exchange server to accomplish. When you send the message from your client application, the message is placed into a temporary location, the *Outbox* in your area of the Exchange Private Information Store. The IS service then looks at the intended recipient of the message and if this user is located on the same server, then it simply places the message into the *Inbox* of the recipient which is stored somewhere else in the same database. Actually, it's not really placed specifically in the recipient's inbox. The message is just held in a big pool of other messages, and an entry in a database table that acts as the recipient's inbox is updated to have an entry point to the new message. If there are multiple recipients of the message, still only one copy of the message is kept, and all of the recipients' inboxes are updated with a pointer to the same message. This is basically all that's required for message transfer on the same server.

So how does the Exchange server work out that the sender and recipient are on the same server? Well, there are a few pieces to this puzzle, but the main player in this whole interaction is the Directory Service. We can get an insight to what happens by looking at some of the attributes of user mailbox account that you don't normally see either from a client or from the Exchange Administrator program. To see these attributes, you need to run the Administrator Program in *raw mode*. You can start up the Administrator in this mode by executing the following command either from a command window or from the *Run* item on the *Start bar*:

```
E:\EXCHSRVR\BIN\ADMIN.EXE /R
```

I've use E: for the location of my Exchange binaries and the ADMIN.EXE program, but you may have used a different directory. You should be able to find where the files are kept by looking at a few of your disk volumes, but in any event its location is specified in the Windows NT registry entry:

```
AdminDest
```

which can be found under:

```
HKEY_LOCAL_MACHINE\SOFTWARE\Microsoft\Exchange\Setup
```

In my example, imagine that I'll be sending a message from *David Kellet* to *Brian Boylan*. If I highlight the entry for *David Kellet* in the Raw Administrator and select *File/Raw Properties* (see Figure 3–1) for David I can see that his *Distinguished Name (DN)* which is defined by the *Obj-Dist-Name* property, is:

```
/o=Digital Equipment Corporation/ou=Redwood/cn=Recipients/cn=DavidK
```

I can also look at the *Home-MDB* property for David (see Figure 3–2). The value of this property on my server is:

```
/o=Digital Equipment Corporation/ou=Redwood/cn=Configuration/
cn=Servers/cn=BVOEXCH2/cn=Microsoft Private MDB
```

The /o=Digital Equipment Corporation part refers to my Exchange Organization name, the /ou=Redwood part is my Exchange site name, and the rest of this *Distinguished Name (DN)* indicates that I'm using the Private Information Store on server BVOEXCH2.

The /cn=Configuration/cn=Servers part indicates the containers under which the server and store reside. (To see how this is represented pictorially, look back to Figure 3–1.)

FIGURE 3–1
Selecting Raw
Properties from the
Administrator
Program

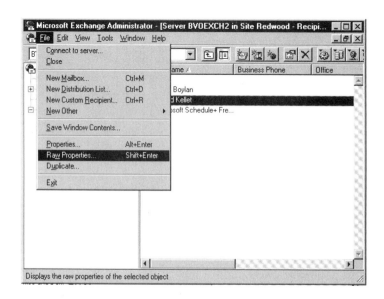

FIGURE 3–2
Raw Properties for
David Kellet

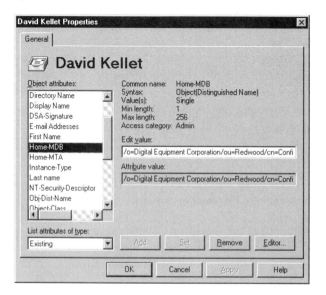

Looking at the *Home-MDB* property for the recipient of the message, *Brian Boylan*, I see that its value is:

```
/o=Digital Equipment Corporation/ou=Redwood/cn=Configuration/
cn=Servers/cn=BVOEXCH2/cn=Microsoft Private MDB
```

They're both the same! So by a few simple lookups to the Directory Service I can tell that both users are on the same server.

Exchange can retrieve this information too. By getting the Distinguished Names and other attributes associated with the recipients, it can work out how to route the message. In this case it's simple since both mailboxes are in the same store on the same server: the Private Information Store.

Since there has been no reason to send the message to another server, the MTA has no cause to be involved. But if the message has to go off of this server, either to another Exchange server, or to an external mail system then the MTA will take the message from the IS and deliver it to its intended destination.

3.4 Message Transfer to Another Server in the Same Site

The situation that arises when a message is sent to a user on another server in the same site is quite similar to the process described in Section 3.3. In this case, when Exchange looks up the attributes of the recipient of the message it can figure out that the recipient lives on another server. The attributes that are important in this case are the *Home-MTA* and the *Home-MDB* properties of the recipient. The Information Store service can readily tell by this stage that it can't handle the activity required to get the message to its destination because it can only deal with local message delivery. But it has a friend that can. The MTA leaps into action at this point and receives the message from the Information Store. Now that it's got the message, the MTA has a more or less relatively straightforward task ahead of it.

Since the other server is in the same site, the local MTA can make a direct connection to the MTA running on that server. In this case, there's no complexity associated with working out a path to the remote server like we'll see later for inter-site transfers. Because all of the servers in a site communicate directly with each other over RPCs, the local MTA simply transfers the message to the other MTA. Upon receipt of the message by the local MTA, the message gets handed over to the Information Store and finally gets delivered to the recipient's mailbox.

3.5   Message Transfer to Another Site

This is the most complex of all the message routing that takes place when a message is sent from one mailbox to another. Again the MTA plays a pivotal role in this transfer since the message must leave the local server. But the MTA has a number of problems to solve before the message can be delivered to the recipient. Unlike the case where a message is sent to another server in the same site, there's no mechanism for the MTA to communicate directly with the destination MTA.

So in order for the message to be delivered to the destination site, a route must be determined which provides a path from the local site to the remote site. In doing this, the MTA identifies all of the connectors that can deliver the message. Once the route has been established then a connector must be selected through which the message will be sent. Based on information associated with the connector, the MTA has a duty to select the best connector for message delivery. These two activities are known as *Route Selection* and *Connector Selection*. In order to get this information, the MTA needs to consult a table that maintains all of the available routes and connectors for the whole Exchange organization. This table is called the GWART.

3.6   The Gateway Routing Table (GWART)

Sites are connected to each other using connectors. The connectors between sites offer routes across which messages can travel to get from one site to another. When you configure a connector there are certain values that you will typically assign to a number of parameters. The most important parameters in terms of message routing are:

- address space;
- cost; and
- connected sites.

Based on the values of all the address spaces, costs, and connected sites properties for all of the connectors throughout the whole organization, every Exchange server maintains its own table which it can search to determine how a message can be routed to remote sites. This is the GWART.

3.6.1   Connector Address Space

The Address Space property is multi-valued, so you may set up more than one address space for any given connector. In essence, the address space defines the type of addresses that this connector will be pleased to accept messages for. Much like a filter, if the address of a recipient matches that address space on a connector, then the MTA knows that it can use this connector to transfer the message. But the address space and the recipient addresses don't need to match exactly. The MTA applies a matching rule based on what's defined as the address space on the connector and the address of the recipient. For example, imagine that we had a connector with an X.400 address space (we'll cover X.400 address in detail in Chapter 4) defined like this:

```
C=US;A=MCI;P=ACME;O=SALES
```

Then any recipient with an X.400 address that started off with these terms would be able to use this connector. So a recipient with an address of:

```
C=US;A=MCI;P=ACME;O=SALES;OU1=NYC;CN=LEO BLOOM
```

would pass through the connector because the higher order terms of the address matched. But a recipient with an address of:

```
C=US;A=MCI;P=ACME;O=MARKETING;OU1=NYC;CN=STEVE DALLAS
```

would have to be routed through a different connector because, in this case, the higher order address terms don't match.

3.6.2   Connector Cost

Each connector has a cost associated with it. The MTA takes the cost of each connector into account when it selects a connector to be used. Using costs on connectors allows you to implement a connecting topology between sites and to control the preferred path for messages to take as they travel from one site to another. The cost that you set on a connector is an arbitrary value and doesn't necessarily relate to the financial cost placed on the message or determined by the route that it takes. Generally speaking, the MTA will always be inclined to select the least cost connector.

For example, assume you have two network connections between sites *LONDON* and *PARIS*. One of those connections is over a 1Mb/s leased line, over which you have implemented an X.400 site connector. The other network link is a 33.6Kb/s dial-up modem connection over which you have implemented a Dynamic RAS Connector. To keep messages zipping between the sites as fast as possible, you'd prefer to use the X.400 Connector all of the time, but you'd really only want to use the RAS connector in times of emergency when the 1Mb/s connection was unavailable for some reason. To set costs on the connectors to reflect this preference, set a lower cost on the X.400 Connector and a higher cost on the RAS connector.

Costs can be set in the range 0 to 100, although the values 0 and 100 have a special significance. By default when you create a connector it has a cost of 1 associated with it. When I set up a connector, I like to set costs in multiples of 5 or 10, partly (strangely?) because it reminds me of line numbers in BASIC programming. Using multiples like this gives space to slot new connectors in at a later date with a preference that places them between existing connectors. If you'd used unary increments (1,2,3, etc.) for preferences and you later wanted to place a new connector in the middle of your existing preferences, you'd have to change values associated with the existing connectors. It is always best to avoid changing things that are established and working well, because changes always run the risk of introducing problems.

Setting a connector with a cost of 0 means that the MTA will *always* try to use this connector; the other connectors will only be used if this connector fails. At the other extreme, setting a cost of 100 on a connector means that it will only be considered for use if all other connectors fail.

Connector costs are cumulative. For example, suppose the path from *Site A* to *Site C* is via *Site B,* and the connector between *Site A* and *Site B* has a cost of 5. Also, the connector between *Site B* and *Site C* has a cost 5 as well. The total cost from *Site A* to *Site C* is 10.

3.6.3 Connected Sites Property

The *Connected Sites* property is only available on some connectors, namely the X.400 connector and the IMS connector. It defines the site that is logically adjacent to your local site. With the Site Connector, the fact that you are connecting to another site is implicit (that's what the Site Connector does!), but if you are using the X.400 connector or the IMS connector, then you may not necessarily be connecting to another site; you could be using those connectors to connect to an external messaging system.

When you connect to another site with the X.400 or IMS connector it's important to set the *Connected Sites* value so that you explicitly tell Exchange that to get a message to a particular site, it can use that connector.

Consulting the GWART provides the list of connectors and their *connected sites* partners so that when a message is to be sent from one site to another, a suitable connector can be easily identified.

3.6.4 How the GWART Is Maintained

Clearly it isn't exactly the same GWART that's used on every server, since the GWART specifies how to route messages from the local site to remote sites and this is slightly different depending on which site happens to be the local site. A component in each site, the *Routing Information Daemon (RID)* is responsible for building the GWART; in NT terms, it's personified in the EMS_RID.DLL file. The RID uses local site information and GWARTs from other sites that are stored and replicated in the Directory to build a consolidated local GWART. From this local GWART, routes are defined across the whole Exchange organization. The local GWART itself is stored in the Directory and thus becomes available to other sites. As well as being stored in the Directory, there is a text copy of the GWART held on the local server. You will find two files in the \EXCHSRVR\MTADATA directory; GWART0.MTA and GWART1.MTA. Respectively, these files represent the current routing table and the routing table just previous to the last change. Alternatively, you can look at the state of the GWART through the Exchange Administrator program by looking at the *Site Addressing* property page and selecting the *Routing* tab. (See Figure 3–3.)

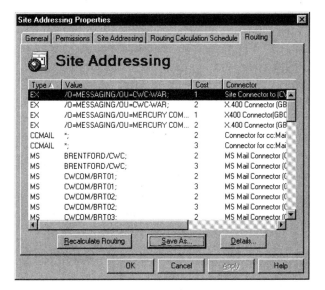

FIGURE 3–3
Viewing the
GWART

The GWART is rebuilt periodically, defined by the values in the *Routing Calculation Schedule* tab on the same property page. By default this is set to occur at 2:00 a.m. everyday, but, of course, you can change it. This might lead you to think that any changes you make to your Exchange environment by way of new connectors or new settings on connectors will only get reflected in the GWART every 24 hours based on the default schedule. However, the *Recalculate Routing* button on the *Routing* tab (see Figure 3–3) can be used to force the GWART to be rebuilt. Every time that you make a change to connectors or connector properties, you can press this button so that changes are included in the GWART and a new GWART is distributed to other servers.

But Exchange is even smarter than that. It detects when a change has been made that will affect routing within a site and will update the GWART accordingly. The refresh rate for the GWART within the site is pretty short, every few minutes, so it doesn't usually take very long after a change has been made to the site's routing properties before the GWART has been rebuilt to reflect this change. Then the new GWART is made available to all other servers in the site.

This covers GWART distribution within the site, but what of making the updated GWART available to servers in other sites? Remember that the GWART is held in the directory, so the frequency with which GWART updates are published outside the site is dependent on the Directory replication schedule between different sites. If the directory replication interval you have between sites is very long then it could take some time before local GWART updates are made available to distant sites and servers. If your Exchange organization is in a state of flux, it's good practice to set up the directory replication schedule so that updates are distributed a number of times during the day. For example, if you are installing new sites and new connectors as part of a roll-out of Exchange, you'll probably want to have this information distributed to other sites as soon as possible so that other users aren't kept out of the picture.

Within a site there is one server in particular that is designated to be in charge of the GWART: the *Routing Calculation Server*. This server is responsible for building the GWART when routing information changes, and then replicating GWART information to all other servers in the site. By default, the first server that you create in a site is designated as the Routing Calculation Server, so if you ever plan to remove this server then you should make sure to reassign the routing recalculation to another server.[*] You can

---

[*]   There are a number of Microsoft Knowledge Base articles which discuss removing the first server in a site and are well worth a visit.

change the Routing Calculation Server from the *General* tab on the *Site Addressing* property page. (See Figure 3–4.)

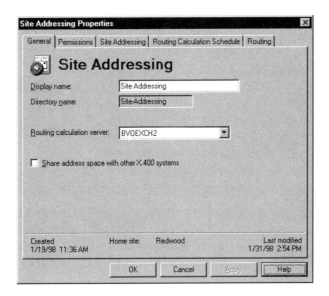

3.6.5   GWART Structure

Although you can view the GWART from the *Routing* tab on the *Site Addressing* page, to really get down to business and understand how the GWART is used for route selection, it's advisable to view the GWART via its manifestation as the GWART0.MTA file.

The GWART comprises three distinct areas, each of which representing a particular address type that Exchange can use to send mail. Each line in the GWART itself will start with an address type that falls into one of these categories. These address types will have an address space, a cost, and a connector (which offers the connection for that address space) and therefore a route is indicated to another site. You can see how each of these items are listed in Figure 3–3. These address types are shown in Table 3–2.

When Exchange determines that a recipient isn't local, i.e., doesn't reside within the same site, the MTA must decide how to route the message to its intended recipient. The MTA scans down though the GWART and searches for an address space that matches the address space of the recipient's address. (We outlined address space matching in Section 3.6.1.) If the MTA can find a match, then the message is routed to the associated connector for that address space.

TABLE 3–2 GWART Address Types

ADDRESS TYPE	DESCRIPTION
EX	*Exchange Distinguished Names (DNs).* This is the native Exchange Address format.
SNADS	For SNADS connector.
PROFS	For PROFS connector.
SMTP	For SMTP users.
cc:Mail	For cc:Mail users.
MS	For MS Mail users.
X.500	To retain replyability after running the Mover Server Wizard.

Figure 3–5 shows two sites with a number of connectors. Most connectors are associated with *AUSTRALIA,* but there are connectors in the other site, *EUROPE,* as well.

FIGURE 3–5
Sample
Connector
Topology

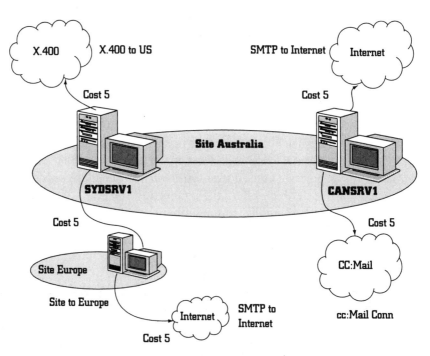

The resulting GWART for this environment would look something like:

```
TYPE         VALUE             COST   CONNECTOR
EX           /O=ACME/OU=EUROPE; 5     Site Connector (EUROPE)
SMTP         *;                5     Internet Mail Connector (CANSRV1)
SMTP         *;                10    Internet Mail Connector (LONSRV1)
X400         C=US;             5     X.400 Connector to US (SYDSRV1)
CCMAILCCM    /PO1;             5     cc:Mail Connector (CANSRV1)
```

3.7 Message Routing

When the MTA sends a message, each recipient is routed individually. This means that the MTA must look at each individual recipient on the TO field of the message and decide how the message should be routed to each one. Potentially, each possible recipient may be located in a separate site, so the MTA may have to perform multiple scans of the GWART in order to work out how to route the message. Fortunately, this isn't always the case and more often than not, a number of recipients will be found in the same site. This minimizes the work that the MTA needs to do when it comes to routing the message. We've already sketched (in Section 3.5) what the MTA needs to do to get the message to its destination. Now let's look at that process in some more detail.

3.7.1 Name Resolution

A recipient address consists of either the Distinguished Name (DN) or the X.400 O/R (Originator/Recipient) address or both. Although we'll discuss it in more detail later, an X.400 address can consist of standard O/R address terms and another component, called a *Domain Defined Attribute (DDA)*.

For a message to be sent outside of the site, a valid X.400 O/R address must be present. This is both important and testimony to the fact that X.400 is used as the native message transport within Exchange—irrespective of what you enter as the address of the recipient, an X.400 address will be used for routing purposes. When you enter a recipient address in the Exchange client you'll probably enter it in one of two ways. You'll either type in the recipient's normal name, like *Kieran McCorry*, and if this user exists in the directory then it is accepted as a native recipient address. Or you might enter a one-off address for the recipient.

Entering a native address won't bother us just for the moment. We'll assume that if the user is in the directory, then an X.400 address exists for that user. If you enter a one-off X.400 address then we've satisfied the requirement of having an X.400 address for the user. But can't you occasionally enter a one-off Internet address? What if your IMS is located in a different Exchange site? Then this message needs to be routed out of the local site to the site where the IMS is located. But I said that a message can only be routed out of the site if it had an X.400 address. How can this be? In this situation, the DDA part of the X.400 address becomes important. The Internet address that you enter is wrapped up in an X.400 O/R address, the DDA part holding the recipient's Internet address.

This is the process that's adhered to for name resolution to take place and for a valid X.400 address assigned to the recipient:

1. If no native address (DN) exists for the recipient, check that the DDA doesn't already hold a DN that may have been created during an earlier pass through the MTA.

2. If a native address (DN) does exist, then read the O/R address for that DN from the Directory.

3. Perform basic checking on the O/R address.

4. If the original DN was invalid or no DN could be located then scan the Directory for a match on the proxy addresses and obtain a DN from there. A fuzzy match may also be performed if a common name or surname exists.

5. If no O/R address can be found, then build one including the entered one-off address as a DDA.

6. If the current O/R address is invalid, then fix it by adding the local GDI[*] information.

You can see that the emphasis is on locating a DN and an X.400 address. When at least one of these have been determined, the GWART can be searched to find a route for the message.

3.7.2   Route Selection

The MTA searches the GWART based on the recipient's address. The MTA will try to locate a group of connectors that may be used to route the message for this recipient so that a choice of routing is available. The search through the GWART is done in a preferential order:

---

[*]   GDI is an acronym for the X.400 Global Domain Identifier.

Distinguished Name

The GWART is only searched for a match on this address type if the Name Resolution phase described above found a DN for the recipient. If one is found, then an exact match on the Organization and the Site is required.

Domain Defined Attribute (DDA)

A DDA such as MSMAIL, SMTP, or CCMAIL might be specified as part of the X.400 address (already generated) for the recipient. An exact, wildcard, or partial match on the DDA value is required with an exact or partial match on the DDA type. Wildcard matches are used in order of the exactness of the match, so an exact match would be first, followed by the wildcard with the next most matching characters, and so on.

O/R Address

An exact or wildcard match on the address space is required. Each field is compared against the contents of the GWART for the individual components of an X.400 address. If a match is not found that conforms to the hierarchy of the O/R address then the message is deemed to be undeliverable.

By the time the GWART has been traversed and the recipient address matched against the GWART's contents, then (hopefully) a group of connectors will have been determined capable of routing the message to the recipient. That was the easy part. Having selected a group of candidate connectors for the message, the MTA sets out to select one connector from the group that will have the honor of routing the message to the recipient's mail server.

3.7.3 Connector Selection

We've seen that the first part of message routing involves building a group of connectors that are known to provide a path to the destination server. Exchange uses quite a sophisticated selection routine on this grouping to decide on the connector that should be used to transfer the message. Taking into account the cost of the various connectors and other factors (like how successful a connector has been in the recent past), the MTA selects a connector that it hopes will offer the most efficient delivery. The selection routine is outlined in Figure 3–6.

FIGURE 3–6
Connector
Selection
Process
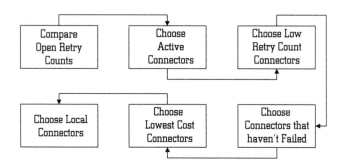

This process is only followed for Exchange server MTA-to-MTA connections over the Site Connector, the X.400 Connector, or the Dynamic RAS Connector. Connections to external systems or connections using the IMS Connector are not subjected to this process and subsequently don't enjoy the same richness of connector selection. This connector selection routine is quite powerful not only because it selects the best connector to transfer the message, but because it can reroute the message after selection if delivery problems occur. Once the message has been handed over to a particular connector, if a problem arises with this connector, the MTA can reroute it to another connector. When the message is handed over to the IMS Connector, in contrast, there's no opportunity for the MTA to reroute the message should a problem be detected with the IMS.

Before any selection tests are applied, the MTA performs a check on the connector that the message took to get to this, the local MTA. If the message arrived from a particular connector, then that connector is excluded from the following selection tests. The MTA carries out this exclusion to stop the message immediately backtracking on itself through the same connector. If the message were to be passed back through the connector that had just brought it here, then the loop detection code would probably jump into action and Exchange would assume that the message was looping. Anyway, there isn't much progress to be made in delivery if you immediately send the message back where it came from!

Compare Open Retry Counts

Each connector has a parameter associated with it called the *Open Retry Count*. When the MTA attempts to transfer a message across a connector, the connector attempts to establish an link between the local MTA and the remote MTA. A successful connection means that there's a channel through which the message can be sent. If the attempt to open the connection has been unsuccessful, then the MTA kicks off an *Open Retry Timer*. When the timer expires, the connector will once again try to establish the link. This process will be repeated a number of times, up to the value defined in the *Max Open Retries* parameter. If a message can only be routed across one connector and the attempts to open a link across that connector have reached the *Max Open Retries* value, then the MTA has no option at this stage but to mark the message as nondeliverable and route it back to the originator.

The MTA maintains a table of connection attempts for each connector in the header of the message that is currently being routed, and it looks at this table as it tries to route the message. The first phase of connector selection involves the MTA choosing a subset of the candidate connectors already determined during route selection. Only connectors whose connection *Open Retry Count* values are less than the value of *Max Open Retries* are selected by the MTA. Other connectors are ignored since they have been unable to establish connections previously. By now the MTA has established a group of connectors that are capable of routing the message to its destination and have not exhausted their connection attempts.

Choose Active Connectors

The X.400 Connector and the Dynamic RAS Connector have *activation schedules* associated with them. Unlike the Site Connector, the IMS Connector, or any other XAPI-based* connector the X.400 and RAS connectors can be configured to only transfer messages at particular times.

There are four possible values that can be set for the *Activation Schedule*: Always Active; Active at Specific Times; Remote Initiated; and Never Active. The Site and IMS Connectors have no way of controlling when messages will be scheduled for transfer and so are *Always Active*, but the X.400 and RAS Connectors might have any one of the above values set.

So, based on the schedule, a connector can be in any one of a number of *Activation States* at any particular time. The states are: Active Now; Active in the Future; Remote Initiated; and Never Active.

The MTA's third task is to examine the list of connectors that it has so far short-listed, and prune this down even further by selecting a connector that is most likely to be active as soon as possible. Obviously, top of the pile are

---

*   XAPI is an acronym for X/Open Application Programming Interface, an API for access to Message Transfer Agents (MTAs) ratified by the X/Open Association.

those connectors that are *Active Now*. If the MTA can find connectors in this state, then this becomes the newest subgroup of connectors that are likely to be used for message transfer. If no *Active Now* connectors can be found, then connectors that will be *Active in the Future* are the next most desirable and the ones that will be active soonest are selected. Coming in at third preference, *Remote Initiated* connectors are chosen only if the quest for *Active Now* and *Active in the Future* has been fruitless. And bringing up the rear, *Never Active* connectors are only selected if nothing better is available. It's clear what the MTA is doing here: Having found connectors that are capable of transferring messages to the destination and have been working reasonably well in the past (*Open Retry Count* within threshold), the MTA tries to find a group of connectors that are likely to be able to transfer messages as soon as possible.

Choose Connectors with Lowest Retry Counts

At this stage the MTA examines the connectors which have made it through the selection process so far. Remember that for every connector that might possibly be used for transfer, there'll be an entry in the connection retry count table in the message header. The MTA scans this table and compares the values for the *Open Retry Count* for the current subgroup of connectors. It selects only those connectors that have the lowest retry count values.

Choose Connectors That Haven't Failed

The process of refining the best connectors to use still hasn't finished. The MTA looks for connectors that currently have an *Open Retry Timer* active. If a timer is active for a particular connector then the MTA can tell that the last connection attempt that this connector made failed. The MTA's logic, in this case, is to ignore a connector that it knows has just failed to make a successful connection; if it failed a short time ago, chances are it will fail next time as well.

Compare Costs

Having run the gantlet of active connector and lowest retry count checks, the MTA should have identified a group of connectors that all appear to be in good health and likely to be able to transfer messages. The overriding selection criterion at this point is to select the connector or group of connectors with the lowest cost. If there is only one lowest cost connector, then this becomes the chosen one. If there are a number of connectors, all sharing a low cost, then selection passes through to the next stage.

Provided a connector is active and isn't in the process of retrying an connection, the lowest cost connector will always be selected. It's only in the case of a connection problem that a lowest cost connector is passed over in preference for a higher cost one.

Choose Local Connectors

The MTA differentiates between *local* connectors and *remote* connectors. A connector is said to be local if it resides on the same server as the MTA. (Its location can be derived from the *Home-MTA* property of the connector.) If the connector is remote, then it lives on another Exchange server in the same site. To send a message through a remote connector means that the MTA has to transfer the message to the other hosting Exchange server. This obviously requires an extra hop for the message, so quite rightly, the MTA will always try to select a local connector in preference to a remote one.

You might recall from our description of Site Connectors (see Section 2.3.1) that we might have defined a local bridgehead server to act as the Site Connector, or we may have opted for the alternative, which is to let any server arbitrarily make the connection to the other site. If you haven't selected a dedicated bridgehead server, then the Site Connector is assumed to be local to your MTA for the purposes of selecting local servers over remote ones.

This is the end of a long and arduous selection process for the message in question. If we reach any of the stages and end up with no connectors that satisfy the selection criteria for that stage, then the message is marked for nondelivery and returned to its sender. (You'll be glad to know the chances of this are pretty slim, though.) Even if a connector is set to be *Never Active* it still has a chance of getting a message handed to it and held in its queue, so there's almost always a candidate connector to route the message. Don't worry about a message that gets sent to a connector that's scheduled to never deliver mail—the message won't stay there, forever and forgotten. Sooner or later a timeout will expire on the message and it will get nondelivered.

3.7.4 Load Balancing

If the MTA reaches the end of the selection process and it's got more than one connector to choose from, then load balancing comes into effect on the connectors. The load balancing algorithm is very straightforward. While there might be some value in selecting a connector based on its current queue size, or the size of the messages, the MTA avoids the complexity associated with working this out. Exchange simply makes random selection from the group of candidate connectors that have made it this far.

Finally, the last form of load balancing relates only to the Site Connector. In discussing this connector earlier, we saw that target MTAs are associated with this connector. If there's a list of MTAs that are capable of receiving the message at the other end of this Site Connector, then the local MTA will select a target MTA based on cost. Similar rules for cost apply to target MTAs as well as connector selection and costs may be between 0 and 100. The MTA uses a *cost-weighted randomization* to select target MTAs with differing costs.

3.7.5 Message Fan Out

Although the message is routed separately for each recipient, this does not mean that a separate copy of the message is sent for each user. The MTA *fans out* the message so that only one copy of the message is sent across any particular connector irrespective of the number of recipients at the other end. For example, imagine that the MTA on a server in site *ASIA* is transferring a message for ten recipients. Let's assume that five of those recipients are on a single server in site *AMERICAS* and the other five are on a single server in *EUROPE* (see Figure 1–4). If there are no problems with any of the connectors between all of the sites, it's likely that the MTA will send the messages to the European server through one connector and to the American server through another connector. Two connectors will be used and only two copies of the message will be sent: one message per connector, not five copies per connector. This approach of transferring a single copy of a message destined for multiple recipients is common and means that network bandwidth and CPU cycles aren't wasted.

It is likely that you might have multiple recipients on a message, and we know that for each recipient the MTA must go through the same process of route selection and then connector selection. If the same final connector group appears for a subsequent recipient on the same message, then the connector used previously for routing to this address space is preferentially selected again. This means that messages to the same address space (probably to users on the same server) all get routed through the same connector. This supports the fan out concept nicely. If we ended up with the same final connector grouping and just randomly selected a connector, then the fan out model would break and we'd end up sending more copies of messages than we need to.

3.7.6 Message Rerouting

When the MTA hands a message off to its chosen connector, it assumes that the connector will deliver the message to the remote MTA. But occasionally connectors fail and are unable to successfully deliver the message. If this occurs, then the MTA, with some notable exceptions, will take the message back from the connector and start the whole process of route selection and connector selection all over again. There's no need to exclude the connector that failed last time round. It will probably be rejected anyhow when the "Choose Connectors that haven't failed" test is executed during connector selection. So, chances are that the MTA will end up with a different final group of connectors for routing.

I made reference to some exceptions to MTA rerouting. We've come across one already earlier in this section when I mentioned that when a message is passed to the IMS Connector, there's no opportunity to get it back within the reach of the MTA should a problem develop with that connector. The same is also true of the Microsoft Mail Connector, the cc:Mail Connector, and basically any connector that's used to provide connectivity to external messaging systems. These connectors are all integrated into Exchange using the EDK (Exchange Development Kit) and maintain their own queues outside of the MTA's control.

Why are these connectors different from the ones that do support rerouting? The differences are subtle, but important. The Site Connector, the X.400 Connector, and the Dynamic RAS Connector are all *native connectors*. They are very closely integrated with the MTA and essentially are just extensions of the Exchange messaging structure. The Site Connector uses RPCs just like Exchange server-to-server intra-site communication, and in terms of communication, the Dynamic RAS connector is basically a dial-up version of the Site Connector. If you're an Internet bigot, try not to be too alarmed with this next statement: The whole Exchange messaging engine is more or less based on X.400 anyhow, so it should come as no surprise that the X.400 Connector is closely integrated as well. The other connectors just aren't as tightly integrated, so the MTA has less control over them.

The other exception to rerouting applies to native connectors with an Activation State of *Remote Initiated* or *Never Active*. The MTA is only capable of rerouting a message if something has gone wrong. As long as no other MTA attempts to connect to the connector in the *Remote Initiated* state, or the schedule is not changed for the connector in the *Never Active* state, then, really, everything is just dandy. This is life as it should be for these connectors and no failure has occurred. No activity means that there's no chance of a connection failure so there's no reason for the MTA to become involved in rerouting the message.

When a native connector fails to establish a successful link with a remote MTA, the message that was being transferred is immediately rerouted by the local MTA. The MTA also increments the *Open Retry Count* parameter for that connector within the message header and an *Open Retry Timer* is initiated so that the connector will attempt the connection again soon (10 minutes in the case of the Site and Dynamic RAS Connectors). If all of the connectors fail to successfully transfer the message and the retry count exceeds the maximum allowed value, then the message is marked for nondelivery and returned to the originator.

However, if the message is successfully rerouted through a different connector, then external and internal trace information in the header of the message is updated by the MTA to indicate that a reroute has been performed. The update to the trace information is very important, since the reroute of the message might cause it to travel back through a connector that it visited earlier. Ordinarily, if a message visited the same MTA twice then this might indicate a looping message. Loop detection code built into the MTA is designed to detect this and remove the message, but in the case of a reroute it's possible that the message might double-back on itself, so loop detection trace information is reset to indicate a special case.

By way of example, let's take a look at Figure 3–7 where we have multiple sites connected via X.400 Connectors. Imagine that a user on server *DOPEY* sends a message to a user on server *HAPPY*. The MTA will route the message to server *GRUMPY* and then try to transfer the message across the connector between *GRUMPY* and *HAPPY*. But what if *GRUMPY* and *HAPPY* don't want to talk to each other and the association fails? The MTA should immediately reroute the message via the alternative (although higher cost) path to *HAPPY*. This means that the message is sent back to *DOPEY*, *SLEEPY* wakes up, receives the message from *DOPEY* and transfers it to at last to *HAPPY!*

This is reasonably straightforward, but it illustrates the fact that circular routing of mail has taken place for this reroute to occur. In normal operation, this kind of circular routing should be avoided and indeed would be detected by the MTA on *DOPEY* as a message loop. In this case, when *GRUMPY* rerouted the message it updated the trace and loop detection information on the message to prevent *DOPEY* being suspicious of a loop.

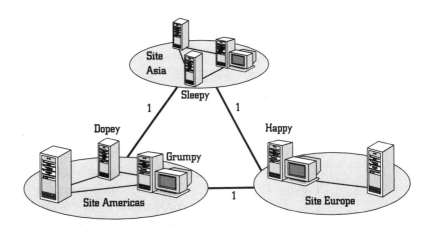

FIGURE 3–7
Message Rerouting

3.7.7 Loop Detection

Exchange uses standard X.400 trace information, although there are some extensions for Exchange-specific operations. Trace information comes in two flavors. *Internal trace* information is used to track the progress of the message as it moves within what the X.400 people call a *Management Domain*. For our purposes, it's probably sufficient to assume that a Management Domain is an Exchange organization. *External trace* information is used for messages that pass between management domains, or in our case, from an external X.400 messaging environment to an Exchange organizational environment and vice versa.

The external trace information is important, but we'll talk more about that later in Chapter 4.

For internal trace information the process is not very complex. Basically, when a message passes through an Exchange MTA, the MTA stamps the message and puts information into the header indicating that the message passed through this MTA. Every time an MTA receives a message it scans the internal trace information, and if it finds its own name there, then it knows that the message has looped. This will generally cause the message to be nondelivered. The only exception to this rule occurs if the MTA finds its own name and more trace information to indicate that the message was either rerouted, redirected (to another recipient), or had a Distribution List expanded (which might genuinely cause it to loop back to the same MTA). In this case, the message is accepted and normal routing takes place.

3.8   Building Resilient Exchange Networks

Understanding some of the ins and outs of how the MTA interacts with the various connectors is pretty interesting in and of itself, but it also lets you build an Exchange environment that is tolerant of server, connector, and network link failures.

There's little doubt that Site Connectors have the simplest requirements for setup and configuration, but as we've seen already they offer little in the way of defining well-known paths for inter-site message transfer. If you're looking to use dedicated connection servers for message transfer, then you've got much more configuration work to do. This free-will policy for routing is to their advantage in terms of resilience, because the default configuration will allow any server in a site to connect to any target server in the remote site when a message is to be sent from one server to another. They interact very closely with the MTA, so if a connector fails, the MTA will be quite happy to reroute the message to another connector for another delivery attempt. Of course, the disadvantage with Site Connectors is their sensitivity to the network, so this might compromise their inherent resilient routing capabilities.

The X.400 Connector may well be the best option for use in an environment where resilience is top of your list. It's certainly less sensitive to the network than the Site Connector and the MTA is just as forgiving with a failed connector association as it is with the Site Connector, so messages won't get stuck in a queue for long periods of time.

Figure 3–8 shows an excellent example of building a reliable and redundant Exchange network based around X.400 Connectors. This may seem rather over-the-top to you, but if you're building a mission-critical messaging environment and you've got the money to do it, this solution may be ideal. In fact it's a modification of an environment that I was involved in planning for a large multinational corporation. You could change bits and pieces to suit yourself, perhaps with an emphasis on the Site Connectors as the primary interconnection mechanism with X.400 components for the last line of defense or a reduced number of SMTP servers. The overall approach merely serves to illustrate the point.

FIGURE 3–8 A
Resilient Exchange
Environment Based
on X.400
Connectors

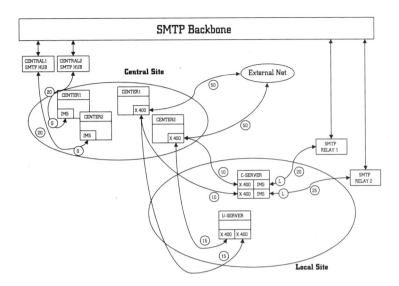

Let's see what makes it tick and why it is inherently resilient:

- Although there's only two sites shown in Figure 3–8, there are actually many sites in the real environment that were removed for the purposes of clarity. In the real implementation there is one *Central Site* (as shown) and a number of other *Local Sites*. Each *Local Site* is actually in another country, but their only connections to each other are via the *Central Site*.

- The underlying network was a hub and spoke affair; the natural hub to the network was at the *Central Site* location. This effectively dictated what the connector infrastructure between all of the local sites and the central sites should be. There is surely no point in having direct local-to-local site connections since the Exchange connection would be passing over the network connection that always went to the *Central Site*. A failure on the link to the *Central Site* would essentially disable all other direct connections to other sites. Maintaining some synergy between the network topology and Exchange topology facilitates a clearer understanding of how messages move across the network from one location to another.

- The *Central Site* is actually split across two different locations (*Center1* and *Center2*) in a major European capital city. The locations are connected via a high-speed network connection (greater than 10Mb/s) so there is no issue with direct RPC communication between the servers in this site.

- Within each location in the *Central Site* there are two dedicated *Connectivity Servers*. One server is dedicated to X.400 connections to each of the *Local Sites* and to external X.400 connectivity while the other server is a dedicated IMS Connector to a corporate-wide SMTP backbone. The duplication of X.400 and IMS connector servers in the central site provides redundancy at the natural hub of the Exchange environment.

- Each *Local Site* has redundancy built into its design as well. Within the *Local Site* there is a dedicated *Connectivity Server* (C-SERVER). The connectivity server provides the main site connection back to the *Central Site* and thus to all other sites as well. All user mailboxes in the *Local Site* are hosted on U-SERVER system.

- The connectivity server hosts two X.400 Connectors each with a cost of 10. One of the X.400 Connectors is linked to the connectivity server in *Center1* back in the *Central Site* and the other X.400 Connector is linked to the connectivity server back in *Center2*. This means two things. Since all inter-site traffic moves through the *Central Site*, we've introduced two X.400 Connectors at the center to eliminate a single point of failure. Should either of the *Central Site* X.400 Connectors (*Center1* or *Center2*) become unavailable, traffic between all sites is still maintained since the remaining server still has connectivity to all of the other sites. Both the X.400 Connectors back to the *Central Site* have a cost of 10 so there's no preference for which connector is chosen. This means that all inter-site traffic is load balanced across the two connectors. The *Center1* and *Center2* servers back in the *Central Site* will share the inter-site traffic between them.

- What if the connectivity server in the *Local Site* fails? If this was the only connection to the *Central Site,* then the *Local Site* would be cut off from the rest of the organization. To cope with this possibility, there are two X.400 Connectors on the user mailbox server in each site as well. The X.400 connectors on the user mailbox server each connect to the *Center1* and *Center2* servers in the *Central Site* so even if the local connectivity server fails and one of the *Central Site* X.400 Connector server fails, mail can still flow from site to site. The X.400 Connectors on the user mailbox server are configured with a cost of 15 so they'll only be used if the X.400 Connectors (cost 10) on the dedicated connectivity server are unavailable.

- The connectivity servers in each site also host IMS Connectors to provide connections to an internal SMTP backbone and to the Internet.

The *Central Site* has two dedicated IMS Connector servers as well to provide SMTP connectivity. Although we'll discuss this later, the IMS connectors are configured so that the ones in the *Local Site* can only be accessed by MTAs in that site (indicated by the *L* for *Local*) and not by any MTA outside of the site. The IMS Connectors in the *Central Site*, however, are configured so that MTAs in any site may use them (indicated by the *G* for *Global*) and their existence is propagated throughout the Exchange environment with the GWART.

- You can see from the diagram that all of the IMS Connectors link into a central SMTP backbone. This means that all sites are implicitly linked over SMTP as well as being linked over X.400.

- While it's true that the IMS Connector is the one which we'd least like to use to link sites together, it's clear that using an SMTP-based inter-site connection mechanism in this environment as a last resort may well be beneficial.

- The IMS Connectors in each *Local Site* have the *Connected Sites* property set on them in just the same way as the X.400 Connectors do. The costs for the IMS Connectors are set quite high at 20 and 25 for connection to the *SMTP Relay1* and *SMTP Relay2* servers respectively. The SMTP relay hosts are located at each site and provide a mechanism for connection into the SMTP backbone.

- In the event that X.400 can't be used for inter-site traffic (only because both X.400 servers in the *Central Site* are unavailable) then the IMS Connectors can be used to provide connectivity between the various sites. Note that there's no reason for IMS-based inter-site traffic to actually pass through the dedicated IMS Connectors in the Central Site. The IMS Connectors in each site can easily communicate with each other via the SMTP backbone.

- The costs on the IMS Connectors are set higher than the costs for the X.400 Connectors on the connectivity server or the user mailbox server within the site so that SMTP will only be used as last resort for inter-site traffic. Additionally, for native SMTP mail within the *Local Site*, the local IMS connectors will always be used because the cost associated with them is either 20 or 25. The IMS Connectors in the *Central Site* have an aggregated cost of 30 because you have to pay the cost of the hop via the X.400 connector (cost 10) to get to them.

- The X.400 connector links from the *Central Site* with a cost of 50, link to an external messaging system. But if these connectors were actually used to connect to another part of the Exchange organization, say an intercontinental link to the United States, then high costs like this would offer a layer of insulation from connector costs in the U.S. environment. You could even set these values much higher, maybe around 80 or 90, if you wanted to be even more certain of maintaining a *them-and-us* barrier. Traffic that is meant for the U.S. part of the environment would always get through irrespective of the cost due to the configuration of the *Connected Sites* and *Address Space* properties.

This topology provides a good deal of redundancy for various components. A lot of servers would need to fail for messaging connectivity between sites to be interrupted. Let's say that you've got a 1 percent chance of any Exchange server going down in a given week. In Exchange terms, only if the two *Central Site* X.400 Connectors failed *and* the *Local Site* connectivity server failed would inter-site connectivity become unavailable. Simple probability theory suggests the chances of this happening are about one in ten thousand.

If you put backup IMS Connectors on the local user mailbox server and backup X.400 Connectors on the *Central Site* IMS servers, then the probability of failure reduces to one in ten million. You could continue adding failover and redundancy paths, but it's important to draw the line somewhere.

The Achilles' Heel in this environment is, of course, the network. If the network link back to the *Central Site* fails then all of the routing redundancy built into the design becomes, well, redundant! That's another problem for someone else to have built redundancy into, but whatever the network design, it pays to keep a close eye on it when designing an Exchange routing and failover topology. And if the user mailbox server fails then you're cut off from the network anyhow.

3.9   Connector Scope

Controlling the conditions under which a connector may be used for transferring messages is not as straightforward a problem as you might think. We've seen from Section 3.7.3 that the MTA primarily bases its decision on which connector to use by comparing the costs of the various connectors, with least cost connectors being favored over higher cost connectors. Section 3.6.2 explains this process and also introduces the special case of the connector with a cost of 100: *only use this connector if all others fail.* A cost of 100 is the maximum cost that you can assign to a connector, and by definition it will be used if no other means of delivering the message can be found.

But what if you want to control not just the order of preference for using a connector, but also the very fact that it is used at all? The example most often cited in relation to this is the use of the Fax Connector.*

Imagine that you have an Exchange organization that spans both the American and European continents, perhaps with servers located in San Francisco and London. Let's assume that the nice system manager in San Francisco installs a Fax Connector on the local Exchange server at lunchtime on Friday. The San Franciscans are no doubt excited with this new connector and they're busy faxing people all over the States for the rest of the day. Life is good in the world of Exchange. The time difference between San Francisco and London is eight hours, so by the time the Fax Connector is up and running in San Francisco most of the Londoners should have gone home for the weekend.

But on Monday morning when the London folks log onto their Exchange server, through the magic of the GWART and directory replication, they'll see the Fax Connector too! Now, Londoners are just as excitable as the folks from San Francisco, so there's no doubt that they will want to use the Fax Connector as well to fax to all of their friends elsewhere in London and its environs. But there's the rub! Every time a London Exchange user sends a fax, it's actually sent from San Francisco to the fax recipient in London. Suddenly life isn't so good in the Exchange world! This is a costly way to fax a friend perhaps just a few miles away, for instead of the cost of the fax call being at a local rate, it's now at an international rate.

Up until Exchange Server V5.5, there wasn't really an obvious way to restrict just how far knowledge of a connector might get propagated. It was basically an all-or-nothing situation. But now there's an option that you can set on the properties of the *Address Space* of a connector that limits its scope (see Figure 3–9).

By default the scope is set to *Organization*. This means that the connector is included in the Organization-wide GWART and users on any server in any site have knowledge of this connector and may send messages through it.

Setting the scope to *This Site* prevents knowledge of this connector being propagated to the GWARTs in other sites, and only users that are homed on

---

*   There are no Fax Connectors as part of the Exchange product, but there are many third party products available that integrate with Exchange to enhance its connection capabilities. Faxination™ from Fenestrae (http://www.fenestrae.com) is a good example of a Fax Connector.

a server in the local site can send messages through the connector. No access is available for users in other sites.

FIGURE 3–9 Setting Scope Restrictions on Address Space Properties

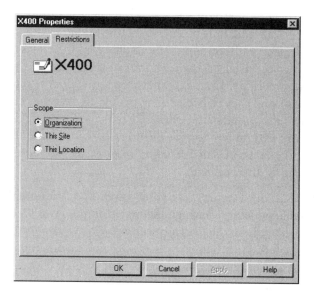

The most restrictive functionality may be achieved by setting the scope to the *This Location* option. This restricts the connector's availability to any servers that share the value of Location on the *General* tab of the server object. Without doubt, this defines the greatest amount of flexibility for message routing when coupled with connector costs.

In Figure 3–8, the IMS Connector in the *Local Site* is set up so that it is local (indicated by the *L*) to the site. This means that only recipients that are homed in the local site can actually see and make use of the connector. But in the case of the IMS Connectors in the *Central Site*, knowledge of these connectors is shared amongst all other sites (indicated by the *G* for *Global*) so that any user in any site may transfer a message through the central IMS Connectors.

The requirement in this environment was to localize outbound SMTP traffic so that Internet-bound mail entered the SMTP backbone as soon as possible without travelling across the Exchange backbone. This is essentially done with costs so that local connectors are favored over remote connectors. If the local connector becomes unavailable for any reason, then Internet-bound mail may be routed via the central connector at a higher cost.

Setting the scope of the IMS Connector in the *Local Site* to *This Site* means that its existence won't be propagated to other sites. This keeps a strict control in place for how messages may be routed through the various IMS connectors and prevents chaotic routing paths for messages becoming available.

3.10 MTA Configuration

Routing messages is without doubt a complex business, and the majority of your efforts in configuring MTA behavior should be oriented in this direction. The MTA itself requires surprisingly little configuration. It's quite capable of running successfully and efficiently straight out of the box. Having said that, it is worthwhile devoting some attention to one or two areas of MTA configuration.

3.10.1 Message Transfer Agent Properties

You can set properties for the MTA by using the Administrator program to select the desired server in the *Servers* container, which you'll find under the *Configuration* container and then double-clicking on the *Message Transfer Agent* icon in the right-hand pane of the Administrator window. Figure 3–10 shows the *General* tab that you should see when you look at the MTA properties.

Local MTA Name

Planning is everything when implementing Exchange and hopefully your plans extend to names for Windows NT servers as well. Unless you've changed this attribute, the MTA should inherit the name of the Windows NT server that it is running on. I think it's a good idea not to mess with this attribute. Having a different value for the name of the MTA and the NT server that it's running on only leads to confusion and steals time when something breaks and you're desperately trying to find the right server to fix. Getting the naming structure right for the NT server first time round should eliminate the requirement to set this attribute. I'd only advise changing the name of the MTA if you're stuck with a server name and you find that you can't make connections to a foreign messaging system because of the default value. If you observe some reasonably simple rules on server naming, you should be in the clear.

In general the value for MTA can be up to 32 alphanumeric characters as well as some special characters like hyphens or underscores and the like. My recommendations for NT server names are straightforward: The name that you choose should be based on a code that you can use within your organization and reflect:

- who owns the server;
- the location of the server;
- its function; and
- how many of these servers you have at that location.

Thus, names like CWCSFOM02 might be mean:

- The server is owned by California Wine Company (CWC);
- Is located in San Francisco (SFO);
- Is a Mailbox server (M); and
- Is the second mailbox server at that location.

Using *M* for mailbox server, *C* for connectivity server, *P* for public folder server, etc., is common practice. Avoid implementing a code that might have the letter *O* next to the number *0*, or having the lowercase letter *L* ("*l*") next to the number *1*. Such schemes only lead to confusion and typographical errors. You'd be amazed at how many hours you can easily spend troubleshooting a problem, only to find later that you'd typed the wrong value in.

Avoid naming codes that are too obscure or longwinded, since this only leads to errors as well. Some characters are most definitely to be avoided. Spaces, underscores, and hyphens, even though they are permitted, are usually bad news in server and MTA names. These characters can have disastrous effects when connecting to other messaging systems that misinterpret them (especially X.400) or using other applications, like Microsoft SQL Server or Microsoft System Management Server (SMS), which don't support them.

Local MTA Password

By default there's no value that gets set for the MTA password. The password is only used if a foreign system needs to specify a password that's associated with the MTA. Some X.400 systems require this, but most will allow you to specify a connection without any need for a password. Avoid using it if you can; it's just one more thing to go wrong if you set a value for it.

Message Size

The default behavior is not to impose any limit on the size of messages that can pass through the MTA. If you specify a value for the maximum size, the

MTA will reject any messages that exceed it and send them back to the origi-nator. Under normal circumstances, I don't see any reason to restrict mes-sage sizes unless you've got some very slow links that you don't want to see clogged up with large messages. If that's the case, then you'd be better off to set size restrictions on the *connectors* rather than on the MTA.

Expand Remote Distribution Lists Locally

This is an important setting. If this box is unchecked then distribution list expansion takes place on the server where the distribution list is homed. By definition that remote distribution list will be on a server in another site. You might recall that messages are routed on a per recipient basis so the dis-tribution list has to be expanded before the message can be properly routed.

Expanding remote distribution lists on the local server ensures that the message will be routed efficiently from the local server to all the servers that have recipients. Expanding the list on a remote computer may only serve to complicate the routing process.

Expansion of very large distribution lists may consume considerable sys-tem resources. If you use a lot of large lists, this may adversely affect the per-formance of the local server. The decision that you make is a trade-off between optimal routing of messages and system performance. Current Microsoft recommendations suggest that if you've got a lot of distribution lists and a lot of servers, then it's wise to home all of the distribution lists on a single server (one distribution list expansion server per 100 normal servers) and make sure you don't set up local expansion. It would also be wise to ver-ify that this distribution list expansion server is located close to the logical center of your routing environment. If your distribution lists are scattered across all of your servers, then it's best to just leave this setting at the default value and rely on the natural order of things to balance out list expansion. Faster CPUs and improved distribution list expansion code in Exchange V5.5 mean that the best course of action is to just leave settings as they are.

Convert Incoming Messages to MS Exchange Contents

Messages are stored in the Exchange Information Store in a combination of MDBEF and MAPI* formats. But some messages, namely those from for-eign messaging systems, arrive in from connectors in their native format, perhaps X.400 format. Leaving this option unchecked means that messages

---

* MDBEF stands for "Microsoft Database Encoding Format." MAPI stands for "Messaging API," and it forms the basis of the Exchange architecture.

remain in their native format and aren't converted. It's probably smart to leave messages as they are. Forcing conversion of messages will only result in increased processor utilization when the conversion takes place.

Only Use Least Cost Routes

This is a new option that appeared in Exchange Server V5.5. Checking this box forces the MTA to use routes that have the lowest cost, irrespective of whether other higher cost routes exist. You could use this option to always force messages through local connectors instead of allowing the use of a connector in another site that might have a higher cost. If the lowest cost route is unavailable for some reason, then Exchange will mark the message as undeliverable and return it to the originator.

FIGURE 3–10
General Properties
of the MTA

The function of the *Recalculate Routing* button is the same as is described in Section 3.6.4.

3.10.2 MTA Site Configuration Properties

While the properties for the MTA described in Section 3.10.1 refer only to the MTA on a specific server, the properties that you set within the *MTA Site Configuration* property page are enforced on all MTAs on every server within the site.

Enable Message Tracking

There's very little of interest on the *General* property page. The only item worthy of mention is the *Enable Message Tracking* checkbox. By default, Exchange keeps very little track of messages as they get sent from server to server. Checking this box instructs the MTA to send a message to the System Attendant every time that it processes a message.

The System Attendant creates and maintains a record of message routing on a daily basis in log files. Each log file relates to a single day and may be found in the EXCHSRVR\TRACKING.LOG. If you look in this directory, the daily log files will be named using a convention of YYYYMMDD.LOG, where YYYY represents the year, MM represents the month, and DD represents the day. Thus, the tracking log file for June 16, 1997 is named 19970616.LOG. Don't forget to enable message tracking on all of your connector servers as well.

Messaging Defaults

The attributes on the *Messaging Defaults* tab are the most interesting of all of the MTA Site Configuration options. Values that you set on this page are used by all of the MTAs in the site when establishing connections with other MTAs and transferring messages between each other. Typically the default values that are assigned to these attributes don't need much changing. I'd only advise making modifications to these settings if you've got some special conditions on your network and you're experiencing connectivity problems. The attributes, along with a description of each one are listed in Table 3–3.

TABLE 3–3 Site-Wide MTA Message Transfer Settings

ATTRIBUTE	DESCRIPTION
RTS Values	RTS values (Reliable Transfer Service) affect the communication exchange between Exchange MTAs when messages are being transferred. Since these values are site-wide, all MTAs within the site observe them. When the sending MTA establishes a link with a receiving MTA in another site, the sending MTA proposes its RTS values. If the receiving MTA's settings are the same, then those values will be used. Otherwise the values used for the communication are determined by the settings for the receiving site.
Checkpoint Size	The value (in KB) controls the amount of data that is sent before a checkpoint is sent. If a data transmission fails, the MTA can restart the transmission but need only resend the data since the last checkpoint. Reducing checkpoint size on unreliable links will decrease the amount of data that needs to be resent in the event of a transmission failure at the expense of sending slightly more data overall. Setting checkpoint size to 0 turns off checkpointing. (Default value is 30KB.)

continued ▸

TABLE 3–3 Site-Wide MTA Message Transfer Settings (continued)

ATTRIBUTE	DESCRIPTION
Recovery Timeout	This is the number of seconds that the MTA will wait for a successful reconnection following a failed transmission. If a connection cannot be reestablished within this timeout period, the MTA will abandon the checkpointed information that it's holding and restart the transmission from the beginning. (Default value is 60s.)
Window Size	As checkpointed data is transmitted, the receiving MTA need only acknowledge receipt of information after a certain number of checkpoints. The Window Size specifies how often (in numbers of received checkpoints) that the receiving MTA must send an acknowledgment to the sending MTA. If no acknowledgment is received then data transfer is suspended. If you experience network connectivity problems, reducing this value will encourage the receiving MTA to acknowledge data receipt more often at the expense of transmission throughput. (Default value is 5.)
Connection Retry Values	Defines the tolerance of an MTA dealing with failed connections between servers, how often, and for how long it will attempt to restart failed connections.
Max Open Retries	The number of times that an MTA will attempt to open a connection before it abandons its attempts. When Max Open Retries attempts are made the MTA will mark the message as undeliverable and return it to the originator. (Default number of attempts is 144.)
Max Transfer Retries	If message transfer across an open connection fails, this attribute specifies the number of times that the MTA will attempt to resend that message across the successful connection before it gives up trying to transfer the message. (Default value is 2.)
Open Interval	The number of seconds to wait following an error opening a connection. (Default value is 600.) Note that 144 open retry attempts are made with a frequency of 600s; this means that the MTA will keep trying to open a connection for 86,400s (24 hours) before the message is nondelivered. You may wish to change some of these parameters if this timeout value for failed messages between Exchange servers is too long in your environment.
Transfer Interval	The number of seconds to wait before the MTA retries a message transfer attempt across an open connection. If your MTAs are distributed across a WAN more than a LAN then you might consider increasing this value if you have message transfer problems.(Default value is 120s.)
Association Parameters	Association parameters determine how messages will flow across open connections and defines the relationship between the cooperating MTAs. Multiple associations may exist within a connection between MTAs.
Lifetime	After a message gets sent across a connection the Association Lifetime defines how long the MTA will keep the idle association open. When another message is transferred across the association the timer is reset. Maintaining open associations for straggling messages reduces the overhead for reestablishing an association for individual messages and helps messages on their way that might otherwise have to wait until the next time a connector is scheduled to be active. (Default value is 300s.)

continued ▸

TABLE 3–3 Site-Wide MTA Message Transfer Settings (continued)

ATTRIBUTE	DESCRIPTION
Disconnect	The amount of time that passes after a Disconnect request is received from the other MTA and the MTA that receives the request shuts down the connection. (Default is 120s.)
Threshold	When an excessive number of messages (more than *threshold*) are queued for delivery across the connection, the sending MTA will establish additional associations across the connection. This means that multiple MTA threads will be dealing with streams of messages transferring across each association. This prevents messages being submitted to the MTA faster than they can be processed. (Default is 50 messages.)
Transfer Timeouts	Settings for transfer timeouts govern how long the MTA will wait before nondelivery notifications are generated for different message types. The MTA may well be retrying connection attempts in order to deliver the message up to the timeout values for connection attempts. The Transfer Timeouts may well occur before the connection attempts are exhausted and thus the message will be nondelivered.
Urgent	How long the MTA will wait (in seconds per KB) before marking the message as undeliverable and returning it to the originator. (Default value is 1,000.)
Normal	How long the MTA will wait (in seconds per KB) before marking the message as undeliverable and returning it to the originator. (Default value is 2,000.)
Nonurgent	How long the MTA will wait (in seconds per KB) before marking the message as undeliverable and returning it to the originator. (Default value is 3,000.)

3.11   The MTA Database

While the Information Store and the Directory Service use a relational database for storing message data, the MTA takes a slightly different approach. A number of files residing in the Windows NT file system constitute the MTA's database. You can see these files in the EXCHSRVR\MTADATA directory named DBxxxxxx.DAT, where the xxxxxx part represents a hexadecimal value. The MTA uses these files to store mail messages, queues, and index information for messages that are currently being processed, and it's important that they are not deleted. It's best to leave those files in the capable hands of the MTA.

Immediately after installation and when some messages have been sent through the MTA, you should see about 35 of these files in the directory. As time progresses, the number of these files will increase. New files are generated by the MTA on an as-needed basis, perhaps to act as an additional queue for MTA operation, or a large message transiting through the MTA may be temporarily written to disk (usually cleaned up after the message has been dealt with).

Don't forget that the MTA needs at least 10MB of free space on the disk where the database resides to ensure correct operation. If less than 10MB of space becomes available, the MTA will shut itself down and won't start until adequate space has been cleared. Exchange V5.5 reuses these temporary files for new message processing. Doing so reduces the overhead associated with deleting files and subsequently recreating them.

3.12   MTA Check Utility

The DB files mentioned in Section 3.11 describe the database that the MTA operates with. Like any other database, although we hate to admit it, there is always the risk of some corruption being introduced. But a corrupt MTA database needn't spell disaster for the MTA. The symptoms of a database corruption may expose themselves in a number of different ways, but it's likely that you'll see the MTA fail to process a particular message, terminate unexpectedly, or fail to start at all.

Don't worry! Help is at hand by means of a handy little tool called the MTACHECK utility. You'll find `MTACHECK.EXE` in the `EXCHSRVR\BIN` directory. MTACHECK performs a number of functions:

- checks the consistency of the MTA queues;
- checks the integrity of all objects used by the MTA; and
- may delete corrupt objects.

Exchange will run the MTACHECK utility automatically under certain circumstances. In the event of an unexpected system failure (such as a power outage), the MTA does not shut down gracefully and may have been interacting with the database at the instant the power failed, raising the possibility of some database corruption. Under circumstance like this, Exchange will automatically run the MTACHECK utility when it restarts. You'll see event information being written to the Windows NT Event Log to indicate that MTACHECK is being executed and the actual output from the scan will be written to the `MTACHECK.TXT` file in the `\EXCHSRVR\MTA DATA\MTACHECK.OUT` directory.

If you experience problems with the MTA then you might wish to run the MTACHECK utility manually from the command line. You'll need to ensure that the MTA isn't running so either shut it down from the *Control Panel/Services* interface or by executing the following command line:

```
NET STOP MSEXCHANGEMTA
```

You can restart it later by replacing the NET STOP command with a NET START. The command to run MTACHECK looks like:

```
\EXCHSRVR\BIN\MTACHECK.EXE /V /F OUTPUT.LOG
```

The /V qualifier makes MTACHECK run in verbose mode so that detailed information is output for each object that's analyzed and potentially fixed. The /F qualifier directs all output to a file as well as to the screen. By default there's no logging of activity performed unless you specify it on the command line.

Sample output from an MTACHECK run can be seen in Figure 3–11.

When MTACHECK runs, it examines all of the queues in the database and if it finds errors it reports information about the error and the action that it took to rectify the situation. Once the queues have been examined, each object in every queue is scrutinized as well. Objects that are in error are removed from the queue and moved to the \EXCHSRVR\MTADATA\MTACHECK.OUT directory. Note that removing corrupted objects (messages) may *repair* queues, but objects are only *removed*. There is no capability to repair a corrupt message.

The summary output from an MTACHECK run will indicate the success or otherwise of the operation. You'll see information indicating the amount of queue repair and corrupt message relocation that took place. In extreme circumstances the database may be unrecoverable, and a message will indicate:

```
Database has serious errors and cannot be reconstructed
```

If this is the case, you might have to rebuild the MTA database from scratch. Don't be too eager to perform this activity. Have a scan through TechNet and if necessary call Microsoft PSS. But if you're not too worried about the messages that you might lose, you can do this by copying the base database files into the \EXCHSRVR\MTADATA directory. These blank database files can be found in the BOOTENV directory in the Exchange Server installation CD. But be warned. Replacing these files will delete all messages currently being held by the MTA. If your MTA database is corrupt then this isn't a big deal anyway, but you shouldn't take this approach lightly.

FIGURE 3–11

Output from
MTACHECK Utility

```
Checking queue XAPIWRKQ (id 01000020)
Checking queue OOFINFOQ (id 01000025)
Checking queue REFDATQ (id 01000026)

Starting object integrity checks
  Checking object 03000002 - OK, on queue 01000026
  Checking object 0A000003 - OK, on queue 01000020
  Checking object 0B000004 - OK, on queue 01000020
  Checking object 0B000005 - OK, on queue 01000020
  Checking object 0C000006 - OK, on queue 01000020
  Checking object 0C000007 - OK, on queue 01000020
  Checking object 06000008 - OK, on queue 01000020
  Checking object 06000009 - OK, on queue 01000020
  Checking object 0600000A - OK, on queue 01000020
  Checking object 0600000B - OK, on queue 01000020
  Checking object 0600000C - OK, on queue 01000020
  Checking object 0600000D - OK, on queue 01000020
  Checking object 0600000E - OK, on queue 01000020
  Checking object 0600000F - OK, on queue 01000020
  Checking object 06000010 - OK, on queue 01000020
  Checking object 06000011 - OK, on queue 01000020
  Checking object 06000012 - OK, on queue 01000020
  Checking object 06000013 - OK, on queue 01000020
  Checking object 06000014 - OK, on queue 01000020
  Checking object 06000015 - OK, on queue 01000020
  Checking object 09000016 - OK, on queue 01000020
  Checking object 09000017 - OK, on queue 01000020
  Checking object 09000018 - OK, on queue 01000020
  Checking object 09000019 - OK, on queue 01000020
  Checking object 0900001A - OK, on queue 01000020
  Checking object 0900001B - OK, on queue 01000020
  Checking object 0600001C - OK, on queue 01000020
  Checking object 0600001D - OK, on queue 01000020
  Checking object 0600001E - OK, on queue 01000020
  Checking object 0600001F - OK, on queue 01000020
  Checking object 06000021 - OK, on queue 01000020
  Checking object 06000022 - OK, on queue 01000020
  Checking object 06000023 - OK, on queue 01000025
  Checking object 09000024 - OK, on queue 01000025

Starting garbage collection of orphaned objects
Database clean, no errors detected.
```

If you've run the MTACHECK utility and everything looks okay but your MTA won't start properly, then the corrupt message may be coming from an external source, probably from an external connector such as the IMS Connector. Messages written to the Event Log should help point you in the right direction to troubleshoot this. Information contained in the Event Description might identify the area of MTA operation where the MTA fails. For example, text containing phrases like *DB Server XFER-IN* or *DB Server DISP FANOUT* might indicate that the MTA was receiving a message from another server or was processing a local message when the failure occurred.

3.13   MTA Queues

You can see queues for the MTA by looking at the *Queues* tab from the MTA property pages (see Figure 3–12). In the *Queue name* drop-down list (which I've selected) you'll see the queues that the MTA is currently maintaining. You should see entries for the Information Stores and for some of the connectors that the MTA talks to. (Other connectors maintain their own queues.) You should also see queues for all of the other servers that the MTA can talk to via RPC communication. However, you'll only see these queues listed if the MTA either has any messages waiting to be sent to these servers or if it has sent some since it was last restarted, otherwise the queue isn't present.

I'd like to tell you what might represent an excessive number of entries to see in any queue, but that's difficult to generalize. Obviously you shouldn't ever see many messages in queues for either the Information Stores or for other servers that your MTA talks to using RPCs. Message delivery from these queues should be fairly immediate. If you do see backlogs of more than 10 or 20 messages for a sustained period of time, then it's likely that you've got a problem. If the queue is to the Information Store then it's possible that the service hasn't started. If the queues are for other Exchange servers then you might want to check network connectivity to the remote servers or it may be that the remote servers are down.

For other connectors, the rules aren't just as clear. Many factors might influence the length of queues that are acceptable in this case. Your messaging system might be very busy and connections to other servers may only be scheduled at certain times of the day, so it may not be that strange to see tens or hundreds of messages in queues like this. You'll know best what represents a problem and what does not. If you see thousands of messages in the queues then I'd suggest that either you do have a connection problem or that you need to increase the frequency of activity for the connector!

FIGURE 3–12
The Queues Tab
from the MTA
Property Pages

Taking an occasional look at the *Queues* tab allows you to keep an eye on queues, but this is hardly effective for production environments. At the very least you should have a dedicated Windows NT workstation running *Performance Monitor* (*PerfMon*) set up to monitor queues on all of your Exchange servers. You can display some of the critical queues on PerfMon windows, but you should also set up alerts that get activated when the queue length exceeds certain thresholds. There is also a range of good third party Exchange server monitoring tools[*] that perform the same functions, and more, which you should consider.

3.14 MTA Connection Tuning

If you find yourself with a few idle moments some day and need to fill in the time, you might do worse (although there are many more interesting pursuits!) than to take a quick look at some of the parameters in the Windows NT Registry. In the Registry you'll find settings that define the behavior of the Exchange MTA.

Most of these parameters can be found within:

---

[*]   NetIQ is an excellent example of an Exchange Monitoring Utility.

```
HKEY_LOCAL_MACHINE\SYSTEM\CurrentControlSet\Services\
MSExchangeMTA\Parameters
```

Maybe you've built an Exchange environment that has dedicated connector servers, or even a dedicated connector site, where the servers mostly act as hubs for message transfer between other Exchange servers. It's possible that you might see significant queues building up on these servers at peak times during the day. The messaging activity might get so intense that the MTA has difficulty dealing with the traffic and a backlog of messages on queues throughout servers may appear both on the dedicated connector servers and on servers that connect to the connector servers.

If you do experience these symptoms, it's likely that you'll need to reach for the surgeon's knife and make some modifications to the odd value or two in the Registry. Many of the out-of-the-box settings for Exchange are just fine for run of the mill installations, but in corporate environments with heavy traffic patterns the default values sometimes just don't cut it.

For pure MTA-to-MTA connectivity, you might want to increase the values for *Kernel Threads* and *RTS Threads*. Much of the MTA activity is multithreaded, so you can easily eliminate any bottlenecks by increasing the number of threads available to do work. The *Kernel Threads* and *RTS Threads* parameters control the number of worker threads that can process messages for connections and the number of threads available to deal with multiple connections at the Reliable Transfer Service level respectively. The default value for each of these parameters is 3 (hex), but you can increase MTA throughput by bumping it up to a maximum of 12 (hex). Try intermediate values first before you opt for the maximum value.

If you're using X.400 connectors over TCP/IP transport to link sites together, then it's possible that you might run out of resources to allow multiple concurrent connections to other MTAs. The parameters of interest here are *TCP/IP control blocks* and *TCP/IP threads,* which control the number of X.400 TCP/IP connections supported and the number of threads per X.400 TCP/IP connection. The default values for these are 14 (hex) and 2 (hex) respectively. You could increase these values up to 200 (hex) for *TCP/IP control blocks* and 4 (hex) for *TCP/IP threads,* but once again, try intermediate values first rather than opting for the maximum.

There are corresponding parameters if you're using OSI TP4 transport or X.25 transport for the X.400 connectors. In this case, the parameters of interest are *TP4 control blocks, TP4 threads, Eicon X.25 connections,* and *Eicon X.25 result threads.* The same default values and recommendations apply, but it's unlikely that you'll need to increase many of these values unless you're running a large Exchange infrastructure across an OSI transport or X.25 network.

A number of other parameters control the MTA's ability to sustain relationships with a number of different MTAs at any one time. These are: *Concurrent connections to LAN-MTAs, Concurrent connections to RAS LAN-MTAs,* and *Concurrent connections to X.400 gateways.* In general these parameters are self-tuning as of Exchange V5.5, so they should adjust themselves based on the requirements of your environment, but you may want to modify them if you're still running an earlier version of Exchange and you're experiencing problems.

Let me finish with a word or two of caution. Connectivity problems between Exchange servers may not be limited by the values of the parameters that I've described, but may be influenced by many other factors. The availability and quality of the network may play an important role in introducing message backlogs between servers, so make sure you're confident that the network link is in good shape before you rush off to make modifications to the Registry. Don't forget the hardware that the MTAs are running on.

Look for obvious Windows NT performance problems first before assuming that the MTA needs tuning. An already overloaded server may just not be physically capable of dealing with the messaging workload. You should see symptoms of this from the Performance monitor: excessive CPU utilization, memory saturation, or perhaps I/O bottlenecks may all contribute to messaging backlogs, so address these first. After close scrutiny, if the general health of your server appears fine, then you can scrub in for the Operating Room and get to work on the Registry.

3.15 Advanced MTA Troubleshooting

From time to time you may get problems with MTA connections between servers. There are a number of areas of investigation that should help you identify and resolve such problems.

Your first port of call should be the *Diagnostics Logging* property page on the MTA entity. Turning on logging for the MTA will cause Exchange to write error, status, and other information to the Windows NT Event log. You can use the Event Viewer to look at the information that's written to the log.

The default logging level for each of the diagnostic categories should be set to *None*. You can select any of these categories and change the logging level to one of *Minimum*, *Medium*, or *Maximum*. It's not always easy to determine which categories to select for logging, but in general if your problems seem to be related to message transfer between servers a good start might be select *X.400 Service*, *Interoperability*, and *APDU*. I'd suggest setting the logging level to *Medium* first of all to zoom in on the area that's causing you trouble. Having done that you can turn the logging up to a higher level if you need to get more information.

Do remember to turn off logging once you've finished investigating problems, since many of the settings can generate a significant amount of information that gets written to the Event Log and quickly clog it up.

Occasionally you may need more diagnostics information than that which gets written to the Event Log. There are a number of other avenues of investigation that are open to you in this case. They all involve other log files. Let's see what they are.

3.15.1 The MTA Text Event Log

The Exchange MTA writes event information (errors, warnings, etc.) to the Event Viewer Application log like most other Windows NT components. In addition to writing to this log, the MTA can also be set up to write to another log file. The MTA Text Event log file doesn't act as an alternative location for event logging: All events continue to be written to the Event Viewer file, and events written to the MTA log file are merely copies of particular events written to the Event Viewer file.

Unlike the Event Viewer Application log file, this MTA Event file is a purely text-based file, so you can use any application (like Notepad or Wordpad) to edit it. It's also easy to access from scripts and applications because of its text-based nature. Only events with a type of ERROR are written to this file; events with the types of INFORMATION or WARNING are written only to the Event Viewer Application log file.

The Text Event log is located in the \EXCHSRVR\MTADATA directory and is named EV0.LOG. This file rolls over so as the file fills, you'll find older messages written to other files called EV1.LOG, EV2.LOG, etc. When the MTA is restarted, the MTA Event log file is cleared and a new EV0.LOG file is created. To preserve copies of the MTA event log across MTA restarts you'll need to make sure to copy the files before stopping the MTA service.

It may not be particularly important to have the MTA writing to this file all of the time, but it is useful if you want to isolate an MTA problem over a period of time. It's also handy if you need to have an application read MTA event information and your application can't read from the Application Event log file.

To enable the MTA Text Event log, set the following registry value to 1:

```
TextEventLog
```

which can be found under:

```
HKEY_LOCAL_MACHINE\SYSTEM\CurrentControlSet\Services\
MSExchangeMTA\Parameters
```

3.15.2 Additional Logging

A few other log files can be useful for troubleshooting: the *Unbounded Event Log*, the *Unbounded APDU Log*, and the *Unbounded Interop Log*. You'll need to have enabled logging to the Text Event Log, so make sure you've performed the steps outlined in previous section.

Unbounded Event Log

This enables uninterrupted logging of information to the EV0.LOG.

Unbounded APDU Log

Information from this setting will go to the BF0.LOG file (found in the EXCH SRVR\MTADATA directory), provided that you've selected maximum logging for the *X.400 Service* and *APDU* categories on the MTA *Diagnostics Logging* tab. The information in this file will be a binary capture of message transfer activity through the MTA. The information in the log won't make much sense to an ordinary human, but you can use the message-decoding tool (*Aspirin*), which you'll find on the BackOffice Resource Kit CD or on the Web.*

Unbounded Interop Log

This writes logging information to the AP0.LOG file (also found in the EXCH SRVR\MTADATA directory). You'll need to select maximum logging for the

---

* You can search for it using what I consider to be the Internet's best search engine: Compaq's Alta Vista Search Engine at http://www.altavista.com.

Interoperability category on the MTA *Diagnostics Logging* tab. This logging operates as a *sniffer* of all transport activity (both incoming and outgoing) carried out by the MTA. This activity can generate substantial amounts of logged information. The file can grow to 5MB in size before the `AP0.LOG` file is rolled over to become `AP1.LOG` and so on.

To enable this logging you'll need to create some new DWORD values under the following key:

```
HKEY_LOCAL_MACHINE\SYSTEM\CurrentControlSet\Services\
MSExchangeMTA\Parameters
```

Create new values for:

```
Unbounded Event Log
Unbounded APDU Log
Unbounded Interop Log
```

Setting the data value for each to 1 to enable them. Don't forget to turn the logging off later either by setting the data filed to 0 or deleting the value.

4

X.400 Messaging: The Basics

4.1   Introduction

Try this for some fun. Mention the words "OSI" and "X.400" to any of your messaging friends. Watch carefully for their reaction. You'll probably be greeted with any one or all of the following: a look of confusion, a trembling mess, hysterical laughter, or a slap in the face. For many years, X.400 provided the only real architecture for reliable message transfer between different mail systems. But it's a complex architecture. It's difficult to understand and difficult to set up. The faint of heart should not take it on.

But there is a real alternative to it—SMTP. Of course, it doesn't cure all of the ills associated with X.400. It has its downsides too. So does this mean we should try to wipe all traces of X.400 out of our heads. Well, yes and no. Maybe the days of implementing widespread X.400 networks are far behind us, but there's still a need for X.400 in the place where we least expect to find it. You've guessed it: in Exchange.

In this chapter we'll explore some of the fundamental concepts behind X.400. That should provide us with enough information to move forward to the next chapter and understand how these concepts are employed by the Exchange X.400 Connector.

4.2   X.400—A Quick History

The X.400 Recommendations (they're actually recommendations, not standards) were first published in 1984 by the CCITT (now called the ITU). Teams of individuals worked on these recommendations for long periods of time, and then eventually went off to meetings and symposia held in interesting places such as Malaga and Melbourne where there are more fun things to do than discuss electronic mail. Anyway, the reasons for going to those places were to agree and release the recommendations. The standards were informally referred to as the *Red Book* because of the color of the cover. George Orwell may have thought that 1984 signaled the end of people's freedom, but that certainly wasn't to be the case for X.400. The recommendations were reviewed in 1988 (the *Blue Book*) and then more recently again, to give the latest edition, the 1992 (the *White Book*) recommendations. Around 1984, the ISO developed its own set of standards that help define the X.400 recommendations, known as the MOTIS (Message Oriented Text Interchange System) 100021 standards. For the best part, the ISO standards and the X.400 recommendations are in agreement, but they do vary a little in some areas. And some vendors have chosen to adhere more closely to one set of rules than the others. Not surprisingly, this can lead to some interoperability problems from time to time, but the problems are minimal.

If you find yourself with too much time on your hands at the weekends, I've got a couple of solutions for you. First of all you could write a book! (That's guaranteed to suck up all of the spare time that you have and then some.) Or else you could read (and maybe try to understand) the X.400 Recommendations. The Red and Blue Books are huge! The Blue Book extends to well over 600 pages, and it's more or less a book of extensions and changes to the original Red Book. What's more, the books themselves are pretty much made up of page after page of logical definitions that make up the components of a Message Handling Service (MHS) written in a special language called Abstract Syntax Notation One (ASN.1). Want an example? Well, we've already met the concept of an X.400 address—that thing called an OR address which Exchange uses for message routing. Figure 4–1 shows how it's defined in ASN.1 format.

FIGURE 4–1

Definition for an
OR Address

```
ORName ::= [APPLICATION 0] IMPLICIT SEQUENCE {
        StandardAttributeList,
        DomainDefinedAttributesList OPTIONAL }

Standard Attribute List ::= SEQUENCE {
        CountryName OPTIONAL,
        AdminstrationDomainName OPTIONAL,
        [0] IMPLICIT X121Address OPTIONAL,
        [1] IMPLICIT TerminalID OPTIONAL,
        [2] PrivateDomainName OPTIONAL,
        [3] IMPLICIT OrganizationName OPTIONAL,
```

```
[4] IMPLICIT Unique UAIdentifier OPTIONAL,
[5] IMPLICIT PersonalName OPTIONAL,
[6] IMPLICIT SEQUENCE OF OrganizationalUnit OPTIONAL }
```

Now that's just the start of it. For each of the constructs defined in Figure 4–1, yet another ASN.1 definition is required to define them, and so it continues for every single component that makes up a message or part of messaging system. It's not hard to imagine why hundreds of pages are needed!

For completeness, let's take a look at the formal structure of a user message, as shown in Figure 4–2.

FIGURE 4–2 ASN.1
Definition for
a User Message

```
UserMPDU ::= SEQUENCE { UMPDUEnvelope, MPDUContent }

UMPDUEnvelope ::= SET {
    MPDUIdentifier,
    originator ORName,
    original EncodedInformationTypes OPTIONAL,
    ContentType,
    UAContentID OPTIONAL,
    Priority DEFAULT normal,
    PerMessageFlag DEFAULT {},
    DeferredDelivery [0] IMPLICIT Time OPTIONAL,
    [1] IMPLICIT SEQUENCE OF PerDomainBilateralInfo OPTIONAL,
    [2] IMPLICIT SEQUENCE OF RecipientInfo,
    TraceInformation }

UMPDUContent ::= OCTET STRING
```

X.400 recommendations are not at all like definitions for Internet and SMTP standards, known as *Requests For Comments* or *RFCs,* which are free and easily accessible off of the Web. To get your hands on these you have to get them from the ITU or the ISO, and they cost quite a few hundred dollars each. Just buying the X.400 recommendations isn't enough, because you'll need to buy a number of other documents that define the bits that help to define X.400! All in all you'll end up spending quite a lot of money to get all of the documentation that you need to give a complete definition of the recommendations. The obstacles associated with getting all of this documentation goes part of the way to explaining why smaller vendors never really set about writing as much software based on the X.400 recommendations as they did for SMTP-based products.

The other cause for the lack of software is the fact that writing against the X.400 standards is so darned complex. Mostly the larger software vendors were able to provide the investment required for X.400 development. When you compare this with the effort associated with pulling down one of the SMTP RFCs off of a publicly accessible FTP site and writing some code against it, it's not hard to see why SMTP development became so prolific.

The X.400 recommendations that are currently in force are listed in Appendix A.

4.3   X.400 Messaging Systems

An X.400 messaging system is made up of a lot of parts. We're going to take a look at those parts in this section. We'll meet a number of terms which are generally used to describe any messaging system, but we'll also meet a number of new terms that are indigenous to the world of X.400. Don't be discouraged by the terminology. I suspect that it's designed to put off the inexperienced, but once you get the hang of the concepts the words aren't really that important. All of the components that we'll meet here have similar partners in the SMTP world, and although they serve more or less the same purpose, the words used to describe them are sometimes slightly different.

The first phrase we need to talk about, I've mentioned already: the *Message Handling Service* or *MHS*. The MHS refers to the complete collection of all the components that make up a messaging environment. Such an environment is comprised of systems or components that store messages and allow you to access them and send mail (*User Agents*) and other components that deal with transferring a message from one part of the MHS to another (*Message Transfer Agents*). The way those pieces fit together is shown in Figure 4–3.

Functionally the *Message Store* (MS) and the *Remote User Agent* (RUA) are the easiest to describe. The MS has a straightforward mission: It receives messages (from somewhere that's not important right now) and stores them. Message Stores usually present themselves as a mailbox or filing cabinet to a user or client application—the RUA. The Remote User Agent is an application that typically runs on a client PC or VT and presents a view of the Message Store to the user, as well as offering the ability to send, read, reply-to messages, and so forth.

This separation of message store and remote user agent functionality isn't seen too often today. It's an architecture that, although well defined in the X.400 standards, didn't really catch on into wide-scale implementation and deployment, although a number of X.400 Message Stores and Remote User Agents are commercially available from companies such as Isocor and MaxWare.

FIGURE 4–3 The
Components That
Make Up an MHS

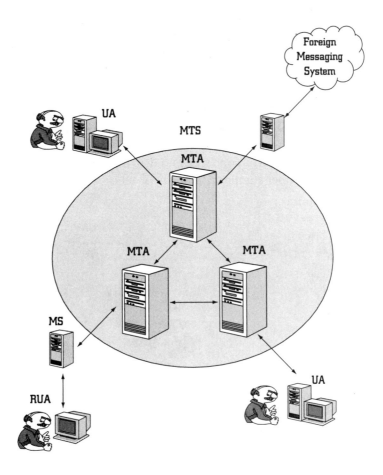

The *User Agent* (UA) is the part of the messaging system that users probably see most often. It's the interface or point of contact between the messaging environment and the person that uses it. In effect it's really a coming together of the Message Store and the Remote User Agent functionality all rolled into one. It's common to see products that implement the architecture in this way. For example, Compaq's Office Server provides a storage facility and an access client all together in the VT interface, as does Uniplex. How the User Agent implements this functionality is entirely up to the vendor. There's nothing to stop the divorcing of the access client component and the message storage functionality into a client/server structure. In fact, both the Office Server architecture and the Uniplex architecture implement this client/server model as well using their TeamLinks clients and OnGo clients respectively. When the functionality is separated out in this way, there's little distinction to be made between the concepts of User Agents and Message Stores/Remote User Agent combinations. However, the strict protocols and APIs which define the interface between the latter are usually not as clear when implemented as a simple User Agent.

When messages are exchanged between users, the path that they take depends on where they are located relative to each other. If the users are located on the same server, this typically means that they share the same User Agent. In this case, it's the responsibility of the User Agent to take the message from one user and deliver it to the other, as shown in Figure 4–4. No other components are involved.

FIGURE 4–4

Sending Messages from One User to Another on the Same User Agent

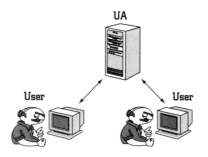

It's a slightly different matter when the users aren't located on the same server and therefore don't share the same User Agent. This means that the sending User Agent must transfer the message to the receiving User Agent. Unfortunately, there's no way for a User Agent to transfer a message directly to another User Agent, but the X.400 recommendations specify a special component that's used to achieve exactly this; it's called a Message Transfer Agent. The Message Transfer Agent accepts messages from a User Agent and will either deliver it directly to another User Agent if it has knowledge of that User Agent or else transfer it to another Message Transfer Agent that does know about the destination User Agent.

MTAs are quite flexible in that they can support connections from multiple User Agents. In this way they act just as a message switch for User Agents. In theory you could connect all of your User Agents together using just one MTA, but it's much more common to see a number of MTAs used on a large messaging network. Typically, you'd use one MTA per geographical region or administrative area. This logically partitions a large messaging network up into a number of zones of message delivery. The regionalized MTAs are then connected together to form a messaging backbone.

The functionality that the Message Transfer Agent offers here is known as *store and forward*. The logic is simple. As a message arrives from one MTA, the local MTA will store it for a predefined period of time if it can't make a connection to the destination MTA or User Agent. If the time period expires and the message can't be delivered the MTA will nondeliver it and send it back to the originator.

FIGURE 4–5

How UAs and MTAs Deliver Messages

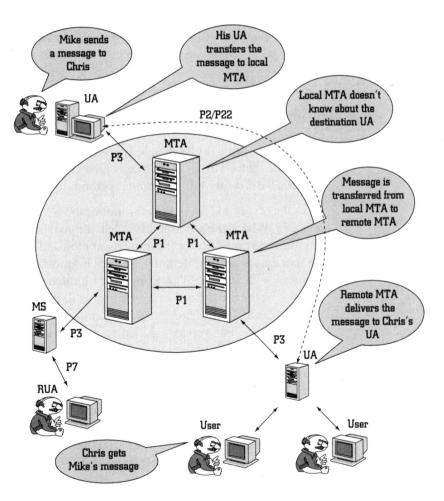

If you've been paying attention to what we covered earlier in this book, you'll no doubt have noticed that the mechanism by which X.400 transfers messages between User Agents and MTAs is very similar to the way Exchange transfers messages. You'll remember that if two Exchange users are located on the same server, then a message sent from one to the other is simply dealt with by the Store service in the same way that a User Agent would control the local delivery. On the other hand, when a message is sent between users on different servers, the Exchange MTA comes into play, accepting messages from the Store and sending them to another server, where the MTA on that server will hand the messages over to the local Store. That process is just like the X.400 model. Where the model differs from X.400 is in relation to the number of User Agents that an MTA can support. Within Exchange there's always a one-to-one mapping between the Store and the MTA, but in the X.400 world, a single MTA can have connections to many User Agents, thus transferring messages between them.

4.4   X.400 Protocols

Apart from showing the route that a message takes between User Agents and MTAs, Figure 4–5 shows something else that's interesting. All of the connections between User Agents, MTA, Message Stores, etc., all have a number beside them. These "P" numbers refer to the X.400 protocols that are used when different MHS components communicate with each other.

In the case of MTA to MTA communication, the protocol that's used is called *P1*. What's the point of this? Well, the goal of the ITU-T and the OSI was to define protocols for the implementation and interoperation of X.400 components between different vendors. This means that an MTA can communicate with another MTA using only a limited number of primitive API operations; they're defined in the P1 protocol. Let's say that you've bought two MTAs one from Vendor *MessageConnect* and the other from Vendor *LetsTalk*. Since both vendors will no doubt have carefully implemented the P1 protocol for both of their products, there's nothing that should stop you from building a messaging environment using both types of MTAs—they should operate together seamlessly.

The P1 protocol defines the structure of the messages that MTAs exchange. You can think of the P1 message as being the equivalent of an *envelope* and a *letter*. The envelope part is the P1 Header and the letter part is the P2 Message (which we'll meet later). See Figure 4–6.

The P1 envelope part contains information that MTAs can use for transfer and delivery of messages. The envelope contains information that (1) identifies the message; (2) provides trace information, originator address, and recipient addresses; and (3) defines the content types, allowable conversions, latest delivery time, alternate recipients allowed, priority flags, security flags, and a host of other information. Figure 4–7 shows a dump of the contents of a P1 envelope for an X.400 message—in this case a nondelivery report that came from an MTA.

FIGURE 4–6
Structure of an
X.400 Message

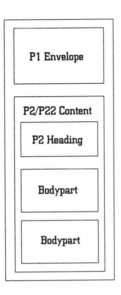

FIGURE 4–7 Dump
of P1 Envelope for
an X.400 Message

```
CONTEXT 1
  <Report>
  SET
    <ReportEnvelope>
    MTS_ID
      <ReportIdentifier>
      GDI
        COUNTRY
          PRINTABLE          Len 2
            "gb" Hex 67 62
        ADMD
          PRINTABLE          Len 2
            "bt" Hex 62 74
```

```
                    PRINTABLE              Len 7
                      "digital"
             IA5              Len 24
               <LocalId>
               "5e3270b411d0576700081c80"
ORNAME
  <ReportDestination>
  SEQ
    <StandardAttributes>
    COUNTRY
      PRINTABLE              Len 2
        "gb" Hex 67 62
TRACE
  <TraceInformation>
  SEQ
    GDI
      COUNTRY
        PRINTABLE            Len 2
          "gb" Hex 67 62
      ADMD
        PRINTABLE            Len 2
          "bt" Hex 62 74
      PRINTABLE              Len 7
        "digital"
    SET
      <DomainSuppliedInfo>
      CONTEXT 0              Len 13
        <ArrivalTime>
        "961216171106Z"
      CONTEXT 2              Len 1
        <RoutingAction>
        Hex 0 Dec 0
CONTEXT 1
  <Extensions>
  SEQ
    CONTEXT 0                Len 1
      <Extension>
      Hex 26 Dec 38
    <InternalTrace>
    CONTEXT 1                Len 2
      <Criticality>
      Hex 00
    CONTEXT 2
      SEQ
```

```
                              SEQ
                                GDI
                                  COUNTRY
                                    PRINTABLE              Len 2
                                      "gb" Hex 67 62
                                    ADMD
                                      PRINTABLE            Len 2
                                        "bt" Hex 62 74
                                      PRINTABLE            Len 7
                                       "digital"
                                  IA5              Len 7
                                    "bvomta1"
                                  SET
                                    <DomainSuppliedInfo>
                                    CONTEXT 0              Len 13
                                      <ArrivalTime>
                                      "961216171106Z"
                                    CONTEXT 2              Len 1
                                      <RoutingAction>
                                      Hex 0 Dec 0
                  SET
                    <ReportContent>
                    MTS_ID
                      GDI
                        COUNTRY
                          PRINTABLE            Len 2
                            "gb" Hex 67 62
                          ADMD
                          PRINTABLE            Len 2
                            "bt" Hex 62 74
                          PRINTABLE            Len 7
                            "digital"
                      IA5              Len 24
                        <LocalId>
                        "5D5D993411D0576700081C80"
                    EITS
                      CONTEXT 0        Len 2
                        <BuiltinEits>
                        " " Hex 20
                    BUILTIN          Len 1
                      Hex 16 Dec 22
                    CONTEXT 0
                      <ReportRecipients>
                      SET
```

```
CONTEXT 0
  <ActualRecipientName>
  SEQ
    <StandardAttributes>
    COUNTRY
      PRINTABLE        Len 2
        "gb" Hex 67 62
    ADMD
      PRINTABLE        Len 8
        "gold 400"
    CONTEXT 2
      <PrivateDomainName>
      PRINTABLE        Len 7
        "digital"
    CONTEXT 3          Len 7
      <OrganizationalName>
      "digital"
    CONTEXT 5
      <PersonalName>
      CONTEXT 0        Len 7
        <surname>
        "McCorry"
      CONTEXT 1        Len 6
        <given-name>
        "Kieran"
    CONTEXT 6
      <OrganizationalUnitNames>
      PRINTABLE        Len 3
        "bvo" Hex 62 76 6f
      PRINTABLE        Len 4
        "exch" Hex 65 78 63 68
CONTEXT 1              Len 1
  <OriginallySpecifiedRecipNo>
  Hex 1 Dec 1
CONTEXT 2              Len 2
  <PerRecipientIndicators>
  "M-(" Hex a8
CONTEXT 3
  <LastTraceInfo>
  CONTEXT 0            ·Len 13
    <ArrivalTime>
    "961216171105Z"
  CONTEXT 1
    <ReportType>
```

```
CONTEXT 1
  <ND Report>
  CONTEXT 0        Len 1
    <ND ReasonCode>
    Hex 1 Dec 1
  CONTEXT 1        Len 1
    <ND DiagCode>
    Hex 0 Dec 0
CONTEXT 5              Len 58
<SupplmentaryInfo>
"MTA has no routing information for this
O/R address. (136)"
```

The protocol that defines the format for a message sent from one User Agent to another (but always via an MTA) comes in two flavors. If the message is structured according to the 1984 recommendations, then the protocol used is P2; if it's the 1998 recommendations or later it's the P22 protocol.

The P22 message (commonly referred to as the *Interpersonal Message*) is the content or letter part of the message as described in Figure 4–6. The P22 message is itself broken down into a number of components. The first part is the P22 Header. Within the P22 Header you'll find some information that's not dissimilar from the data that's held in the P1 part. You should see fields that define information about the originator, the recipients, references to optional information like phone numbers, free text names, etc. Most of this information is optional, but one part, the Message Identifier, is mandatory and is used by the User Agents to uniquely identify the message.

The originator and recipient address information that's held in this part of the message isn't used by the MTAs for routing the message; only the addressing information that's held in the P1 envelope is used for that. So why is it included in this part? Well, strictly speaking, it's not actually required apart from being used by User Agents to fill in fields on a display form when you read the message to indicate where it's come from. If you think about the style you use when writing an official letter to some company (perhaps to apply for a new job), you specify name and address information twice as well. Firstly, you'll put the address of the recipient on the front of the envelope and you *should* put your own address on the back flap of the envelope or, if in the United States, the return address goes on the front cover as well. You duplicate this information in the content of the letter when you put your own address information on the top of the first page and the address of the recipient there as well.

After the P2 header, the content part of the message includes a P2 body. The body is composed of one or more *bodyparts*. Each bodypart is basically an attachment to the message and has some tagging information associated with it to describe its type. This tagging information is also listed in the P1 header so that the MTA can make a decision on the delivery to the User Agent based on what content types the User Agent can handle.

The supported content types are shown in Table 4–1.

For a simple text message there's typically just an IA5 text bodypart, but when complex attachments (say Word documents or Lotus 1-2-3 spreadsheets) are used there'll be a number of different bodyparts tagged either as BP14 if the message has come from a 1984 X.400 system or BP15 if the message has come from a 1988 system. There are no tags which define the actual format of the attachment, just the type. But for 1984 systems, typically an IA5 string is used to define the actual format. Providing the target system understands the extra IA5 field (hence, the *Bilateral* definition), the content format tagging can be accurately maintained.

TABLE 4–1   1988 X.400 Bodypart Types

BODYPART TYPE	CONTENT TYPE
0	IA5 Text Bodypart
1	Telex Bodypart
2	Voice Bodypart
3	G3 Facsimile Bodypart
4	G4 Class 1 Bodypart
5	Teletex Bodypart
6	Videotex Bodypart
7	Nationally Defined Bodypart
8	Encrypted Bodypart
9	Message Bodypart
10	Forwarded IP Message Bodypart
11	Simple Formatted Document Bodypart
12	TIF1 Bodypart
13	Mixed Mode
14	Bilaterally Defined Bodypart
15	Externally Defined Bodypart

For 1988 systems there are typically an agreed set of Object Identifiers (OIDs) used to tag the format of the contents. These are privately maintained by some vendors for proprietary formats, but a number of publicly defined OIDs are maintained by international bodies, specifically the Electronic Messaging Association's Message Attachment Working Group (EMA MAWG).

The 1992 revision of the X.400 recommendation introduced yet another bodypart, the *File Transfer Bodypart* (*FTBP*). The other bodyparts (BP14 and BP15) designed to aid the identification of complex documents never really got off the ground. The FTBP approach is based on the OSI FTAM[*] model and some of the concepts of the Internet MIME standard (which we'll meet later) where filename information is stored with the message, rather than relying on tagging systems which MTAs and User Agents use to infer the document type.

Part of the FTBP bodypart holds information on the attributes of the file or document in question. So the attributes part of the bodypart would hold information like that shown below.

```
NAME:   JobPlan.MPP
CREATED:10-APR-1998 by Tommy Byrne
MODIFIED:11-APR-1998 by Bob Palmer
```

The FTBP approach is the one favored by Microsoft Exchange. Integration is quite straightforward if the X.400 systems you're interoperating with support FTBP, but since it's relatively new not all do. In that case, you're constrained to working in either BP14 or BP15 mode, but we'll cover more on this later.

Figure 4–8 shows a dump of the P2 content part of an X.400 message. In this case, the message went through a gateway (look at the originator address) and has one Externally Defined Bodypart (BP15).

FIGURE 4–8 Dump of P2 Content for an X.400 Message

```
CONTEXT 0
  <IPM>
  SET
    <Heading>
    IPM_ID
      ORNAME
```

---

[*] File Transfer, Access, and Management. An OSI-based approach for file transfer.

```
                        SEQ
                          <StandardAttributes>
                          COUNTRY
                            PRINTABLE          Len 2
                              "gb" Hex 67 62
                          ADMD
                            PRINTABLE          Len 2
                              "bt" Hex 62 74
                          CONTEXT 2
                            <PrivateDomainName>
                            PRINTABLE          Len 7
                              "digital"
                          CONTEXT 3           Len 7
                            <OrganizationalName>
                            "digital"
                          CONTEXT 6
                            <OrganizationalUnitNames>
                            PRINTABLE          Len 3
                              "bvo" Hex 62 76 6f
                            PRINTABLE          Len 6
                              "bvorly"
                      SEQ
                        <DDAs>
                        SEQ
                          PRINTABLE          Len 8
                            <Type>
                            "XMRROUTE"
                          PRINTABLE          Len 27
                            <Value>
                            "MCCORRY(a)BVO(a)TURBVO(a)A1"
                    PRINTABLE        Len 10
                      <UserRelativeId>
                      "E1IEG3AWJO"
                CONTEXT 0
                  <Originator>
                  ORNAME
                    SEQ
                      <StandardAttributes>
                      COUNTRY
                        PRINTABLE          Len 2
                          "gb" Hex 67 62
                      ADMD
                        PRINTABLE          Len 2
                          "bt" Hex 62 74
```

```
                        CONTEXT 2
                          <PrivateDomainName>
                          PRINTABLE          Len 7
                            "digital"
                        CONTEXT 3            Len 7
                          <OrganizationalName>
                          "digital"
                        CONTEXT 6
                          <OrganizationalUnitNames>
                          PRINTABLE          Len 3
                            "bvo" Hex 62 76 6f
                          PRINTABLE          Len 6
                            "bvorly"
                   SEQ
                     <DDAs>
                     SEQ
                       PRINTABLE          Len 8
                         <Type>
                         "XMRROUTE"
                       PRINTABLE          Len 27
                         <Value>
                         "MCCORRY(a)A1(a)TURBVO(a)BVO"
                  CONTEXT 0        Len 14
                    <FreeFormName>
                    "Kieran McCorry"
                  CONTEXT 1        Len 15
                    <TelephoneNumber>
                    "+44 1232 384066"
                CONTEXT 2
                  <PrimaryRecipients>
                  SET
                    CONTEXT 0
                      <ORDescriptor>
                      ORNAME
                        SEQ
                          <StandardAttributes>
                          COUNTRY
                            PRINTABLE              Len 2
                              "gb" Hex 67 62
                          ADMD
                            PRINTABLE              Len 2
                              "bt" Hex 62 74
                          CONTEXT 2
                            <PrivateDomainName>
```

```
                        PRINTABLE              Len 7
                          "digital"
                        CONTEXT 3         Len 7
                          <OrganizationalName>
                          "digital"
                        CONTEXT 6
                          <OrganizationalUnitNames>
                          PRINTABLE              Len 3
                            "bvo" Hex 62 76 6f
                          PRINTABLE              Len 4
                            "exch" Hex 65 78 63 68
                   SET
                     <ORname Extensions>
                     SEQ
                       CONTEXT 0              Len 1
                         Hex 1 Dec 1
                       CONTEXT 1
                         <CommonName (Printable)>
                         PRINTABLE          Len 14
                           "Kieran McCorry"
                 CONTEXT 0          Len 28
                   <FreeFormName>
                   "Kieran McCorry (on Exchange)"
                 CONTEXT 1              Len 2
                   <NotificationRequest>
                   "'" Hex 60
                 CONTEXT 2              Len 1
                   <ReplyRequested>
                   Boolean FALSE
             CONTEXT 8
               <Subject>
               TTX              Len 5
                 "test4" Hex 74 65 73 74 34
             CONTEXT 12          Len 1
               <Importance>
               Hex 2 Dec 2
             CONTEXT 13          Len 1
               <Sensitivity>
               Hex 3 Dec 3
             CONTEXT 14          Len 1
               <AutoForwarded>
               Boolean FALSE
       SEQ
         <Body>
```

```
CONTEXT 15
  <ExternallyDefined>
  CONTEXT 0
    OBJECT_ID              Len 4
      Hex 56 01 0b 0b
    CONTEXT 0
      SET
        INTEGER            Len 1
          Hex 01
        INTEGER            Len 1
          Hex 06
    EXTERNAL
      OBJECT_ID            Len 4
        Hex 56 01 04 0b
      CONTEXT 0
        GENERAL            Len 11
          Hex 1b 28 42 0f 74 65 73 74 34 0d 0a
```

While the P2 and P22 protocols define the structure of an X.400 message for its transfer between two User Agents, another protocol actually specifies the protocol for the interconnect between a User Agent or Message Store and an MTA. This protocol is called the P3 protocol. P3 defines the mechanism by which a message is submitted or received to/from the MTA. Having said that, it's important to note P3 is usually not implemented by most vendors. An alternative and more popular mechanism for this type of communication is made available by a simpler and richer protocol called XAPI (the X.400 Application Programming Interface) defined by the XAPIA (X.400 Application Programming Interface Association). XAPI is preferred to P3 because it allows the User Agent or Message Store to be more selective about the messages it's willing to receive or process, whereas the P3 protocols insists that those components accept the message first, process all of it and then decide whether or not to accept it.

You should be able to buy User Agents from any vendor and, providing they all correctly support the P3 or XAPI protocols, there's no reason why they shouldn't be able to connect to any of your MTAs.

Finally, let's mention the P7 protocol. We tend not to see this protocol too much because it defines the interconnect between a Remote User Agent and a Message Store. To be frank, this mode of operation is not too common since most implementations use the combined functionality of the User Agent rather than segregating the functionality. P7 allows the Remote User

Agent to examine messages stored in the Message Store and to retrieve them selectively as well as offering functionality that will allow the submission of messages. This concept is similar to the IMAP4 model for Internet messaging.

# 4.5	X.400 Originator/Recipient Addresses

We've already talked about the fact that addresses are used when a message is sent from one user to another in an X.400 messaging environment. Specifically, these addresses are called *Originator/Recipient* (O/R) addresses in X.400-speak.

O/R addresses are hierarchical in nature. They consist of a fixed number of terms that serve to uniquely identify an individual in a global context. When looking at various X.400 systems, you may come across different forms of X.400 address. Several exist, namely *mnemonic, numerical, terminal,* and *postal.* They all use a common set of terms at some point in the address, but also have some special terms for each address type. The address format that we're most interested in is the mnemonic format. It's this format that's the most common and used for most purposes. It's pretty long, but once you get the hang of it, it all makes sense. As an example, here's my X.400 address:

```
C=GB;A=GOLD 400;P=DIGITAL;O=DIGITAL;OU1=BVO;S=MCCORRY;G=KIERAN
```

Looking at the individual terms, you'll see that the address starts off with a C or COUNTRY term. All addresses are rooted with a country identifier, the actual code being defined in ISO standard 3166-1:1997 (see http://www.iso.ch). The C term is mandatory for an O/R address and must always be specified. Next in the hierarchy is the A or ADMD (Administrative Management Domain) term. The ADMD term relates to the public X.400 carrier to which your P or PRMD (Private Management Domain) is connected. The PRMD part relates to your private implementation of an X.400 network. Within the PRMD you'll be able to send messages around your organization, which might consist of one or more MTAs and User Agents. Arbitrarily, within the PRMD, you can then specify an O or ORGANIZATION term, and below that up to four levels of nesting for ORGANIZATIONAL UNIT (OU1 through OU4). Finally, the address is terminated with an S (or SURNAME) and a G (or GIVENNAME) which holds the person's first name. An I term may also be used to hold INITIALS. The structure is illustrated in Figure 4–9.

FIGURE 4–9
Hierarchical
Structure of O/R
Addresses

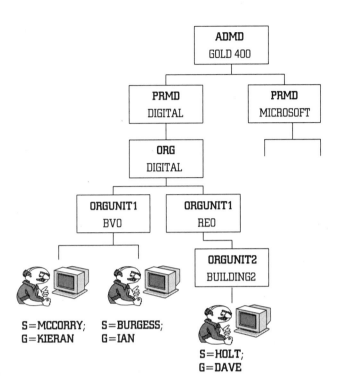

You can see from the figure how the collection of all the terms uniquely identifies any one individual. You don't need to have all of the O/R terms in your address, but some are required, namely the C, ADMD, and then any combination of PRMD, ORG, ORGUNIT, or name terms. Different PRMDs (companies) may interconnect with each other by plugging into an ADMD, typically run by a national telecommunications provider. The ADMD term exists within the context of COUNTRY, and typically ADMDs communicate with each other across national boundaries to provide an international X.400 messaging environment.

While this is useful for uniquely identifying a person within a country, it does of course present a problem for multinational organizations that operate out of different countries. For example, a colleague of mine in DIGITAL has the following X.400 address:

```
C=US;A=ATTMAIL;P=DIGITAL;O=DIGITAL;OU1=ZKO;S=STJEAN;G=BOB
```

Strictly speaking, according to the ISO view of the world, PRMDs should not be able to communicate with each other across national boundaries, but the ITU-T view of communication more or less sanctions this. To counter this, some recent moves by the ISO have introduced a country code of WW (Worldwide) so that a multinational can "relinquish" any nationality and operate transparently across the globe. Having said that, most X.400 implementations allow for some degree of multi-homing, so that user accounts and MTAs can simultaneously exist with multiple addresses.

The 1988 version of the recommendations suggested a replacement for the G (or GIVENNAME) and S (or SURNAME) terms. Instead of separately dealing with these parts of the name you could use a CN (or COMMON-NAME) term. This is useful when an X.400 address is referring to an object rather than a person (say CN=CONFERENCE ROOM 1, which is difficult to assign G and S terms to), but it's important to note that 1984-based X.400 systems don't support the CN term. This means that a 1988 X.400 system must convert addresses from CN to G and S when connecting to a 1984-based system. If the address isn't converted then it's usually encapsulated in a catchall address term, the *Domain Defined Attribute* (DDA). This is more or less ignored by the X.400 MTA and just passed on with an address, the intention being that when the address gets to the other end (the other domain), some message system within that domain will be able to understand it. On X.400 backbones, it's common to see SMTP addresses wrapped as DDAs and transported across the network.

For example, the following address is in 1988 format:

```
C=US;A=ATTMAIL;P=BDPL;O=DESIGN;CN=NIALL M TIPPING
```

But when converted to 1984 style it would look like:

```
C=US;A=ATTMAIL;P=BDPL;O=DESIGN;S=TIPPING;G=NIALL;I=M
```

Or in DDA format it might look like:

```
C=US;A=ATTMAIL;P=BDPL;O=DESIGN;DDA:COMMONNAME=NIALL M TIPPING
```

You'll find that Exchange uses address structures that include DDAs from time to time; we'll meet some of them later.

5

Understanding the Exchange X.400 Connector

5.1 Introduction

The previous chapter outlined some of the fundamental concepts behind the X.400 Message Handling Standards. Of all the Exchange Connectors, the X.400 Connector has the reputation of being the most daunting one. True, there are many property pages associated with it, nine in fact, and there are no helpful wizards to guide you though the configuration process. In this chapter we'll examine the necessary preparation that must be carried out to facilitate the use of the Exchange X.400 Connector and study in detail the options and settings that are associated with Connector setup.

My approach to covering this connector will demystify the X.400 Connector. I will not merely describe what each of the settings mean, but explain the effects that you'll see as a result of setting them one way or another.

5.2 X.400 Needs a Transport

Suppose you are responding to a job listing. Think of that letter you've written. Once you put it in the mailbox, you assume that it's going to get delivered to the recipient. But someone needs to move the letter from the mailbox to its destination. For the Postal Service, this transport is provided by a mail carrier who is either walking or driving along in a truck.

You can think of the X.400 Connector as the mail carrier too. It is responsible for the sequence of actions required to deliver the X.400 message to the intended recipient once you hand it over. It too needs a transport, and Exchange offers a number options here.

FIGURE 5–1

Selecting an MTA
Transport Stack for
the X.400
Connector

These are listed below and also shown in Figure 5–1 from the *File/New Other/MTA Transport Stack* option in the Administrator program.

- X.25 (TP0) Transport;

- RAS Transport;

- TCP/IP (RFC1006) Transport; and

- TP4 (OSI) Transport.

Providing these options for transport makes the X.400 Connector a very flexible animal indeed. The first step you need to take is to plan how you'll connect your X.400 Connector to its destination. Basically, you can use the X.400 Connector in one of two ways: Either you can use it to act as Site Connector to link two Exchange Sites together within the same Organization, in which case you've set up the link and you'll set up a Directory Replication Connector on top of it. Or you can use the connector to link to another X.400 messaging system. So long as the other system supports the X.400 rules (be they 1984, 1988, or 1992) you should have no trouble connecting. The other system can be any mainstream X.400 messaging product, HP OpenMail, Uniplex, MAILbus 400, Lotus Notes, Microsoft Mail X.400 Gateway, or even an Exchange server in another Organization (perhaps a different company).

If you're linking Sites together using an Exchange X.400 Connector then chances are you'll be running TCP/IP on your network. In that case you'll select the TCP/IP MTA Transport Stack. This is the simplest way to connect X.400 Connectors together.

If you're connecting to any other X.400 system then your choices may be limited based on the version of the X.400 recommendations that the vendor's implementation supports. Bear in mind that X.400 is an OSI application, and as such, was originally designed to run over the OSI protocol suite. This includes the TP4 OSI protocol and the X.25 protocol. It soon became apparent though, that TCP/IP was emerging as the dominant network protocol, and accordingly, the 1988 version of the X.400 recommendations introduced support for TCP/IP as a legitimate transport using RFC1006 (the ability to run OSI applications over a TCP/IP transport). If the other X.400 implementation supports RFC1006 then you can use the TCP/IP stack. Otherwise you'll be limited to either the X.25 or the TP4 transports. It's less likely that you'll have to use these with modern internal networks, but there are still occasions when it's almost impossible to avoid them. Connecting your Exchange server to a public X.400 ADMD service, for example, probably requires the use of an X.25 network, since RFC1006-based connections to ADMDs are few and far between. Even connections to the Microsoft Mail X.400 Gateway are not possible over TCP/IP, so you're forced to use either X.25 or TP4. (Of course, the best method for connecting to Microsoft Mail is by using the Exchange Microsoft Mail Connector.)

If you use an OSI-based stack you'll enter information on the configuration which serves to identify the X.400 Connector when it connects to other systems. OSI applications like X.400 talk to each other directly and assume that the lower order parts of the model are there to provide the environment for communication. (Figure 5–2 shows the seven-layer model and how an OSI application traverses down one stack, across a physical network connection, and up the other.)

In OSI terms, the information that you enter makes up a *Presentation Address*. The presentation address is composed of a number of parts that map directly onto the OSI seven-layer model and typically you'll see it referenced on OSI systems in this style:

```
<PSAP>/<SSAP>/<TSAP>/<NSAP>
```

For example, on the UNIX OSI system on which I run an X.400 MTA, the Presentation Address that other X.400 MTAs use to talk to mine is:

```
MTA/MTA/MTA/SABLE.BVO.DEC.COM
```

The term PSAP is an acronym for *Presentation Services Access Point*, and the same rules apply for SSAP, TSAP, and NSAP where the S refers to Session, the T to Transport, and the N to Network respectively. You'll also see the terms *P-Selector*, *S-Selector*, *T-Selector*, and *N-Selector* used to refer these components.

FIGURE 5–2 OSI
Seven-Layer Model
Communication

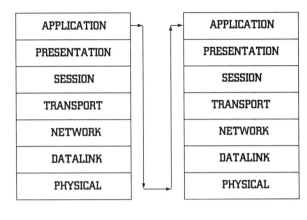

We'll take a brief look at configuring each of the transport stacks in the next few sections, apart from the RAS MTA stack; we've met that already in Section 2.3.2. But we won't go into too much detail on any of the transport technologies, which is beyond the scope of this book.[*]

5.2.1   Configuring the Eicon X.25 Stack

If you want to use X.25 to connect Exchange to another X.400 system, you must use the Eicon X.25 hardware and software. No other products are supported, at least not by any versions up to Exchange V5.5 SP2. Make sure that you've installed the X.25 host adapter card and then configured up the X.25 software. This is by no means a trivial task: X.25 isn't the easiest transport protocol to get to grips with, so make sure you know what you're doing here. It's best if you use an X.25 expert for this activity, but failing that you might be able to get by using some books on the subject and taking your lead for the configuration from the support person at the other side of the X.25 connection, especially if you're connecting to a public service. You can get to see some of the Eicon documentation on the Web (http://www.eicon.com) if you want to get started immediately.

---

[*]   Clear and concise descriptions of these technologies can be found in *X.400 and SMTP: Battle of the E-Mail Protocols* by John Rhoton (Digital Press).

Once you've configured X.25, it's a simple matter of selecting the X.25 Transport stack from the dialog (as shown above in Figure 5–1), selecting a server in your Site on which to run it, and filling in the fields on the dialog. You'll need to give the stack a name. It's common to use the name of the transport and the name of the server that it's hosted on, so for my server with the X.25 Connector I'd use X.25 (BVOJEN) since BVOJEN is my server's name.

You'll have to enter a few X.25-specific values on the *General* tab of the X.25 transport stack. Whatever form of X.25 network you're connecting to, either the network provider or the person who administrates the private network will have given you some connection information. This will include values for *Call User Data* and the *X.121* address.

Since this is an OSI-based transport, you'll also be prompted to enter P-Selector, S-Selector, and T-Selector values. In theory you can leave these values blank if you're not running any other OSI applications on your server, in which case there's no need to be able to uniquely identify the OSI application that you need to talk to. In practice, however, I always like to put some values in here. You never know what might happen to your server in the future, and in some cases X.400 implementations from other vendors sometimes expect to see these values. In Exchange, you can specify up to 4 text characters for the P-Selector, 16 for the S-Selector, and 32 for the T-Selector. Alternatively, you can specify hexadecimal characters instead of text, in which case the preceding maximum numbers are doubled. I recommend that you use something short for these values and always use the same values for each of the fields on all of the systems that you're building. Whatever values you put in for the stack on the local system, you'll need to specify on the X.400 Connector on the remote system that you're connecting to so that your system is correctly identified. Keeping the values constant like this greatly reduces the possibility of misconfiguration and many hours of painstaking troubleshooting. My personal favorite, which I use on all systems, is:

```
P-Selector: X400
S-Selector: X400
T-Selector: X400
```

Figure 5–3 shows those settings for the TCP/IP Connector. This naming structure is simple and avoids confusion.

You don't need to worry about changing any settings on the *Permissions* tab, since the default values should be just fine for normal management purposes, but if you wish to assign permissions to individual users or groups, you can use this tab to set administrative privileges up. The *Connectors* tab will be blank immediately after you set the stack up, but as you create X.400 Connectors you'll select the transport stack which you wish to use for each one and the list of connectors which rely on the stack will increase accordingly. With the stack set up this far, you're all set to go set up the X.400 Connector at this stage.

FIGURE 5-3

Configuring the
TCP/IP Transport
Stack

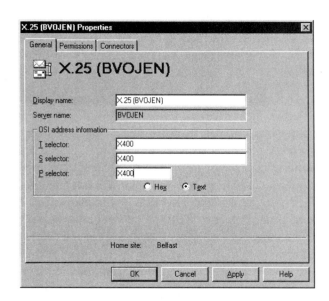

5.2.2   Configuring the TP4 Stack

If you wish to use TP4 (an OSI connectionless-oriented protocol), then you'll need to install this protocol separately. Much like X.25, it's not a native network protocol that's built into Windows NT, but unlike the Eicon software, it's supplied free on the Microsoft Windows NT Server CD. (You can search for the TP4SETUP directory on the CD, copy the files onto a floppy, and then add the protocol from the *Network* option in the NT Control Panel.) When you've got the protocol installed and set up, you should find that values for the local address and local NSAP are already configured as shown in Figure 5-4. There isn't much to do here.

When you've got the protocol installed, then you can select the TP4 MTA stack from the dialog box as shown in Figure 5-1. You'll need to set up values for the P-Selector, S-Selector, and T-Selector in the same way as you did for the X.25 stack, but exactly the same rules apply—it's just a different transport that you'll use.

FIGURE 5–4 TP4
Protocol Properties

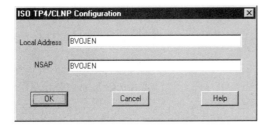

5.2.3 Configuring the TCP/IP Stack

Far and away, this is the easiest transport stack to use. The TCP/IP protocol is built into Windows so it's just a matter of selecting the TCP/IP MTA stack from the dialog in Figure 5–1. Once you've selected the stack you'll have to configure the P-Selector, S-Selector, and T-Selectors just like the other stacks.

5.3 Using the X.400 Connector

We've spent a lot of time exploring the concepts behind X.400 and understanding what it needs in order to function. Now we'll take a look at actually configuring it. When you select the option to create a new X.400 Connector, using the *File/New Other/X.400 Connector*, the first thing you'll have to do is select which MTA transport stack you'll be running the connector across. You should select one of the stacks that you configured earlier, but chances are it will be TCP/IP unless you're connecting to an external X.400 system.

5.3.1 The General Tab

There are nine tabs on the X.400 Connector configuration. The first one which requires configuration is the *General* tab, see Figure 5–5.

You'll need to complete the values for Display Name and Directory Name on this tab. It's wise to try to develop a standard naming scheme for connectors. The approach that works best for most implementations is a scheme that contains an indication of the connector type, where the connector originates, where it terminates, and some kind of numeric identifier to differentiate between multiple connectors from the same system. Try using the following syntax:

```
<type> <source> <target> nn
```

where,

<type>	is X.400 (X.400 Connectors) or DRPC (Site Connectors);
<source>	is Source Exchange Server name (X.400 Connectors)
	is Source Site name (Site Connectors);
<target>	is Target Exchange Server name (X.400 Connectors)
	is Target Site name (Site Connectors); and
nn	is a 2-digit number in the range 01–99

FIGURE 5–5

X.400 Connector
General Tab

Most of the values on the *General* tab are self-explanatory. For example, in the *Remote MTA Name* and *Remote MTA Password* you should enter the values for the remote or target MTA to which you're connecting. If you're using the X.400 Connector to connect to another Exchange server then the values that you need to enter in these fields equate to the name and password of the remote Exchange server. The remote MTA name should be the same as the NT name of the remote server (unless you've explicitly changed it during the Exchange configuration) and the value for the password should be null.

If you're connecting this X.400 Connector to an external X.400 system, then the values for the MTA name and password will be defined somewhere in the configuration of the remote system. (We'll see later how the settings should be configured to connect to a DIGITAL MAILbus 400 MTA.)

By default, the radio button for *Message Text Word Wrap* will be set to *Never*. You should keep it set this way unless you've got special requirements within your messaging environment. By this, I mean that if you're using the X.400 connector to connect to a non–Exchange messaging system *and* the clients it supports aren't intelligent enough to automatically wrap message text, then you'll need to force the connector to do the wrapping for the remote system. If you do this, the most common wrap position that gets set is position 79 (since dumb clients or VT terminals can usually only display 80 characters across the screen). Be sure you only set this if you really need to, otherwise intelligent clients will wrap the message text anyway and you'll see ugly formatting of messages, as in Figure 5–6. The first terminal shows a dumb client failing to wrap the text at all, while the second terminal shows text which is being wrapped twice (once by the Connector and again by the user agent).

FIGURE 5–6

Rendering of Text
after Wrapping
in the X.400
Connector

If you're using the X.400 Connector to hook up to another Exchange server, then you can be pretty confident that the clients on the other server will be able to interpret MAPI messages. When you send a message from a MAPI client like Outlook to another user on the same server that has the same type of client, the message will be rendered in exactly the same way that you constructed it. What this means is that all the formatting on the message (bolding, italics, underline, font style and size, etc.) and icon placement is maintained. Similarly, when you send mail across the X.400 Connector to similar clients on a system that supports MAPI, Exchange maintains the *richness* of the content in a single message, provided the *Remote clients support MAPI* option is checked (as shown in Figure 5–5). In this case you can be sure that the recipient will get a message that looks exactly like the one that you sent. Exchange uses a mechanism called *Transport Neutral Encapsulation Format* (TNEF) to keep the format of messages as they travel along a connection, and having this box checked means that TNEF message format is maintained as the message is sent. If you keep the box checked and the receiving mail system is not MAPI-aware, then Exchange will strip all of the rich text formatting and icon placement information into a separate attachment—the infamous WINMAIL.DAT file that you'll see in such circumstances. If you try to open this file you'll find it to be more or less unreadable. It's a binary file and doesn't have any information in it that can be used by normal user agents.

If you know for certain that the receiving mail system isn't MAPI-aware (likely if you're sending to an external X.400 system) then you should make sure that this box is not checked. The net result of this is that the extra formatting is removed from the message and no confusing attachment is sent along with the message. Let me assure you that no important content is lost from the message in this case. All of the textual content is maintained and embedded messages and documents are preserved as separate attachments to the message.

FIGURE 5–7
Sharing a Single
X.400 Connector
between MAPI/
Non–MAPI Users

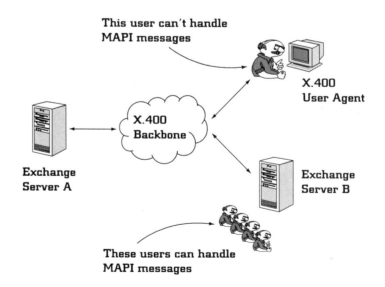

In some cases, this option may cause you some headaches. If you've got an X.400 Connector that you use to route messages to an X.400 backbone which has in turn connections to non–Exchange systems and to other Exchange systems, then you'll have to accept the lowest common denominator format and keep the option turned off. See Figure 5–7.

From the diagram, this means less pretty messages for the Exchange users on server B, but if the MAPI checkbox was enabled on server A then the users on the X.400 User Agent system would constantly get messages with what appeared to be meaningless attachments. This may not seem like a big problem until you total up the cost of every call to the Help Desk from one of those X.400 users when they call up to say that they've got a mail message with an unreadable attachment.

5.3.2 The Permissions Tab

Earlier versions of Exchange didn't have this tab. So if you're desperately looking for it on your X.400 Connector and it's not there, then it's just because you're not running an up-to-date version; there's no need to seek medical advice. Having said that, the advice that you should seek is on upgrading your version of Exchange Server to the most recent version.

FIGURE 5–8
X.400 Connector
Permissions Tab

The *Permissions* tab let's you control the access that Administrators have to the X.400 Connector. In a large and distributed organization you might have Administrators at key locations, and while you may want them to have complete control over servers in their own location, you might also want to restrict what they can do to a connector (X.400 in this case) at your location.

On the *Permissions* tab shown in Figure 5–8, you can see in the top list box that there are some accounts with permissions set for this object by default. As the administrator of this system it's up to me to specify who does and who doesn't have administrator access to this connector. I never actually modified the access rights for this object to include the NT account HughesBA in the access list, but I do know that HughesBA is a member of the Exchange Admins group that was set up in the User Manager for Domains for this NT domain. Because HughesBA is a member of that group, he's inherited the rights to modify this object.

You can add specific Windows NT accounts to which you want to grant access by clicking on the *Add* button in the lower part of the tab and assigning a *Role* to the newly specified account. Typical roles such as *Admin* and *Permissions Admin* are available, but you can create custom roles that include a given set of *Rights*. The rights that are available to be set are:

- *Modify User Attributes,* which allows the holder to modify the user attributes that are associated with this connector, i.e., who is and who isn't allowed to send mail through the connector;

- *Modify Admin Attributes,* which allows the holder to modify administrator settings on the connector;

- *Delete,* which allows the holder to delete the X.400 Connector; and

- *Modify Permissions,* which allows the holder to change the Permissions settings.

In general you shouldn't need to mess with this setting too much unless you have distributed administration and you want to be very specific about what rights you'll grant to administrators. As always, simplicity is best. If you've got sets of administrators that you can trust, it's best to bundle them into specific groups and either let them have access through inherited permissions or set roles on the Groups.

5.3.3   The Schedule Tab

The *Schedule* tab hosts four radio buttons that control how often the X.400 Connector attempts to send messages. The radio button options and the schedule grid are shown in Figure 5–9.

FIGURE 5-9
X.400 Connector
Schedule Tab

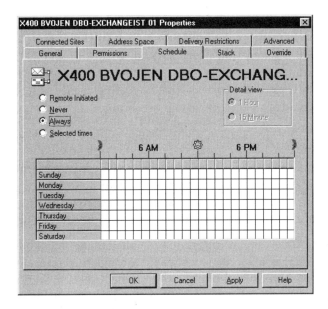

Of the four options, the most common settings that you're likely to need within your environment are either the *Always* setting or the *Selected Times* setting. Setting the schedule to Always means that any messages that need to get sent across the connector are transferred as soon as they arrive from the MTA. There's no delay for any message transfer under normal circumstances, and this represents the optimal setting for your environment if you've got high enough available bandwidth between all of your systems.

On the other hand, you may feel compelled to use the *Selected Times* option instead. This is attractive because it allows you to schedule the times when the connector will be able to transfer messages. Let's say you schedule the connector to transfer messages every hour on the hour. This means that any messages that get sent during the hour get queued up until the connector wakes up. This limits the constant flow of messages across the network and is useful if you're concerned about the capabilities of your network to sustain a constant message flow. Of course, the flip side of this setting is that if you do have a heavy message traffic workload and you restrict the flow so that transfer takes place every hour you may be causing short bursts of heavy utilization on the network links. Instead of a constant trickle of messages across the network which you might see with an "Always" setting, messages will back up and when the scheduled time arrives, a rush of messages will go out across the link. This may even be more troublesome than an Always setting.

There's little that you can do about this apart from setting a schedule that backs up messages until a time when you know that you have the network to yourself and won't impact other network users. Setting the connector so that it only transfers messages after 6:00 p.m. and before 7:00 a.m. might do the trick. But this means that no mail gets sent during the day. No doubt this would be unacceptable to most companies.

Alternatives exist. The simplest option is to keep the setting at Always and upgrade the capacity of your network links if the cost isn't prohibitive. If you can't do this, then it may be possible to implement prioritization of traffic on the network. If you've got dedicated Exchange servers (you should have) and smart routers, another alternative might be to lower the priority of IP traffic between your Exchange servers in preference to other traffic.

Two other settings are possible. Setting the connector to *Never* means that messages will never be sent through this connector and in fact the MTA connector selection process described earlier in Section 3.7.3 will ignore it if any other connector possibilities exist. The other possible setting is *Remote Initiated*. When set, the local connector will never attempt to open a connection to the destination X.400 MTA. But when a connection is established by the remote X.400 MTA partner in this relationship, the local connector is then happy to transfer its messages through the link. The local connector always waits until prompted by the remote connectors before outbound message transfer takes place. This is a classic master/slave scenario and is useful in environments where message transfer needs to be driven from a central source. For the remote initiated connection mechanism to work, you'll need to have both X.400 connectors set up to use the *Two Way Alternate* setting which we'll meet later. But make sure that you don't inadvertently set both the local *and* remote connectors to Remote Initiated. If you do, then neither connector will ever initiate a connection to its partner.

5.3.4 The Stack Tab

The *Stack* tab provides one of the greatest opportunities for wasting time. If you get any of the settings wrong on this page, chances are you'll spend a considerable amount of time troubleshooting your connection to the other X.400 system.

It's important to remember that all of the information that you set on this page relates to the other X.400 system to which you're trying to connect.

If you're using the TCP transport stack you'll see the *Stack* tab appear like the one in Figure 5–10. The upper part of the tab asks you to specify either the host name or the TCP/IP address or the remote system to which you wish to connect. You can just put the TCP/IP address into the *Address* field, but this isn't very pretty or meaningful to most normal people. It's much better if you can enter the fully qualified DNS hostname (like DBO-EXCHANGEIST.DBO.DEC.COM as shown in Figure 5–10). This is much more readable than a string of numbers. Exchange will use DNS or a lookup to a *hosts* file in order to perform the address translation. Using the hostname is also more tolerant of network reconfiguration. For example, if you move the remote X.400 system from one floor to another, it's possible that its TCP/IP address might change as it moves into a different subnet. It's also likely that it'll keep the same name. Using the fully qualified hostname insulates you from these subtle network changes. Of course, it's important for the network administrator to update DNS or provide some means of notification for everyone to update their *hosts* files if DNS isn't being used.

FIGURE 5–10
X.400 Connector
Stack Tab

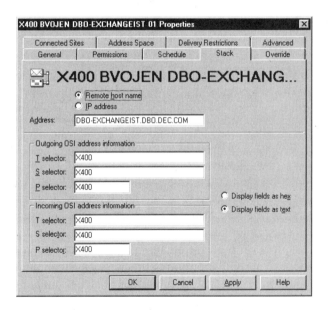

There is one drawback to using the fully qualified hostname rather than the TCP/IP address that's often mentioned. Every time that the Exchange server establishes a connection to the remote X.400 system, an address lookup must be performed to get the actual TCP/IP address. For this lookup there's a small performance penalty to pay, but in most cases, I'd say that the value that's derived from having a readable address that is easier to manage and maintain far outweighs the very small time delay that's introduced by the performance of a lookup.

If you're connecting the X.400 Connector to another Exchange server, then you'll need to fill in the values for the *Outgoing OSI address information* and the *Incoming OSI address information* fields with the values that you set for the transport stack on the remote system. For example, if you set the values of the *T selector*, *S selector*, and *P selector* to *X400* on the remote system as I suggested in Section 5.2.1 (see Figure 5–3), then you should set the corresponding attributes to the *X400* value for both the *Outgoing OSI address information* and the *Incoming OSI address information* sections. If you decided not to enter any values for the stack attributes on the remote system, then you can keep the values blank in both of these sections on your local system. There's nothing in the rules to say that you must have values in this section, but if the system you're connecting to has values set for these attributes then you must set them up on the local X.400 Connector to correspond with what's been set up remotely.

If you're linking your X.400 Connector to a non–Exchange system, then it will be quite likely that the remote system does have values for these attributes. In that case you'll have to enter the values for the remote stack in these sections as well.

You may be puzzled at this stage as to why the OSI attributes that you specify here are grouped into both *Outgoing* and *Incoming* sets since, on Windows NT at least, there's only one set of OSI attributes that are required to be set up on the stack. While this is true for Exchange and Windows NT (and in fact for most other X.400 systems that you'll be connecting to), in some cases foreign X.400 systems have the ability to use one set of OSI attributes for incoming connections and a different set of attributes for outgoing connections. If the system that you're connecting to operates in this way (ask the administrator of the remote X.400 system), then you should set the *Outgoing OSI address information* attributes to match the incoming attributes on the remote system and accordingly, set the *Incoming OSI address information* to match the outgoing attributes on the remote system. These two sets of OSI attributes can often be confusing to users the first time they try to set the connector up, and the temptation is to assume outgoing attributes refer to the local system stack values, and the incoming attributes refer to the remote system attributes. All the settings on this tab refer to attributes on the remote system.

If you're entering text values for the OSI address information, make sure that you've set the *Display fields as text* radio button, otherwise only hex characters will be allowed. In most cases, text values should be used but for older remote X.400 systems, the OSI attributes on these systems may only be specified in hex. If that's the case then select the *Display fields as hex* button and enter the appropriate value. When you've got the values entered you can toggle the radio buttons to see the attributes in their text and hex forms.

So far we've just talked about setting values for the X.400 Connector when we're using a TCP/IP transport stack. But remember that there are other transports that can be used for the Connector. If you're using a transport other than TCP/IP then you'll be presented with a slightly different version of the *Stack* tab. The tab is more or less the same as the TCP/IP version except for how you specify the address details of the connection to the remote system. The OSI attribute information will be required. If X.25 is your transport of choice then the *Stack* tab will allow you to enter *X.121 Address* of the remote system, the *Call User Data* and the *Facilities Data* for the connection. If native OSI (TP4) is your thing, then you'll be prompted for the NSAP address of the remote system, rather than the TCP/IP address. All other attribute settings follow the same rules as discussed above.

5.3.5   The Override Tab

In most cases you shouldn't ever need to go near the *Override* tab for the X.400 Connector. Essentially the attributes that you set on this tab override the default values under which the Exchange MTA operates. If you're making a connection from a foreign (non-Exchange) X.400 system then you may be asked to specify the name of the X.400 MTA to which you're connecting. If you remember the earlier discussion about the close integration between the Exchange MTA and X.400, then no prizes go out for guessing that the X.400 MTA is the same as the Exchange MTA; you'll want to give the name of the Exchange MTA as the X.400 MTA to which your remote X.400 system will connect.

Typically you can just leave this as it stands. So in the case of my server, I'd tell my remote X.400 system that the Exchange X.400 MTA was called *BVOJEN*. This is, of course, the Windows NT host name for the system. But occasionally the hostname may contain characters that you don't want to have in your X.400 MTA naming scheme. (Underscores and hyphens are the usual culprits.) If this is the case, you can override what the X.400 connector presents as its MTA name by entering a value in *Local MTA Name* field of the *Override* tab.

Passwords are another common cause of upset. In most cases you will avoid putting passwords onto the MTA characteristics of your Exchange server, but some non-Exchange X.400 implementations might mandate that a password be specified. Using passwords really only complicates the process of establishing connections between X.400 systems, and introduces more opportunity for things to wrong. If you're really concerned about security, then their use may be essential, but if possible don't use them.

If you're connecting to such an X.400 system you have two alternatives: You can either set a password on the MTA and then make sure that all other Exchange servers know about this password if they need to, or you can avoid all the problems with reconfiguring the MTA and merely set up a password for inbound X.400 connections using the *Local MTA password* field on the X.400 Connector. These fields are shown in Figure 5–11.

There are several other default MTA settings which you can override on this tab. You might recall that most of the default MTA connection parameters are set on the *Messaging Defaults* tab of the *MTA Site Configuration* option (see Section 3.10.1).

The values for the connection parameters that exist on the *Messaging Defaults* tab are also used for X.400 connections. When we discussed these parameters back in Section 3.10.2, we learned that for the most part the parameters could be left at their default values. The same holds true when we're using X.400 connections between MTAs. In most cases you shouldn't have to tamper with them too much. But if you find that messages are getting delayed or you come across connection errors in the Windows NT Event Log, you may wish to modify some of the parameters. (See Table 3–3 for advice on how to modify the parameters to overcome certain transmission problems.)

FIGURE 5–11
X.400 Connector
Override Tab

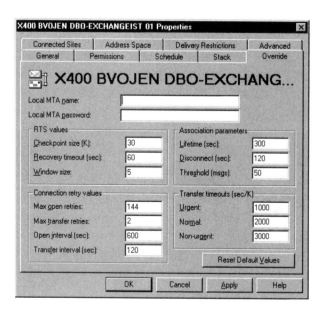

5.3.6 The Connected Sites Tab

Depending on how you intend to use the X.400 Connector, this tab may or may not be relevant to you. Connections to foreign X.400 systems don't require that you enter any data onto the fields on this tab—you can just skip it and move on. Why? Well, the *Connected Sites* tab is only useful if you're using the X.400 Connector to connect to another Exchange server, which necessarily will be in a separate site.

There's another tab on the X.400 Connector which we'll come to soon: the *Address Space* tab. Setting values in that tab dictates which messages will be routed from the local X.400 MTA to another. So providing that you've got two X.400 Connectors properly configured on two Exchange systems with the Address Spaces set up in order, this is all that you need to send X.400 messages from one Exchange system to another. Providing this kind of connectivity is just like linking Exchange to some other foreign messaging system that supports X.400 connections; there's no added value derived from the fact that we're linking one Exchange system to another. Our case is slightly different though: We want more than just the ability to send messages from one box to another. If we want to properly link two Exchange systems (and sites) together, not only do we need to configure the Address Spaces, but we need to tell each Exchange server hosting the X.400 Connector that the link between the two X.400 MTAs also represents a connection between the two sites. Having the sites properly linked together means that we'll be able to perform Directory Replication later and provide access from one site to any Connectors which may be held in the other site and vice versa.

FIGURE 5–12

X.400 Connector Connected Sites Tab

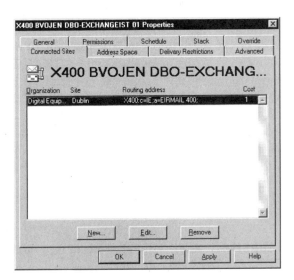

In a sense it's the values that you set on the *Connected Sites* tab that bind different sites together into a single Exchange organization. Making that special bond between the two sites isn't that difficult. Click the *New* button on the tab (as shown in Figure 5–12) and you'll be asked to enter the details that specify the Organization and Site Name of the site to which you wish to connect (see Figure 5–13).

FIGURE 5–13

Connected Sites
General Tab

The *Organization* field should be filled in already because although its value relates to the Organization of the remote site it is assumed to be the same as the Organization of the local site, which makes perfect sense, of course. The only hard bit of work that's required of you is to specify the name of the remote site. In my case, that's *DUBLIN*. So with this configuration information available, Exchange now knows that this Connector handles messages that need to be sent to site *DUBLIN*. There's just a little further effort that's required. Although we know that messages for *DUBLIN* are handled by this Connector, we need some way to determine what characteristics of an address indicate that a message is bound for the *DUBLIN* site. On the *Routing Address* tab (see Figure 5–14), we can indicate the higher order part of the X.400 address which should mean that messages are bound for this site. In my case, I've instructed Exchange that any X.400 OR addresses that begin with:

```
C=IE;A=EIRMAIL400;P=DIGITAL;O=DIGITAL;OU1=DBO
```

need to be sent through this Site Connector. (I got these settings from the Site Addressing Defaults for the Dublin site.)

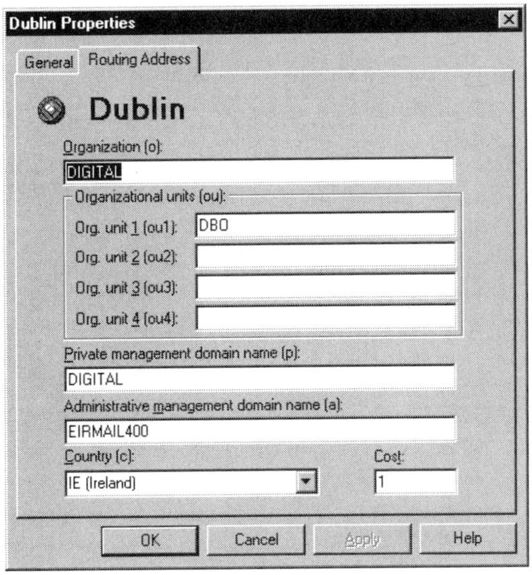

FIGURE 5–14
Connected Sites
Routing Address
Tab

You'll notice that the cost for this site connection is *1*. I'd advise you to set the costs in multiples of ten so that more flexibility is inherent in the design of the message routing network. Remember that these connection instances get pooled together and amalgamated into the single routing table: the GWART.

Bear in mind that the X.400 Connector typically works on a one-to-one mapping principle. That is, your X.400 Connector only connects to one other X.400 Connector on one other single Exchange server. This means that you can only use it to directly link your site to the site in which the target server resides. The fact that you can use the *Connected Sites* tab to create multiple Site Connections can get rather confusing. When you create the connection, use the *New* button just once to establish the relationship between your site and the target site. You shouldn't set up connections to other sites? Remember that we've already specified the server that this X.400 Connector links to, specifying its Stack information. How then could you connect to multiple sites when you can only connect to one server and the server you're connecting to can only live in one site? And why then can the *Connected Sites* tab display connections to multiple sites? The answer is quite straightforward: If the Site that you are connecting to has downstream connections to other Sites, then when you establish the Site Connection between your local site and the remote site and then enable directory replication, you'll see the other sites listed as available through this Connector. You don't have to explicitly enter them.

For example, look at the site connections that are shown in Figure 5–15. Assuming that these sites are connected with X.400 Connectors, the *Connected Sites* tab should read as follows.

FIGURE 5–15

Downstream Site
Connections

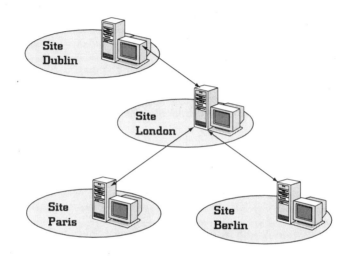

On the *LONDON* server the X.400 Connector to the *PARIS* server should have its Connected Sites list only contain *PARIS*. In the same way, on the *LONDON* server the X.400 Connector to the *BERLIN* server should have a Connected Sites list that lists only *BERLIN*. But on the *DUBLIN* server, the X.400 Connector to the *LONDON* server should have a Connected Sites list that contains *LONDON*, *PARIS*, and *BERLIN*, even though the Connected Sites tabs would only have been set up with the single value of *LONDON* when the sites were first connected. This list would have been fully populated later when directory replication first took place.

5.3.7   The Address Space Tab

Having filled in the *General* and the *Stack* tabs, you've been able to identify the remote end of your X.400 Connection. And if you just want to make a site connection to another Exchange server, then all you need do is fill in the *Connected Sites* tab. With this data, you've given all the information that's required to link one site to another. The particular details of any X.400

addresses (e.g., an OU1 of *DUBLIN* or an OU2 of *NORTH*) that you might use to identify individual sites actually isn't required for messages to flow across the Connector. However, if you're using the X.400 Connector to link to another X.400 MTA (not necessarily an Exchange server), then you will need some way to determine which messages should get routed through a particular Connector. To indicate which addresses an X.400 Connector is prepared to service, you must set values on the *Address Space* tab, as shown in Figure 5–16.

FIGURE 5–16

X.400 Connector
Address Space Tab

If you left the address space blank (as it is in Figure 5–16), then all X.400 messages will get routed out through this Connector unless a more specific address space is defined on another Connector.

By clicking on the *New* button, you can configure more explicit address spaces that route mail through this connector. For example, if I were to configure my X.400 Connector such that I wanted to send messages that were addressed to users, with an address part of:

```
C=IE;A=EIRMAIL400;P=DIGITAL;O=DIGITAL;OU1=DBO
```

then I could explicitly define an address space on this connector by setting the values as shown in Figure 5–17.

FIGURE 5–17
Setting an Address
Space on the X.400
Connector

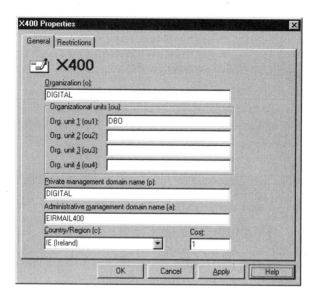

In a large deployment of Exchange, it's likely that you will either connect to some form of X.400 backbone to provide connectivity to legacy systems or to an external X.400 provider. If you've got multiple points of contact in a number of different countries, you'll want to set up X.400 connectors in each of the main countries where you have a relationship with the X.400 service provider.

So let's say you ran a company and had connections to X.400 service providers in the United States, Ireland, and the United Kingdom. In this case, you'd want to make sure that any X.400 messages for outside recipients that went to the United States were handled by the U.S. X.400 Connector; any messages for outside users in Ireland went to the Irish X.400 Connector, and so on. The simplest way to achieve that is to set up address spaces and merely specify the C part of the address. Not only does this make logical sense from a routing point of view, it's also desirable because the cost for X.400 messages that travel internationally from one national service provider to another is quite high. Using a routing design like this optimizes the message flow. Many large organizations, including Compaq, structure their connections like this.

When you were setting up the *Connected Sites* tab, I said that you could only specify one Site to connect directly to, even though the buttons on the tab suggested that you could enter more values there. The buttons on the *Address Space* tab suggest the same thing. But in this case, it does make perfect sense to add multiple address spaces, because the target X.400 server that you connect to may provide connections to a number of different X.400 domains. Let's think about that fictitious company that you're in charge of. You may also want the U.K. X.400 Connector to take care of messages that are addressed to users in France because you know that the target server for the U.K. X.400 Connector can either cheaply or easily route messages to the French X.400 domain. No problem. Simply add an address space for C=FR to the U.K. X.400 connector and you're all set.

You'll also see that a cost can be associated with each address space. In Figure 5–17, the cost is 1, but once again, you'd probably want to set the costs in multiples of 10 so that it's easier to make changes to the routing topology of your organization. With the French connection, you could set a cost of 10 for the French address space on the U.K. Connector, and create another address space for French recipients on the Irish Connector with a cost of 20. This would ensure that an optimal path would always used, but in the event that the U.K. connection was unavailable, Exchange would use the higher cost Irish Connector instead.

FIGURE 5–18

Setting Scope
Restrictions on an
X.400 Address
Space

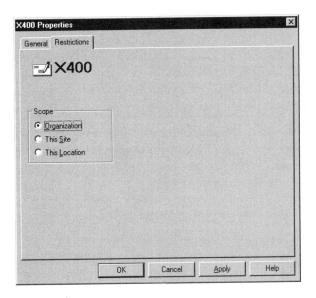

Back in Section 3.9, we came across the concept of limiting the scope of a Fax Connector so that it was only accessible to a limited number of users. It's possible to apply the same scope restrictions to almost all of the Connectors; the *Restrictions* tab (see Figure 5–18) on the X.400 Connector, which is visible when creating or editing an address space, allows you to do this. Setting the scope to *Organization* exposes the Connector to all servers in the entire Exchange Organization; setting it to *This Site* limits its availability to only servers located in the same Site as the Connector server; and setting the scope to *This Location* restricts its availability to only users that connect to servers with the same location value as the one on which the Connector is running.

It's worth pointing out that it's possible to create different types of address spaces over an X.400 Connector, although it's most likely that you'll only ever be creating X.400 address spaces as we've described above. When you click on the *New* button to create a new address space, you'll be presented with a choice of address space types. Usually you'll choose X.400, but you may choose another. It's difficult to envision exactly why you might want to create a non–X.400 address space, but one scenario springs to mind. Let's assume that you've got a central Site called *CENTER*, and in it you have an SMTP Connector to the Internet. Perhaps you don't want to advertise the fact that it's possible to send Internet mail into your organization, so you've set the scope of the SMTP Connector to *This Site*. If you've got a number of other Sites (let's call them *SITE01* to *SITE99*) connecting to this Site over X.400 Connectors, they won't have any idea that there's an SMTP Connector anywhere in the organization. But if you did need to let just *SITE53* get access to SMTP, then you could set up another X.400 Connector to link it to the *CENTER* Site and set the scope on that Connector so that it can't be seen outside of *SITE53*. This approach overcomes the restrictions in granularity of the scope control over Connectors.

You can deal with other address space types apart from the default ones (X400, SMTP, and MS) by selecting *Other* and entering in the values that you need. Other address spaces that you could be interested in might relate to Fax or Pager connectors.

5.3.8   The Delivery Restrictions Tab

One of the advantages that the X.400 Connector has over some of its peers is that you can restrict usage of the Connector to named individuals. This is done by using the *Delivery Restrictions* tab as shown in Figure 5–19. These restrictions relate to the sending of messages out through the Connector. Specifying restrictions for a particular user means that the person won't be able to *send* messages, but it doesn't imply that there's a restriction on the messages that can be *received* through the Connector for the named user.

FIGURE 5–19 X.400
Connector Delivery
Restrictions Tab

You can implement the restrictions by using the *Accept messages from* or *Reject messages from* list boxes. By default, everyone is allowed to use the Connector and in most cases this is how you'll want to implement it. However, if you do have a requirement to prevent a small number of users making use of the Connector, then you can list them in the *Reject messages from* list box, while keeping the access open for all other users with the *Accept messages from* setting at *All*. If you want to prevent access from everyone, with only a few restrictions, then use the *Accept messages from* list box to specify those users you are prepared to allow to use the Connector.

In the example I've shown, I've got access to the Connector open to everyone in the Organization with the exception of Tony Redmond and Frank Clonan (those mailboxes must be in the Global Address List).

5.3.9   The Advanced Tab

Settings on the *Advanced* tab are grouped into MTA Conformance, X.400 Link Options, Message Size, GDI settings, and message text settings. The tab is shown in Figure 5–20.

Determining which type of MTA to conform is pretty straightforward and governed completely by the target MTA to which you'll be connecting. For the most functionality, it's best to set the MTA conformance to 1988 Normal mode, which is how most of the more modern MTAs tend to behave. Connecting to another Exchange server is, of course, a breeze. The 1988 normal mode of operation is the order of the day, and it's the default value in any case.

FIGURE 5–20

X.400 Connector
Advanced Tab

However, if you'll be connecting to an older MTA then you may have to use a setting of 1984 mode. This means that connections from your Exchange X.400 MTA will be downgraded (if they can) to deal with the lower level of functionality that's found in 1984-based MTAs. This usually isn't too serious but can sometimes result in interoperability problems with OR addresses (1988 OR addresses support Teletex strings, 1984 doesn't), content and tagging issues, or the presence of critical fields (e.g., *critical for delivery*). What do I mean by interoperability problems? Well, usually this manifests itself by a *nondelivery notification* (NDN). You should get some clues in the NDN to indicate what the problem was, but sometimes not. So if you're connecting to 1984-based system and start to get unexplained NDNs, one of the above issues could be the cause. At a time like that, you'll need to be able to capture the message in question and decode it to give you an idea of what's gone wrong.

Then there's the 1988-X.410 mode of operation. X.410 relates to the public message transfer service and *"specifies the general, operational and quality of service aspects of the public international message transfer service."*

Unless you're connecting to a public service provider, you're probably unlikely to come across this mode of operation. However, it is, of course, possible that the X.400 system that your company uses internally, and to which you're trying to connect, is the same type of system that some public service provider is using. If that's the case, then make sure that you set the Exchange X.400 Connector to conform to X.410 as well.

In the X.400 link options grouping, you again need to be aware of the type of target X.400 system that you're connecting to. If the target system behaves as a 1984-based system, then it won't be able to make any sense of 1988 BP15 bodyparts. In this case you should uncheck the *Allow BP-15 (in addition to BP-14)*. With the box unchecked, all attachments are encoded as BP14 bodyparts and thus are acceptable to 1984-based systems. With the box checked, attachments are encoded as BP15 bodyparts. Actually, Exchange doesn't send the BP15 bodypart as an externally defined bodypart but creates it in the File Transfer Bodypart (FTBP) that we discussed earlier. If that's the case, you should also make sure that the target X.400 system is capable of understanding FTBP bodyparts, since not all 1988-based systems possess this knowledge. For connections to another Exchange server, you should make sure to send BP15 (FTBP) bodyparts.

Exchange uses its own structure for representing messages when they travel from one Exchange MTA to another. This format is called the *Microsoft Database Encoding Format*, but it's often abbreviated to MDBEF. The option *MS Exchange contents* as shown in the link options grouping is synonymous with MDBEF. So long as you're using the X.400 Connector to connect directly to another Exchange X.400 Connector it's quite okay to leave the *Allow MS Exchange contents* box checked because the target Exchange X.400 MTA will be capable of understanding a message in MDBEF format. But if you're connecting to a non–Exchange system, then you should uncheck this box, since it's not very likely that any external X.400 implementation will be able to make any sense of an MDBEF message. It's also important that you uncheck this box even if the target MTA is an Exchange one, but there are intermediate X.400 MTAs on the way. In such a case you might be connecting your Exchange server to someone else's Exchange server over a public X.400 service. The risk in this configuration is that the intermediate MTA may become confused with the MDBEF content which it is trying to forward. A nondelivery is likely to result from such a situation.

When you uncheck the box, Exchange converts the MDBEF format message into the standard X.400 P.22 format (if it's a 1988-based connection) or

P.2 format (if it's a 1984-based connection). There's no great loss in functionality or message integrity from this conversion, but like everything, there is a price to pay. The process of conversion is quite CPU-intensive, so there is a slight performance hit for all the messages that have to be converted. Some analyses show an overhead of about 20 percent of CPU time. Such a load won't bring your Exchange server down to its knees with poor performance, but if you have a lot of traffic going through the Connector and conversions must take place, then it may make some more sense to put the Connector on a dedicated system rather than leaving it on system with user mailboxes. If you do, then the Connector is just stealing CPU cycles that could potentially be put to better use servicing user requests.

The proper setting for *Two way alternate* is also dependent on the target X.400 implementation to which you are connecting. When an X.400 MTA initiates an association to another MTA to send messages, the initiator of the association sends all of the messages that have to be sent and the association is terminated. If the system that received the messages in the previous association has messages to send as well, then it has a responsibility to initiate another association to allow those messages to be sent. Now, X.400 MTAs are, of course, able to deal with multiple associations at the same time so this doesn't mean that the operations must take place in a lock-step fashion. That is, there's no risk that system A with lots of messages to send to system B will prevent system B from sending messages until A is finished. However, in order to make exchange of messages slightly more balanced, the two-way alternate approach allows the initiating MTA to send a message and then request that the receiving MTA send a message that it may have. This process continues with each MTA taking turns to send messages to each other. If the target system that you're connecting supports this functionality, then you should ensure that the box is checked. Otherwise leave it unchecked.

If you inadvertently check the box when the target MTA can't deal with two-way alternate, you'll as likely as not see all message flow between the systems be prevented.

Although the MTA setting for message size governs the maximum size of a message that can be sent from Exchange MTA to Exchange MTA, you can impose a further limit on the maximum message size that you send to an X.400 MTA. In some cases, you may want to impose limits like this if you're connecting across a public network and the line speed is slow. For example, it's not uncommon to find many connections to public X.400 service providers over X.25 connections that only support 9.6Kb/s transfer rates. In a case like that, you may not want to allow very big messages to be sent out which might potentially tie up the connection for a long period of time during the day.

You may think that there's a smart way around this: What if you set up two X.400 Connectors, one that dealt with small messages and one that dealt with large messages? Could you configure the "small" Connector to only be active during daytime, and the "large" Connector to be active at night when demand is lower? The theory here being that if a user sends a large message, then it will be queued to the inactive "large" Connector and delivery is deferred until later. As of Exchange V5.5 SP2 this functionality is available, but it won't work on any earlier versions.

Selecting the correct format for message text is usually a no-brainer. In most cases you should be able to take the default value of IA5 (International Alphabet 5), which defines an ASCII-based text scheme that is more or less universally implemented by most X.400 MTAs and X.400-based systems. This means that outbound text messages are encoded using this scheme, and if you've selected the *Convert Incoming Messages to Microsoft Exchange Contents* on the MTA, then inbound messages are converted using these settings as well. A number of options are available under this drop-down box, and unless the target system that you are connecting to has specific requirements or you intend to use country-specific versions of the IA5 structure, you should leave this option as it is.

And finally on the *Advanced* tab, you should set a value that is appropriate for the GDI (or Global Domain Identifier). When X.400 messages leave one X.400 routing domain and transit into another, the GDI field is stamped in the X.400 message header to indicate where it has been. A receiving MTA that knows it exists at an X.400 domain boundary and is accepting a message from a foreign X.400 domain will check the GDI to make sure that it's not the same as its own. Although the algorithm is slightly more complex than this, if the MTA were able to find its own GDI in the message header, then it would know that the message had been looping. As such, Exchange must stamp its own GDI on every message.

By default, the GDI will be generated from Site Addressing, so that yields a GDI that is specific to the details of your Exchange environment. Typically, the GDI is based on the C, ADMD, and PRMD terms that you use in your X.400 addresses. Exchange will automatically build X.400 addresses and a GDI that is mapped directly to the Organization and Site names of your Exchange implementation. Just as you've probably used a different scheme for X.400 addresses, you'll probably also want to use the same terms for the GDI.

For example, the default X.400 addresses that Exchange would build for my system would be:

```
C=US;A= ;P=Digital Equipment;O=Redwood
```

which derives from an Organization name of Digital Equipment Corporation and a Site name of Redwood. But as you've seen in many of my examples so far, I've used X.400 addresses of the form:

```
C=GB;A=GOLD 400;P=DIGITAL;O=DIGITAL;OU1=BVO
```

So when it comes to selecting the GDI to be used, I'd manually choose to use the C, ADMD, and PRMD terms as above rather than the Site defaults.

If you're using a space in the ADMD part of the GDI, you should be aware of the fact that a space character can legally be represented as either a numeric or a printable string character and the X.400 recommendations allow both. Some older versions of Exchange used to nondeliver the message if the ADMD part of the GDI had a space in it which was encoded as a numeric rather than a printable string, so watch out. (This is one that took me a few hours to track down!)

5.4   Using a Flat Address Space

One approach to implementing an X.400 addressing scheme within your Exchange environment is to build addresses that map onto individual Sites using the OU1 term. For example, Figure 5–21 shows a possible OR addressing scheme for a company called Ornothobic Ltd.

If these Sites are linked together using X.400 Connectors, you may be forgiven for thinking that each Site must be uniquely identified using an X.400 OR address for each Site, and this would of course mean that all user mailboxes in each Site would have to adhere to that naming scheme. Clearly if you used a Site Connection other than the X.400 Connector (perhaps the Site Connector or the SMTP Connector) then this problem would not arise.

But really there is no problem in a pure Exchange environment. If you flip back to Figure 4–2, where we give the ASN.1 definition for a user message, you may notice an optional attribute called *PerDomainBilateralInfo*. This attribute holds information that is arbitrarily defined by the X.400 messaging domain through which the message is travelling. Exchange holds certain information in this attribute that allows you to share the X.400 address space between MTAs located in different sites.

The result of this is that it's not mandatory to implement an addressing scheme like the one shown in Figure 5–21. If your company wishes to implement a much flatter structure, as demonstrated in Figure 5–22, then there's no reason why this can't be done.

FIGURE 5–21
Mapping Sites to
Organizational
Units

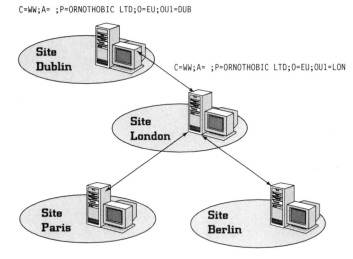

`C=WW;A= ;P=ORNOTHOBIC LTD;O=EU;OU1=DUB`

`C=WW;A= ;P=ORNOTHOBIC LTD;O=EU;OU1=LON`

`C=WW;A= ;P=ORNOTHOBIC LTD;O=EU;OU1=PRS`

`C=WW;A= ;P=ORNOTHOBIC LTD;O=EU;OU1=BLN`

FIGURE 5–22
Organizational
Units with a Flat
Address Space

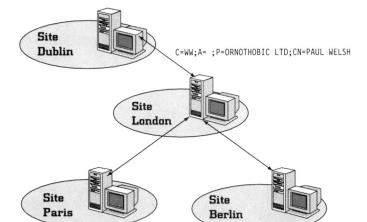

`C=WW;A= ;P=ORNOTHOBIC LTD;CN=CONOR BRADY`

`C=WW;A= ;P=ORNOTHOBIC LTD;CN=PAUL WELSH`

`C=WW;A= ;P=ORNOTHOBIC LTD;CN=NIALL TIPPING`

`C=WW;A= ;P=ORNOTHOBIC LTD;CN=FIONA RICE`

6

Understanding SMTP and DNS

6.1   Introduction

Today most people take Internet mail for granted. You sit at home, press a few keys to write a message to your cousin who lives on the other side of the world, press the *Send* button, and you *expect* that the message should reach him or her within a few minutes. If it doesn't, then you'll want to know why. When the first traces of the Internet appeared in the 1960s in the guise of the ARPAnet (Advanced Research Projects Agency), I doubt if any of its pioneers ever imagined that it would become such a commodity.

But few people realize just how complex a set of operations must take place so that the message gets from one computer to another. Fewer still probably care. John Q. Citizen isn't really too interested in what happens after he presses the Send button; he's not intrigued at how his mail server manages to determine which host to connect to try to deliver the mail. Nor does he understand the conversation that goes on when his mail server says "Hel(l)o" to the other server. And I guess he doesn't give a hoot about how an ugly sender address is turned into something more beautiful before the message is transmitted. But as a messaging system integrator, *you* care! It's the reason you get up in the morning, isn't it?

Understanding the principles of the Simple Mail Transfer Program and how it uses other TCP/IP application protocols in the background forms the basis of what we cover in this chapter.

6.2   Where Does SMTP Come From?

Most people would agree that X.400 and SMTP are two radically different approaches to the problem of sending mail between one computer and another. While the protocols and rules that they use for message exchange have little in common, it's perhaps a little surprising to see that both approaches enjoy pretty much the same attitude towards components and topologies.

By this, I mean, that many of the terms used to describe X.400 messaging components are the same as the terms used to describe SMTP components. I guess we shouldn't be too surprised. After all, both technologies are aimed at providing a solution to the same problem, and both have had some of the greatest brains in the business directed at building specifications for reliable message transfer systems.

We've already discussed the standards-making bodies for X.400 (the CCITT and the ISO), and you'll be delighted to know that similar, although less formal, bodies exist for Internet standards. It's the role of the Internet Engineering Task Force (IETF)* to facilitate and control the process of defining documents known as *Internet-Drafts* (I-Ds). These I-Ds outline the rules and standards that implementers should follow when designing their products to allow the greatest amount of interoperability. They can sometimes exist for an extended period of time, and if so they are generally accepted as standards. However, most get discussed during IETF forums and through IETF Working Groups, undergo considerable modification, then become full-fledged RFCs.† The status and relevance of an RFC, i.e., whether or not it is in force, is defined in the current edition of the *Internet Official Protocol Standards* document. RFCs are usually authored by leaders in the field of the technology to which the RFC relates, and typically draw on panels of industry and academic experts. Once the RFCs have been approved, they are released to the public domain and anyone may access them and begin building products to the RFC specification.

Although there are many RFCs which relate to various aspects of messaging (including interoperability with X.400), the ones of most interest to us are:

- RFC-821, SMTP—Simple Mail Transfer Protocol;
- RFC-822, Standard for the Format of ARPA Internet Text Messages;

---

* You can reach it online at `http://www.ietf.org`.
† An RFC, or Request for Comment, is a de facto standard published by the IETF. There are many locations on the Internet where you may browse through the RFC standards. I normally use `http://www.cis.ohio-state.edu/hypertext/information/rfc.html` but you can easily find others by querying a Web Search Engine such as `http://www.altavista.com`.

- RFC-1521, MIME (Multipurpose Internet Mail Extensions) Part 1 (Format of Message Bodies); and

- RFC-1522, MIME (Multipurpose Internet Mail Extensions) Part 2 (Message Header Extensions).

The original RFCs (821 and 822) were published back in 1982, when sending text messages was all that anyone thought would ever need to be done. RFC-821 describes the process that's required for the transmission of messages between systems, while RFC-822 defines the structure of the text message itself. But as document technology advanced and it was observed that X.400 didn't really take the lead that it should have for dealing with complex attachments, newer standards to deal with the issues emerged. These were the MIME RFCs, which were published more recently in 1993. Essentially, MIME represents a set of extensions to the existing rules for representing message content within SMTP messages and has gained widespread acceptance since its inception. But more about that later.

Unfortunately the phrases used to describe SMTP mail components occasionally lack some consistency. You'll often see the terms *SMTP mail* and *Internet mail* used interchangeably. Further, in terms of addresses there's usually little distinction made between the expressions SMTP address, Internet address, and RFC-822 address. Strictly, speaking it should be referred to as an RFC-822 address, but that usage is less common.

6.3 SMTP Networks: Components and Topology

Many of the terms that we've already met during our discussions on X.400 mail are also used to describe components that make SMTP-based mail systems. In much the same way that X.400 employs MTAs to transfer messages and UAs to read or store messages, SMTP uses the same names to describe the components that transfer messages and allow you to read them.

SMTP MTAs accept mail from a UA by polling specific locations on disk and looking for messages. When a message is detected, the TO: recipient is analyzed and the MTA will attempt to deliver the mail. This may involve contacting another MTA running on another system. In such cases, the MTA establishes an IP connection to the other MTA using Port 25. When the mail reaches its final destination, the last MTA in the set of relays passes the message onto the UA.

On UNIX systems, the MTA is generally realized as a program called *sendmail*, but may be casually referred to as an *SMTP* or *Internet mailer*. In

Exchange terms, the SMTP MTA is known as the *Internet Mail Service* (IMS).[*]

Message structure is more or less the same for SMTP messages as it is for X.400 messages. Each message is composed of a header and body. (You can see this structure in Figure 6–3.) The message is basically split into two parts. Any text at the start of the message is deemed to be part of the header, and the blank line signifies the end of the header and the start of the body. Some header fields must be present, namely the creation time, the originator identity, and a destination address. Anything else that's present is optional, although most implementations usually insert a generous sprinkling of fields.

As defined in RFC-822, the message body (of which there can only be one) is a sequence of 7-bit ASCII characters. This allows the use of the first 127 defined characters, typically all the normal printable characters that you'd see on a U.S. keyboard. What's missing from this are the extended ASCII characters (from character 128 onwards), which require 8-bits for representation. So if you need to use foreign characters (e.g., if you were sending a message to your French colleague and you wanted to start your message with *Salut Michèle* and close it with *A Bientôt*), then you'd be in trouble because most foreign characters can't be represented with a 7-bit ASCII value. Similarly, complex documents (executables, word processing files, etc.) all make use of 8-bit ASCII characters.

6.4   MIME—Bringing SMTP Mail Up-to-Date

Although SMTP mail as defined in RFC-821 and RFC-822 did its job well, it really only met a relatively short-term objective. The transfer of simple single mail messages was about all that SMTP mail was capable of dealing with. The proliferation of PCs and requirements to send complex documents and attachments meant that changes had to be made to the original SMTP specifications. These changes came in the form of the MIME standards.

There are essentially two methods that can be used to allow the existing global SMTP MTA infrastructure to be capable of supporting 8-bit ASCII messages. Changes to the specification of SMTP could be mandated such that each MTA would have to be upgraded to a more sophisticated software implementation. This would be a mammoth task and would no doubt be

---

[*] Exchange versions earlier than V5.0 used the term IMC (Internet Mail Connector) to refer to the SMTP MTA.

met with long delays in the introduction of the new MTAs and periods of instability on the Internet. There would also obviously be a time during which some Internet MTAs were 8-bit aware while others were still only 7-bit aware. Such an approach is doomed to failure.

The MIME approach to dealing with increasing message requirements is ostensibly quite straightforward. Rather than meddle with the existing infrastructure, the MIME standards would have 8-bit ASCII messages and attachments encoded so that they could be represented in a 7-bit format. The encoding algorithm is usually *base64* but sometimes the old UNIX favorite *uuencode* is used, depending on configuration settings. In essence, binary files were encoded so that they appeared to be simple text files. A MIME message reads just like a text message with all of the interesting parts seemingly running into one long body text. This means that there is no problem sending the message across an SMTP network because it's treated just like any other text message, albeit a long one. When the message arrives at the destination MTA, that MTA takes on the responsibility to convert the text-based MIME message back into its native parts. Not all message body-parts need to be base64-encoded. If the message cover memo or attachment is already a simple 7-bit sample of text, then there's no need to encode for transmission. Doing so it would just impose extra overhead anyhow, since base64-encoded MIME messages are typically 33 percent larger than their binary representations.

MIME has to do slightly more than just encode 8-bit files though. It also has to provide a mechanism for tagging MIME contents, preserving filenames, and dealing with multiple attachments in a single message. All of its features, and the means by which it does them, are described in RFC-1521. I'd suggest you look there if you want to get a deeper understanding of MIME.

All of these aspects are illustrated in Figure 6–1. Notice the *Content-Type* header section of the message. This indicates that the message is composed of multiple parts. In order to separate one part of the message from another, a MIME MTA will generate a one-off unique string (or boundary) that can be used as the delimiter between attachments in the message. The boundary string is declared in the header of the message. The receiving MTA can then simply parse the whole text body line by line and recognize a different message part whenever it encounters the boundary string.

```
From daemon Thu Aug  6 11:54:16 1998
Received: from eur-rmc.vbo.dec.com by sable.bvo.dec.com;
(5.65v3.2/1.1.8.2/23Feb96-1148AM)
        id AA23241; Thu, 6 Aug 1998 11:54:15 +0100
Received: from DBOIST-MSXCL ([16.183.240.197])
        by mail.vbo.dec.com (8.8.8/8.8.8) with ESMTP id MAA24731
        for <kmc@sable.bvo.dec.com>; Thu, 6 Aug 1998 12:55:24
+0200 (MET DST)
Received: by dboist-msxcl.dbo.dec.com with Internet Mail
Service (5.5.2217.0)
        id <Q244G2DH>; Thu, 6 Aug 1998 12:03:55 +0100
Message-Id: <1DA0270C0F05D2119D7B0000F805504901C3F4@dboist-
msxcl.dbo.dec.com>
From: Kieran McCorry <Kieran.McCorry@digital.com>
To: "'kmc@sable.bvo.dec.com'" <kmc@sable.bvo.dec.com>
Subject: MIME message
Date: Thu, 6 Aug 1998 12:03:54 +0100
Sensitivity: Company-Confidential
Mime-Version: 1.0
X-Mailer: Internet Mail Service (5.5.2217.0)
Content-Type: multipart/mixed;
        boundary="----_=_NextPart_000_01BDC129.E7281B3B"

This message is in MIME format. Since your mail reader does not
understand this format, some or all of this message may not be
legible.

------_=_NextPart_000_01BDC129.E7281B3B
Content-Type: text/plain;
        charset="iso-8859-1"

A Word file is attached.

Regards
Kieran

------_=_NextPart_000_01BDC129.E7281B3B
Content-Type: application/msword;
        name="salary_plan.doc"
Content-Transfer-Encoding: base64
Content-Disposition: attachment;
        filename="salary_plan.doc"
Content-Location: ATT-1-2EC38FBF632CD2119D800000F8055049 -ENCODED.DOC
```

```
OM8R4KGxGuEAAAAAAAAAAAAAAAAAAAAAPgADAP7/
CQAGAAAAAAAAAAAAAAAABAAAAIQAAAAAAAAA
EAAAIwAAAAEAAAD+////AAAAACAAAAD/////////////////////////////
//////////////
AADxcxcAMQAAAAAAkySOKAACAQIAAAAEAAAA/////
wAAAACTJOZkEIBEZXNrdG9wAAAAAAAAAFOT
AKBE10YAPABAABAAAAAAAEAAAAAAAAAUARABvAGMAdQBtAGUAbgBOAFMAdQBtAG
OAYQByAHkASQBu
...
...
...
AGYAbwByAGOAYQBOAGkAbwBuAAAAAAAAAAAAAAA4AAIB////////////
AAAAAAAAAAAAAAAA
c29mdCBWb3JkIERvY3VtZW50AAoAAAABNU1dvcmREb2MAEAAAAFdvcmRQuRG9jdW
11bnQuOADOObJx
AAAAAAAAAAAAAAAAAAAAAAAAAAAAAAAAAAAAAAAAAAAAAAAAAAAAAAAAAAAAAAAA
AAAAAAAAAAAAAA
AAAAAAAAAAAAAAAAAAAAAAAAA==
```

```
------_=_NextPart_000_01BDC129.E7281B3B
```

Each message part has tagging information associated with it so that the type of the part can be deduced by the receiving MTA. The tags are produced by the sending MTA, which usually performs a lookup against some kind of MIME mapping table. If you look at the last part in the sample message, you'll see that it's tagged as *application/msword*. This *tuple* is the MIME type and sub-type pair, and in this case, there are no prizes for guessing that this is a Word document. For this message part, the filename of the original document is also maintained in the MIME header (content disposition) and you can see that it's called *salary_plan.doc*. There's some more information in this part of the MIME header that is of interest to us. We're explicitly told for this message part that it's to be handled as an *attachment*. Alternatively, you may see a value of *in-line* from time to time, but this is more common for text-type message parts. For a text message, if it's marked as in-line then the recipient of the message will see it rolled into the main cover memo part of the message and not explicitly dealt with as a real attachment to the message.

The receiving MTA will be able to use all of this information when it reconstitutes the attachment. If the filename is not passed on (some gateway implementations don't provide it) the MTA should provide a default file-name such as *att1.doc*.

The current list of MIME types and sub-types is maintained by the IANA.[*] If you take a look at this list, you'll notice that some major file types aren't registered. For example, there's no registered type for *application/ msaccess*, although you might expect one. Of course this begs the question, "How do you tag an Access file?" Well, according to the MIME rules, a binary file for which no explicit tag exists should be tagged as *application/ octet-stream*. This is an indication that it's a binary file but there's little else to tell us just what type of file it is. In most cases the name of the file should be passed along with the octet-stream sub-type so a smart MIME MTA should be able to work out the file type based on the filename suffix.

RFC-1521 allows other sub-types to be defined provided that they are only used privately between cooperating parties. In such cases the sub-type should start with an "X-". Under no circumstances should private sub-types be sent to other parties that are not privy to the "X-" tagging agreement. Thus, a private sub-type for an application that generates files with a suffix of *.myt* would look like:

```
Content-Type: application/X-mytype;
        name="my_doc.myt"
Content-Transfer-Encoding: base64
```

Although we've only scratched the surface of the MIME specifications, we've covered enough of the basics to allow us to understand how the Exchange IMS functions and how we can use it to connect to other SMTP messaging systems.

6.5   SMTP Made Simple!

Actually, there's nothing very complex about the SMTP protocol at all. It is what it claims to be: the Simple Mail Transfer Protocol. In reality, it's just a conversation between two SMTP programs using a very basic language. The SMTP system that initiates a connection is called the *Sender* and the host that accepts the connection is called the *Receiver*. The Receiver always listens on TCP/IP Port 25 for incoming connections.

The language consists of 14 basic commands defined in Section 4.1 of RFC-821. (We'll take a look at some of the most basic commands in the fol-

---

[*]   Internet Assigned Numbers Authority (visit them on http://www.iana.org). The current list of registered types and subtypes is shown in Appendix B.

lowing example.) The Sender role in an SMTP conversation doesn't need to be performed by a special SMTP program. Any user on a TCP/IP system with access to a TELNET program can pretend to be an SMTP Sender and take part in the conversation. In the example shown in Figure 6–2, I've connected from my UNIX system (sable.bvo.dec.com) to an Exchange's SMTP program (the IMS) running on a system that I know my friend Ian Burgess has a mail account on. The conversation in Figure 6–2 is pretty straightforward.

FIGURE 6–2

SMTP Conversation to the Exchange SMTP Program

```
# telnet dbo-exchangeist.dbo.dec.com 25
Trying 16.219.81.142...
Connected to dbo-exchangeist.dbo.dec.com.
Escape character is '^]'.
220 dbo-exchangeist.dbo.dec.com ESMTP Server (Microsoft
Exchange Internet Mail Service 5.5.2232.0) ready
HELO sable.bvo.dec.com
250 OK
MAIL FROM:<kmc@sable.bvo.dec.com>
250 OK - mail from <kmc@sable.bvo.dec.com>
RCPT TO:<ian.burgess@dbo-exchangeist.dbo.dec.com >
250 OK - Recipient <ian.burgess@dbo-exchangeist.dbo.dec.com >
DATA
354 Send data.  End with CRLF.CRLF
Hello Ian,

This is just a test please ignore it.

Kieran
.
250 OK
QUIT
221 closing connection
Connection closed by foreign host.
```

The rules of transmission are straightforward: Make the connection to the SMTP port (25), identify yourself (HELO *<hostname>*), say who the mail is from (MAIL FROM:*<originator's address>*), say who the recipient is (RCPT TO:*<recipient's address>*), tell the Receiver to expect the content of the message (DATA) and then enter the information, finishing with a "." on a line by itself and a carriage-return. If you're concerned that the IMS on your Exchange server (or any other SMTP MTA for that matter) isn't functioning correctly, then try to TELNET to Port 25 on that server. It's a surefire way to determine if the SMTP component is running properly.

The information that I've sent in the DATA section is really the message body, but a real SMTP mailer will send more information than that. When you read an SMTP message, there's typically a lot more information that goes along with it. This information is held in the message header, and depending on the client that you use to read the message some or all of this information may not be displayed. For example, Figure 6–3 shows the header text that accompanies a message sent from an Exchange server across the SMTP network to a UNIX host, in this case, it's my sable.bvo.dec.com system.

FIGURE 6–3

SMTP Headers
Exposed in a
Message to a UNIX
Client

```
From daemon Wed Aug  5 16:28:04 1998
Received: from eur-rmc.vbo.dec.com by sable.bvo.dec.com;
(5.65v3.2/1.1.8.2/23Feb96-1148AM)
        id AA23122; Wed, 5 Aug 1998 16:28:03 +0100
Received: from DBOIST-MSXCL ([16.138.204.197])
        by mail.vbo.dec.com (8.8.8/8.8.8) with ESMTP id RAA11447
        for <kmc@sable.bvo.dec.com>; Wed, 5 Aug 1998 17:29:14 +0200
        (MET DST)
Received: by dboist-msxcl.dbo.dec.com with Internet Mail
Service (5.5.2217.0)
        id <Q244GHK3>; Wed, 5 Aug 1998 16:37:47 +0100
Message-Id: <1DA0270C0F05D2119D7B0000F805504901C3EC@dboist-
msxcl.dbo.dec.com>
From: Kieran McCorry <Kieran.McCorry@digital.com>
To: "'kmc@sable.bvo.dec.com'" <kmc@sable.bvo.dec.com>
Subject: Test message
Date: Wed, 5 Aug 1998 16:37:46 +0100
Sensitivity: Company-Confidential
Mime-Version: 1.0
X-Mailer: Internet Mail Service (5.5.2217.0)
Content-Type: multipart/mixed;
        boundary="----_=_NextPart_000_01BDC086.FE88225B"

This message is in MIME format. Since your mail reader does not
understand
this format, some or all of this message may not be legible.

------_=_NextPart_000_01BDC086.FE88225B
Content-Type: text/plain;
```

```
                  charset="iso-8859-1"
        Hello

        Did you get this?

        Regards
        K


        ------_=_NextPart_000_01BDC086.FE88225B--
```

All of the text in that message up to where the body of the message starts with "Hello," is inserted by the sending SMTP mailer. There's no magic means by which it's inserted either. It's just entered as text after the sending mailer issues the DATA command, so for all intents and purposes it's just like the rest of the text in the message. There's a responsibility on the receiving mailer to recognize the text as something special (header fields), and mailers can easily do this. Recognition is easily done because the header field is well-formed: the field title, then a colon, then the field text. This structure is defined in Section 3 of RFC-822. For example, in Figure 6–3, the subject text is preceded with *Subject:*. It's exposed to the reader using the standard mail client in UNIX but smarter clients will usually process this information before the user gets a chance to see it in its native format. When the client does header processing, the information is usually presented in some other, usually more visually appealing way. For example, the Outlook client represents a Priority field of type Urgent as a red exclamation point.

There are some other headers shown in Figure 6–3, in relation to MIME types, but we'll cover those later.

6.6   SMTP Host Name Resolution

We all know that computers are relatively stupid entities compared to the sophistication of the human mind. One of the symptoms of this is that computers tend to deal more effectively with numbers while you and I find names easier to understand and remember.

In my SMTP communication example, shown in Figure 6–2, I've used telnet to connect to a system called dbo-exchangeist.dbo.dec.com. While I know that this refers to a system that runs in my office in Dublin, the system from which I am connecting, *sable*, isn't able to visualize dbo-exchangeist in the same way. Because it would rather deal with a number, it consults a database to convert the name `dbo-exchangeist.dbo.dec.com` to a numeric IP address. Since SMTP is an application protocol that runs over a TCP/IP network, it should be no surprise that it uses TCP/IP addresses to make contact with its SMTP partner. All SMTP MTAs (including the Exchange IMS) will do this same conversion and they'll do it in one of two ways: using the *hosts file* or using a *Domain Name System* server.

6.6.1   Using the Hosts File

There's no particular complexity associated with a hosts file. It's simply a straightforward text file which correlates hostnames with TCP/IP addresses. Figure 6–4 shows a sample Hosts file that comes from a UNIX system.

FIGURE 6–4

Hosts File from a
UNIX System

```
# HISTORY
# From Silver: AG_BL6
#
# @(#)$RCSfile: hosts,v $ $Revision: 1.1.3.2 $ (DEC) $Date:
1992/04/16 10:55:55$
#
# Description:  The hosts file associates hostnames with IP
addresses.
#
# Syntax:  nnn.nnn.nnn.nnn hostname.domain.name
[alias_1,...,alias_n] [#comments]
#
# nnn.nnn.nnn.nnn       the IP address of the host
# hostname.domain.name  the fully qualified hostname, including
the domainname
# alias_n                other names or abbreviations for this host
# #comments              text following the comment character (#)
is ignored
#
127.0.0.1 localhost
16.138.112.6 sable.bvo.dec.com sable mail.bvo.dec.com
16.138.112.31 bvojen2.bvo.dec.com bvojen2
16.138.112.9 newtoy.bvo.dec.com.bvo.dec.com newtoy
# BIND server
16.138.112.55 antrim.bvo.dec.com.bvo.dec.com antrim
# BIND server
```

The structure is straightforward and self-explanatory; with any particular TCP/IP address you'll see that you can associate multiple hostnames. On

UNIX systems, the Hosts file is usually located in /etc and on NT systems, usually in \WINNT\System32\drivers\etc. When an SMTP MTA or the IMS needs to send mail to a user on another host, it can consult the host file to perform resolution. You can see that there's an alias for my UNIX system "sable," which is *mail.bvo.dec.com.* This means that there's no need for a person's mail address to be directly tied to the machine name that their account resides on, so it's possible to use more generic addresses.

Of course, the problem with the Hosts file is that it's a static entity and is available only to the SMTP MTA running on the same system. In theory then, to send mail to anyone on the Internet you'd need to have a Hosts file that included the TCP/IP addresses and machine names of every computer that's out there. That's not particularly feasible. Enter DNS.

6.6.2 Using the Domain Name System

Rather than distribute a flat and unstructured Hosts file that would grow to millions of entries, the Internet forefathers adopted a more structured and scalable approach to the problem of unique naming.

Since every organization has the responsibility of maintaining its own computers, it makes sense that ownership of the addresses and names be maintained by each organization as well. DNS allows an organization to create a structure for naming systems within the confines of that organization or *domain.* For example, Digital Equipment Corporation owns the domain names digital.com and dec.com. An organization can then name their systems within this naming domain. For example, kramer.digital.com, would be a legitimate name for a computer owned by DIGITAL.

Large organizations tend to break their naming structure down to a number of *subdomains.* Within DIGITAL, we use a subdomain that corresponds to the mailstop of each location. The subdomain for Dublin, Ireland is dbo.dec.com, while the subdomain for Valbonne, France is vbo.dec.com. (See Figure 6–5.) The global DNS is structured like an inverted tree. Companies tend to exist within the .com domain, while universities and the like fall within the .edu domain. There are a whole host of domains that cover various groupings, and a listing of all of them is outside the scope of this book. A quick browse on the Internet should provide a reasonably complete list of all the domain types that are out there.

FIGURE 6–5 The
DNS Hierarchy

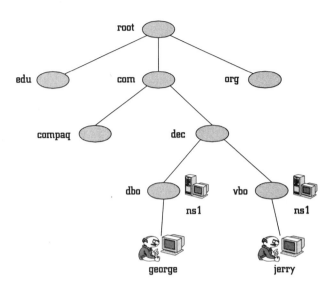

DNS uses two concepts to describe groupings of computers: the *subdomain* and the *zone*. The difference between the two concepts is slight, but very important. In the example shown in Figure 6–5, the subdomain for *dec* includes all other subdomains underneath that part of the tree. However the zone for *dec* refers only to systems at the *dec* level: responsibility for the rest of the subdomains is partitioned for each of the other subtrees.

Within each zone, one computer will exist which has knowledge of all the machines within that zone. This computer, called a *nameserver*, is able to map the TCP/IP address to the *fully qualified hostname* (e.g., dbo-exchangeist.dbo.dec.com) of a system and is said to be *authoritative* for that zone. In Figure 6–5, the nameserver for the dbo.dec.com zone is called ns1.dbo.dec.com and for vbo.dec.com it's called ns1.vbo.dec.com.

At a higher level in the structure, nameservers for the dec.com domain have knowledge of all of the nameservers for the various subdomains below them. The subdomain nameservers correspondingly have links back up to the domain nameservers above. For example, if I'm connected to the computer george.dbo.dec.com and I need to make a connection to the computer jerry.vbo.dec.com, I'll need the address of jerry. The following sequence of operations will probably take place:

- george.dbo.dec.com contacts its nameserver ns1.dbo.dec.com.

- It's likely that the nameserver for dbo.dec.com won't hold this address mapping since it's only interested in dbo.dec.com addresses, unless it performed the query some time earlier and it's held in the cache.

- However, this nameserver knows that the nameserver for dec.com may have knowledge of the name and so the request is escalated to it.

- If the dec.com nameserver hasn't got the address in its cache then it will direct the querying nameserver to the nameserver for vbo.dec.com and obviously the vbo.dec.com nameserver will know about all hosts within its subdomain.

- ns1.vbo.dec.com returns the result of the query back to ns1.dbo.dec.com, which sends the final results back to the requesting client, george.dbo.dec.com.

Thus, the name is resolved to a TCP/IP address and contact can be made. This form of query escalation and referral works not just inside the DNS implementation of a single company, but across companies and all DNS domains. That's the whole point of it. Obviously this is a simplification of how the process works. Various forms of caching take place, and secondary nameservers can be used to eliminate the single point of failure problem.

It's obvious that DNS provides a flexible and scalable way to get the TCP/IP address of any computer that exists on the Internet, since it works today for the millions of computers that are registered in DNS. In the DNS scenario that I've described, we've only looked at the process of hostname resolution. In the case of a general SMTP MTA or Exchange IMS sending mail to a simple mail address such as neumann@jerry.vbo.dec.com where the hostname is explicitly specified, then this process of resolution is all that's needed. The SMTP program simply uses either DNS or the hosts file.

Sometimes it is useful to be able to control the process by which name resolutions take place. For example, you may want to specify that mail to the hostname relay.acme.com is always resolved to a particular address (say 19.183.224.99). Maybe this is the central hub for your SMTP network. If it is, you may not want to put this into your DNS database in order to limit the scope of who can resolve this name. One solution would be to localize the resolution by placing it in the local HOSTS file, which can only be seen by the local machine.

The order of resolution can be controlled by various parameters on the different platforms. On Windows NT, when an SMTP program like the IMS needs to resolve a hostname it checks the HOSTS file, then DNS, then WINS, then it does some broadcasts to locate the host, then LMHOSTS, and finally another check of DNS (if it's enabled for Windows name resolution). By default the resolution process is in line with what we might want to do since HOSTS is checked before anything else. The resolution precedence can be controlled by modifying values in the Registry:

`SYSTEM\CurrentControlSet\Services\Tcpip\ServiceProvider.`

In here you'll find values for `DnsPriority`, `HostsPriority`, `LocalPriority`, `NetbtPriority`. These all have hexadecimal values associated with them. The lower the value in relation to the others, the earlier it gets checked in the resolution process.

Controlling the process on UNIX is pretty straightforward as well. When SMTP tries to send a message to another SMTP host it performs the *gethostbyname* function to resolve the address. The order of resolution is enforced by the `hosts` key in the `/etc/svc.conf`. By default it's the hosts file first, then the DNS database.

6.6.3   Structure of the DNS Files

Many mixed messaging environments continue to employ UNIX as the primary vehicle for providing DNS services. Of course, DNS server facilities are available on Windows NT, but UNIX has for a long time provided a robust and secure platform for this activity. In examining the implementation of DNS in this section we'll respect the fact that UNIX remains the operating system of choice for DNS implementations. We'll also look at how the DNS server components are implemented on Windows NT so that a complete picture can be seen.

A number of files are used by a nameserver to perform address resolution. Of all of the files, the one of most interest to us at this stage is the hosts database, but we'll mention some others in this discussion.[*] It's important to understand the concepts described here: familiarity with them will make for an easy time when you come to implement SMTP backbones for Exchange environments.

To map hostnames to TCP/IP addresses, a special file is used which is similar in structure to the hosts file that we've encountered earlier. This DNS hosts file, typically called *db.hosts*, maps the local hostnames to TCP/IP addresses. Within the file, *address records* (or *A records*) are used for this purpose, but the file can contain other types of records as well, some of which we'll meet later.

---

[*]   A full description of the operation of DNS and its associated files is outside the scope of this book. A useful reference point is Albitz and Liu, *DNS and BIND,* 2nd ed. (1997). (Visit them at `http://www.oreilly.com`.)

Figure 6–6 shows the structure of the DNS database file that I use for DNS hosts registered locally in the DNS zone bvo.dec.com. Although it is a pretty simple hosts.db file, it does manage to contain most of the concepts that we are interested in.

FIGURE 6–6

Sample
hosts.db File

```
;
; Data file of hostnames in this zone.
;
@          IN           SOA     newtoy.bvo.dec.com.
postmaster.newtoy.bvo.dec.com. (
                         2004    ; Serial
                         300     ; Refresh - 5 minutes
                         60      ; Retry - 1 minute
                         1209600 ; Expire - 2 weeks
                         43200 ) ; Minimum - 12 hours
           IN     NS     newtoy.bvo.dec.com.
           IN     NS     antrim.bvo.dec.com.
           IN     NS     us1rmc.bb.dec.com.
;
; Host Definitions
;
localhost          IN    A         127.0.0.1
newtoy             IN    A         16.138.112.9
hank               IN    A         16.138.112.10
bobbi.bvo.dec.com. IN    A         16.138.112.11
;
; Aliases
;
mailhub            IN    CNAME     hank
```

Start of Authority

The *IN* term that you see for all of the records in this file indicates that the records are of the *Internet* class. There are other classes for records but this is by far and away the most common. The first record, *SOA*, indicates the *Start of Authority* for this zone. It says that the primary nameserver for the zone is *newtoy.bvo.dec.com.* (Note the period that terminates the hostname—it's important!) If you need to send mail to someone who's responsible for managing the zone, then you can direct it to *postmaster@newtoy.bvo.dec.com* (the fact that the address shown in Figure 6–6 has a period rather than an "at" sign is intentional).

For the time being, let's just ignore the values that are contained within the parentheses in the SOA record. These are timeout values for records used mostly by secondary name servers. Before we describe how the timeout values are implemented, it's useful to be familiar with the concept of those secondary nameservers.

Secondary Nameservers

Secondary nameservers can be used for redundancy purposes and for load balancing. In Figure 6–6, the *NS* records (which follow the SOA record) indicate the valid nameservers for this zone. In this we already know that the primary nameserver is the local host, newtoy. But the other systems that are listed— antrim.bvo.dec.com and us1rmc.bb.dec.com —are the secondary servers. This means that should the primary server become unavailable for any reason, then any one of these two systems may be used for lookups instead. In terms of load balancing, there's no reason why you wouldn't be able to use these systems as well as newtoy for name resolution.

Of course, the primary nameserver is the definitive source for information for address lookups in the bvo.dec.com zone. When you make changes or additions to the hosts database on the primary nameserver, it knows immediately of the changes and can pass this on to any clients that make a request of it (provided it's restarted). However, secondary nameservers need some way of knowing when a change has occurred to the information on the primary nameserver so that they too can keep their information up-to-date. Accordingly, this is done in one of two ways.

Serial Numbers and Time Intervals

Every time a secondary nameserver starts up, it checks with the primary nameserver to see if there have been any modifications to the databases. A very simple mechanism is used to determine if there have been changes and the mechanism relies on good system management practices by the system administrator. (That could be you!)

In the SOA record you'll see a value for a field called *Serial*. In my example it's set to 2004. Every time that a change is made to the databases, you should update this field to the next value: just add one. When the secondary nameserver starts up it always contacts the primary nameserver and compares its value for the Serial field with the primary's. If the primary has a higher Serial number than itself, then it assumes that all of its zone information is out-of-date and gets a new copy of the zone information from the primary. What happens if the secondary nameserver doesn't restart very frequently? In this case, there's a risk that it won't get up-to-date copies of information from the primary by using the Serial number update mechanism. To cope with this, a set of timeout values are associated with the validity of the zone data.

The next most interesting field is the *Refresh* interval. In our example it's set to the default value of 300 seconds. This field tells the secondary nameserver to query the primary every five minutes and check to see if the Serial number has changed. If it has, then the secondary performs a zone refresh. If the secondary nameserver has encountered any problems trying to contact the primary, then the *Retry* field becomes important. In our example this value is set to 60 seconds. After a failed refresh query, the secondary will attempt a new query every minute until connection is reestablished.

Let's say you had a hardware problem on your primary nameserver and it was out of service for an extended period of time. In this case the value of the *Expire* field is critical. Expire dictates the length of time that a secondary nameserver will continue to supply potentially out-of-date information. In our case, the Expire interval is set to 1209600 seconds (two weeks). This means that if your secondary nameserver can't contact your primary nameserver for its regular refresh check (every five minutes) it will be prepared to hold on to its existing zone data for up to two weeks. After that time it gives up and flushes out the zone information it has and assumes that it is now invalid. This means that you've got a two-week window in which to work on your out-of-commission primary nameserver before all of the nameservers for your zone give up!

We've seen in Section 6.6.2 how a querying DNS server (not a primary or secondary), which doesn't have knowledge of host in a particular zone may request that information from one of the primaries or secondaries. Although we only mentioned it indirectly, the querying server will actually cache the lookup information locally so that subsequent lookups for this information may be responded to efficiently. As always, the problem with caching information is that it can quickly become stale. Secondary nameservers deal with the data validity problem by asking for a zone update check every *Refresh* seconds, but other DNS servers deal with cache updates using the *Time-to-Live* (*TTL*) field. This is the last field shown in Figure 6–6, which in our case is set to 43200 seconds (twelve hours). The effect of this setting is that when a DNS server caches a lookup it is only valid for twelve hours, after which time it expires and the next time the same lookup request is processed by the server either the primary or a secondary nameserver must be consulted to satisfy the request.

The TTL field is important when you change any settings that relate to how messages are delivered to your mail system. If you do make changes, and we'll see some examples of changes on the Exchange IMS later, you need to make sure that your environment is still capable of dealing with old definitions for a period of time as defined by the TTL.

Address Records

The next section of our sample hosts database shows the types of definitions that we expect to see in such a file. Each record in this part of the database has a hostname, listed on the left hand side of the file, which is mapped to a TCP/IP address, listed on the right hand side of the file. These are called *Address* (A) records.

Even though the hostnames that are listed along the left hand side of the file are in their shortname form, the fact that this is the zone file for .bvo.dec.com implies that this subdomain part is appended to the short form name. Note that all of the short form names as shown in the file aren't terminated with a period.

Note that there is an explicit entry for another host, bobbi.bvo.dec.com and this is terminated with a period. Either means of representing the fully qualified domain name for the host is acceptable, but clearly one method involves more typing than the other.

If you'd foolishly left out the period when you typed in the mapping for bobbi.bvo.dec.com, you'd find that DNS knew nothing about a host called bobbi.bvo.dec.com, but it would have assumed that you meant to refer to a host called bobbi.bvo.dec.com.bvo.dec.com. It would be unlikely that this was what you really meant!

Canonical Name Records

There may be occasions when you'd like a system to be known by more than one name. Let's say you'd been using the system hank.bvo.dec.com for some time but subsequently decided to use it as your main Exchange server for receiving Internet mail. You may decide the name hank.bvo.dec.com is not all that informative a name after all, and think mailhub.bvo.dec.com is perhaps more appropriate.

In such a situation, the easiest thing to do is set up an alias for `mailhub` so that it maps to `hank`. In this example, we've used the *Canonical Name (CNAME)* record to provide this mapping. It is also possible to use another A record to map `mailhub` directly to the TCP/IP address, but most SMTP implementations prefer to see CNAME records in DNS when they resolve aliases in mail headers. If you've just used more A records, then the text you see in mail headers can sometimes be confusing.

6.7 Mail Exchanger Records

The previous section described some of the more common *resource records* that you can expect to see in use with DNS. One type of record which we didn't mention is the Mail Exchanger. It's so important that it deserves a section to itself.

Having looked at how DNS is used to ferry messages from one SMTP system to another, it all seems pretty straightforward. Well, there's actually a little bit more to it than that—but this is the really interesting part. If you're used to receiving or sending any Internet mail at all you'll know that many RFC-822 addresses are pretty short and don't seem to be of the same structure that I've described above. In short, most RFC-822 addresses don't include a hostname: they're typically of the form:

```
Firstname.Lastname@company.com
```

although it's likely that you'll see other domains of the form `.org`, or `.edu`. You can e-mail me, for example, at:

```
Kieran.McCorry@digital.com
```

which we'll call a *pretty address*, but you can also use the *technical address* which accurately reflects the system on which my mailbox resides:

```
Kieran.McCorry@dbo-exchangeist.dbo.dec.com
```

In the SMTP conversation example that I've shown above in Figure 6–2, we used the full name of the mail system, `dbo-exchangeist.dbo.dec.com`, to identify the user and it appears that SMTP requires this in order to connect to the right system directly to deliver the mail.

It makes perfect sense that at some stage in the delivery of a message a connection is made to the system on which the user's mailbox resides. Since you can address me as `Kieran.McCorry@digital.com` and know that a message you send with that address gets to me eventually, then at some stage the SMTP mechanism must translate the Kieran.McCorry@digital.com form of the address to the one which includes the hostname, Kieran.McCorry@dbo-exchangeist.dbo.dec.com.

Ostensibly, a Mail Exchanger (MX) record is used to provide this mapping between the pretty address and the technical address that I've described above. I can't define the MX record for digital.com because I don't have any authority for that zone, but it's likely that the records for that zone would look like those shown in Figure 6–7.

FIGURE 6–7

Sample MX
Record
Definitions

```
;
; Mail Exchangers
;
digital.com.   IN   MX 400     mail1.digital.com.
               IN   MX 400     mail2.digital.com.
               IN   MX 300     europehub.vbo.dec.com.
               IN   MX 200     dublinhub.dbo.dec.com.
               IN   MX 100     dbo-exchangeist.dbo.dec.com.
```

The mechanism is reasonably straightforward. Each MX record defines a host which runs an SMTP mailer of some description and each host either accepts an SMTP message on behalf of a local recipient, or else forwards it on to another host.

6.7.1 Using MX Records for Mail Flow

In Figure 6–7 there are five definitions assigned for the MX record of digital.com. Each definition has an associated *preference value*, in our case ranging from 100 to 400. Although this may seem a little counterintuitive, the lowest cost record is the preferred one. Since these are DNS records they are published out to the Internet so they you can see them from your mail system, providing you've got DNS configured.

Here's a possible flow of events when you send mail to me:

- You address mail to Kieran.McCorry@digital.com

- The local SMTP system queries DNS and asks for a resolution of digital.com

- DNS returns the mapping of dbo-exchangeist.dbo.dec.com because it's the lowest cost

- If `dbo-exchangeist.dbo.dec.com` is available and accepting connections then the message will be delivered directly that system

- If there's a problem contacting `dbo-exchangeist.dbo.dec.com`, then the local SMTP system tries to connect to the next lowest cost host, in this case `dublinhub.dbo.dec.com`

- If that server can't be contacted, then the next lowest cost system is selected, `europehub.dbo.dec.com`

- And if that server can't be contacted, then the next lowest cost server is selected, either `mail1.digital.com` or `mail2.digital.com`

- Finally, if none of the MX record specified hosts can be contacted your local mail system will hold on to the message for a specified period of time and regularly try to resend the message

So what happens if one of the intermediate hosts is selected when a message is sent from your system to mine. Let's assume that all the lower cost hosts are unavailable and the only systems that can be contacted are either `mail1.digital.com` or `mail2.digital.com`. Since both of these hosts have the same preference value, good implementations of SMTP should actually randomly choose one of the specified hosts. This makes for good load balancing and is the reason why you'll often see multiple mail relays for large organizations with the same preference values. However, many SMTP implementations don't observe this protocol and you'll often find that the first record to be returned by a lookup is the one that is selected.

In this case, we'll assume that `mail1.digital.com` actually receives the message. When `mail1.digital.com` gets the message, it realizes that the recipient isn't local and therefore consults DNS again to determine how best to process the message. When the MX records are returned, the mail relay will look for its own name in any of the MX records and subsequently ignore any other records that have the same or lower preference (higher cost) values. The forwarding mailer does this so that there's no chance of mail looping or being sent back out to a host that is logically further away from the ultimate destination. The `mail1.digital.com` system will hold on to that message and continue trying to contact a lower cost host until the message times out, at which point it will be sent back to the originator.

Establishing a hierarchical mail infrastructure similar to that shown in Figure 6–8 may make sense for your organization. One single point in the infrastructure may act as a sole connection to the Internet, while regional mail hubs can be used to transfer inbound mail into each geography where Exchange servers will be located. This downstream method of routing prevents mail backlog on important servers and helps distribute mail flow in a localized and equitable fashion.

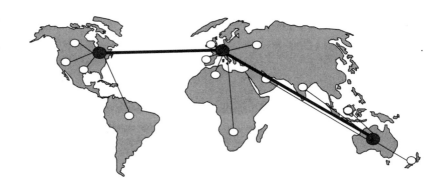

6.7.2 The Effect of Firewalls

Almost all organizations place a great deal of importance on the IT infrastructure. An infrastructure that is so vital to the operation of an organization needs protection and typically a firewall is used to prevent unauthorized access from unwanted guests. At the very least, a screening TCP/IP router may be used.

The environment and servers that I've described in Figure 6–7, in common with most other large organizations, can be considered as containing both internal and external systems. In our example, the regional mail hubs and our trusty mail server, `dbo-exchangeist.dbo.dec.com` can all be considered internal systems, while the external hosts are `mail1.digital.com` and `mail2.digital.com`. (See Figure 6–9.)

Since all of the hosts in the `dec.com` subdomain lie inside the firewall they should not be accessible to a general SMTP messaging system on the Internet. Accordingly, even though the MX records for these hosts may be visible to the outside world, no such systems should ever be able to connect to them. This means that mail inbound from the Internet to the `digital.com` domain will always be routed through either `mail1` or `mail2`.

In general, if you wish to provide Internet mail access for your Exchange server or any other mail system, you should always provide an MX record for it and for another host that can be used as a relay on the exposed side of your firewall. The only alternative to this is to punch a hole in your firewall to let any connections to Port 25 pass through the firewall unimpeded, but this defeats the purpose of the firewall in the first instance!

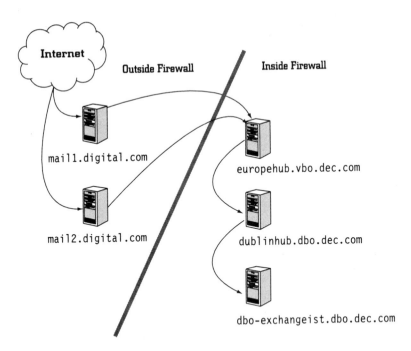

FIGURE 6–9 Mail Relay Systems in Relation to a Firewall

6.7.3 **Wildcard MX Records**

Under normal circumstances you shouldn't need many MX records for any messaging environment that you set up. Typically, organizations tend to strive for the flattest possible format for addresses, such as `digital.com` and `microsoft.com`. However, under some circumstances you may be encouraged to implement a naming structure that tracks a company's organizational or physical topology. Consider a company that has branches and mail servers at every major airport. In designing a messaging infrastructure, you might be forced to implement an SMTP naming structure that incorporates a location code in the address, which might yield such mail addresses as:

- `@nyc.speedy.com`
- `@lon.speedy.com`
- `@la.speedy.com`
- `@sf.speedy.com`
- `@par.speedy.com`

If you think it is tedious to read each and every one of these mail address formats, it's also just as tedious to build MX records for them, especially since each and every one of them may well point to the same mailserver within your organization. DNS comes to the rescue here to some extent, because it allows you to build a wildcard MX record that would cover all of those addresses. Your DNS hosts database file would look something like that shown in Figure 6–10. While this does meet the requirement of dealing with mail addresses of the form @nyc.speedy.com, it will also route mail for addresses of the form @queens.nyc.speedy.com or even a host or domain that doesn't exist so it can lead to problems.

FIGURE 6–10
Sample Wildcard
MX Record

```
; Wildcard Mail Exchangers
;
*.speedy.com.        IN   MX 100      mail.speedy.com.
```

6.8 Mail Hosting

Large organizations will typically have a permanently connected link to the Internet so they can define their lowest cost MX records to point directly to their firewall mail host. There may well be at least one higher cost MX record that points to a mail relay in another organization, perhaps your service provider, which can store mail for you in the event that your systems become unavailable.

But for the smallest of organizations, those that cannot justify the cost of a permanent and dedicated link to the Internet, there needs to be some way of having another permanently connected host store mail destined for them until they can pick it up. Therein lies the concept of mail hosting.

It's a simple enough architecture. For example, consider the small business *Svahn Trading Inc.*, which has mail users that can be addressed from the Internet as firstname.lastname@sti.com. For our purposes, let's assume that this small business only has a dial-up link to an Internet service provider. Any mail that gets sent to the sti.com domain is stored temporarily by their ISP, until the mail server in *Svahn Trading Inc.* dials the ISP's mail server and requests that all messages stored for them should now be forwarded.

Getting the mail delivered to the ISP is the easy part of the mail hosting problem. It's just a simple application of using MX records to have mail sent to a particular SMTP address sent to a particular system on the Internet. The only difference in this case is that the system isn't owned by your company, it's the property of an ISP, and then the ISP hangs on to the mail until you connect to them and ask for it.

Asking for the mail represents the tricky part. The ISP mail server typically doesn't store the messages and then initiate a connection to your mail server to send them. Instead, it's a "pull" technology from the small business side that is required, so while the ISP holds onto the messages, it's up to you to connect to the ISP's system and request the messages. RFC-1985, fully entitled *SMTP Service Extension for Remote Message Queue Starting* defines a protocol that allows an SMTP client to connect to a server and request that any messages it may be queuing for the client be released to it.

6.8.1 Dequeuing to a Single Local Host

This is exactly the functionality that is required by our occasionally connected mail host in the sti.com domain. It's implemented by using an additional verb in the SMTP command set, ETRN[*] (*Extended TURN*), which has single parameter: the name of the domain to which messages are to be dequeued. The TURN command can be used for this purpose simply by establishing a connection over SMTP such as we've seen earlier, declaring its identity, and then requesting the TURN. For example, the sequence of commands in Figure 6–11 should be sufficient to connect to an ISP mail host and request that all mail stored for the host myserver.sti.com be then sent across the link.

FIGURE 6–11 Using the TURN Command to Deliver Mail

```
telnet mail.myisp.com 25
HELO myserver.sti.com
TURN
QUIT
```

However, the sequence of commands in Figure 6–11 is inherently insecure because the same session is used by the ISP mail host to send the messages back to the requesting SMTP client. There's an assumption made that the host name that it is given on the HELO command is actually the hostname of the system that's initiated the connection. The ISP server performs no checking to verify that the requestor actually is who it purports to be. Of course, it may not be, and the cold reality is that there's nothing to stop me from connecting to an ISP and downloading someone else's mail.

It's for this reason that many ISP systems don't actually accept the TURN command. But the ETRN command overcomes this security weakness. Rather than just turning the SMTP conversation around when the ETRN command is issued, the ISP mail server creates a new SMTP session to the

---

[*] ETRN supersedes its predecessor, the TURN command that is defined in RFC-821.

host specified on the command. When the server receives the command, and if there is queued mail for the requesting host, it will respond immediately to the client to let it know that the appropriate mail queue has been started, at which point the client can continue with other SMTP commands or close the connection. In any event, the ISP server then initiates a new connection to the client. Figure 6–12 shows a likely conversation using the ETRN command.

FIGURE 6–12

Using the ETRN
Command to
Deliver Mail

```
telnet mail.myisp.com 25
Trying 19.214.74.142...
Connected to mail.myisp.com.
Escape character is '^]'.
220 mail.myisp.com ESMTP Sendmail 8.8.8/8.8.8 Thu 25 Feb 1999
21:55:50 +0100 (MET)
EHLO myserver.sti.com
250-mail.myisp.com Hello myserver.sti.com [12.43.28.1],
pleased to meet you
ETRN myserver.sti.com
250 Queueing for node myserver.sti.com started
QUIT
221 mail.myisp.com closing connection
Connection closed by foreign host.
```

6.8.2 Dequeuing to Multiple Local Hosts

The ETRN command is actually quite flexible in its syntax. If, for example, you are connecting to an ISP and you need to request that the queues for several hosts are started, there's no need to specify each host individually. For example, the command:

```
ETRN @sti.com
```

could be used to de-queue messages for any hosts within that domain, possibly:

```
mail1.sti.com,
relay.sti.com,
mailbox.sac.calif.sti.com
```

6.8.3 Alternatives to ETRN

We'll see later how ETRN can be used by the Exchange IMS for dial-up connections to an ISP. However, for the ETRN mechanism to work, the ISP vendor must be running Sendmail V8.8 or higher.[*] Any ISP worth its salt will be running this revision, but you may find yourself in a situation where the system you're connecting to only runs a lower version.

In such circumstances we're still faced with the same problem: encouraging the ISP mail host to start dequeuing messages to your local mail relay, which has just become available on the dial-up connection. In some cases, the ISP may execute a script of some description whenever you establish the dial-up connection. One of the commands within that script might be:

```
sendmail -q
```

which tells Sendmail to start flushing the queue immediately. But some other Sendmail implementations (and Sendmail V8) allow you to specify explicitly the domain names or hosts to be de-queued with:

```
sendmail -qRmyserver.sti.com
```

The `finger` command can also be used in a script to initiate processing of queued messages. With this mechanism you'll need to specify your mail server details and the name of the ISP server as follows:

```
finger myserver.sti.com@mail.myisp.com
```

but in general, your ISP will undoubtedly have a solution that works best for you.

You can get more information on ISP message delivery techniques at `http://www.swinc.com`.

---

[*] You can get the latest version of Sendmail or more information about it from `http://www.sendmail.org`.

7

Understanding the Exchange Internet Mail Service

7.1   Introduction

Few organizations implement an Exchange environment without connecting it to some other mail system. Exchange provides native connectors to communicate with a whole variety of messaging systems, but perhaps the most versatile and useful of them all is the connector that links Exchange to the world of SMTP. This connector used to be called the *Internet Mail Connector,* but it received a makeover in Exchange V5.0 both in terms of its functionality and its name and is now named the more descriptive *Internet Mail Service* (IMS).

The IMS isn't just a connector to another a mail system. It's a critical component in the Exchange Server model that facilitates communication to the majority of computers elsewhere in the world. The IMS is more than a connector; it is a core piece of messaging switching technology closely integrated with Exchange. Although Exchange Server V5.5 is built around X.400 technology, it is fairly obvious that the primary messaging technology in use today is based on SMTP. It's the responsibility of the IMS to provide the rich set of SMTP functionality that's required to successfully allow Exchange to interact with the increasing number of other SMTP-based systems around.

7.2   Basic Operation

The IMS is a store-based connector. This means that the IMS uses the Store as the temporary repository for messages in transit. This is quite different from the X.400 Connector, which communicates directly with the MTA. Without looking in detail at the effect of the various IMS parameters, let's take a quick peek at how the IMS deals with message flow.

7.2.1   Inbound Message Flow

When a message is received, the IMS stages the message in a dummy folder in the Store while it processes it. As a result of the processing, the message may wind up going in any one of a number of directions: perhaps staying in the Store if the intended recipient is local; perhaps being passed to the MTA if the message is intended for a recipient on another server; or even being routed back out again through the same IMS.

FIGURE 7–1

Inbound Message Flow to the IMS

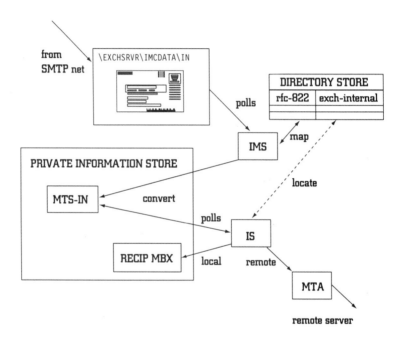

Figure 7–1 shows the potential paths that a message might take as it is received from an SMTP network and processed by the IMS. One of the first actions that the Port 25 component of the IMS takes as it receives the message is to write a copy of the message to disk. In the case of an inbound message, the message copy is written to the EXCHSRVR\IMCDATA\IN directory. The location of this directory is system definable: You may have specified its location during the Exchange installation, or you may subsequently change it using the Performance Optimization Wizard. Whatever means you use to define it, the single most important factor to bear in mind is its *Location* in relation to the other Exchange data storage locations. We'll see more about this shortly.

After receiving the message, the IMS inspects the recipient addresses on the message header and basically decides whether to accept the message for processing for each of the recipients. Clearly the goal of the IMS is to deliver the message to an Exchange recipient, but first the SMTP address supplied on the message header must be converted into something Exchange can understand. The IMS essentially performs a reverse lookup in the Directory, providing the SMTP address as a key and attempting to find an Exchange directory entry that has an address that matches.

If a match isn't found, then a nondelivery notification is sent back to the originator of the message for that particular recipient address. Assuming that the lookup goes well, the IMS picks up the message from the IMC-DATA folder where it is held in SMTP/MIME format and converts it to Exchange's native format, MDBEF. When the conversion has been completed, the message is placed in a virtual folder within the Store named MTS-IN. At this point, the real work of the IMS is more or less completed and it will have no further part in the delivery of the message.

But to complete the picture, we need to understand how the message is ultimately delivered to the recipient. Every few seconds, the Store service polls the MTS-IN folder for new messages awaiting delivery. As the Store processes messages, it consults the Directory to determine where recipients are located. If the message is destined for a user located on the same server as the IMS, then the Store service has a relatively simple job to perform. It merely moves the message from the MTS-IN folder to the inbox of the intended recipient. (In fact, this is actually just a modification to a set of pointers in both folders: the message doesn't really "move.") If the intended recipient is on another server, the Store service can't deliver the message directly but passes it to the MTA, which then becomes responsible for its delivery.

That may not be the end of the relationship between the IMS and this message. Its transfer to another server may mean that it is delivered across a site connector that uses an IMS as its vehicle for delivery.

If you expect your IMS to be busy, then it's likely that there will be a significantly high number of IO operations as IMS-processed messages produce IO load to the IMCDATA folder, lookups to the Directory database, and operations against the Store database and transaction logs. In such a case, make sure that the IO subsystem is capable of performing well in an environment where IO load is significant. There are many texts and sources of information that deal with the subject of hardware sizing for IO servers, which falls beyond the scope of this book. However, a few ground rules that make sense to bear in mind may be offered:

- At the very least, make sure that the IMCDATA area and other data-bases are located on disk volumes that are adequately protected against hardware failure. RAID5 configurations provide sufficient redundancy but can compromise write performance unless write-back caching is enabled on the controllers. If you do enable write-back caching, then make sure that the caches are suitably protected with battery backup.

- For relatively busy IMS servers, where you expect to process thousands of messages per day, try not to colocate the IMCDATA area with all of the other Exchange data locations. Separate physical volumes for IMCDATA, store database, transaction logs, directory database, and message tracking logs are a better approach.

- For the highest performing IMS servers—those where you might expect to process tens of thousands of messages per day—the utmost care should be taken when sizing the systems. RAID0+1 configurations should be used since they offer the greatest performance and redundancy characteristics. Such configurations should be realized with high performance controllers and the disks that make up the RAID0+1 set should be split across those controllers to balance the load.

7.2.2 Outbound Message Flow

A similar message flow can be identified for messages that are being delivered out through the IMS connector.

In the configuration shown in Figure 7–2, a message is submitted to the Store via the client in the normal way. This is the standard mechanism for sending a message from a MAPI or HTTP-based client; the message is first placed in the Outbox of the originator and the Store then begins the process of delivering it to its intended recipient.

In our case, the MTA may be called into action if the IMS is present on the same server as the originator of the message. In such a case, the message is transferred to the system that hosts the IMS and the message is passed to connector as if it were local.

Sending outbound is pretty much the reverse process that we've seen for receiving a message in through the IMS. On the IMS server, the message is placed into the MTS-OUT virtual folder within the Store. Periodically, the

IMS polls this virtual folder and when it finds a message residing there, it springs into action. It's first task is to perform a content conversion, this time from MDBEF into MIME format so that the message can be interpreted by its intended recipients. If the IMS finds more than one message in the MTS-IN folder, these are all processed within one poll cycle. Messages aren't left behind until the next poll is initiated.

FIGURE 7–2
Outbound Message
Flow from the IMS

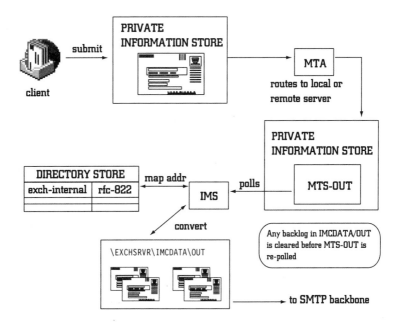

Having converted the content of the message, the IMS now sets about converting the originator address of the message. At this stage, the originator address will be represented in native Exchange format, but for the message to be reply-able, the address should be in SMTP format. The IMS consults the Directory and maps the Exchange address for the user into the preferred SMTP address.

That's pretty much all the hard work that's required of the IMS at this point. The message is now written to the NT file system \EXCHSRVR\IMC-DATA\OUT folder, where the SMTP service component picks up the message and begins the process of transferring the message over the SMTP protocol to other SMTP hosts.

7.3   Configuring the Internet Mail Service

By default, the IMS is installed when you install Exchange, but it is not configured unless you explicitly do it. You need to select the option to configure it from the Exchange Administrator program using *File/New Other/Internet Mail Service.*

7.3.1   The Ever Helpful Wizard

Selecting this option encourages one of those helpful Microsoft Wizards to leap to your assistance and do all the dirty work of configuring the IMS for you (see Figure 7–3).

FIGURE 7–3 IMS Configuration Wizard

Previous versions of Exchange didn't make the configuration quite so simple. Before the Wizard came along you'd have to manually configure the IMS by changing settings on the individual property pages. While this was confusing for the average system administrator with little knowledge of SMTP, it was, in its defense, quite a flexible way to tune the configuration for the experience integrator. The configuration wizard asks a number of questions that quickly guide the installer through the setup. You'll need to know the answers to the following questions:

1.   The server in the Site on which you wish to install the IMS. By default it will be the local server to which you are currently connected through the Exchange Administrator program but it could be any server in the Site.

2.   Whether you wish to use DNS to perform host name resolution or whether you wish to forward mail to a general purpose relay host. If you only intend to use this IMS for message delivery within your complete messaging environment, then the DNS option may be enough. If you're going to be routing messages out through a firewall, then you'll most likely have to point the IMS to the firewall's SMTP service and let it perform the lookups and delivery.

3.   Whether you wish to allow mail to all Internet addresses or just a subset of addresses. You can restrict the domains to which you'll allow messages to be sent, but in general you'll just allow all mail to go through.

4.   The Internet domain you wish to have built into addresses for recipients in the local Site. This will default to a combination of the Site and Organization name, but you'll generally have to change it to something more meaningful.

5.   A mailbox to be used to receive nondelivery notifications for messages that get sent to your system but can't be delivered to a recipient.

6.   The name of the Exchange service account and its password.

That's just a brief overview of the questions and possible answers. As you can see, we haven't really gone through them in too much detail. But don't worry, you don't need to get everything right just when you run the wizard. Once the wizard configuration has completed, the IMS is created for you and all of the configuration settings you've just given are easily changed on the property pages, which is where the real configuration can begin.

Actually, I don't like the IMS wizard. I prefer to just whiz (if you'll pardon the expression) through the wizard-based configuration with more or less the first values that spring to mind. Of course, I try to make them as close as possible to the settings that I really want, but I'm quite prepared at this stage to accept whatever the wizard gives me. When the wizard has finished casting its spell, then I use the settings on the individual property pages to configure the IMS how I really want it.

7.3.2 IMS Configuration Prerequisites

There are just a few things that you need to make sure of before you can comfortably configure the IMS. We've talked about many of these things already, but now is the time to put them into action.

Obviously TCP/IP needs to be properly installed and configured on the system, but you do need to make sure, now more than ever before, that you're *not using DHCP to obtain a TCP/IP address for the Exchange server that will be hosting the IMS*. It may seem like a mistake that you couldn't make, but I have seen it done and it can lead to hours of confusion when mail delivery to your IMS begins to crumble over the next few days.

You should also make sure that DNS has been configured at least as a client on your IMS server. The IMS configuration process checks for this and if DNS isn't properly configured for lookup then you may run into problems during configuration.

Finally, make sure that at the very least the appropriate A records exist in your DNS configuration, but having the MX records defined at this point is smart as well. You can, of course, configure the DNS environment later, but it is wise to have the infrastructure in place before you enable the IMS service. In this way, if curious users do manage to sneak out messages through the IMS just after you've finished configuring it, you've got some guarantees that the messages can be replied to. There's little worse than having to explain to people why they receive nondelivery notifications for messages inbound to the IMS whenever it's apparently possible to send messages out.

7.4   Using the IMS Connector

Rumor has it that everyone feels much more comfortable with SMTP and the IMS because *we all understand* SMTP, don't we? But I bet the first time you look at the IMS property pages, you too may turn away feeling just a little perplexed and wondering what to do next. In this case, it isn't really because the IMS has a lot of very new terminology associated with it, but it just looks scary because there are so many things that can be configured with it.

This is where its power really lies. There's a wealth of flexibility in the IMS settings and in the remainder of this section we'll go through each property page and discuss in some detail exactly what the ramifications are when you change any of the settings.

7.4.1   The General Tab

There isn't really too much to talk about on the *General* tab. You're presented with the name of the computer on which this IMS installed, but hey, that's probably something which you knew already.

The only setting of interest is the *Message size*. Changing the setting from *No limit* to a value for *Maximum* controls the maximum size of a message that can be sent either inbound or outbound through the connector. It's easy to dream up maximum sizes that you'd be prepared to tolerate within your environment. From a management point of view, you might decide that 3MB is the maximum message size that you'd like to see going through the connector. If you can decide on such a policy and enforce it, then great. But remember that message sizes used for communication between employees and across companies are growing every week. One company I've worked with recently has a policy for maximum message size for Internet messages of 20MB. That may seem quite high to you, but I've seen this same Internet gateway refuse messages because they exceeded that limit by a factor of two or three, and many of these messages were definitely business related!

You should also consider that as complex messages pass through the SMTP connector they get converted to MIME format and this can typically cause the message to grow by a third of its size, so a 10MB PowerPoint file can suddenly become 15MB.

FIGURE 7–4
IMS Connector
General Tab

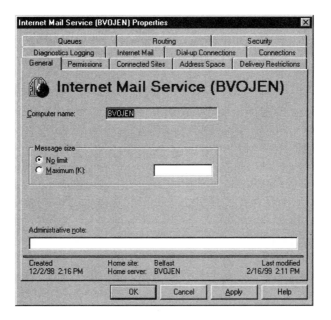

In many cases, the value that you set for the IMS will be determined by the network links that you have more than anything else. This is especially true for internal gateways where the Exchange IMS is used for connections to other legacy systems. The links within your organization may be towards the lower end of the bandwidth chart, and if you're dealing with heavy traffic volumes, it pays to control the interoperability.

Connections to the Internet are a different story. Bandwidth to your ISP shouldn't be too limited, so you should be able to deal with reasonable maximum size messages. What do I mean by a reasonable maximum size message? For me that's about 20MB: your bandwidth may vary.

7.4.2 The Permissions Tab

The *Permissions* tab that is displayed for the IMS Connector bears a striking resemblance to the *Permissions* tab that can be seen for the X.400 Connector (see Section 5.3.2). It serves the same purpose, allowing you to control access that Administrators may have to this connector. Much like the *Permissions* tab on the X.400 Connector, this tab is a relatively new arrival in Exchange; it first appeared in Exchange Server V5.5, so you won't see it if you're running an earlier version of the server.

FIGURE 7–5
IMS Connector
Permissions Tab

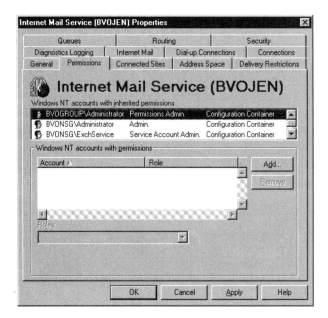

To understand the operation of permissions, take a look at the tab as shown in Figure 7–5. In this environment, you can see that two different administrators have management access to this connector: the Administrator from the *BVOGROUP* domain and the Administrator from the *BVONSG* domain. But careful inspection of the tab will indicate that they both have slightly different administrative roles. You can see that the *BVO-GROUP* Administration account has a *Permissions Admin* role, which allows that holder to modify user attributes for the connector, modify administration settings, delete the connector, and modify permissions on the connector. (These are also described back in Section 5.3.2.)

The *BVONSG* Administration account has *Admin* permissions. This is really a subset of *Permissions Admin*. In this case, the *BVONSG* Administrator can do all that the *BVOGROUP* Administrator can but is restricted from modifying the permissions on the connector, the unique difference between *Permissions Admin* and *Admin* roles.

Why the difference for these two administrators? The answer is simple. The server on which this connector is hosted, *BVOJEN*, resides in the *BVO-GROUP* domain, so it makes sense that an Administrator for this domain should have the fullest set of rights to control it. But this server is connected to another server that exists in a different site and a different Windows NT domain. The name for the other domain is *BVONSG*, so while the administrator for that domain has management access to the *BVOJEN* Exchange IMS Connector, it is slightly more restricted.

7.4.3 The Connected Sites Tab

We've already seen in an earlier chapter about the different options available for linking sites together. One option, but not the most preferred, is the IMS Connector. In describing the operation of the connector in Section 7.2, we saw how much conversion that an Exchange message must undergo (from MDBEF to MIME and vice versa) as it gets routed into and out of the IMS. When this conversion is applied to all of the Exchange system traffic, directory replication, and public folder replication between sites, it's obvious why other inter-site connection mechanisms are preferred. Nevertheless, it is possible to use the IMS, and provided the address space is correctly configured (which we'll look at later) there's no reason why sites can't be linked together.

FIGURE 7–6
IMS Connector
Connected Sites
Tab

Using the example shown in Figure 7–6, you can see that we've used the IMS Connector on *BVOJEN* to link to the site Orlando. To create this site connection, it's a matter of clicking on the *New* button at the bottom of the tab and filling in the fields on the resulting dialog boxes. The first box that appears asks for the Organization name and Site name of the site to which you wish to connect (see Figure 5–11). To connect to the Orlando site, I entered *Digital Equipment Corporation* for the Organization and *Orlando* since I know this to be the site name of the remote location.

FIGURE 7–7
Connected Sites
Routing Address
Tab

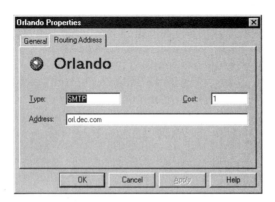

On the *Routing Address* tab of the *New* option, you can then enter the SMTP address details of the target site: in this case type SMTP, and address or1.dec.com, you can see this in Figure 7–7.

In this example, I've set the cost to 1, but you should carefully work out what the costs should be and what impact it will have on the other connectors that may exist in your environment.

Although it's relatively easy to set up the IMS as a Site Connector, you should be careful with it. Apart from the fact that its use can impose significant load on the server itself, directory and public folder replication especially can produce a very large number of messages that get sent between sites. If you're sending directly to the target IMS across your network, then this is reasonably acceptable because you won't really catch sight of the multitude of messages that get generated. But if you direct your local IMS to a mail relay so that you piggy-back off of your company's SMTP network, you'll see a significant increase in the number of SMTP messages that get sent across your backbone. This may cause the backbone administrators in your company to scream and hurl abuse at you as they suddenly see all of this traffic flowing through their systems. The replication messages can be pretty big, and they get even bigger as they become MIME-encoded. This can quite easily begin to clog up an SMTP backbone, especially if it lacks much headroom for growth. I've even seen companies that have implemented virus checking systems on their SMTP backbone watch their systems grind to a halt and have messages backed up for days because of all the replication messages that those scanners have to process!

7.4.4 The Address Space Tab

The IMS can be configured to route messages for all SMTP/Internet addresses or just a particular subset by choosing specific values on the *Address Space* tab which act like a filter. In many cases, it's likely that the IMS will be opened up to all SMTP addresses using a wildcard address like the one shown in Figure 7–8.

If the Scope on this connector is set to Organization (as it is in Figure 7–8), then a configuration like this means that the connector can be used by any server in the entire Exchange network. Alternatively, the visibility of the connector can be limited by setting the Scope to one of the values described in Section 3.9.

FIGURE 7–8
IMS Connector
Address Space Tab

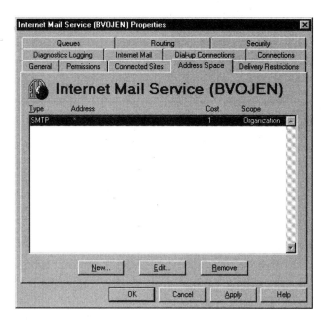

But the whole point of the Address Space settings is to control which messages get routed through the connector even when it can be seen by any server in the Exchange organization. In the example I've shown, this particular connector routes messages for all Internet domains. Consider though, what might happen if a company maintained a private IMS Connector to one of its trading partners and wished to use this Connector for all of its communication with the partner, rather than the normal Internet-based link.

By way of example, take a look at Figure 7–9. The Exchange servers in the Argyle Company are ims1, ims2, and mbox. Now let's assume that mail users on the mbox server wish to send mail to someone that works for the JD Company. Technically, there are two possible routes a message can take to get from mbox to the JD Company, whose mail domain is jd.com. Ideally, it might make sense for ims2 to handle such messages, rather than have them follow the alternative route through ims1. If this were to be the preferred route for the messages then the IMS Connector on ims2 should have an address space:

    *@jd.com

perhaps with a cost of 5. Note that just setting the address space to jd.com isn't enough and will cause messages for *user@jd.com* not to be accepted through the IMS Connector on ims2. In our example, the address space on ims1 might be:

*

with a cost of 5 as well. It's important to understand that even if the cost on this complete wildcard address space was less than the cost for the *@jd.com address space on ims2, that this would make no difference to the routing of messages. Essentially, Exchange works left to right in parsing the address string of the intended recipient and comparing this with the routing options that exist in the GWART. In our example, messages destined for *user@jd.com* will always be routed through ims2. The only way to counter this full match requirement is to use a similar matching address space on ims1. If such an address space is configured locally on the ims1 server with a lower cost, then it will accept messages for *user@jd.com*.

FIGURE 7–9
Using Address
Space Filters

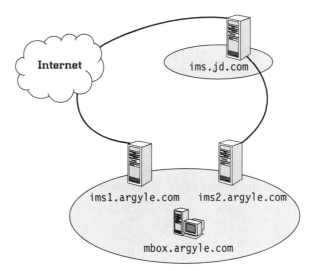

Using the address space filters to control how messages are routed through connectors is pretty straightforward, but the subtleties in terms of the order of address pattern matching and costs can be enough to cause you a few hours of delay and confusion when setting up IMS Connectors. There are two other factors that can contribute to this confusion when configuring connections in a real world environment, and if you want to make sure that those hours of confusion don't become days, then read on.

It's important to remember that merely adding a new address space or changing the cost on an existing one doesn't necessarily mean that messages will get routed through the IMS based on these parameters. The MTA makes routing decisions based on information that's held in the GWART. Whenever you make changes, make sure to either force a routing recalculation from the *Message Transfer Agent General* tab or from the *Routing* tab in *Site Addressing* properties. (I prefer the latter, since I can see the contents of the GWART in the window at the same time.) All of this holds true for parameters within the context of one site, but if you make changes to address spaces on IMSs that exist in different sites, then it's also important to force a directory replication cycle to take place between all of the sites. Only after doing this can you be sure that routing decisions are being based on address space information that is fully up-to-date.

7.4.5   The Delivery Restrictions Tab

Like the X.400 Connector, it's possible to control the list of users that can use a particular IMS Connector. By default, the IMS accepts messages from all users in the Exchange organization and processes them. Looking at Figure 7–10, you can see that I've modified the operation of this IMS so that certain users are prevented from using it.

FIGURE 7–10 IMS Connector Delivery Restrictions Tab

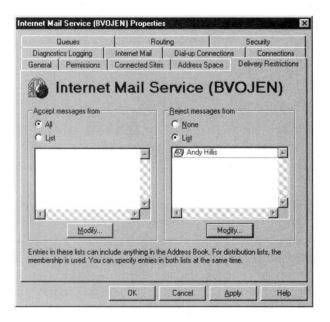

In this example, I've been selective about who I want to prevent from using the connector and as such I've indicated that in general I'll allow messages from all users, but in particular I'll reject messages from a list of users. In this case it's just one: Andy Hillis. So the behavior of the IMS is now such that any messages that Andy tries to send through this IMS will be rejected and sent back to him with a message indicating that he's prevented from using this IMS Connector, similar to the following:

```
'manager@jd.com' on 11/23/98 1:52 PM
  A restriction in the system prevented delivery of the message.
  MSEXCH:MSExchangeMTA:Boston:IMS2
```

If you think back to the arrangement of servers and connections that we had in Figure 7–9, it's interesting to see the behavior of delivery restrictions when there are two IMS serving the same address space. Let's assume that we had defined an address space of:

```
*@jd.com
```

on both the ims1 and ims2 servers, with costs of 2 and 1 respectively. Under normal circumstances, messages sent by a user to *user@jd.com* would get routed through the ims2 server, since this represents the most efficient way (least cost) to send the message. But what happens if we now place a delivery restriction on the ims2 server such that user Andy Hillis isn't permitted to route messages through? The net result of this is that if Andy now tries to send a message to the jd.com domain the message gets successfully routed to the other IMS Connector on the ims1 server. Even though the cost for using ims1 is higher, Exchange recognizes that Andy doesn't have the permissions for the ims2 and forces the message to take a different route.

It's also important to understand the implications for routing if the defined address spaces aren't exactly the same. Consider that the IMS Connector on ims2 remains as before, serving the address space:

```
*@jd.com
```

with a cost of 1, while the connector on ims1 has the original address space:

```
*
```

with a cost of 5. In this case, when a delivery restriction on Andy Hillis is applied at ims2 to prevent his sending mail through it, the same rules as those seen in Section 7.4.4 apply. The address space match must be exact, so even though ims1 has a completely wildcarded address space (*) it will not route the message through its connector.

Once again, the correct operation of the IMS Connector with respect to delivery restrictions is time dependent, so make sure that the same precautions are observed as those for setting address spaces: namely, make sure routing is recalculated when any changes are applied and directory replication is performed between sites. It shouldn't be necessary to stop or restart any Exchange services, such as the IMS or the MTA, but if you're not prepared to wait for a number of minutes after making a change make sure to cycle these components.

7.4.6 The Diagnostics Logging Tab

If you're having trouble confirming the path that messages take as they move through your organization and exit through IMS Connectors, it's useful to enable some of the diagnostic logging options on the connector. There are, of course, a variety of other reasons why you might wish to enable this logging, especially if you see the IMS or another SMTP system having difficulty delivering a message through the connector.

By default, all of the logging options are disabled, as shown in Figure 7–11, but serious errors are written to the Windows NT Event log in any case.

FIGURE 7–11
IMS Connector
Diagnostics
Logging Tab

If you do enable any of these logging options to troubleshoot a problem, remember to disable them again after you've found the cause of the problem. Many of the options cause a significant amount of logging to be performed, some of it to the Event Log and some of it to other locations in the NT file system. Not only does this gradually eat up useful space on your disk volumes, but it also has a considerable impact on the performance of the connector. Writing logging information to disk for every message that goes through the connector is not the most effective use of CPU cycles or IO operations.

Table 7–1 shows the various options for logging on the IMS Connector and a description of what happens when this option is selected. If you do decide to troubleshoot a problem, you can set the logging level to medium on most of the categories to generally zoom in on the one that is causing problems and then use a maximum setting on what you believe to be the troublesome one. Setting all of the logging options to maximum right at the start of an investigation phase can sometimes produce just too much information, which is actually counterproductive to finding the real cause of a problem.

TABLE 7–1   IMS Connector Diagnostic Logging Options and Descriptions

OPTION	DESCRIPTION
Initialization/ Termination	Setting this option records the startup and shutdown status of the IMS Connector to the Windows NT Event Log.
Addressing	Shows errors encountered during the resolution of originator and recipient names and addresses against the Directory Service. These errors are reported to the Windows NT Event Log.

Message Transfer	Records the movement of messages between the IMS and other MTA queues, e.g.,
	
	`A message from <df@belvedere.com> in`
	`temporary file`
	`D:\exchsrvr\imcdata\in\FQN8MSYB was`
	`received from`
	`Bastion.belvedere.com with 1 local`
	`recipients.`

SMTP Interface Events	Records connection events between the IMS Connector and other SMTP hosts to the Windows NT Event Log.

continued ▶

TABLE 7–1 IMS Connector Diagnostic Logging Options and Descriptions (continued)

OPTION	DESCRIPTION
Internal Processing	Shows failures to create temporary resources during message processing.
SMTP Protocol Log	Records a complete log of communication between the IMS and the SMTP service to which it is connecting, e.g., see Figure 7–12. This log is maintained in \EXCHSRVR\IMCDATA\LOG.
Message Archival	Retains a copy of all messages sent through the IMS Connector in \EXCHSRVR\IMCDATA\IN\ARCHIVE and \EXCHSRVR\IMCDATA\OUT\ARCHIVE.

FIGURE 7–12 SMTP
Protocol Log

```
2/23/99 3:39:05 PM : <<< IO: |HELO mail.belvedere.com|
2/23/99 3:39:05 PM : <<< HELO mail.belvedere.com
2/23/99 3:39:05 PM : >>> 250 OK
2/23/99 3:39:05 PM : <<< IO: |MAIL From:<df@belvedere.com>|
2/23/99 3:39:05 PM : <<< MAIL From:<df@belvedere.com>
2/23/99 3:39:05 PM : >>> 250 OK - mail from <df@belvedere.com>
2/23/99 3:39:05 PM : <<< IO: |RCPT To:<peter@jd.com>|
2/23/99 3:39:05 PM : <<< RCPT To:<peter@jd.com>
2/23/99 3:39:05 PM : >>> 250 OK - Recipient <peter@jd.com>
2/23/99 3:39:05 PM : <<< IO: |DATA|
2/23/99 3:39:05 PM : <<< DATA
2/23/99 3:39:05 PM : >>> 354 Send data.  End with CRLF.CRLF
2/23/99 3:39:05 PM : <<< IO: |Received: by mail.jd.com;
(5.65v3.2/1.1.8.2/23Feb96-1148AM)
 id AA08952; Tue, 23 Feb 1999 15:27:41 GMT
Date: Tue, 23 Feb 1999 15:27:41 GMT
From: Deirdre Fitzpatrick <df@belvedere.com>
Message-Id: <9902231527.AA08952@mail.belvedere.com>
Apparently-To: peter@jd.com

Peter,
Don't forget to call round.
|
2/23/99 3:39:05 PM : <<< IO: |.|
2/23/99 3:39:05 PM : >>> 250 OK
2/23/99 3:39:06 PM : <<< IO: |QUIT|
2/23/99 3:39:06 PM : <<< QUIT
2/23/99 3:39:06 PM : >>> 221 closing connection
```

7.4.7 The Internet Mail Tab

The *Internet Mail* tab has evolved through a number of different versions of the IMS Connector. New areas of functionality have been quietly introduced onto this tab, and if you weren't paying careful attention you won't really have noticed them. Essentially its function remains the same, defining some of the characteristics of mail sent through the connector and controlling how the IMS deals with certain situations or destinations for outbound mail. But the evolution of the connector has allowed the IMS to become more granular in how it deals with message interoperability on a per domain basis. Figure 7–13 shows the V5.5 *Internet Mail* tab.

FIGURE 7–13
IMS Connector
Internet Mail Tab

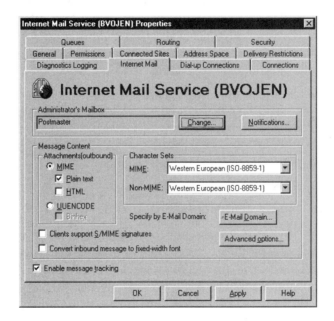

Our first point of interest is the value for the *Administrator's Mailbox.* The mailbox specified in this field will be the lucky recipient of a whole host of notification messages whenever a message is received by the IMS but can't be successfully delivered to a local recipient. Perhaps the message can't be delivered because the address of the recipient has been slightly misspelled, e.g., spelling *Keiran* instead of *Kieran.* In such cases a copy of any nondelivery notification will be sent to this mailbox. In our example, I've used a special mailbox account called *Postmaster,* which I've created for the singular purpose of receiving such messages.

My advice to you is to do the same. You can use the *Change* button to select a different mailbox. Try to use a special purpose one rather than just selecting any other mailbox. Using an Administrator account for this purpose isn't a smart idea, since the chances are it will just get filled up with messages and get in the way of normal operation. If you do create a dedicated mailbox for receiving delivery notifications like this, then you can use the same mailbox for all of the IMSs in your organization. Whatever mailbox you specify to be the location for delivery notifications, do make sure that there's a management process in place to check it regularly. There's little point in saving such messages if your system administrators never check to see what's been delivered there.

Using the *Notifications* button, you can select which types of nondeliveries will generate notifications to the Postmaster mailbox. You can take the catch-all option, which will generate notifications for any type of nondelivery, or you can be more refined, generating notifications for any or all of the following nondelivery events:

- An e-mail address could not be found;

- Multiple matches for an e-mail address were detected;

- Message conversion failed;

- Destination host could not be found;

- Protocol error occurred; and

- Message timeout exceeded.

This tab is also used for controlling the content type of any attachments that get sent through the IMS. For outbound attachments, you can specify the mechanism that gets used when the IMS encodes the message for transmission across an SMTP network. In general, any connections to other SMTP hosts will operate in line with the MIME standards, so it's advisable to check off the radio button that specifies MIME encoding so all message attachments are MIME encoded by default. If you do specify MIME encoding, a check box gives you a further choice which indicates whether plain text messages are MIME encoded (tagged as TEXT/PLAIN) or sent out untagged. Similarly, a check box exists which allows you to encode HTML messages (tagged as TEXT/HTML) or again sent out untouched. Most systems on the Internet today are quite MIME-aware, so sending out plain text with a MIME tag is a fairly safe approach to take. As well as that, HTML is fast becoming the message content of choice for many mail clients, so it's more common now to see TEXT/HTML tags as well. It's unlikely that you'd want to

UUENCODE all message content. That's a format that's rarely used now on the Internet for general message transfer.

As well as specifying the encoding mechanism that is used for complex attachments, you also need to specify the type of character set that will be used for both MIME and non–MIME messages. When a message is transferred through the IMS the content type is converted from the Exchange internal format to/from the character set that you specify in these fields. The value shown in this example is the standard Western European character set (ISO-8859-1),[*] which provides support for characters commonly found in Western European languages, including accents, tildes, umlauts, etc. This is usually sufficient for interoperability with most national character sets, with the notable exception of some Eastern countries. Receiving message text encoded in a different character set (other than US-ASCII) may result in some characters being lost or undisplayable.

If all of the client population that you're supporting is capable of supporting S/MIME signatures (such as Outlook 98), then you may wish to check the box that reads *Clients support S/MIME signatures*. When set, the S/MIME signature is properly preserved and interpreted by the S/MIME-aware client. Otherwise, if you don't want to preserve the signature, leave this box unchecked and the signatures will be removed by the IMS. If you are preserving the signatures but some or all of your clients aren't S/MIME-aware, it's not a very critical problem—the messages can still be read, but the S/MIME signature is retained as an unsightly attachment at the end of the message. That's not a huge problem, since all of the message content is still readable by the user, but it can generate unnecessary and unwanted calls to your helpdesk.

Unless 100 percent of your user population is running with S/MIME-aware clients, it's a good idea to keep this option turned off. If you are in the midst of a migration, it makes sense to strip the signatures out until all of the clients get upgraded to S/MIME-aware versions and only then enable the check box.

And if you wish to go further with modifying the contents of inbound Internet messages to accommodate your client population, it's possible to make sure that all inbound content is converted to a fixed width font by checking the box on the lower left-hand corner of the window.

---

[*] There are numerous ISO character sets that can be used for encoding text and are defined in International Standard Field 35.040, Character sets and information coding. You can see them at http://www.iso.ch/cate/35040.html.

Of course, in messaging environments, especially those connected to the Internet, it's the mix of different types of messages that present the most fun and challenges. Although all of the settings and options we've described so far on this tab apply to all connections to the Internet through this connector, it's possible that you may wish to apply certain rules to certain domains. For example, a particular domain that you send mail to may be unable to process MIME-encoded messages but is able to deal with UUencoded messages. From the options for attachment encoding, it looks like this is an all-or-nothing setting: configure attachments to be encoded as MIME and this is applied to all domains. But not so! You can specify particular options for particular domains by using the *E-Mail Domain...* button. This will allow you to create specific rules for specific domains, by *Adding* a domain as shown in Figure 7–14, and then setting the values, as shown in Figure 7–15.

FIGURE 7–14
IMS Connector
E-Mail Domain
Main Window

FIGURE 7–15 IMS
Connector E-Mail
Domain Settings

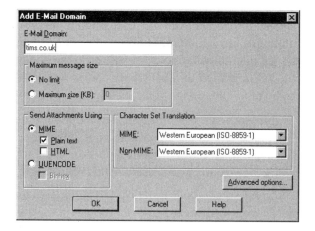

A number of other options exist on the *Advanced options* screen. This is available both at the global level for all messages sent through the IMS and similarly as an E-Mail domain specific setting. You can use the settings on this screen to control whether out-of-office responses, automatic replies, or display names (display text associated with an entry in an address book) are sent to specific domains. In general you may wish to prevent these being sent but for certain trading partners, for example, it can be useful to have them enabled. You can also use settings on this screen to force line breaks into messages. Again, this is not something that you should do in general, but if you are regularly communicating with users in a particular domain that are perhaps using VT terminals to read mail, this may be useful.

Finally, note that there's a separate check box to have message tracking enabled for the IMS. Even if you've already turned it on for the MTA, you must explicitly enable it for operation on the IMS.

7.4.8   The Dial-Up Connections Tab

If you're using RAS connections to reach an Internet Service Provider (ISP), you'll need to make some settings to this tab to accurately reflect the desired characteristics in your environment. The available connections that are displayed represent the RAS connections that you've already defined in the RAS phone book, so you'll need to have information already set up in Exchange.

As you can see in Figure 7–16, you can use settings on the *Dial* group to control when and how often you connect to your ISP to retrieve or send mail. Most ISPs will hold onto messages for a significant period of time, usually a number of days, so you need at the very least to be sure to connect at least once within this time period.

The window of time that you have to collect any stored mail needs to be determined from your ISP, but at the very least you'd probably want to be doing it a few times per day. You can adjust the schedule times so that the connection is made at a specific time every day or every so many hours or minutes. It's difficult to give firm recommendations for this frequency, but generally, if you've more than a handful of users and mail is important to them, avoid anything less than connecting once an hour. You can choose to be quite responsive for the sending of mail by selecting the option that makes a connection to the ISP when any mail is queued outbound. By coupling this with a low value for the *"at most every xx minutes,"* you can be sure that mail will be sent to your ISP shortly after it is sent by the user. The problem here is that if you select this option and you hardly ever send mail then you won't be making any connections to your ISP to retrieve incoming mail, so you could lose some.

FIGURE 7–16 IMS Connector Dial-Up Connections Tab

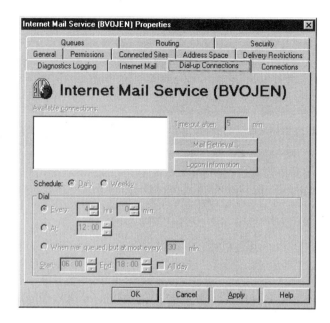

Your options are simple: if you wish to be responsive you can either make an explicit connection every 15 or 30 minutes or so, or you can be less aggressive with outbound mail and *accept* the fact that inbound mail may wait at your ISP for quite a while until connections are made.

The window of operation of these settings is controlled by the Start and End time values. These define when the other settings are active. For example, you may want the IMS to connect every 30 minutes to the ISP to check for messages, but only during the hours of 9:00 a.m. to 6:00 p.m. You can define this window using those settings.

Clicking on the *Mail Retrieval* button displays a screen that presents you with the various options for initiating mail transfer from the remote host. (If you haven't installed the Remote Access Service, then you won't be able to get to this screen.) We've already discussed some of the mechanisms for getting an ISP mail server to start dequeuing messages and, in Figure 7–17, you can see how these options are realized in Exchange. One of four options can be selected to control how mail is sent from the ISP system when a connection is made:

FIGURE 7–17

Mail Retrieval
Option for Dial-Up
Connections

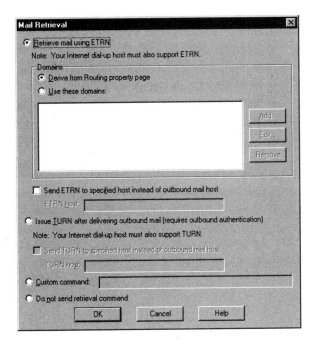

1. **Retrieve mail using ETRN.** If you select this option you can make use of the fact that the ETRN mechanism allows mail for a number of hosts or domains to be de-queued with a single request (see Section 6.8). Exchange will automatically work out which hosts should be catered for if you select the *Derive from Routing* property page option (more about this tab later), since the settings on that property page define the inbound domains that this IMS covers. Alternatively, you explicitly define the hosts that you want de-queued.

    Some ISP services balance their inbound and outbound traffic loads, so the host that you connect to for the outbound mail transmission may not be the same host that delivers messages inbound to you. In that case, sending an ETRN command to the connected outbound host would achieve nothing, but the ETRN mechanism implemented in the IMS allows you to explicitly specify the host which will receive the command.

2. **Issue TURN after delivering outbound mail.** If your ISP only supports TURN, then it's available from the IMS. Note that some ISPs that do actually implement TURN will require a form of authentication. If that's the case, then you'll need to specify an account name and password, which should be entered on the IMS Connector Security tab.

3.   **Custom Command.** Alternatively a command can be executed *on the local system* (i.e., your Exchange server), which would encourage the ISP server to de-queue messages. This command may well be ISP-specific. A common approach is to use a client/server utility that sends a message to an ISP server process to indicate that a connection has been made, at which point the server process initiates a message to de-queue.

4.   **Do not send retrieval command.**

As you make the initial dial-up connection to the ISP, you will probably be required to provide authentication to the ISP server to confirm your identity. This can either be done at the RAS level (in the connection script) or you can use the *Logon information* button on the main *Dial-up Connections* tab to reach the screen (shown in Figure 7–18) that allows you to specify logon information.

Again on the main page, above the two buttons we've just described, there's a setting that defines the time out value. We've discussed how we can use an event to trigger the ISP to deliver messages once a connection has been established. By far, this is the most robust way to have inbound messages delivered, because the IMS is taking positive action to have the messages de-queued, although a less definitive action/response approach can be taken. One way to do this might be to have the ISP configured to attempt delivery to your host every hour on the hour. Of course this approach assumes that you will be connected in time to receive the de-queue from the ISP. If you're not, then no mail is delivered and we haven't achieved anything. To tie in with the ISP, you could configure the IMS to make a connection at the same time, again every hour on the hour. This seems like a reasonable idea, but the issue of time synchronization crops up here. What if your clock is even thirty seconds slower than the clock on the ISP system? By the time you've connected, the ISP mail relay will already have tried to deliver the mail and you'll have to wait for another hour before trying again.

Using the timeout field, you can specify that after a connection is made, the connection remains open for a number of minutes (five minutes, by default). So you make the connection at 11:58 a.m., with a timeout value of five minutes, in anticipation of the ISP making a delivery attempt at 12:00 p.m. This gives a safety net of a few minutes either way to capture the mail.

Note that the timeout value refers to the waiting that's implemented after the last successful exchange of messages. When a connection is made and outbound messages are sent, the IMS will wait a further amount of time as defined by this value for inbound mail to be delivered.

FIGURE 7–18
Logon Information
Dialog Box

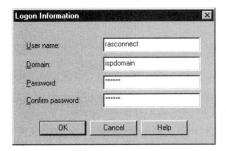

There are no real constraints on how long the timeout value should be, but in general and for timed delivery mechanisms, it should be long enough to allow outbound as well as inbound delivery to be completed. It's also important that the timeout not be longer than the interval in which the ISP server initiates mail delivery. For example, if the ISP mail server is configured to attempt a delivery every 30 minutes and the timeout interval is set to 35 minutes, then after the first delivery, the timeout will not have expired before the ISP server tries to deliver again. The net result of this is that the connection is never dropped and your phone bill gets very high.

7.4.9   The Connections Tab

The whole point of the IMS connector is to get messages from the local system to another system using the SMTP protocol. The *Connections* tab controls and dictates this part of the functionality more than any other. As the first part of this control, you can see from the *Transfer Mode* settings in Figure 7–19 that it's possible to have the IMS operate in one of several modes. In most circumstances, and especially where messaging volumes are not particularly high, the IMS usually runs in *Inbound and Outbound*, but in certain circumstances you may wish to have dedicated IMS servers performing dedicated functions. For load balancing reasons you may elect to have one server only handle outbound mail while another handles inbound traffic. This is a common enough scenario, especially in environments where traffic volumes are particularly high (perhaps tens of thousands of messages per hour).

If you need to shut the IMS down, perhaps to move its storage locations to another disk or move the whole IMS to another server, you can achieve this without shutting down all of Exchange. Use the *None* option for the transfer mode. This gracefully shuts down the IMS and flushes any messages queued in either direction.

Depending on your environment, you may wish to modify the settings on the *Advanced* tab. This controls how connections to and from other hosts are controlled, in terms of number of inbound connections that can be maintained simultaneously, number of outbound connections simultaneously, number of outbound connections to a single host simultaneously, and the number of messages that may be delivered per connection instance. Typically the default values of 30, 20, 10, and 8 respectively are sufficient. In organizations with the very highest of message transfer levels you may wish to raise these settings. You'll need to clearly understand the behavior of other systems that connect to your IMS before you consider making any changes here. For instance, you'd need to know that other systems were being rejected from making connections inbound, that you had so much traffic that the IMS wasn't processing multiple connections fast enough, etc. You may be able to get much of this information from Performance Monitor figures, but data about external hosts being delayed will be hard to come by, and for that you'd have to rely on someone telling you. If your IMS is connected to only one mail relay host, then you may wish to increase the value of the maximum number of messages per connection if you see delays in message delivery. This won't solve a problem of saturation, but it may slightly improve the situation by reducing the overhead associated with opening and closing new connection sessions.

If you are using the IMS in any form of outbound mode, then you'll be concerned with the settings on the *Message Delivery* group. These options determine how the IMS makes connections to other SMTP servers when it attempts to deliver a message.

If your IMS is directly connected to the Internet and there's no firewall blocking the way, then you can elect to have mail addresses looked up directly in DNS. In this mode of operation, the IMS will use DNS to resolve e-mail addresses for users, either resolving MX records or fully qualified domain names. In this case, the IMS is responsible for delivering messages directly to the target mail servers. Similarly, if you're only using this IMS connector to service internal addresses (you'd have set this on the address space), then you probably won't be concerned with a firewall configuration, and again can use the *DNS* option for delivery.

Even if you are using a firewall, it may be possible to allow the *DNS delivery* option for external mail. If you want to operate your mail system in this way, you could allow message traffic to pass through the firewall between the Internet and your primary IMS system. This would be a simple matter of using a filter on the firewall configuration to allow traffic on Port 25 (the

SMTP port) to the TCP/IP address of your IMS server. This configuration should be avoided if at all possible: It's a much better idea to simply have the mail relay service on your firewall handle all external communications rather than allowing any connections from the Internet to slip through to your Exchange system.

FIGURE 7–19
IMS Connector
Connections Tab

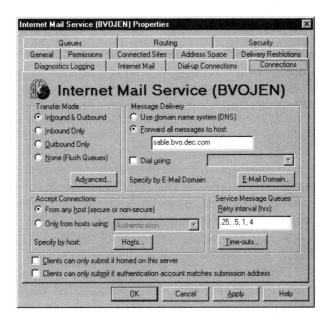

If you do tend toward the more secure option, then you'll have to configure the firewall to forward all messages to a particular host, which as you can see from Figure 7–19, is the approach that I've taken on my own server. In this case, I've simply asked the IMS to deliver all outbound messages to host sable.bvo.dec.com, which is a system running Sendmail. The tasks of resolving addresses and looking up MX records are now delegated to this host. There has often been much discussion about the benefits of using a TCP/IP address to reference the mail relay host rather than a fully qualified domain name. Using a TCP/IP address should reduce the number of lookups required whenever the IMS is required to make an outbound connection. However, a combination of LAN colocation of the DNS server, DNS caching, and readability almost always convinces me to use the domain name form. In most cases, when your IMS connection is for messages to the Internet, the specified host will be a firewall server running SMTP. However, you may have your mail service configured so that you're using an SMTP backbone of some form within your organization. (We'll see more of this in the next chapter.) If that's the case then you may be concerned with redundancy in the configuration of your IMS to an SMTP relay. You can compensate for this either by using an MX record to point to the mail relay, or by using a comma-delimited list of names. For example, you may point the IMS to a mail relay with an MX record of mailrelay.acme.com, with the following record definitions:

```
mailrelay.acme.com.      IN        MX 10        mail1.acme.com.
                         IN        MX 10        mail2.acme.com.
                         IN        MX 10        mail3.acme.com.
```

This should have the IMS use mail relays mail1.acme.com through mail3.acme.com in a load balanced and randomly selected fashion. Alternatively, if you don't wish to use MX records for this purpose, you can use a simple list, such as:

```
mail1.acme.com, mail2.acme.com, mail3.acme.com
```

Now when the IMS forwards messages to the relay host, it will cycle through those hosts in a round robin fashion; if resolution for one host fails, it is ignored and the same message is attempted to be delivered to the next relay. Up to eight such hosts can be defined.

In a similar fashion to some of the other settings on this connector, you're not forced to accept these settings for all messages. You can use the *E-Mail domain* settings to control the particular settings that are used for particular destination domains.

As you can see in Figure 7–20, any mail for the domain shaggy.com is handled by the mail relay eur-relay.vbo.dec.com, while any mail for the domain scooby.com is handled by a DNS lookup. Furthermore, these settings also relate to any subdomains for that domain, so messages addressed to:

```
home.shaggy.com
```

and

```
office.shaggy.com
```

will be routed via the eur-relay.vbo.dec.com mail server as well, without explicitly defining them as routes. If you need to handle one of these addresses differently from the handling for the parent domain, you'll have to explicitly add it to the list of domains and make sure that it is higher up in the hierarchy than the rules for the parent domain. On each of the subdomain settings, it's also possible to select that messages for that subdomain are queued up to await a de-queue request by means of an ETRN command. This allows the Exchange to act in an ISP role.

FIGURE 7–20
IMS Connector
E-Mail Domain
Settings

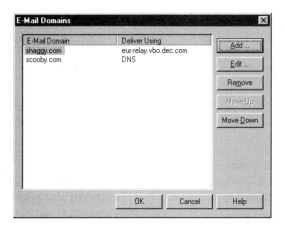

Previous versions of the IMS connector allowed you simply to specify which hosts you would or wouldn't accept connections from merely by quoting their TCP/IP addresses, but new features in Exchange V5.5 enhanced this functionality considerably. It's now possible to accept connections from all hosts as a matter of course or you can specify by default that connections will only be entertained for hosts that use one of *authentication, encryption,* or *authentication/encryption.*

If you select authentication, then the *Simple Authentication and Security Layer* (SASL)[*] facility is used to have the connecting remote host authenticate itself to the IMS. SASL provides a way to implement authentication with connection-based protocols, in this case the SMTP protocol, using a variety of encryption mechanisms (including Kerberos, CRAM-MD5, etc.), but Exchange only implements either a plain text password or a Windows NT password mechanism that is valid only when the two communicating servers are NT systems.

The plain text authentication mechanism is straightforward to implement. You should ensure that an account exists on a domain that the IMS server has access to which you'll use for authenticating the inbound connec-

---

[*]   SASL is defined in RFC-2222.

tion. When an authenticated SMTP connection is to be made, the remote system quotes the username and password information as the connection is established. You may wish to think carefully before implementing this mechanism, since the username and password pair that is exchanged is quoted in plain text across the SMTP link, although it is base64 encoded. Figure 7–21 shows an example SASL conversation between client and server; I've shown the base64 decoded data in italicized parentheses, although this does not appear during the data exchange.

FIGURE 7–21
SASL Plain Text
Authentication
Example

```
220 bvojen.bvo.dec.com ESMTP Server (Microsoft Exchange
Internet Mail Service 5.5.1960.3) ready
helo
250 OK
auth login
334 VXNlcm5hbWU6         (Username:)
c2FzbGNvbm5lY3Q=         (saslconnect)
334 UGFzc3dvcmQ6         (Password:)
b3Vyc2VjcmV0             (oursecret)
235 LOGIN authentication successful
```

In addition to just specifying that the remote system authenticates itself, it is also possible to encrypt the communication between the SMTP client and server. Exchange can use the *Secure Sockets Layer* (SSL) mechanism to provide public key/private key encryption between the cooperating parties in the conversation. This ensures that all exchange of SMTP information between the Exchange IMS and the remote server is fully secure. To use SSL encryption you'll need to already have the X.509 public certificate for the other half of the SMTP connection. This certificate gets installed on the Exchange server and is used in the initial conversation that takes place between each of the communicating SMTP partners.[*]

When communication is first established and public keys are exchanged, the client system will authenticate the server. When the authentication has been successful, the client and server agree on a random secret key, called the *master key*, which is used to encrypt all further communication for the session.

---

[*] You can get X.509 keys from many sources on the Internet. Just search at your favorite search engine. Alternatively, one of the major providers can be found at http://www.verisign.com.

The rules that are put in place at this level apply generally to all inbound connections, but once again it's possible to balance this by specific rules that only apply to specific servers or groups of servers.

Taking a look at Figure 7–22, there are two rules in place for specific hosts. Both rules have the explicit TCP/IP address specified and both have a full 255.255.255.255 mask. This means that the TCP/IP address must match exactly before the rule is appropriate. You can be less specific with the rule if you wish, using only, for example, 255.255.255.0 as this mask. In the case of the first rule, this would mean that any address in the 16.183.112 domain would be a valid candidate for the rule to be applicable. The action for each of the matching addresses can be either an *accept* or a *reject* of the connection and you can further refine the settings in the same way that you could globally for either authenticated or encrypted communication.

FIGURE 7–22
IMS Connector
Accept/Reject
Specific Hosts

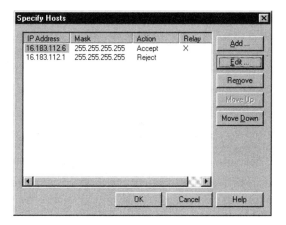

This is a powerful mechanism and is often implemented by organizations that use their IMS connectors extensively for generalized communications, but which have particular requirements for secure connections to a small number of other SMTP systems.

In other environments, organizations may wish to use the IMS to provide interconnectivity services between different mail systems but restrict the IMS to be only used for this purpose. In many large companies, it's common to see SMTP being used by a variety of different departments or development groups as a transport for new department-wide information services or linked into web applications. Enterprising individuals usually determine pretty quickly how they can direct their applications to the nearest SMTP server to act as a relay. Before you realize what's happened, the IMS connector you were using to provide connectivity between Exchange and another mail system is also being used by a number of applications in a production environment. The best approach to take is to lock the access down to authorized hosts only just as soon as you've put the infrastructure in place.

The settings for *Service Message Queue Retry interval* define how long the IMS waits between attempts to deliver SMTP messages. These settings assume (1) the validity of the address on the SMTP message and (2) that it was resolvable by the IMS but when the SMTP connection was made, it failed to be successful. A number of values are specified, indicating a time in hours. The first value defines the delay between the first unsuccessful attempt at delivery and the first retry attempt, the second time defines the time between the first retry attempt and the next retry attempt and so on. When the last retry interval is reached (in this case four hours), a delivery is attempted every four hours until the message is delivered or it times out. For IMS servers that make their connections over dial-up lines, these times may be suitable, but for permanently connected IMS servers, I'd tend to bring at least the final retry interval down to an hour to ensure a reasonably speedy message delivery.

Working hand in hand with these settings are the timeout intervals, which are set by default at 24, 48, and 72 hours for urgent, normal, and nonurgent messages respectively.* It's quite common to see these timeout values changed in many environments. In cases where mail delivery is of paramount importance for urgent messages, the 24-hour interval is often reduced to four or six hours. However, it is also quite common to see the delivery timeout for normal messages increased to 72 hours. Quite simply, problems on mail relay systems take place from time to time and they are often noticed and rectified pretty quickly. However, when problems occur on systems at a weekend, up to two full days can elapse before corrective action is taken. Consider a problem on a mail relay that occurs at 8:00 p.m. on a Friday evening, blocking SMTP traffic. It may take until 8:00 a.m. on Monday morning before staff return to work and rectify the problem, but with a timeout of 48 hours for normal messages, nondelivery messages start to get generated after 8:00 p.m. on the Sunday evening. Of course, this situation should rarely take place, and when it does, support staff should be automatically notified of problems on the mail system either by manual moni-

---

* Urgent, normal, and nonurgent SMTP priorities map to High Importance, Normal, and Low Importance messages in Exchange.

toring procedures or automated alert systems (typically pagers integrated into system management products). However, some organizations can't afford to run such services 24 hours a day, and for the sake of messages being stuck in a queue for an extra 12 hours on a Sunday evening, this may be a tradeoff between user complaints that you're prepared to live with.

In any event, a separate notification timeout value is also available on this tab. The previous timeout values defined the time that a message could remain in a queue and be retried before a nondelivery notification was issued for it. While it's good that the IMS will retry the delivery of a message for up to 72 hours, it would not be so good if the message remained undelivered for this period of time and the originator knew nothing about it, thus assuming it had been delivered almost immediately. The IMS provides a notification facility *Notify sender for queued mail* so that a warning message can be sent back to the originator to indicate a problem with delivery. For urgent messages this is set to every four hours, every 12 hours for normal messages, and every 24 hours for nonurgent messages. The settings are only enabled for urgent messages, but I like to have them enabled for all message classes. Basically, if I send a normal message and it's not delivered within 12 hours I'd like to know about it.

Two more check boxes are provided at the bottom of the tab that relate to clients that submit their messages directly to the IMS. Both these settings require that either authentication or authentication and encryption are in use. The submitting client *must* authenticate itself, and the IMS uses the authentication information to verify that the client has an account homed on the local server. If no such account exists then, the message cannot be accepted. In a similar vein, and in an effort to control message spoofing, the second box may be checked to ensure that the submitting client properly reveals its identity. When this box is checked and a message is submitted, the IMS compares the RFC-821 From address (part of the message envelope) with an SMTP alias on the account that they have authenticated with. If no RFC-821 From address is present, then the RFC-822 From address (part of the message header) is used for the comparison instead. When the check is made, the message is rejected if the RFC-821 or RFC-822 addresses don't match the alias on the authenticated account. In this way, it's impossible to connect to the IMS and send a message with a false From address.

7.4.10 The Queues Tab

The IMS also includes a *Queues* tab, which allows you to see if messages are backlogged either inbound or outbound in the IMS. There are four queues that can be inspected:

- Inbound messages from the Internet awaiting conversion (these messages haven't yet been delivered into the MTS-IN folder);

- Inbound messages from the Internet awaiting delivery to recipients (these messages are in the MTS-IN folder);

- Outbound messages for the Internet awaiting conversion (these messages are in the MTS-OUT folder); and

- Outbound messages for the Internet awaiting delivery (these messages have left the MTS-OUT but haven't been handed off to the SMTP delivery system).

FIGURE 7–23
IMS Connector
Queues Tab

Typically you should only see entries in the queue if message delivery is backed up for some reason. Entries in the awaiting conversion queue will probably indicate that the IMS has been unavailable for some time and has only recently been started, while problems actually delivering messages over the SMTP transport will manifest themselves with entries in the awaiting delivery queue. If a message delivery is attempted but has been unsuccessful, the message will be placed back into the awaiting delivery queue and retried periodically as defined by the values on the *Connections* tab. The message will remain there until the next retry attempt, but it may leave the queue earlier if another message delivery is attempted to the same domain and is successful. In this case, this better news about the destination domain is used by the IMS so that the next time a message is delivered to this domain, the queued message is delivered as well.

Entries on the inbound queues will typically indicate problems with other Exchange components, either the Directory Service or the Information Store, since failure on these subsystems will generally prevent further processing of inbound messages. It's also likely that any such problems on these components will have appeared after the IMS has started, since problems on these components will generally prevent the IMS from starting under normal circumstances.

7.4.11 The Routing Tab

More than any other component of this connector, the facilities provided for routing messages on this tab allow the IMS to perform the role of a fully fledged SMTP switch. In versions of Exchange before V5.0, the IMS (then called the IMC) could merely gateway SMTP messages into and out of the Exchange environment. However, with the V5.0 release of Exchange server, the functionality to reroute incoming SMTP traffic was introduced.

Essentially this mechanism allows the IMS to analyze the domain part of an inbound message and potentially reroute it to another SMTP server. This allows an Exchange server to become an intelligent mail relay.

As well as providing functionality for the rerouting of SMTP traffic, the routing capability on the IMS is also used by POP3 and IMAP4 clients to allow delivery to users outside of the Exchange environment. In short, if you have any POP3 or IMAP4 clients and you wish to allow them to send mail to non-Exchange recipients, then you *must* enable the IMS to perform rerouting of messages.

When a message is received by the IMS and rerouting of messages is enabled, the domain name part of the address is compared to the domain name list in the *Routing* property page. If a match is found, then the associated routing action is performed for that message. The message will either be accepted inbound or rerouted to an external host. You can see an example of a number of rewrite rules in Figure 7–24.

FIGURE 7–24
IMS Connector
Routing Tab

Exact matches are looked for first and the appropriate routing action taken. If no exact match can be found, then a subdomain comparison is performed. A subdomain comparison will attempt to match a complete subdomain, rightmost part first, and if one is found then that routing action is performed. Finally, if no match can be found then the message is rerouted to the domain specified without any host-specific redirection. Confused? You won't be after this example, which is based around the rerouting terms in Figure 7–24.

Messages are routed as shown in Table 7–2.

In all cases, if a match is found on the rightmost part of the domain name, then any subdomains underneath that hierarchy are also subject to the rerouting action. Specifying a pound sign (#) in front of the domain part implies that the rewriting rule applies if and only if an exact match is obtained for this domain. In such cases, subsequent inexact comparison operations are not carried out.

If you intend to use the IMS to act as an intelligent mail relay, then you'll need to plan carefully how to deal with the various addresses that the IMS may be presented with. In a sense, the routing functionality in the IMS allows you to redirect mail to a specific host in the same fashion as an MX record operates, but without the associated flexibility and redundancy. No specific ordering of the entries in the routing table is required, and you can see that unlike many other tables, there's no option to *move up* or *move down* the domain names. Matches are simply performed on an exact or inexact basis, so if there are specific subdomains that you need to handle, these must be explicitly entered. The Add function doesn't allow you to enter duplicate domain parts either.

TABLE 7–2   IMS Rerouting Actions for Various Domains

`user@bvojen.bvo.dec.com`	An exact match is found for the domain part and this message is routed inbound.
`user@mail.bvo.dec.com`	An exact match is found for the domain part and this message is routed inbound.
`user@unix.bvo.dec.com`	An exact match is found for the domain part and this message is rerouted to the mail server `sable.bvo.dec.com`
`user@dec.com`	An exact match is found for the domain part (identified as `#dec.com`) and this message is rerouted to the mail server `us-relay.mro.dec.com`
`user@paris.dec.com`	An inexact match is found on the subdomain part of `dec.com` and this message is rerouted to the mail server `eur-relay.vbo.dec.com`
`user@hq.center.rome.dec.com`	An inexact match is found on the subdomain part of `dec.com` and this message is rerouted to the mail server `eur-relay.vbo.dec.com`
`user@exchange.mail.bvo.dec.com`	An inexact match is found on the subdomain part of `dec.com` and this message is routed inbound.
`user@compaq.com`	No match is found for this domain and the mail is rerouted out to the `compaq.com` domain.

In any event, it is very important that the IMS knows to route inbound any domain names that may be associated with Exchange mailboxes or recipients, otherwise mail is simply routed straight back out of the connector.

7.4.12 The Security Tab

We've already seen on the *Connections* tab how the IMS can handle authentication and encryption that may be required for specific domains. That was simply a matter of specifying the host details and indicating what the security requirements were for connections with that host. However, those settings dealt only with inbound connections from the host or domain and didn't provide any mechanism for specifying that particular security levels should be put in place for out bound connections.

To do this, you can use the settings on the *Security* tab. With the IMS, it's a simple matter of selecting the domain name for which you wish to apply the appropriate security access. In the example that I've shown in Figure 7–25, it's important to understand that the security settings can apply to domain names that reference either fully qualified host names or MX records.

FIGURE 7–25
IMS Connector
Security Tab

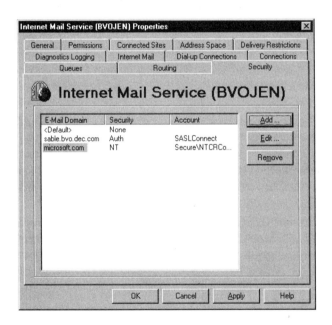

As you can see, sable.bvo.dec.com is a fully qualified hostname, actually a UNIX host that's internal to my network. I've chosen to use SASL to authenticate myself to this server. But for microsoft.com, which is an MX record that points to several mail servers,[*] I've chosen to use NT authentication.

---

[*] You can see what servers microsoft.com resolves to using the NSLOOKUP utility:
```
nslookup >set type = mx and
nslookup > microsoft.com
```

There are some points to be aware of with this configuration. If you're using an MX record in the E-Mail Domain definition, you need to be sure that *all* of the hosts that service the MX record are capable of dealing with the authentication request from your Exchange server.

Furthermore, for the domains that you have set up secure access, your Exchange server must be able to make a direct connection to the target system. This has a number of repercussions, especially the fact that you can't use any SMTP relaying to get to these domains and have an authenticated link. So using the *Forward message to host* option from the *Connections* tab won't initiate a secure connection to the target system unless there's a chain of security set up between all of the systems potentially involved. When a message is forwarded to an intermediary such as what happens when using the *Forward* option, then the security requirement is ignored and a normal connection attempt is made. However, if the Exchange IMS attempts to make a connection directly, even by resolving an MX record, then a secure connection attempt takes place irrespective of the actual host to which the connection is made.

FIGURE 7–26

IMS Connector
Security Definition

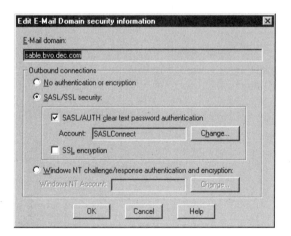

As you can see in Figure 7–26, I've decided to set up SASL authentication for my UNIX host, `sable.bvo.dec.com`. This is a simple matter of entering the host name, selecting the required authentication and encryption requirement, and then specifying the user name and password that will be presented at the remote server.

More or less the same information is required for a Windows NT challenge/response authentication configuration. I've decided to use this mechanism for communications that I'll make to any mail servers representing the Microsoft domain. When connecting to another Exchange system over TCP/IP, it makes sense to use the Windows NT authentication mechanism, since this provides the greatest degree of security.

In summary, using secure access between servers is something that certainly can be implemented but must be designed and put into place very carefully. Widespread use of SASL communication across the Internet is something that may materialize in the future, but for the moment, secure access is pretty much restricted to internal networks and backbones and communication with trading partners.

8

Connecting Exchange to
Corporate Backbones

8.1   Introduction

We've looked at much of the technology basics associated with Exchange, X.400, and the SMTP connectors in earlier chapters, but in this chapter it's time to put this technology framework into effect.

The thrust of many integration projects usually involves implementing a backbone of some description, typically either X.400 or SMTP, but increasingly, SMTP is the backbone of choice for most organizations. In this chapter we'll look at some real life examples of connecting to corporate backbones, both X.400 and SMTP, and the issues that arise when these kind of connections are made. Looking just at the technology and at the connector components themselves gives us a broad understanding of what needs to be done to get some form of interoperability in place, but often this doesn't cover some of the more subtle issues that crop up. More often than not these issues relate to address manipulation, replyability, and interoperability of delivery and read notifications. While Exchange possesses facilities for much of this functionality, when a multitude of different messaging systems are involved, this often needs to be complemented with other backbone products more attuned to these issues.

Rather than describe such environments in an abstract way, the approach taken in this chapter uses some specific products that are commonly used in backbone environments. For the X.400 environment, I've described the connections to Exchange using Compaq's MAILbus 400 product and for connections to SMTP backbones I've used Innosoft's PMDF[*] product. PMDF is a widely used SMTP switch that couples great functionality with ease of use, a combination not often found in the world of

---

[*]   You can find more information about Innosoft's PMDF product at http://www.innosoft.com.

SMTP messaging. As well as providing great features, PMDF runs on a variety of different platforms, including Windows NT, Solaris, Digital UNIX, and OpenVMS. This combination means that PMDF is often ideally suited for environments that have multiple messaging systems on multiple operating system platforms.

We've set the scene; now let's see how we can set this technology to work.

8.2   Connecting to X.400 Backbones

Exchange has a big advantage over most other X.400 implementations. It's fronted by an easy to use management interface, the Exchange Administrator program, and it can do some things using wide-area X.400 connections that other X.400 systems can't.

What it can do is to make intelligent routing decisions across its backbone of X.400 site connectors so that if one link presents an obstacle to routing messages, for example, a server is down, an alternative route can be taken. Load balancing across pure X.400 backbones can't easily be achieved and is not defined in the ISO recommendations. In terms of building a reliable infrastructure, there's no substitute for implementing native Exchange connections from site to site. As an Exchange network designer, what this should tell you is that there is little point in building an Exchange environment on top of an X.400 backbone from another vendor, one like that shown in Figure 8-1.

Some might argue that using an X.400 backbone to interconnect Exchange sites makes sense because it leverages an existing investment in backbone technology, allows routing across an already established and stable backbone, and makes use of added value services on the backbone such as virus checking, accounting logs, etc. While this may well be true, it does bring with it some problems. The basic functionality of Exchange and inter-site communication will be preserved, so users can send messages to one another across such a backbone. However, if one site has an IMS connector and users try to send to it across the backbone, then messages don't get properly transferred and the mail doesn't get delivered. This is a function of the way that messages get constructed as they go across the backbone to and from Exchange. In short, the best approach to take in this case is to connect Exchange servers together directly using native Exchange connectors.

This doesn't mean that Exchange shouldn't connect to an X.400 backbone! There are, of course, times when this is very desirable and it's especially so when a self-contained Exchange environment needs to communicate with other X.400-aware mail systems—exactly the scenario we're interested in when we talk about Exchange connectivity.

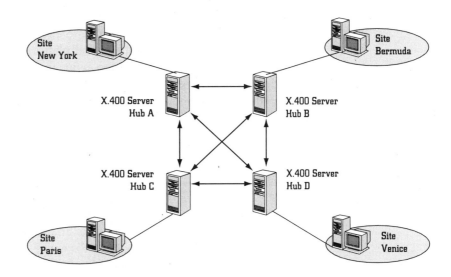

FIGURE 8–1
An X.400 Backbone for Exchange Site Connections

It's true that Exchange supports many of the X.400 recommendations very strongly, but some environments have particular X.400 requirements that aren't met by Exchange. For example, Exchange supports the X.400 P1 protocol, but doesn't allow for connections from other systems using XAPI User Agent connections, P3 (for X.400 Message Stores), or P7 (for X.400 Remote User Agents). While these represent less popular environments, some organizations do have them and in such cases, connectivity is provided using X.400 backbones.

Many organizations have invested significant effort into developing X.400 backbones as a platform for integration, and although SMTP has become the preferred interconnection mechanism today, some will no doubt wish to exploit the infrastructure they've already developed.

8.2.1   Making Connections to MAILbus 400

Many people familiar with messaging systems from Digital Equipment Corporation (now called Compaq Computer Corporation),[*] such as ALL-IN-1

---

*   Visit Compaq at http://www.compaq.com.

or MailWorks, may well have had occasion to work with MAILbus 400, Compaq's X.400 backbone product set. Making connections from ALL-IN-1 or MailWorks to Exchange can only be achieved over either X.400 or SMTP, and if you choose the X.400 method then this section is important to you.

MAILbus 400 runs on both the OpenVMS and Tru64 UNIX operating systems, but its configuration mechanism is platform independent, using the Network Control Language (NCL) to define the connection parameters and routing instructions to Exchange. The complete configuration of MAILbus 400 is quite complex and involves many components, including OSI, TCP/IP, and X.500, and a full discussion is beyond the scope of this book. However, the configuration of MAILbus 400 is completely described in the product documentation set, specifically the *MAILbus 400 Planning and Setup* guide.

To establish an X.400 link to Exchange from MAILbus 400, you'll need to set up a *peer MTA entry* on a local MAILbus 400 system. This provides the connection to the Exchange X.400 connector and routes messages from the MAILbus 400 environment through to Exchange. The following commands, as shown in Figure 8–2, which are executed from the MTA startup script, start_mta.ncl, define such a connection to Exchange.

FIGURE 8–2

MAILbus 400
NCL Peer MTA
Definition

```
create mta peer mta [type=manually configured, name="BVOJEN"]
set mta peer mta [type=manually configured, name="BVOJEN"] -
  application context mts transfer
set mta peer mta [type=manually configured, name="BVOJEN"] -
  pres add """MTA""/""MTA""/""MTA""/
RFC1006+16.183.112.31,RFC1006"
set mta peer mta [type=manually configured, name="BVOJEN"] -
  local name "BVOMTA1", -
  local password [type=ia5, ia5 string="MYPASSWORD"]
set mta peer mta [type=manually configured, name="BVOJEN"] -
  peer name "BVOJEN", -
  peer password [type=ia5, ia5 string="secret"], -
  peer domain "BVOEXCH-DOM"
enable mta peer mta [type=manually configured, name="BVOJEN"]
```

The following points describe the actions for each of these commands: ·

- The initial `create` commands defines a peer MTA (the Exchange X.400) connector. It has to be `manually configured` because it's a third party X.400 implementation.

- The `application` context `MTS transfer` commands indicate that the connection to the Exchange X.400 connector fully supports the 1992 MHS Standards.

- The terms within the presentation address refer to the settings for the P-Selector, S-Selector, and T-Selector for the Exchange stack (see Section 5.2), finally the TCP/IP address of the Exchange server is quoted. The RFC1006 term indicates that this connection will take place over the TCP/IP protocol.

- The name of the local MTA (i.e., in the MAILbus 400 environment) and its password. These values should coincide with the settings for *Remote MTA name* and *Remote MTA password* on the *General* tab of the X.400 Connector (see Section 5.3.1). This system can also be known as the *boundary MTA,* since it hosts the connection to the foreign system, in this case Exchange.

- The peer name and password should coincide with the name and password of the Exchange server on which the X.400 connector resides. This is found on the settings for the Exchange MTA, but can be overridden on the X.400 connector itself (See section 5.3.5). In this case, the Exchange MTA is called `BVOJEN` and the password used is `secret`. The peer domain is an X.400 concept that MAILbus 400 uses to name (locally) the routing domain which is represented by Exchange.

- Finally, the peer MTA is enabled to make it available.

FIGURE 8–3
MAILbus 400 OR
Address Routing
Instructions

```
create mts "/c=gb/o=digital/mts=digitalmts" oraddress -
    "c=gb;a=bt;p=digital;o=digital;ou1=exch "
set mts "/c=gb/o=digital/mts=digitalmts" oraddress -
    "c=gb;a=bt;p=digital;o=digital;ou1=exch " -
    routing instruction -
        [action=transfer to domain, -
            server domain="BVOEXCH-DOM"]
```

After setting up the MTA connection, you'll need to define the routing information on the MAILbus 400 side so that MAILbus 400 knows what to do with specific OR addresses. This is pretty much the same concept as defining an address space on the X.400 connector. You'll also need to define the following routing instructions in MAILbus 400, as shown in Figure 8–3 (above).

Before we cover each of the command settings in detail, I should explain the use of the mts terms in the definitions. MAILbus 400 stores its configuration data for message routing in a particular subtree, or naming context, within an X.500 directory. The naming context for this particular configuration is identified with a name of:

```
/c=gb/o=digital/mts=digitalmts
```

This is an arbitrary setting, and you should give it a value of something that accurately reflects your MAILbus 400 environment.

These instructions indicate that any X.400 messages with an OR address of:

```
c=gb;a=bt;p=digital;o=digital;ou1=exch
```

are to be routed to Exchange. The address processing mechanism that MAILbus 400 uses is from left to right, so any OR addresses that start with this partial address, e.g.,

c=gb;a=bt;p=digital;o=digital;ou1=exch;cn=tommy byrne
c=gb;a=bt;p=digital;o=digital;ou1=exch;ou2=dublin;cn=frank clonan

are subject to the same routing instruction. The *action* on processing such a message is that it is transferred to the domain BVOEXCH-DOM, and there's another set of MAILbus 400 commands that link the BVOEXCH-DOM to the peer MTA, like those in Figure 8–4.

FIGURE 8–4
MAILbus 400
Domain Routing
Instruction

```
create mts "/c=gb/o=digital/mts=digitalmts" domain
"BVOEXCH-DOM"
set mts  "/c=gb/o=digital/mts=digitalmts" domain
"BVOEXCH-DOM" -
     different ccitt domain false, -
     routing instruction -
         [action=transfer to domain, -
             boundary mta="BVOMTA1"]
```

This routing instruction explicitly tells MAILbus 400 that the boundary MTA for this domain is BVOMTA1, so any messages that are being processed on any X.400 MTA in the MAILbus 400 environment must be transferred to this boundary system if they are to be routed to Exchange.

MAILbus 400 knows that messages that get routed into this domain, BVOEXCH-DOM, must eventually get sent over to Exchange because the peer MTA entry for the Exchange server explicitly identifies this domain in the peer MTA definition.

With the setup that we've covered so far, this is sufficient for transferring messages between the two environments of MAILbus 400 and Exchange. We've already seen (from Section 4.4) that X.400 messages are composed of an envelope and a number of bodyparts, and that bodyparts are tagged with a content type. Many Compaq messaging systems (such as OfficeServer or MailWorks) use MAILbus 400 to identify messages between systems with the Externally Defined Bodypart (BP15) tag, while Exchange uses the newer FTBP mechanism. In addition to just providing the linkage between MAILbus 400 and Exchange for message routing, to achieve good fidelity for message transfer you'll need to tell MAILbus 400 to convert BP15 bodyparts through to FTBP bodyparts. You can do this by specifying a content type filter on the OR address like that shown in Figure 8–5.

FIGURE 8–5

MAILbus 400 OR
Address Content
Type Settings

```
set mts "/c=gb/o=digital/mts=digitalmts" oraddress -
    "c=gb;a=bt;p=digital;o=digital;ou1=exch" -
content information [maximum content length = 0, -
content types=( -
    "{1 3 12 2 1011 5 5 0 1 22 1}"), -
encoded information types=( -
    "{2 6 3 4 2}", -
    "{1 3 12 2 1011 5 5 1 0}")]
```

This content type example uses the OID value

{1 3 12 2 1011 5 5 0 1 22 1}

to convert BP15 bodyparts to FTBP when sending to Exchange. Messages coming in the opposite direction, that is, from Exchange to another MAILbus 400 messaging system should have their content types converted in the opposite direction and for that you can use a content type OID value of

{1 3 12 2 1011 5 5 0 1 22}.

If you want content types to pass through untouched, then the OID value of

{1 3 12 2 1011 5 5 0 1 22 0}

will allow this.

For each content type that you specify for a particular mail system, you also need to specify which EITs within that content type that you'll be prepared to accept. These too act like a filter, so depending on the list of acceptable data formats that you specify messages may or may not get delivered.

As you can see in Figure 8–5, I've defined two EITs that I'll be prepared to accept when messages are being delivered to my Exchange system. The EITs defined are for IA5 text and any EIT, so in this case all data formats would get through because of the catchall "any EIT" at the end of the list.

Typically, MAILbus 400 will look at the content information defined for a particular OR address and compare that with content information held in the envelope part of the message. Depending on what MAILbus 400 sees as being acceptable content types for a particular address, it makes a decision to do one of the following:

- Deliver the message, since the content types or EITS are acceptable to the receiving system;

- Nondeliver the message because the content types or EITS are not acceptable to the receiving system;

- Nondeliver the message because the content length exceeds that defined for the receiving system; or

- Attempt to convert the bodyparts to a format acceptable to the receiving system.

In a complex environment[*] where you use MAILbus 400 as a backbone to connect multiple and different types of systems together, you'll need to carefully consider the acceptable content types and EITs for each messaging system. Doing this as a specific part of an interoperability design exercise will allow you to build an environment where every mail system can successfully interpret the attachment types that it receives. The conversion capabil-

---

[*]   A complete description of using MAILbus 400 to provide such an interoperability is beyond the scope of this book, but is well covered in the *MAILbus 400 Tuning and Problem Solving* guide.

ities of MAILbus 400 prove very useful in mixed environments, where proprietary attachments can be converted to something more useful in the target environment. This is particularly true in the ALL-IN-1 or Office-Server world, where MAILbus 400 can be configured to convert WPS-PLUS messages to text that's readable in an Exchange environment.

8.2.2   Redundant Connections

While a MAILbus 400 backbone to link multiple messaging environments together can be useful for providing rich handling of content types and conversions, it is less functional in terms of providing redundant routing between one environment and another.

X.400 uses a rigid routing model to define the path that messages take from one point to another. Unlike Exchange and, as we'll see, SMTP, the rerouting of messages isn't possible; once a message sets out on a particular course it adheres to this route in order to get to the target systems. If a problem occurs at any stage during the transfer of the message, its delivery will be delayed until the connection to the next hop becomes available again or the message times out.

FIGURE 8–6

Message Routing in an X.400 Backbone

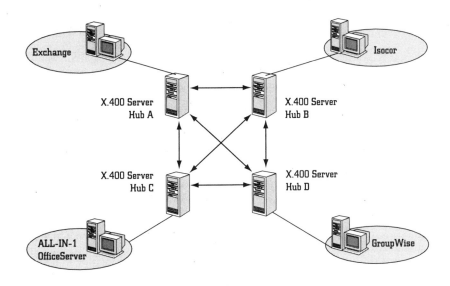

Consider the route that a message might take to get from the Exchange environment to the GroupWise environment shown in Figure 8–6. Of course, all of the X.400 hub servers may communicate with each other directly, but in setting up the X.400 environment you'll define a set path that a message will take to get from one messaging environment to another. In our example, it's likely that the path that the message would take to get to the Novell GroupWise environment to the Exchange environment is to pass through *Hub A* and then be routed directly to *Hub D,* where it can be passed off to the GroupWise system. What happens if for some reason the *Hub D* server becomes unavailable? If that's the case, then messages will simply queue up on the *Hub A* server until *Hub D* comes back online again.

There's no concept of failover routing or associating costs with particular links, so there's no way to dynamically control the route that a message will take as it flows from one X.400 system to another. The routing rules are defined statically in the configuration of the X.400 environment and can't be changed unless you modify the configuration data for all of the X.400 systems.

Exchange gives you some control over the redundancy of connections to an X.400 backbone. While there's no redundancy from the backbone to Exchange, it is possible to configure some redundancy in the opposite direction, that is, from Exchange to the backbone. This is simply done by having multiple points of contact into the backbone at various places in the Exchange organization. With these links and appropriate costs you can cater for availability issues in one direction at least.

While X.400 environments don't provide the kind of redundancy we'd like to see for routing messages, there are some measures that you can take to compensate for this weakness. MAILbus 400, in common with some other X.400 implementations, supports the concept of an *MTA set.* An MTA set is a collection of MTAs that operate together and provide high availability services. If one MTA in the set should become unavailable for any reason, the remaining MTAs in the set can take on the workload of the failed system.

And, depending on operating system platforms, it may be possible to offer a clustered approach to X.400 services, if MTA sets are not available. Most X.400 implementations don't natively support clusters (be they Windows NT clusters, UNIX clusters, or OpenVMS clusters) but with some innovative scripting, it's possible to build a degree of cluster awareness into many backbone products.

Neither of these approaches go any real way to provide a redundant backbone built around X.400 standards, but they do provide a means to increase the availability of the environment.

8.3 Connecting to SMTP Backbones

Two aspects of SMTP make it a very desirable technology for building backbones: (1) almost all messaging systems support the SMTP protocol and either have gateways or SMTP functionality built into their product sets, and (2) without doubt, SMTP is *the* most talked about messaging technology on the planet today.

Almost all organizations that are considering implementing a new backbone insist on building a solution on *open standards* using *industry standard components*. Without fail this means SMTP.

As well as providing the de facto technology for standards, SMTP backbones also bring some advantages that X.400 backbones lack. The new functionality that's most useful is the inherent redundancy that you get with an SMTP backbone because of the MX-record-based routing model.

8.3.1 Using Exchange as an SMTP Backbone

We've already seen many of the features of the IMS Connector and how functional it can be when connecting to SMTP backbones. One of the areas that we should now explore is how good Exchange actually is at being an SMTP backbone itself. First let's determine what general features we should expect to see from such a backbone:

- Ability to reroute messages based on domain names;
- Ability to reroute messages based on a full address;
- Ability to rewrite address information (inbound and outbound);
- Ability to connect to other SMTP systems with redundancy; and
- Convert and/or relabel content for messages in transit.

By way of example, let's look at the possibilities of using an Exchange backbone to link several messaging systems together for the Bauby Company and how its features can be used to build a reliable backbone in such an environment. We'll assume that the environment is like that shown in Figure 8–7.

In this environment, the hub servers are all Exchange systems and all run the IMS connector. The four messaging environments that they connect to all have SMTP gateway systems that are directly connected to the backbone. The Exchange environment that we're using to form the hub should have no relationship whatsoever to the Exchange environment to which users in the

Bauby Company connect. Our backbone Exchange environment will be disconnected from the users' Exchange environment (in Exchange organizational and site terms) and no routing or user information will be shared between them. It's possible that all of the hub servers may exist within the same site (if available bandwidth between the locations is good) or they may be in separate sites if they're physically located in different geographies (and bandwidth is less than ideal).

FIGURE 8–7
Using Exchange as
an SMTP Backbone

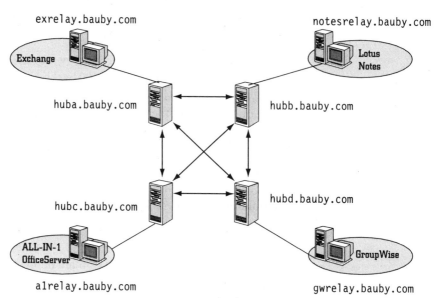

exrelay.bauby.com

notesrelay.bauby.com

huba.bauby.com   hubb.bauby.com

hubc.bauby.com   hubd.bauby.com

alrelay.bauby.com   gwrelay.bauby.com

Rerouting Messages on Domain Names

The *Routing* property page exposes the functionality that allows Exchange to reroute a message based on the domain name (as we've seen in Section 7.4.11). A prerequisite for such an environment is that users in each messaging system have some unique parts to their address that will identify them. It's probable that if you were building such an environment that you'd decide on a naming scheme similar to that shown in Table 8–1.

Each hub in the backbone takes on the responsibility for connecting to each end messaging system. In our environment it's only coincidental that we've got four hubs and four different messaging systems; it's unlikely that this is how it might turn out in practice, and generally we find that each hub is responsible for connecting to several different end messaging systems.

TABLE 8–1 Naming Structures for an SMTP Backbone

MESSAGING SYSTEM	DOMAIN NAME
Exchange	`@ex.bauby.com`
Lotus Notes	`@notes.bauby.com`
ALL-IN-1/OfficeServer	`@a1.bauby.com`
Novell GroupWise	`@gw.bauby.com`

How would messages be routed in such an environment? The important routing concept to follow is that an end messaging system never makes a direct connection to another end messaging system. Inter-end-messaging-system traffic is always routed through a backbone node. Further, it's common practice to only have one point of contact to each end messaging system, as shown in Figure 8–7. This means that any messages addressed to `first.last@gw.reuters.com` will always be routed through Hub D, irrespective of where its origin. This means that messages will always take two hops across the backbone to reach the destination environment. It's prudent to do this because we're implicitly putting in place a well-defined path for messages to follow. It's useful to control message flow in this for management, reporting, and troubleshooting reasons. You always know what path a message has taken to get to its destination so if there's a problem with its delivery, it's fairly straightforward to trace its progress. Furthermore, it's easy to trawl through message logs to generate usage tables for a particular environment, since all messages are routed through that one hub.

In terms of Exchange, the routing properties for each IMS connector would be slightly different, reflecting the hub node's juxtaposition to the end messaging system. In our environment, you could use a routing table like that in Table 8–2.

TABLE 8–2 IMS Connector Routing Definitions for Each Hub Server

HUB NODE	ROUTING INFORMATION	
	Domain	*Action*
huba.bauby.com	@ex.bauby.com	Route to: exrelay.bauby.com
	@notes.bauby.com	Route to: hubb.bauby.com

continued ▸

TABLE 8–2 IMS Connector Routing Definitions for Each Hub Server (continued)

HUB NODE	ROUTING INFORMATION	
huba.bauby.com (continued)	@a1.bauby.com	Route to: hubc.bauby.com
	@gw.bauby.com	Route to: hubd.bauby.com
hubb.bauby.com	@ex.bauby.com	Route to: huba.bauby.com
	@notes.bauby.com	Route to: notesrelay.bauby.com
	@a1.bauby.com	Route to: hubc.bauby.com
	@gw.bauby.com	Route to: hubd.bauby.com
hubc.bauby.com	@ex.bauby.com	Route to: huba.bauby.com
	@notes.bauby.com	Route to: hubb.bauby.com
	@a1.bauby.com	Route to: a1relay.bauby.com
	@gw.bauby.com	Route to: hubd.bauby.com
hubd.bauby.com	@ex.bauby.com	Route to: huba.bauby.com
	@notes.bauby.com	Route to: hubb.bauby.com
	@a1.bauby.com	Route to: hubc.bauby.com
	@gw.bauby.com	Route to: gwrelay.bauby.com

Rerouting Messages on Full Addresses

Most environments don't like to publicize their internal addressing structure. While addressing structures that contain some system-specific information make life easy for determining which messaging system a message should be routed to, the structure tends to complicate the address and generally make it look ugly. Usually, most organizations will settle on a flat address structure, often along the lines of the following:

```
firstname.lastname@organization.com
```

In our environment, it's likely that the decision makers will go for a naming structure that looks like:

```
firstname.lastname@bauby.com
```

which we'll call the *pretty address*. In common with most other companies, the visibility of the *expanded address*, perhaps one like:

```
firstname.last@notes.bauby.com
```

is to be avoided at all costs. Mail users, both internal to the Bauby Company and on any internal system, should never be presented with this style of address, either as a reply-to address for the originator of a message or in a directory service lookup. In common with external users, internal users should always be able to address their colleagues using a pretty address and be confident that somewhere on the backbone the address will be rewritten to an expanded address form suitable for routing. This constitutes the principle of *centralized naming,* which we'll cover in more detail.

We've already built our interoperability environment on the basis of Exchange making an intelligent routing decision using an expanded address. To complete the picture, we need some way for a user to send a message using a pretty address, have Exchange convert this to an expanded address, and subsequently route it.

In fact, Exchange is quite happy to do this using *custom recipients*. A custom recipient is just a means of providing an alias in the Exchange directory for an external recipient. It's simply a mapping between a display name and an e-mail address for an external user and it's common to find many of these in a typical Exchange environment. For example, you might have a custom recipient for *Bill Clinton* that maps to the SMTP alias *Bill.Clinton@whitehouse.gov*. But the custom recipient entry that we use to route messages based on a pretty address is slightly different insofar as it has two SMTP aliases and should look like the one shown in Figure 8–8.

FIGURE 8–8
Custom Recipient
Entry E-Mail
Addresses for
Alexandre Dumas

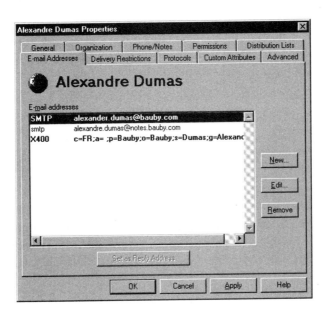

Close inspection of the custom recipient in Figure 8–8 shows that the entry has a primary SMTP alias of:

```
Alexandre.Dumas@bauby.com
```

This means that mail sent to this address will be picked up by this custom recipient.

FIGURE 8–9

Customer Recipient
Entry General Tab
for Alexandre
Dumas

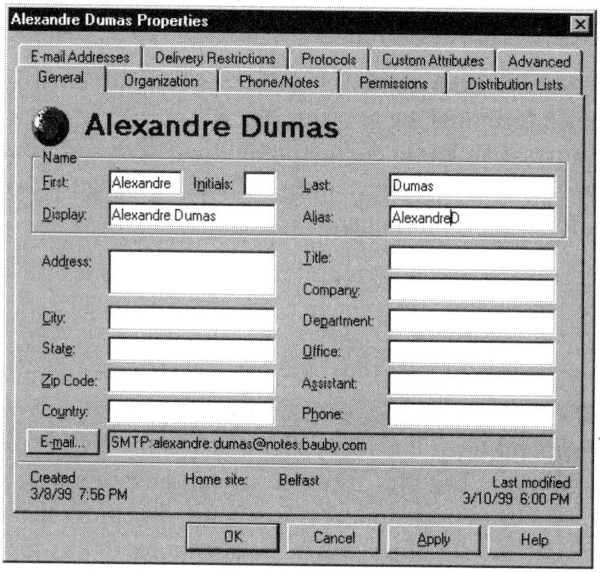

Looking carefully at Figure 8–9, you'll see that the SMTP address associated with this custom recipient is Alexandre.Dumas@notes.bauby.com. The net result of such settings means that a message can be routed into Exchange (through the IMS) using the secondary address:

```
Alexandre.Dumas@bauby.com
```

and upon receiving it, Exchange will immediately route it out again, but this time re-addressed to the value specified on the *General* tab:

```
Alexandre.Dumas@notes.bauby.com
```

Unfortunately, the settings that we constructed in Table 8–2 only apply to messages that are being routed into the IMS. We now find ourselves in the position of having a message within Exchange which is being routed out through an IMS. In this situation, we also need to have a set of address space definitions so that Exchange knows (from an internal perspective) which IMS to route the message to. It's likely that you'd set up address spaces on the various servers, costed as shown in Table 8–3.

For the purposes of the example, let's assume that each address space has a cost of 10 associated with it, and that all of the hub servers are in the same Exchange site. (Even if they are in different sites, the cost for the inter-site link is arbitrary and shouldn't interfere too much with the cost for the address space if it's kept to a low figure, perhaps less than five.)

TABLE 8–3   IMS Connector Address Space Costs for Each Hub Server

HUB NODE	ROUTING INFORMATION	
	Address Space	*Routing*
Huba	@ex.bauby.com	Cost 10 (local) to exrelay.bauby.com
	@notes.bauby.com	Cost 10 (remote) via hubb.bauby.com
	@a1.bauby.com	Cost 10 (remote) via hubc.bauby.com
	@gw.bauby.com	Cost 10 (remote) via hubd.bauby.com
Hubb	@ex.bauby.com	Cost 10 (remote) via huba.bauby.com
	@notes.bauby.com	Cost 10 (local) to notesrelay.bauby.com
	@a1.bauby.com	Cost 10 (remote) via hubc.bauby.com
	@gw.bauby.com	Cost 10 (remote) via hubd.bauby.com
Hubc	@ex.bauby.com	Cost 10 (remote) via huba.bauby.com
	@notes.bauby.com	Cost 10 (remote) via hubb.bauby.com
	@a1.bauby.com	Cost 10 (local) via a1relay.bauby.com
	@gw.bauby.com	Cost 10 (remote) via hubd.bauby.com
Hubd	@ex.bauby.com	Cost 10 (remote) via huba.bauby.com
	@notes.bauby.com	Cost 10 (remote) via hubb.bauby.com
	@a1.bauby.com	Cost 10 (remote) via hubc.bauby.com
	@gw.bauby.com	Cost 10 (local) via gwrelay.bauby.com

As you can see from Table 8–3, irrespective of which server the re-addressed message exists on, it will always get routed to the hub node nearest to the end mail environment. As well as specifying the address spaces on each IMS, the Routing properties for each IMS also need to be updated so that messages addressed to bauby.com are now routed inbound by the IMS.

Take the example of the Exchange user Edmond Dantès, who sends a mail to Alexandre.Dumas@bauby.com. When Edmond sends the message, it gets routed out from his Exchange environment via the exrelay.bauby.com server directly to the huba.bauby.com backbone server. The IMS accepts the message for Alexandre.Dumas@bauby.com and passes it through to Exchange where it is redirected to Alexandre.Dumas@notes.bauby.com. Exchange determines that this address space is serviced by hubb.bauby.com and the message is passed internally to this server. Upon receipt of the message, the IMS on hubb.bauby.com processes the message and delivers it to notesrelay.bauby.com.

Rewriting Addresses

As we've seen, the principle of routing mail on full addresses using custom recipients relies on Exchange's ability to rewrite addresses for the recipient of a message. However, we're also interested in understanding how Exchange can rewrite the address of the message originator.

This is straightforward if the sender of the message is an Exchange user. The IMS simply looks up the originator of the message in the directory and searches for the primary SMTP address of that user. When Exchange is the originating mail system this may serve our purposes, but if we are simply using Exchange as a backbone or relay service then the address rewriting process is slightly more complex. Exchange actually does provide a facility for rewriting originator addresses as well as recipient addresses, but this requires some modifications to the Windows NT Registry. We'll look some more at these Registry settings later.

Provide Redundant Connections to Other SMTP Systems

The Exchange backbone environment that we've outlined so far shows how straightforward it can be to build a backbone using Exchange servers and setting the appropriate costs on address spaces. In our example, we only created a single address space on each hub server for the primary mail environment to which that server was connected.

Some redundancy could be built into this backbone by having other hub servers cater for the same address space but with a higher cost. In the event that the most desirable hub server wasn't available, the higher cost server would come into play, acting as the hub server for that mail environment.

Converting and Relabelling Message Content

Unfortunately, this is one area where the Exchange IMS connector isn't replete with functionality. On occasion, it can be desirable to intercept messages as they go through a backbone and manipulate either the content of the message, its attachments, or merely just the tagging on those messages. The IMS, doesn't provide a great deal of flexibility for performing this kind of operation, so if this is a function you really must have, then you'll need to look at alternative SMTP backbone technologies.

8.3.2 Building Redundant SMTP Backbones

When organizations set out to build large-scale SMTP backbones to connect their messaging systems together, one of the most important factors in the design is the ability for the mail still to get through even if some of the systems in the backbone suffer a catastrophic failure.

There's little point in having a wonderfully functional and high performing environment linking thousands of users if a single failure on one disk brings mail transfer within the company to a sudden halt. There are, of course, many steps that the backbone designer can take when configuring individual systems to ensure protection against failure. Typically, these measures include RAID-based disk arrays, dual redundant disk controllers, redundant power supplies, and, if the operating system permits, clustering. But these measures only address disaster on the microscopic scale, where perhaps a component may fail. The backbone designer needs to take a macroscopic view as well, and take into account the repercussions that ensue when a whole building suffers a disaster or a major network link becomes unavailable.

In such circumstances, redundancy needs to be built into the architecture of the backbone itself. This implies multiple points of contact between the messaging systems being interconnected. Companies often deploy such backbones using interface points in major geographical regions. It's common to see backbones with three major sites: one in the United States, one in Europe, and one in Asia Pacific, but mere geography isn't always the driving factor. Network, management, and cost of operations are other contributors that affect the balance of the design. Although such an approach is costly (because you end up duplicating the environment a number of times), it's desirable because you end up with an infrastructure that supports higher levels of capacity and improved performance.

A Typical Design for a Globally Redundant Backbone

Using SMTP, it's very straightforward to build this kind of redundancy on a global scale. All that's needed is just a little creative thinking using MX records.

Let's take as an example a company called *Zeitgeist Information Ltd.* Zeitgeist has two mail environments: Exchange and Lotus Notes, with users spread all over the world. To provide reliable communications between the two environments, Zeitgeist has decided to put an SMTP backbone in place to link the environments, and for the backbone, it will use Innosoft's PMDF SMTP product. We'll analyze later some of the factors that led to this decision. Figure 8–10 shows a possible topology for the Zeitgeist backbone.

FIGURE 8–10
Zeitgeist's
Worldwide
SMTP Gateways

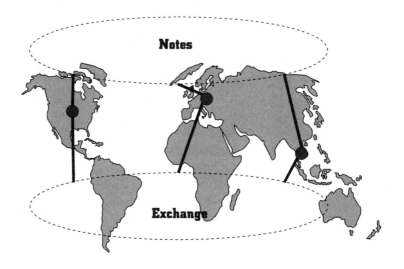

With a correct design, a backbone such as this provides two main features that any company may find useful:

1. **Localized gateway usage.** In the United States, when a Notes user sends to an Exchange user, the mail is routed through the local U.S. gateway. In Europe, when a Notes user sends to an Exchange user, the mail is routed through the local Europe gateway. And in Asia Pacific, the same local routing takes place.

2. **Global Failover.** Should the United States gateway fail, the Europe
or Asia Pacific gateway can take on the routing responsibility. Similar redundancy agreements exist for the Europe and Asia Pacific
gateways.

Let's look in detail at some of the construction parameters for this global
gateway environment.

There are three instances of the gateway located in the United States,
Europe, and Asia Pacific. Each gateway consists of three separate components: a dedicated IMS Connector server which is called the *EGATE* node, a
dedicated SMTP relay called the *CGATE* node, and a dedicated Notes SMTP
MTA server called the *NGATE* node. (The *EGATE*, *CGATE*, and *NGATE*
names are derived from *Exchange gateway*, *Center gateway*, and *Notes
gateway*.)

FIGURE 8–11
Zeitgeist
Backbone
Gateway
Components

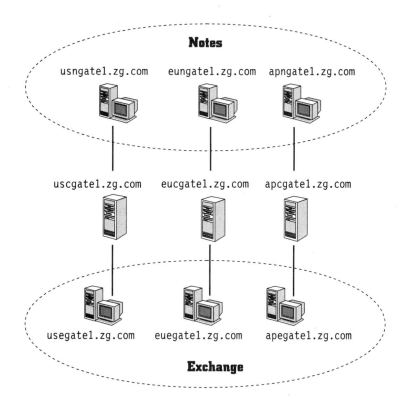

Simple Routing

In Figure 8–11, each gateway instance NGATE node connects directly to its partner CGATE node, which in turn connects to its partner EGATE node. Mail sent from Notes to Exchange is addressed as:

```
firstname.lastname@zeitgest.com
```

in line with the standard requirement to have a simple addressing structure. When the mail is relayed to the CGATE node, mandatory address translation takes place here which maps the address into a form that can enable a routing decision to be made. This form is as follows:

```
firstname.lastname@ex.zeitgeist.com
```

The CGATE system can route the mail directly to its partner EGATE system, which upon receipt of the message relays the mail to the required Exchange server. A similar routing process takes place for mail flow in the opposite direction.

Localized Connector Selection

Mail sent from one environment to the other is always routed via the *nearest* NGATE or EGATE system. For Notes, this can be implemented using *Connection Records* so that lowest cost SMTP MTA is always selected, unless availability problems prevent it. Similarly, connector scope and cost coupled with inter-site routing costs can be used within the Exchange environment to ensure that the optimal IMS Connector is always selected or an alternative used if connection problems dictate.

It's important to understand that only connection problems to a Notes SMTP MTA or Exchange IMS will induce rerouting within the native mail environment. You can read a connection problem to mean a failed network link to the SMTP component on the server or any inability to route messages to the server itself. In the case of Exchange for instance, if a message can be routed through to MTA on the server that hosts the IMS, problems with the IMS itself will not allow for rerouting (since the IMS is a store-based connector). These restrictions apply to Exchange's native Notes connector as well, and Notes itself exhibits this behavior.

Redundant Backbone Connections

For a truly redundant design it's imperative not only to provide failover from the end messaging system to the first point of contact with the backbone, but on all of the backbone components themselves. One of the benefits of using a pure SMTP environment is that MX records can be used to their fullest potential.

Each gateway in our environment must be configured to talk to its partner. For example, if we simply use the hostname of the CGATE component when configuring the NGATE system, we'll get no redundancy since the NGATE systems will always try to communicate directly with its continental CGATE partner. Using an MX record overcomes this because we can use different MX records for each instance of the gateway to reference each gateway component, as shown in Table 8–4.

TABLE 8–4 MX Record Definitions for the Zeitgeist Backbone Connections

GATEWAY INSTANCE	ROUTING INFORMATION		
	Component	*Points To*	*Which is an MX record defined as*
U.S.	Usngate1.zg.com	Uscgate.zg.com	Pref 10 uscgate1.zg.com
			Pref 20 eucgate1.zg.com
			Pref 30 apcgate1.zg.com
	Uscgate1.zg.com	Usngate.zg.com	Pref 10 usngate1.zg.com
			Pref 20 eungate1.zg.com
			Pref 30 apngate1.zg.com
		Usegate.zg.com	Pref 10 usegate1.zg.com
			Pref 20 euegate1.zg.com
			Pref 30 apegate1.zg.com
	Usegate1.zg.com	Uscgate.zg.com	Pref 10 uscgate1.zg.com
			Pref 20 eucgate1.zg.com
			Pref 30 apcgate1.zg.com
EU	Eungate1.zg.com	Eucgate.zg.com	Pref 10 eucgate1.zg.com
			Pref 20 uscgate1.zg.com
			Pref 30 apcgate1.zg.com
	Eucgate1.zg.com	Eungate.zg.com	Pref 10 eungate1.zg.com

continued ▸

TABLE 8–4 MX Record Definitions for the Zeitgeist Backbone Connections (continued)

GATEWAY INSTANCE	ROUTING INFORMATION		
	Component	*Points To*	*Which is an MX record defined as*
EU (continued)			Pref 20 usngate1.zg.com
			Pref 30 apngate1.zg.com
		Euegate.zg.com	Pref 10 euegate1.zg.com
			Pref 20 usegate1.zg.com
			Pref 30 apegate1.zg.com
	Euegate1.zg.com	eucgate.zg.com	Pref 10 eucgate1.zg.com
			Pref 20 uscgate1.zg.com
			Pref 30 apcgate1.zg.com
AP	Apngate1.zg.com	Apcgate.zg.com	Pref 10 apcgate1.zg.com
			Pref 20 eucgate1.zg.com
			Pref 30 uscgate1.zg.com
	Apcgate1.zg.com	Apngate.zg.com	Pref 10 apngate1.zg.com
			Pref 20 eungate1.zg.com
			Pref 30 usngate1.zg.com
		Apegate.zg.com	Pref 10 apegate1.zg.com
			Pref 20 euegate1.zg.com
			Pref 30 usegate1.zg.com
	apegate1.zg.com	apcgate.zg.com	Pref 10 apcgate1.zg.com
			Pref 20 eucgate1.zg.com
			Pref 30 uscgate1.zg.com

The net result of using connection definitions in this way is that you get quite a high degree of redundancy with respect to the links from one gateway component to another. In this environment, we always route messages through a CGATE system because special address rewriting can take place there, which we'll look at later.

A backbone such as this could withstand quite a number of system failures and still have messages delivered from one system to another. As an example, consider a message sent Exchange to Notes by a European user:

- The mail leaves the Exchange environment through the euegate1.zg.com server.

- It should get routed to the eucgate1.zg.com server, but if this is unavailable, it will get rerouted to the uscgate1.zg.com server.

- The address conversions take place and the message is then destined for the usngate1.zg.com server. Let's assume that this is unavailable.

- The next choice system is the eungate1.zg.com server, but let's assume this has failed too!

- The MX preferences suggest that the alternative route to Notes is through the apngate1.zg.com server, and the message will be routed this way.

In theory, the backbone environment shown in Figure 8–12, provide n^3 possible routes from source environment to destination environment, where n is the number of instances of the gateway.

FIGURE 8–12

Zeitgeist Backbone Gateway Components with Inherent Redundancy

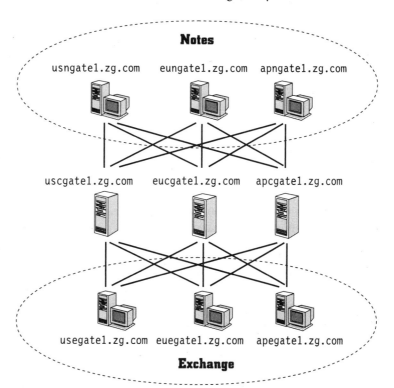

Up to two thirds of all the gateway components can be unavailable at any one time and mail will still be delivered. While such an architecture provides optimized routing for message delivery and higher overall throughput due to its multi-gateway nature, each gateway instance should be capable of supporting the full inter-system traffic load in the event that a significant number of other components are unavailable. If each instance isn't sized for the complete workload, then messages may be become significantly backlogged during degraded operation. This is one of the implementation tradeoffs that should be decided upon during a design phase if implementation costs are significant.

8.3.3 Centralized Addressing: Guaranteeing Uniqueness

We've already touched on the concept of centralized naming when we saw the common need of most organizations for a flat and unified addressing structure tempered with the need for an internal addressing format which makes message routing straightforward.

The backbone architectures that I've shown in Figure 8–7 and Figure 8–12 may look different in some respects, but they have much in common. What's especially relevant, from the perspective of centralized naming, is the fact that both topologies implement a shared address space model. The flexibility and redundancy in the message routing model that's shown in Figure 8–12 is only achievable because addressing information for mail is consistent across each of the CGATE systems. On the U.S. CGATE, messages addressed to:

```
Karen.Scott@zeitgeist.com
```

get rewritten to:

```
Karen.Scott@ex.zeitgeist.com
```

and exactly the same mapping takes place on both the European and Asia Pacific CGATE systems.

But to implement such a model requires some degree of sophistication. Guaranteeing uniqueness of mail addresses across multiple systems is no easy feat. The Exchange Administrator does this to some extent, and you can see it in action if you try to assign an SMTP address to a mailbox or custom recipient when that SMTP address is already assigned: you'll get an error message to tell you that the address is already in use by another user.

It's important to note though this uniqueness checking is only enforced by the Administrator program. There's no uniqueness checking intrinsic to the Exchange Directory schema itself for the SMTP mail address attribute which prevents duplication. If you load entries into the directory via the LDAP protocol and duplicate the SMTP address field, you'll get no warning or error message to indicate the gravity of your transgression. Similarly, if you add two users with the same SMTP address in different sites at the same time, they'll both appear in the Directory with a duplicate address when the next directory replication cycle completes.

So Exchange does go some way to enforcing unique addressing within its own environment, but obviously there's no way it can check other mail systems for a clash. In mixed environments, you can cut down on the likelihood of a name clash by using an internal address structure that includes an indication of the messaging system. In the case of the Zeitgeist organization, two users, both called *Colin Bateman,* would be uniquely identified with the SMTP expanded addresses:

```
Colin.Bateman@notes.zeitgeist.com,
```

and

```
Colin.Bateman@ex.zeitgeist.com
```

But this doesn't help us give unique pretty addresses to these users, since both would be known as:

```
Colin.Bateman@zeitgeist.com
```

To alleviate this problem, we'll have to take an approach whereby one user's address is differentiated from the other's. Using initials is the normal approach, and if this fails, appending a numeric identifier is usually acceptable.

Implementing this approach means a single authoritative source for generating unique SMTP addresses must be used. Typically this means employing a single authoritative directory culled from all of the other directory sources associated with each messaging environment. The single directory (more often than not an LDAP directory) can be used to store users' personal details and their SMTP address. In many environments an entry can be created for the user and a script of some kind run against the directory data to create a unique address. You can see an example of such a script in Appendix D. This is, of course, the essence of directory synchronization, which we'll discuss in detail in Chapter 9. Here we are brought to the very core of centralized addressing: a single or distributed (but consistent) database that maps pretty addresses to expanded addresses. This database allows all mail to be addressed, both externally and internally, in a flat and regular format (e.g., @zeitgeist.com) but converted and routed internally with an expanded format (e.g., @notes.zeitgeist.com).

However, this is only half of the problem. It's one thing to look up an address for an intended recipient of a message and map it from its pretty address to its expanded address, but the originator information on the message must be rewritten as well. Consider the situation where the Zeitgeist user Conor Brady sends a mail message to Karen Scott. When the message begins its journey, the originator and recipient information will read:

FROM: Conor.Brady@notes.zeitgeist.com
TO: Karen.Scott@zeitgeist.com

As it passes through the CGATE, the TO: address will get mapped through to its expanded format of:

TO: Karen.Scott@ex.zeitgeist.com

However, we also need to map the originator's address from its expanded form to its pretty form, so that when the message arrives at the intended recipient, the FROM: field reads:

FROM: Conor.Brady@zeitgeist.com

and is in line with our addressing requirements.

Exchange can offer this functionality by selecting one of the possible SMTP aliases as a reply-to address, but this doesn't help in mixed environments, where a decision on an addressing structure can't be made unilaterally. If you're connecting to another messaging environment through a firewall, you can usually enlist the services of the SMTP component of the firewall to flatten address structures. In these cases, firewalls usually just strip off extraneous information and leave a well-defined rightmost domain name, such as zeitgeist.com. While this may seem like a neat solution to the problem of creating pretty reply-to addresses, it's fraught with problems because it doesn't deal with name duplication, and it can easily produce an address that's ambiguous. The only real solution to this problem is to use a centralized database that takes care of reverse address mapping in the same way as forward addresses.

8.3.4   Forward and Reverse Address Rewriting Techniques

The mechanism and flexibility by which forward and address rewriting is achieved is, unsurprisingly, closely related to the technology that's used for the backbone environment. Although both Exchange and PMDF can provide this service, the richness of functionality offered by PMDF is worthy of careful consideration.

Using Exchange for Address Rewriting

We've already seen how Exchange can be used to perform forward address translation. The procedure for doing so is relatively simple. You create a custom recipient entry for the target recipient, assign an SMTP alias that matches the address that you're sending to (the pretty address), and set the custom recipient to redirect messages to the target address (the expanded address), as shown in Figure 8–8 and Figure 8–9.

Performing reverse address rewriting is slightly more complex. If you take another look at Figure 8–8, you can see that there are two values for the SMTP addresses, which relate to the primary and secondary SMTP addresses respectively, and are often represented as:

```
SMTP:  Alexandre.Dumas@bauby.com
smtp:  Alexandre.Dumas@notes.bauby.com
```

The difference here is subtle. These values tell Exchange that if it processes any mail and the originator address on the message is:

```
Alexandre.Dumas@notes.bauby.com
```

then this address should be rewritten as:

```
Alexandre.Dumas@bauby.com
```

as it leaves the Exchange IMS Connector. To get this to work, there are a couple of registry settings that need to manipulated. First, if it's not already there, you'll need to go the Registry key:

```
HKEY_LOCAL_MACHINE\SYSTEM\CurrentControlSet\Services\
MSExchangeIMC\Parameters
```

and set the entry:

```
Name:  AddressRewrite
Type:  REG_DWORD
Value: 1
```

This tells Exchange to use the values for the SMTP primary and secondary address to rewrite the RFC-821 From header. This is the originator's address on the envelope part of an SMTP message, and chances are you won't ever see this on a message unless you're looking at an SMTP log file.

To get the RFC-822 From field rewritten you'll need to set the following Registry key:

```
Name:  ResolveP2
Type:  REG_DWORD
Value: 64
```

Setting the value to 64 only resolves the RFC-822 From field, but there are a number of other header fields that can be rewritten as well if they're present. If you want to rewrite all of these headers, then you should set the value to 1. If you want to be selective for the headers that you'll rewrite, then refer to TechNet Knowledge Base Article Q174755, which describes each of the possible settings.

When the RFC-822 From field is resolved, two rewrites actually take place. The SMTP style address is rewritten with the values you've specified for the SMTP primary alias, but additionally, the RFC-822 Personal Name field is rewritten with the Display Name value of the custom recipient.

Exchange will process many fields when it parses the headers on a message, as well as just the originator address being written, and *sideways recipients* will also be rewritten. This means that when you receive a message, any other addresses on the TO: or CC: lines will also be rewritten so that expanded addresses will be replaced with pretty addresses. At no time should a user ever see an expanded address form in the header of any message.

In a normal Exchange environment (i.e., one that's hosting mailbox users and not one that's being used just for backboning, as in this example), setting the ResolveP2 Registry entry has an interesting effect. When mail is sent in through the IMS to a local Exchange mailbox recipient, the IMS will check for the presence of a custom recipient for the originator of the message. If one is found, the Personal Name and SMTP address of the sender, which would normally be displayed when the message is read, is overridden and the Display name of the custom recipient is shown instead. If you maintain a lot of custom recipients for external users that you frequently communicate with, it's smart to set this parameter and modify sender addresses so that they're more aesthetically pleasing.

Using an Exchange backbone to perform address translation certainly has its benefits if part of your organization already has an Exchange environment. It's a technology that you'll already be familiar with and thus training and management costs should be lessened. That's the positive side of using an Exchange backbone. As ever, there are some gloomier aspects to consider as well.

Because Exchange performs all of its address translations using custom recipients, this means that these are objects that you must manipulate in order to make modifications to addresses, add, or delete users. Custom recipients aren't the easiest objects in the world to tamper with in bulk, primarily because of how Exchange maintains them as part of the Directory. This means that any code or scripts that you use to manage the translation entries must deal with the Directory directly, either through the Administrator Import/Export feature, or using LDAP access. (We'll see later, when we discuss directory synchronization, what techniques can be used to perform this manipulation.)

Using PMDF for Address Rewriting

PMDF provides quite sophisticated mechanisms for address rewriting. Indeed, the whole concept of centralized addressing is at the core of the PMDF model of messaging, and modifying addresses both inbound and outbound through the PMDF MTA is easily achieved.

There is little doubt that PMDF provides a wealth of features in this area and many others relating to SMTP messaging. What follows here is only a sketch of a subset of PMDF functionality that's relevant to connecting different messaging systems together and perform address rewriting.

Simple Address Rewriting

Applying catch-all address rewrite rules is done using the core PMDF configuration file, `pmdf.cnf`.[*] For example, if Zeitgeist uses PMDF as a backbone to provide Internet connectivity to their mail systems and have their users referenced as:

```
firstname.lastname@zeitgeist.com
```

---

[*]   The complete pathname for this file differs according to implementation platform. For example, on the UNIX platform this file is correctly referenced to as `/pmdf/table/pmdf.cnf`, while on OpenVMS it's referenced as `PMDF_TABLE:PMDF.CNF`. For a full description of PMDF configuration you should check the PMDF documentation set, available from Innosoft.

they may also wish to provide routing capabilities for other forms of the address, such as us.zeitgeist.com, emea.zeitgeist.com, and ap.zeitgeist.com if they have gateway instances connecting their internal environment to the Internet in three geographical regions (United States, Europe-Middle East-Africa, and Asia Pacific).

Having these secondary forms of address can often be a useful mechanism for providing an unofficial address syntax that quickly and efficiently directs inbound Internet mail to a nearby gateway. When a message addressed like this reaches the PMDF system, rules in the configuration file can quickly normalize it to the standard zeitgeist.com format. Such a PMDF rule would simply look like this:

```
us.zeitgeist.com       $U@zeitgeist.com*
```

and normal address rewriting to an expanded form can then take place.

Rewriting Forward Addresses

Exchange uses a Custom Recipient entry to map a pretty address form to an expanded form. In effect, this is really a lookup to a database where the lookup is keyed on the pretty address and the expanded form is returned.

PMDF provides a similar facility using a number of approaches, the most flexible of which is the *Directory Channel*. A rule in the configuration file, like this one:

```
zeitgeist.com         $U%zeitgeist.com@DIRECTORY-DAEMON
```

instructs PMDF to direct any inbound messages addressed to

username@zeitgeist.com

for processing through a *Directory Daemon*. The Daemon is responsible for processing the address of the recipients on the message and rewriting them from their pretty form to their expanded form, if appropriate.

The Directory Daemon can consult a number of different databases to perform the translation, including an indexed sequential database and an LDAP or X.500 directory. The indexed sequential database (which PMDF refers to as a *crdb database*) represents the highest performing option and is probably the easiest to deal with. Directory entries are manipulated in a text

---

*   The $U term references the username, or left-hand-side of the @ sign.

file that bears the name of the domain for which the rewrites will be performed (e.g., `zeitgeist.com.txt`). Take a look at the file extract in Figure 8–13, which shows some entries in this file.

FIGURE 8–13
Directory Database
File Extract

```
Prosper.Merime      ProsperM@ex.zeitgest.com
Georges.Bizet       GeorgesB@ex.zeitgeist.com
Don.Jose            Don_Jose/AND/ES@notes.zeitgeist.com
Tatiana.Troyanos    Tatiana_Troyanos/MAD/ES@notes.zeitgeist.com
```

What this extract tells us is that any message addressed to an individual in the `zeitgeist.com` domain which matches on the left-hand-side of this file will be mapped to the addressed on the right-hand-side of the file. For example, mail sent to

```
Don.Jose@zeitgeist.com
```

is redirected to

```
Don_Jose/AND/ES@notes.zeitgeist.com
```

Once a text file has been constructed, a couple of PMDF commands are used to build the indexed sequential version of this file and the forward address mapping database is complete. The commands you'll need are platform specific, but on UNIX you can build the database using the following commands:

```
pmdf crdb –duplicates zeitgeist.com.txt /pmdf/directories/z.c.tmp
pmdf renamedb /pmdf/directories/z.c.tmp /pmdf/directories/zeitgeist.com
chown pmdf /pmdf/directories/zeitgeist.com.
```

These commands will build a temporary database from the text file, rename the temporary database (thus minimizing the amount of time that the database will be in an indeterminate state) and then set the appropriate protections on the file so that it's usable.

Building the file shouldn't take too long. A file with about 20,000 entries in it will take about fifteen seconds to build on the average UNIX platform.

Essentially this is the same mechanism that Exchange uses for address rewriting, but the ability to manipulate the data using just a simple text file is very appealing to the messaging integrator. Furthermore, for every domain that you wish to perform address rewriting against, you can create a separate instance of the directory database. These databases can be maintained by hand if the number of users in your mixed environment is low, but it's much more likely that you'll have an automated process for maintaining it. The mechanism that you'd use will probably be intimately linked with the directory synchronization process, and it's a straightforward matter to write a script file that will interrogate a central LDAP directory of all of your users and generate a directory file. (To make life easier for you, I've included a sample script for the Zeitgeist company which does just this in Appendix E.)

Rewriting Reverse Addresses

A very similar mechanism to that used for forward addresses is employed by PMDF for reverse address mapping. Again a text file is used to maintain the expanded address forms and map them to a pretty address form. As mail is processed through the PMDF MTA en route to its destination, PMDF looks up the originator and any other recipients for each instance of the message that it processes. If a match is found in the Reverse Database for an address, the original address is replaced with the new one. An example of a Reverse Database for the Zeitgeist environment is shown in Figure 8–14.

FIGURE 8–14   Reverse Database File Extract

```
ProsperM@ex.zeitgest.com  Prosper.Merime@zeitgest.com
GeorgesB@ex.zeitgeist.com  Georges.Bizet@zeitgest.com
Don_Jose/AND/ES@notes.zeitgeist.com  Don.Jose@zeitgeist.com
Tatiana_Troyanos/MAD/ES@notes.zeitgeist.com  Tatiana.Troyanos@zeitgeist.com
```

The Reverse Database file is very similar to the Directory Database file, but its implementation is slightly different. There's no reverse file specific to each domain being catered for; all reverse entries are located in the same file, called reverse.txt. Unlike the Directory Database, you can see from the file extract in Figure 8–14 that the complete pretty address needs to be specified, not just the username part. Since there is only one file used by the Reverse Database this is unsurprising: addresses could be reversed for multiple domains. The Reverse Database is also an indexed sequential format and it needs to be converted from its text representation into its database format before it can be used by PMDF. A similar set of commands is used for this task.

Controlling Localized Routing

The benefits of implementing a centralized naming policy in an integration environment are many. Mail routing is well defined across all platforms and users see a consistent addressing structure irrespective of their messaging environment. This is just how Nature intended it to be.

But there is one particular side-effect of centralized addressing that can be upsetting in some environments: When a message is received by a recipient in one particular environment, any other sideways recipients on that message will be displayed on the TO: or CC: with their pretty address format. By way of example, take a look at the message that's sent from Prosper Merime to Don Jose and Tatiana Troyanos in Figure 8–15.

FIGURE 8–15
Unlocalized Routing
with Centralized
Addressing

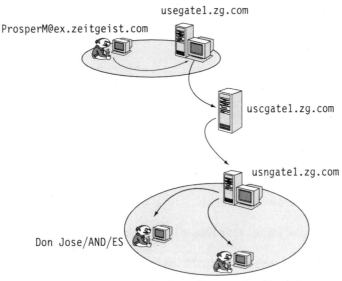

When the message is first sent from the Exchange environment, the originator's address is:

ProsperM@ex.zeitgeist.com

and it's addressed to two Notes recipients:

Don.Jose@zeitgeist.com,
Tatiana.Troyanus@zeitgeist.com

As the message is processed on the center system, where address rewriting takes place, for the instance of the message which is being delivered to Don Jose, the originator address is rewritten (by a reverse database) to:

Prosper.Merime@zeitgeist.com

And the recipient address for Don Jose is rewritten to:

```
Don_Jose/AND/ES@notes.zeitgeist.com
```

The address for the other recipient, Tatiana Troyanus is untouched by this process since this instance of the message is only processed for Don Jose.

As the message reaches the Notes SMTP MTA, `usngate1.zg.com`, the expanded address for Don Jose will be converted (depending on configuration settings) to a native Notes address, in the form:

```
Don Jose/AND/ES
```

While this is perfectly legal, think about what will happen when Don Jose replies to all recipients on this message. One instance of the reply message for Prosper Merime will be routed across the backbone, via the `uscgate1.zg.com` system to be delivered to Prosper Merime's Exchange mailbox—which is just what you'd expect. However, another instance of the message, the reply message to Tatiana Troyanus, will also be routed back up to the `uscgate1.zg.com` server where the address gets rewritten to its expanded form of:

```
Tatiana_Troyanus/MAD/ES@notes.zeitgeist.com
```

and it's then routed back into the Notes environment before it can be delivered to Tatiana Troyanus. The unpleasant side-effect of this otherwise perfect addressing scheme is the inefficient routing of a reply to a message that has traversed the backbone and has co-recipients in the same messaging environment. This is perfectly normal behavior for any form of backbone and in some cases won't cause a problem. If the network bandwidth between all of the messaging environments and the nearest backbone hub system is sufficient, then this may not be too much of an issue within your environment. However, if network bandwidth is an issue, or load on the hub server is high, or you just plain don't like the fact that replies take this "long way home," then you'll need to do something about it.

If you're using Exchange as a backbone in this instance, you'll be out of luck. In fact, most backbone systems can't perform any magic to alleviate this problem. Fortunately for us, PMDF isn't one of those systems.

The root cause of the problem in this example is that from Don Jose's perspective, Tatiana Troyanus's address is in its pretty form when it should really be in a native Notes format. If we were able to modify the reverse address settings for Tatiana Troyanus's as it passed through the backbone, perhaps we could make sure that that address was also converted from its pretty form to its expanded form and would thus be correctly handled by the Notes SMTP MTA. The only problem is that if we change the settings for this address in the Reverse Database then the address conversion for a message that's actually sent by Tatiana Troyanus won't be correctly reversed.

PMDF overcomes this problem by allowing you to specify different reverse mappings depending on where the message is going to. Without looking at too many of the details of how PMDF needs to be configured for this, enough information can be gleaned from looking at the more sophisticated Reverse Database file as shown in Figure 8–16, which is required.

FIGURE 8–16 Destination-Specific Reverse Database Extract File

```
Notes|ProsperM@ex.zeitgest.com  Prosper.Merime@zeitgest.com
Exch|Prosper.Merime@zeitgest.com  ProsperM@ex.zeitgest.com
#
Notes|GeorgesB@ex.zeitgeist.com  Georges.Bizet@zeitgeist.com
Exch|Georges.Bizet@zeitgeist.com  GeorgesB@ex.zeitgeist.com
#
Notes|Don.Jose@zeitgeist.com  Don_Jose/AND/ES@notes.zeitgeist.com
Exch|Don_Jose/AND/ES@notes.zeitgeist.com  Don.Jose@zeitgeist.com
#
Notes|Tatiana.Troyanos@zeitgeist.com  Tatiana_Troyanos/MAD/ES@notes.zeitgeist.com
Exch|Tatiana_Troyanos/MAD/ES@notes.zeitgeist.com  Tatiana.Troyanos@zeitgeist.com
```

What can we tell from this file? Looking at the database entries for Prosper Merime, the Exchange user, the following rewrites will be performed:

- When a message is sent by Prosper Merime to a Notes user, the Notes-specific mapping is used (the one preceded by `Notes|`) and Prosper's expanded address will be rewritten to his pretty name.

- When Prosper is a co-recipient on a message that's sent to another Exchange user, the message will be sent towards Exchange and thus the Exchange-specific mapping is used (the one preceded by `Exch|`). In this instance the Prosper's pretty name is converted to his expanded address.

The number of reverse mappings that you need to maintain for each user is directly proportional to the number of messaging systems you connect with your backbone. For instance, if you had five different messaging systems, then you'd need five address mappings for each user.

The concept of destination-specific address mapping is a little intimidating at first, but once understood, it becomes obvious that it's a very powerful tool indeed. Many mixed messaging environments have strict requirements for address mappings, and the flexibility that's available with PMDF for specific addressing in this way can be indispensable.

Managing such a file by hand obviously isn't feasible, especially when many hundreds or thousands of users are involved. But in the same way that a complex Directory Database can be built automatically from a central LDAP directory, so too can a complex Reverse Database like this. You can find a sample script to build such a file for the Zeitgeist environment in Appendix E.

8.3.5   Modifying MIME Tags for Messages in Transit

As well as rewriting addresses for originators and recipients of messages as they pass across a backbone, there is occasionally a requirement to modify the content on messages. At its very fundamental level, we may find that compound messages have incorrect MIME tags on their attachments for one reason or another. At the most extreme level, it's possible that the actual content type of the attachments may be unacceptable to the destination mail system. To cope with this, on the backbone we need some mechanism to be able to tamper with either the message tags or with the content.

Dealing with incorrect tagging on messages usually presents one of the most significant problems that a messaging integrator needs to deal with. It's common to see messages traverse a backbone with attachments whose integrity is preserved between systems but which are incorrectly tagged and can't be easily read by the recipient. How many times have you been frustrated when you've received a message with an attachment labeled ATT1.UNK and you've then had to go through the process of exporting it to your desktop and associating an application with it before you can read it? Some messaging clients are extra-smart and use file sniffing technology to determine the file type of an attachment when you attempt to open it if it's not correctly tagged. Although this is useful, it's a case of cure rather than prevention and it's not a feature that you can rely on to be available for all client systems.

Tagging problems crop up in two forms: filenames and MIME tags. The nature of the tagging issue determines the lengths that you must go to in order to compensate for it. Most messaging clients, Exchange and Outlook are no exception, rely on the filename type suffix of the attachment in order to determine how to deal with it when you double-click on it. Remember that the MIME header for a message can include the filename of the attachment so it's a relatively easy task for the IMS or any other SMTP/MIME system to preserve this information and present it to the user as the filename for the attachment.

Dealing with Incorrect Filenames

Occasionally, either the filename may not be supplied or it may not be meaningful to the system on which the message is being received. For example, Compaq's Message Router, which can provide messaging transport services for OfficeServer or MailWorks, doesn't have any facility for storing the filename of an attachment. Similarly, consider what happens when you send an attachment with a long filename (including spaces) from your Windows NT workstation to a mail client on UNIX. How useful is that filename information to a UNIX messaging client? In this sense, the value of a filename in a mixed messaging environment is rather subjective.

More information on the type of the attachment is also maintained in the MIME header. For example, a Word document should be tagged as APPLICATION/MSWORD, but this is usually only meaningful to the messaging server on SMTP gateway and generally never interpreted by messaging clients (with the exception of POP3 and IMAP4 clients). This information can be very useful, though, in circumstances where the filename of the attachment is incomplete. In these cases we can generally use the MIME information to reconstruct part of the file name. Clearly we can't reconstruct all of the filename, but the part we're most interested in is the file type and typically almost all SMTP/MIME gateways have a set of tables that map MIME types to file extensions.

Exchange can do this reconstruction by using a setting in the Registry. By default, the IMS will maintain the filename extension on any message that it receives inbound, but this behavior can be overridden. On previous versions of the IMS, there was a separate property page for MIME types which mapped tags to filename extension values. These mappings have now been relocated with the IMS and are to be found by selecting the *Properties* of the *Protocol* object within *Configuration* in the Exchange Administrator. If a message should be received from a remote system and the filename extension is missing, you can insist that the IMS inspect the MIME type tag for this message and reconstruct the extension. To do this, you'll need to visit the following Registry location:

```
HKEY_LOCAL_MACHINE\SYSTEM\CurrentControlSet\Services\
MSExchangeIS\ParametersSystem\InternetContent
```

and set the value:

```
Name:  RemapExtension
Type:  REG_DWORD
Value: 2
```

This instructs the IMS to provide a file extension (based on the MIME type) to any attachment that doesn't already have one. Setting this value to 1 will always remap the extension, irrespective of what's already there. This value isn't to be recommended since it does little to honor the filename information provided by the originating system, but in some environments its use may be desirable. (Setting the value to 0 disables its use altogether.)

Dealing with Incorrect MIME Tags

So far we've discussed only the use of the attachment filename and how we could reconstruct it should something have gone awry. However, in some environments we may also be interested in inconsistencies in the MIME tags on messages as well. Although all of the official MIME tags should be registered and maintained by the IANA, it's still common to see messages tagged incorrectly.

The most obvious example is to see messages still being tagged as APPLI-CATION/OCTET-STREAM (the catch-all binary tag) whenever a valid MIME tag for that content type exists. Other examples include the Lotus Notes SMTP MTA 4.6.2, which tags Excel documents as APPLICATION/MXEXCEL when the correct tag should be APPLICATION/VND.MS-EXCEL. Even the Exchange IMS V5.5 breaks the rules by tagging Access files as APPLICATION/MSACCESS when no MIME type is actually registered for it.

These are clear deficiencies of the originating messaging systems and we may or may not have some control over it. If the originating system is part of your environment and connects to your backbone, the most obvious way to deal with the problem is to modify the MIME tables so that the correct values are sent. However, if you don't have control over those remote systems or don't wish to interfere with their settings (to ease any upgrade fears), then it's possible, with PMDF at least but not with Exchange, to retag the messages as they pass along the backbone. Consider the following example set of PMDF relabelling commands:

```
out-channel=Exch; in-type=application; in-subtype=octet-stream;
in-parameter-name-0=name; in-parameter-value-0=*.doc;
out-type=application; out-subtype=msword; relabel=1
```

These commands will examine messages passing through the backbone destined for Exchange (out-channel=Exch). If the message is received with a MIME tag of APPLICATION/OCTET-STREAM but the filename extension is determined to be of type .DOC, then this file is relabeled to have a new set of MIME tags for APPLICATION/MSWORD.

Clearly this is a very powerful tool. PMDF's relabelling facilities allow you to deal with almost all of the MIME tags associated with a message, so quite complex mappings can be performed. Some SMTP instances will also provide application version information in the MIME header (e.g., Word V4, Word V5), which is also available for interpretation. Being able to interpret the version information means you could apply your own private MIME tags to messages within your environment to aid interoperability where mixed versions of an application are in use. For example, if your environment was using two different versions of Word you could define MIME tags for APPLICATION/X-MSWORDV6 and APPLICATION/X-MSWORDV7 when messages get sent between systems. This may allow you to go some way to identify the Word version to the recipient of the message. This would be useful in the situation where the recipient of the message used Word V6 but received a Word V7 document. At least they'd know what the problem was when Word reports an error on attempting to read the document.

Dealing with Message Content

Generally it's a bad idea to interfere with message content as a message passes across a backbone. In most cases it is both right and proper to preserve the integrity of the message and be faithful to the wishes of the originator of the document. Content conversion can usually produce unwanted results since conversions can be lossy, and context and information can be altered. Equally undesirable is the effect of reconverting documents to their original format when they are being sent back to the originator. This can produce much confusion since it's likely that content and geometry of the document will have been altered in some way. Unless both parties know that conversions have taken place, much discussion can result.

But if specific circumstances dictate that only certain attachment types are valid for one of the messaging systems in your environment, it is possible to use PMDF to invoke a converter to convert the unacceptable content type to something useful to the recipient. For example, let's say you had a group of users on a VT-based messaging system that could only read text documents but not complex formats. The following PMDF conversion command (on UNIX) might cause Word documents to be converted to text:

```
in-chan=VTLegacy; part-number=1; in-type=application; in-subtype=msword;
service-command="/pmdf/bin/convert.sh $INPUT_FILE $OUTPUT_FILE"
```

It's important to understand that PMDF doesn't supply a full suite of conversion tools, but many are commercially available (from Keypak, for example) and can be easily integrated into a PMDF implementation.

8.3.6   Balancing the Load for Outbound Messages

The topology and size of your Exchange environment may well dictate how many connection points that you have between Exchange and your own backbone or to the Internet. Unless your Exchange environment is quite small and restricted to just one location, it's highly unlikely that you'll maintain just a single IMS Connector. What's much more likely is that you'll have multiple points of connection to an SMTP, as in the example of the Zeitgeist Company, which maintains three connection points.

We've already discussed mechanisms for controlling access to IMS Connectors which include connector scope, routing costs, and address space restrictions. Your task as a messaging system designer will be to tailor these settings to match the requirements for your environment, influenced by other factors such as site design, bandwidth, redundancy, and cost.

In the case of the Zeitgeist environment, it's likely that the outbound routing of messages from Exchange to the SMTP backbone should always be through the nearest IMS Connector. For a large Exchange design this is usually most easily catered for using costs for site connectors and the IMS itself.

The topology shown in Figure 8–17 caters for this reasonably well. Let's assume that the aim is to always use the nearest IMS for outbound message processing in a geographical region, but if that IMS isn't reachable then an alternative should be selected. The costing/site model shown here should facilitate this requirement. Let's say that we're sending mail from Asia Pacific Site 1. The local IMS has a cost of 2 so this will be selected. Mail sent from A.P. Site 2 will also use the A.P. IMS connector, since the cumulative cost to reach it is 12. Other regional Exchange sites could similarly make use of the A.P. IMS connector in a preferential fashion if they connected in this way. In the event that the A.P. IMS connector should become unavailable, the next nearest IMS connector to be selected would be the E.U. connector with a cumulative cost of 57 from A.P. Site 1 and 47 from A.P. Site 2. And in the worst case scenario, the U.S. IMS connector could be selected at a cost of 62 and 52 from A.P. Site 1 and A.P. Site 2 respectively.

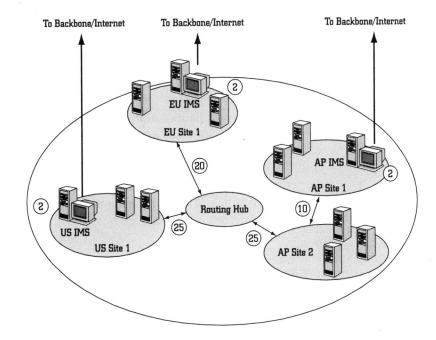

FIGURE 8–17
Multiple IMS
Connection
Points

Such a costing model makes a number of assumptions of course. This particular model assumes that the European location is the natural hub of the network and that's why the E.U. IMS connector is cheaper than the U.S. IMS connector from the Asia Pacific perspective. We're also assuming that no other major factors are influencing the Exchange routing design, but obviously some factors need to be accounted for in any major design. The use of a routing hub, or central Exchange backbone, makes sense for global deployments and helps to provide the routing flexibility in the Exchange environment. We're also assuming that with the Asia Pacific environment, Exchange sites are directly interconnected, but there's nothing to stop the use of regional hubs and still provide the same flexibility in the overall routing architecture.

To have the same localized outbound delivery and redundancy would be considerably more difficult to achieve using address spaces or connector scopes, but certainly some degree of this could be achieved. This is very much a simplistic view of using the IMS connector. Your environment may dictate that a larger number of IMSs are in use, but the overriding design feature should always be for the closest IMS to be selected.

8.3.7   Balancing the Load for Inbound Messages

Implementing a number of Exchange IMS connectors for outbound message processing and having a particular Exchange site or server maintain an affinity with a particular IMS connector is relatively easy to do using costs and routing models. Clearly these are models over which you have some control. On the other hand, routing messages inbound from the Internet to an Exchange environment, or any internal SMTP environment for that matter, and optimizing their direction, is considerably more complex. The problems stem from the nature of the SMTP address in use, and typically the shorter, prettier address is problematic because it doesn't contain any clue to indicate to which IMS connector it should be routed. Consider a mail from the Internet addressed to:

```
Don.Jose@zeitgeist.com
```

While we can certainly have MX records that indicate which IMS connectors to contact for this address, there's no way that we could know how to route the message directly to the IMS closest to this user. Unfortunately, there's no brilliant solution to this problem, but there are four different techniques that can be used smooth the bumps.

Splitting the Address Space

Consider this addressing scheme for the Zeitgeist Company environment, as shown in Figure 8–17. If we choose a scheme that includes some geographical information, so that users are addressed as:

```
firstname.lastname@us.zeitgeist.com
firstname.lastname@eu.zeitgeist.com
firstname.lastname@ap.zeitgeist.com
```

then these addresses can be easily resolved to determine which IMS connector they should route. We could simply use MX records that look like these:

```
us.zeitgeist.com.    IN    MX 10    usegate1.zg.com.
eu.zeitgeist.com.    IN    MX 10    euegate1.zg.com.
ap.zeitgeist.com.    IN    MX 10    apegate1.zg.com.
```

This doesn't really provide any redundancy into the design should one of the IMS connectors become unavailable, so it would be wise to define secondary IMS servers for each of the MX records. In this case, the records would look like this:

```
us.zeitgeist.com.    IN    MX 10    usegate1.zg.com.
                     IN    MX 20    euegate1.zg.com.
                     IN    MX 30    apegate1.zg.com.
eu.zeitgeist.com.    IN    MX 10    euegate1.zg.com.
                     IN    MX 20    usegate1.zg.com.
                     IN    MX 30    apegate1.zg.com.
ap.zeitgeist.com.    IN    MX 10    apegate1.zg.com.
                     IN    MX 20    euegate1.zg.com.
                     IN    MX 30    usegate1.zg.com.
```

Using this approach, inbound mail from the Internet is always routed directly to the IMS connector nearest to the recipient of the message, and there's redundancy built into the MX records so that delivery can always fail over to another IMS server. If Zeitgeist had any concerns about the available bandwidth on their internal network, especially with messaging traffic between the major continental land masses, then this approach is without doubt the most appealing.

But if there is a downside to this approach; it is that most organizations prefer to go with an addressing scheme that omits the geographical information. It may also be difficult to implement from an internal perspective if you're using a backbone and have a number of other messaging systems connected to it. In this case, it may be harder to determine the location of each user and thus provide them with an optimized SMTP address. However, if sensible naming structures have been used for the messaging servers, then it may well be quite straightforward to determine this information. Fortunately, for Exchange users, Exchange sites will probably be located within regions and Site Addressing properties can be used to generate meaningful addresses.

Use Primary and Secondary MX Hosts

If there is an overwhelming desire to maintain a flat and simple addressing structure, such as:

```
firstname.lastname@zeitgeist.com
```

then two approaches are available for controlling the flow of inbound messages. The first of these approaches is to select a primary location for receiving inbound mail and have the other locations only act as backups. In our example for Zeitgeist, it would be prudent to select the European location to be the primary recipient for mail since it is the physical hub of the network. In this case, we could define the following MX records:

```
zeitgeist.com.        IN    MX 10      euegate1.zg.com.
                      IN    MX 20      usegate1.zg.com.
                      IN    MX 20      apegate1.zg.com.
```

This is certainly the approach taken by many large organizations today and it does have its benefits. Using a single primary interface to the Internet makes management and problem tracking more straightforward, and the simpler addressing scheme is easier to manage and pleasing to the eye. However, this approach doesn't do anything to help balance the load of inbound messages across multiple servers, and the single euegate1.zg.com server must be able to handle the entire messaging load. Many larger companies that expect many tens or hundreds of thousands of messages per day will use multiple servers at a single location to compensate for this. If that's the case, the MX record definitions that you'll need to make may look like these:

```
zeitgeist.com.        IN    MX 10      euegate1.zg.com.
                      IN    MX 10      euegate2.zg.com.
                      IN    MX 10      euegate3.zg.com.
                      IN    MX 10      euegate4.zg.com.
                      IN    MX 20      usegate1.zg.com.
                      IN    MX 20      apegate1.zg.com.
```

This approach will make extensive use of the internal network to route messages received centrally, so you need to be sure that your network is optimized for this type of message flow if you implement this approach. Using a single location to receive incoming mail also introduces a number of other concerns. Apart from optimizing your internal network so that it's capable of dealing with large volumes of messages fanning out from one location, you should also be sure that your Internet Service Provider is capable of providing you with an Internet connection with sufficient bandwidth to cope with your expected traffic flow. The availability of high bandwidth connections is typically one reason why many multinational companies tend to locate their primary Internet connections in the United States, but the situation in Europe is improving all the time. But don't just stop there. Looking further than your connection to the ISP, you should also look at the connectivity that your ISP has to the nearest Internet hub. It may be possible for your ISP to provide you with a 2Mb/s connection, but they may also be providing this same bandwidth to many hundreds of other customers. If the ISP itself only has a 50Mb/s link to the nearest Internet hub, then you may find yourself with a bottleneck that's outside of your control.

Similarly, if you're using ATM to connect to your ISP, make sure that the service you buy relates to the Committed Information Rate (CIR) and not just the capacity figure.

Use Equal Cost MX Records

Using equal cost MX records should balance the load across all of your IMS connectors, the definitions for which should look like this:

```
zeitgeist.com.     IN    MX 10      euegate1.zg.com.
                   IN    MX 10      usegate1.zg.com.
                   IN    MX 10      apegate1.zg.com.
```

The theory, in this case, states that a sending SMTP system should have three equal cost MX records returned to it and one of the hosts should randomly be selected to receive the mail. While the load is balanced across multiple hosts, and the potential of a bottleneck between the IMS and the ISP, or even at the ISP is reduced, this approach doesn't help ease the burden on your internal network. Given the random nature of the MX record selection, a mail sent to the A.P. IMS Connector has a 66 percent probability that it should be routed to either the E.U. or U.S. Exchange environments, so the net utilization of the internal network remains the same as the approach using just a single location to receive mail.

Actually, this approach has another twist associated with it. While the theory suggests that sending SMTP systems should randomly select a host from the list of MX records returned, many systems don't implement this properly and simply select the first host in the list. Clearly this is something that you have no control over since it's a defect in the implementation of other SMTP systems. But it can lead to a situation where the first host in the list of MX records gets a higher percentage of messages passed to it than the other systems. If you do implement this mechanism, you should carefully monitor the messaging loads on all servers and be prepared to improve the configuration of the de facto primary IMS server if it becomes overloaded.

Use Round Robin DNS

An alternative approach to using the potentially flawed equal-cost MX record mechanism to load-balance messaging throughput is to use *round robin DNS*. To implement this approach, a single MX record is defined as follows:

```
zeitgeist.com.     IN    MX 10      mail.zg.com.
```

which points to a generic host name, `mail.zg.com`, that is to receive mail for this domain. The generic host name is further defined by three Address records that all point to different TCP/IP addresses:

```
mail.zg.com.        60        IN        A  17.129.12.10
mail.zg.com.        60        IN        A  17.130.128.63
mail.zg.com.        60        IN        A  17.12.2.4
```

where

17.129.12.10 is the TCP/IP address of `euegate1.zg.com`

17.130.128.63 is the TCP/IP address of `usegate1.zg.com`

17.12.2.4 is the TCP/IP address of `apegate1.zg.com`

I've specified an explicit time-to-live value of 60 seconds on the Address records, so that if they do get cached on a nameserver that doesn't support the round robin scheme, they'll get timed out quickly.

With this mechanism, only a single MX record is provided to the sending SMTP system, but when the TCP/IP address of the host is resolved, the DNS nameserver rotates the address values that it returns. In this way, DNS guarantees that the three IMS mail hosts are cycled through and used equally for receiving inbound mail. You'll need to be running a version of DNS which supports round robin (BIND 4.9.3 or higher) but using this approach means that you take control for cycling through the mail systems: you're not at the mercy of the sender's SMTP implementation. Of all the approaches, this one balances mail volumes best. Whatever approach you take, be sure to check that the ISP you select has sufficient bandwidth back to the Internet for your expected message traffic volume.

8.4   Moving Users between Servers

Moving users between one server and another is a relatively straightforward task, at least from the point of view of moving accounts and mailbox data. However, if you need to maintain SMTP address information for the users, then you'll need to be careful about the sequence of operations for the move so that no mail is lost and no nondelivery notifications are generated.

Consider the example of moving users from one Exchange server with its own IMS, where the users were referenced as:

```
firstname.lastname@us.bauby.com
```

to another server, where the mail addresses are, by default:

```
firstname.lastname@fr.bauby.com
```

In our example, the original server (which we'll call USEXC1) on which these users were located will be decommissioned, and as part of the migration to the new server (which we'll call FREXC1) the MX records that referenced the original server will be repointed to the new system.

What steps should you take as part of the move to ensure the smoothest possible migration?

- The IMS on the new FREXC1 system should be configured so that the Routing properties now accept us.bauby.com as well as fr.bauby.com.

- Migrate the mailboxes from the old server, USEXC1, to the new server, FREXC1, but keep the old IMS in place so that it can still accept messages for these mailboxes. The mailbox migration should be phased, with users moving over to the new server in groups.

- Before the migration of each group, you should suspend the operation of the IMS until the group migration is completed, and then ensure that directory replication has taken place between the two servers before the IMS is started up again. Controlling the migration in this way means that there's no chance of being caught in a no-man's land where the original IMS is temporarily unable to identify the intended recipient of the message.

- When all users have been migrated, you can change the value on the MX record for us.bauby.com so that it now points to the new FREXC1 server. Once you make the changes to the MX record, it will take some time for other servers on the Internet to be aware of the new value. Other DNS servers may well have cached the value of the MX record, and depending on the configuration of your DNS, it can take around twelve hours for the old value to become invalid. Only after the old setting has timed out, is it possible to decommission the USEXC1 IMS.

8.5   Delivery Notifications

The behavior of delivery notification requests in the mixed messaging world is very difficult to predict. What we can be pretty sure of is that when a message is sent between systems, either to or from Exchange, nondelivery notifications will be generated if the message fails to be delivered.

For positive delivery notifications, two methods are generally used on the Internet. Older systems rely on a field in the header of an SMTP message to request a delivery notification, so you might see a field that looks like this:

```
Return-receipt-to: Tommy.Byrne@compaq.com
```

SMTP implementations should be able to interpret this correctly and generate a notification message to indicate that the message was successfully delivered. However, not all SMTP messages *do the right thing* when they receive such headers, and often you'll find that delivery notification requests like this are ignored.

In an effort to improve the rather sporadic handling of SMTP delivery notifications, several RFCs[*] have been defined which dictate a new mechanism for notification handling. These RFCs, commonly referred to as the NOTARY recommendations, outline a strict mechanism for notification request handling.

Essentially, when a NOTARY-aware SMTP system connects to another SMTP system, it should check for the presence of the DSN keyword in response to the EHLO keyword. If the keyword is present, the originating mail can request a NOTARY delivery notification when specifying the recipients of a message. For example, the following the SMTP command:

```
RCPT TO:<Frank.Clonan@compaq.com> NOTIFY=SUCCESS, FAILURE, DELAYED
```

instructs the receiving SMTP system to generate a delivery notification if the message is successfully delivered, not delivered, or if there is a delay in its processing. (Any subset of these conditions is also a valid request.)

If the receiving SMTP system can't accept NOTARY notification requests, then the sending systems should indicate to the message originator that it relayed the message to an non–NOTARY-aware SMTP system.

Exchange indicates support for the NOTARY recommendations since it presents the DSN keyword, but you'll find mixed results when it's used in a very heterogeneous environment. From an originating point of view, the IMS uses both the NOTARY notification mechanism and the Return-receipt-to: field in the message header when a message is sent with a deliv-

---

[*]   These RFCs are: RFC-1891: SMTP Service Extension for Delivery Status Notifications; RFC-1892: The Multipart/Report Content Type for the Reporting of Mail System Administrative Messages; RFC-1893: Enhanced Mail System Status Codes; and RFC-1894: An Extensible Message Format for Delivery Status Notifications.

ery notification request. From a consultant's perspective, it's best to set customer/user expectations pretty low with respect to the level of integration that can be achieved for delivery notifications.

8.6   Read Notifications

If delivery notification request handling is poorly implemented across different mail system platforms, then read notification request handling can be considered to be even worse. Many systems implement read notification requests using a proprietary mechanism, but there is an RFC specification, RFC-2298, that defines a mechanism for inter-system working.

Similar to the older mechanism used for return receipts, RFC-2298 uses the `Disposition-notification-to:` fields in the header of an SMTP message. Upon receiving a message with such a header, the recipient's mail system should respond with a mail message indicating the actions that have been performed on the message. Typically, the response will indicate that the message was *displayed*, or some other processing took place on it.

The IMS's support of RFC-2298 is poor, and no standard means of ensuring the integrity of read notifications between Exchange and non–Exchange platforms is available. As is the case for delivery notifications, customer/user expectations for the inter-working of read notifications should be set very carefully indeed when a multitude of different system types are involved.

8.7   Time Synchronization

Like a forgotten relation at Christmas time, time synchronization is almost always overlooked in a messaging integration project. Actually, there is a great value to be had from ensuring that system clocks on different messaging servers, gateway systems, and backbone nodes are all pretty much in agreement on the real time.

As messages pass from one system to another, over X.400, SMTP, or any protocol, the systems involved in the transfer, stamp the message with the current time. Amongst other times, the timestamps on the message are useful in the event that something goes wrong with the delivery of a message and you have to trace back through the route that the message took in order to identify the problem. Scanning through mail log files to monitor the path of a message as it moves from one system to another is also difficult. A system that's sending the message may indicate that it passed the message off at say, 10:15 p.m., yet when you look at the log files on the receiving system, there's no sign of the message being received at that time because the clocks are off by a few minutes.

Synchronizing time within a Windows NT environment can be achieved using the built-in time synchronization feature. If you've got a single NT system from which you want to synchronize all other NT systems, you can schedule a batch job to run on each NT computer that executes the following command:

```
NET TIME \\<computername> /SET
```

This at least will synchronize all NT systems from one definitive NT time source, but in a mixed messaging environment many different platforms can often be involved. And it's the very fact that many different systems are involved that the time on all of the different systems should be regulated. To synchronize time between multiple platforms, you'll probably need to use products that adhere to the *Network Time Protocol* (*NTP*). NTP is defined in RFC-1129 (Internet Time Synchronization: Network Time Protocol) and it defines a mechanism for synchronizing system clocks on different computers.

A number of computers on the Internet set the time on their systems from precision clock devices or use radio clocks to get the real time from an official source. These systems are know as *Tier 1 time servers* and they act as NTP servers to other systems known as *Tier 2 servers.* The Tier 1 servers usually have access restricted to them so that only Tier 2 servers can connect and request the right time, but Tier 2 servers are usually able to receive synchronization requests from just about anyone.

For example, I synchronize the clock on my internal system with a Tier 2 server that's hosted within Compaq. When the synchronization job runs, I see the following messages:

```
connecting to usno.pa-x.dec.com using SNTP
resolved address (204.123.2.72)
received time (ping 600 ms), error -90 ms
Monday, January 11, 1999 09:17:22
```

In any sizeable environment, you could do worse than to dedicate one small system to synchronize its clock with a Tier 2 server, and have this local system act as the definitive time source for your complete environment. NTP software exists[*] (much of it freeware or shareware) for almost all oper-

---

[*] You can find more information on NTP Time Synchronization software at:
    http://www.eecis.udel.edu/~ntp.

ating system platforms so there's no reason why your UNIX or NT systems that either make up or connect to your messaging backbone couldn't have their clocks synchronized by requesting the right time from your local time server.

8.8   Virus Checking

Virus checking should be performed at any point in your messaging environment where there is an external connection to another messaging system. A number of virus checking products exist, some specifically for Exchange (which connect to the Information Store) while others are more generic and can be integrated into any SMTP messaging environment. For the greatest flexibility, and to reduce all fears about interoperability with Exchange versions (after upgrades and service packs), I tend to prefer those virus checkers that operate at the pure SMTP level.

Apart from the obvious features of a virus checking system, there are a few other aspects of such programs that can typically be of interest to the messaging integrator and be of great value to your user community. These include:

Inserting Disclaimer Text. Most SMTP virus scanning products will allow you to insert some text onto the end of the cover memo of your message. The text usually reads something like: *"The contents of this message are intended solely for the recipients as stated above. Any views expressed in this message are those of the individual sender, except where explicitly indicated otherwise."* Usually such text is included in messages for legal reasons.

Lexical Scanning. Some virus checkers either provide this facility or let you integrate another product in the scanner, which allows lexical scanning of message content. This feature means you can check messages (both inbound and outbound) for obscene words or phrases or for references to pornography.

Large Message Parking. Many scanners provide a facility whereby you can control the delivery of large messages. If you have limited bandwidth internally and a very high volume of traffic, you can configure the virus checker to defer the delivery of messages over a predetermined size, until a specific time. For example, you may prohibit the delivery of inbound messages over 20MB between the hours of 8:00 a.m. to 6:00 p.m., so that delivery doesn't interfere with other user traffic.

Similarly, outbound delivery can be curtailed so that large messages aren't sent until a particular time if you don't wish to tie up the network links to your service provider during peak users.

One of the common areas of concern for large messaging environments is that the virus checking solution will introduce some form of bottleneck into the environment. Certainly this may be true if a substantial backbone environment capable of processing many tens of thousands of messages per day is fronted with a poorly configured Windows NT system, but if common sense is applied this shouldn't be the case.

Properly configured systems should be used in all cases, applying the same logic that's used to build messaging backbone systems to virus checking systems. Dual processor systems are typically used, with appropriate memory configurations (usually not less than 128MB) and RAID sets for the IO subsystems. If it's impossible to sustain the message traffic volume using just one virus checking system, then multiple virus checkers can be used, with equal cost MX records used to split the load.

9

Synchronizing with the Exchange Directory

9.1   Introduction

One of the greatest assets for any messaging system is the provision of functional directory service. Despite all the richness of a messaging environment, its use can be difficult if there's no way to simply address a user. In most environments, and Exchange is no exception, the directory service usually has no problems referencing all the users on the same messaging system. In Exchange, it's the Global Address List (the GAL), which provides this capability. The GAL is populated from mailbox lists from each individual Exchange site, and Exchange servers across the organization communicate with each to share their directory information. As all of the servers communicate with each other, a single consistent view of mail users with the complete Exchange organization is formed.

But as well as just being able to reference other Exchange users, many Exchange environments have a requirement to see external users represented within the GAL as well. In Exchange parlance, these external users are maintained as *custom recipients*, and we've already met them when we discussed address rewriting in Chapter 8. To the native Exchange user, these custom recipients are addressed in just the same way as other Exchange mailboxes and they can be simply selected from the GAL. Fortunately, if you create a custom recipient on one Exchange server, the same directory replication mechanism that distributes mailbox information is also responsible for distributing custom recipient information. Create an entry for an external user in one site, and it's available to other sites shortly thereafter.

Custom recipients can easily be created manually. Simply use the Administrator program and you can create an entry for an external user by a few mouse clicks and entering in some basic information, typically the first name and surname details of the recipient and, of course, a mail address.

While manual mechanisms are sufficient for small environments, in large mixed environments where thousands of external entries and regular changes are the norm, automated processes must be used.

Exchange does provide directory synchronization services for some companion messaging products such as Lotus Notes, Microsoft Mail, and the like using its proprietary connectors. However, there's no generic tool for sophisticated synchronization. In spite of this, there are several ways of accessing the Exchange directory that lend themselves quite comfortably to directory synchronization processes. In this chapter we'll explore many of these techniques and look at some examples from the relatively esoteric world of directory synchronization.

9.2   Synchronization Models

Several different models can be used to synchronize information from one directory environment to another, but all models hinge around one central concept: the ability to detect changes.

9.2.1 Full Import and Export Synchronization

Consider a simple mixed messaging environment where only two mail systems, Exchange and some *other system*, are involved. At its simplest level, the Exchange Directory can be kept in synch with the other directory if regular full extracts from the other directory are provided. This means that a process is put in place whereby a complete dump of the other directory is frequently loaded into the Exchange Directory database.

If we adopt this approach, then in order to reflect changes from the other directory, perhaps when people on that messaging system have left the organization, we need to flush all of the synchronized entries out of the Exchange Directory and add them back in all over again. Failing to flush the entries out before we load the latest batch would mean that no entries would ever be removed from the Exchange Directory, and the directory information that we maintain would become stale.

This model is by no means an ideal one, and is to be avoided for several reasons:

- Constant deleting and unloading of all of the synchronized entries puts undue stress on the receiving Exchange network. Two sets of operations are required: one set of delete operations, and one set of add operations. If many tens of thousands of directory entries are involved, it may not be possible to complete all of the synchronization tasks within a reasonable amount of time. (Synchronization times of seven or eight hours are common, although this is usually governed by hardware configurations.)

- Deleting and then reloading all of the entries not only puts stress on the target Exchange Directory server, but considerable stress can be placed on the network, as the Directory Replication mechanism distributes all of the deletions and then additions to every other Exchange server in the organization.

- Deleting entries and then readding them, even when the entry data is identical, causes links in personal address books (PAB) and distribution lists to be problematic. When a user tries to send a message to, for example, a PAB entry that was created before the GAL entry was deleted and recreated, the message will be undeliverable.

9.2.2 Transactional Synchronization

The ability to detect changes that have occurred in a source directory and only reflect those in the target directory represents the most sophisticated form of directory synchronization. Considering our *other system*, as described above, our ideal synchronization model is to provide a set of transactional updates to the Exchange environment. Rather than a complete dump of the other directory being loaded into Exchange, our real concern is being able to deliver a set of files that show:

- Deletions from the other directory;

- Additions to the other directory; and

- Modifications to entries in the other directory.

Unfortunately, few directory services provide any such facility for determining such changes and only producing a set of transactions. The extra logic that's required for sophisticated synchronization like this either has to be written as part of a synchronization project, or by the use of existing differencing tools. The least cost option, of course, is to use the existing tools rather than reinvent the wheel, and we'll look at tools that provide this functionality later in this chapter.

Adopting a transactional approach provides the most efficient means for synchronization in so much as the amount of information that has to be exchanged is minimized and the amount of disruption to the target directory is reduced. Once again though, the notion of tradeoff appears. Merely applying transactional updates to a target directory can be fraught with risk if one of the sets of transactions isn't applied. In such a case, those transactions are lost and there's usually no way for the target directory to know that this has happened.

9.3   Accessing the Directory with the Administrator Program

Normally, the Exchange Administrator program gives you a GUI-based view of the Exchange environment, but it has another personality as well. The ADMIN.EXE program can be executed from the DOS environment with command line options that allow it to act as an interface directly to the Exchange Directory.

Using ADMIN.EXE in this mode allows you to export mailbox information from the Directory into a comma separated value (CSV) file or to import information into the Directory using either add, delete, or modify commands. This functionality provides a framework from which a directory synchronization solution can be constructed.

Using the Administrator Export functionality, Exchange users can be exported to a text file and this file used to load some other mail system. It's likely that the export file will have to be manipulated in some way to make its contents acceptable to the target mail system, but this is usually a straightforward task. In the reverse direction, recipient information from another messaging system can usually be represented in a CSV format, and this file can then be loaded into the Exchange Directory to create a number of custom recipient entries.

9.3.1   Exporting from Exchange

Performing the export from the Exchange Directory is the easiest of the two mechanisms to look at first. The export operation is run from a DOS command line and should be similar to this command:

```
ADMIN.EXE /E C:\exchsrv\dir_mbx.csv /N /O C:\exchsrv\direxp.opt
```

This instructs the Exchange Administrator to run in Export mode (/E) and it will produce a file called:

```
C:\exchsrv\dir_mbx.csv
```

that will hold the details of the mailboxes. The CSV file should exist before the export operation is commenced and the first line in the file should indicate which Exchange Directory fields are to be exported for each mailbox record. Although certainly not exhaustive, this first line or filter, should at the very least export the following fields, which are considered the minimum for a directory export operation:

```
Obj-Class,First name,Last name,E-mail Addresses
```

The /N qualifier controls the export operation so that no status dialog box is displayed during the export activity. If you're running the export interactively you may wish not to specify this qualifier so that you get an indication of how far the export operation has proceeded.

Finally, the /O qualifier specifies the name of the file which holds optional settings for the export run. The export options file should typically look like that shown in Figure 9–1.

FIGURE 9–1
ADMIN.EXE Export
Options File

```
[Export]
DirectoryService=DIRSRVR
Container="Recipients"
ExportObject=Mailbox
InformationLevel=Full
ColumnSeparator=44
MVSeparator=37
QuoteCharacter=34
```

where,

- `DirectoryService` specifies the name of the Exchange server to contact for the export operation,

- `Container` specifies the name of the Exchange container to export,

- `ExportObject` specifies the type of objects to be exported, and

- `InformationLevel` specifies the degree of logging to be performed.

In addition to the first four options, which represent the standard control settings, I've specified three more parameters in this option file that control how export data is represented. Usually, fields in the exported data are separated with commas, quoted fields are delimited with double-quotes, and multivalued fields are delimited with percentage signs. While this is normally acceptable, there may be cases when you want to change the default delimiters. It's common to want to do this if one of the fields that you'll be exporting contains one of the characters that is used as a delimiter by default. Display Name is the usual culprit in cases like this. Consider what might happen if the Display Name field already contains a comma (in the case where your Display Names are formatted as *Lastname, Firstname*). When the export information is presented, the Display Name field is wrapped in quotes so that the comma isn't interpreted as a column separator. If you were writing code to parse the export file, this makes the tokenizing of the field data that much more complex because you now have to distinguish between commas in the Display Name and commas as field separators.

As an alternative to this, you can explicitly control which characters are used as separators for columns, multivalued attributes, and for quoting field values using the `ColumnSeparator`, `MVSeparator`, and `QuoteCharacter` fields respectively. To control the characters that are used for each of these functions you need to specify the decimal ASCII code for each character. In the example I've used above, I've specified a comma (44), percentage sign (37), and double-quote (34) character for each of those fields.

Running such an export could produce a CSV file structured similarly to that shown in Figure 9–2.

FIGURE 9–2
ADMIN.EXE Export
Output Data Obj-
Class, Firstname,
Lastname, E-Mail
Addresses

```
Mailbox,Gary,Adams,SMTP:ga@asm.acme.com%X400:c=us;a=;p=acme;cn=ga;
Mailbox,Wes,Otow,SMTP:otow@ldc.acme.com%X400:c=us;a=;p=acme;cn=otow;
Mailbox,Sohrab,Mans,SMTP:sm@lc.acme.com%X400:c=us;a=;p=acme;cn=sm;
Mailbox,Mike,McKenna,SMTP:mm@lhc.acme.com%X400:c=us;a=;p=acme;cn=mm;
Mailbox,Steven,Freer,SMTP:sf@fse.acme.com%X400:c=us;a=;p=acme;cn=sf;
```

Having produced such a mailbox export file, it's possible to move this data onto another mail system and after some preprocessing have it loaded into another directory. However, you should note some of the restrictions that this mechanism imposes. When the directory export is requested, some information must be supplied, which instructs the export procedure which server to connect to. Upon selecting a server to be used, the highest level of container that can be exported is the Recipients container. So for any given export instance from a particular server, only the recipients from the site of which the server is a member will be exported. This means that if you have several Exchange sites in your environment, you must connect to each site individually and perform an export.

Although this may not present a huge problem for most organizations, in those environments where bandwidth is a particularly scarce commodity and many sites have been implemented, this directory export process may be cumbersome.

9.3.2 Importing into Exchange

The import process into the Exchange Directory uses more or less the same mechanism as the export process, except that instead of starting off with an empty CSV file (apart from the field names) a fully populated CSV file is provided.

The data in the import CSV file should be populated from the directory on the source messaging system and should contain mailbox information, which is to be uploaded into the Exchange Directory. The sophistication of your directory synchronization model determines the type of operations that you need to handle during this import run. Additions and removals of external users are usually simple, mapping straight to *Creates* or *Deletes*, while modifications can be more complex perhaps mapping directly to *Updates*, but occasionally requiring a delete and an addition to achieve the modification.

The command syntax for an Exchange Directory import operation is very similar to that used for exports:

```
ADMIN.EXE /I C:\exchsrv\foreign.csv /N /O C:\exchsrv\dirimp.opt
```

In this case, the /I command qualifier is used, thus indicating that an Import operation is to be carried out. The /N qualifier is used, again, to indicate that no progress dialog box should be displayed during the operation, and the /O qualifier indicates the options to be used for this operation. The options file for an import operation should be very similar to that used for an export, and an example of this file is shown in Figure 9–3.

FIGURE 9–3
ADMIN.EXE Import
Options File

```
[Import]
DirectoryService=DIRSRVR
Container="Foreign Recipients"
InformationLevel=Full
ColumnSeparator=44
MVSeparator=37
QuoteCharacter=34
```

If the desired result of the import operation is to add a number of custom recipients to the Exchange Directory, then the structure of the CSV file should look something like that shown in Figure 9–4.

FIGURE 9–4   ADMIN.EXE Import Add Data

```
Obj-Class,Mode,Directory Name,Alias Name,Display Name,E-mail Address
Remote,Create,Jim White,WhiteJ,Jim White,SMTP:jwhite@pol.acme.com
Remote,Create,Pete Black,BlackP,Pete Black,X400:c=us;a=;p=acme;cn=pb
Remote,Create,Steve Adams,AdamsS,Steve Adams,SMTP:sa@foobar.com
```

Again, while not providing a complete list of the fields, which you might wish to add to a custom recipient entry, the fields shown here represent the minimum amount of information that you need. These instructions indicate that *Create* operations are to take place for each of the records in the load file, each record representing a *Remote* entry, which equates to a custom recipient. The target address of the custom recipient is specified with the *E-mail Address* field, one of the most critical fields for a foreign entry in the directory.

Looking at the fields we've decided to populate, you may notice that the *E-mail Addresses* field is missing. (I've just specified the *E-mail Address* field.) If you don't specify values for this multivalued attribute, the custom recipient entry that you create inherits values for it from the Site Addressing defaults on the Exchange server into which you're importing. Under some circumstances this may be problematic because you're assigning addresses that may be meaningless for the entry that you are creating. It's always a wise practice to assign all the relevant values for this attribute just in case any stray values can lead to confusion or misrouting of mail. At the very least you should create entries with dummy addresses just so that you're working with known values.

Deleting custom recipients from the GAL is just as easy. The file structure is exactly the same for *Delete* operations except that the *Mode* of operation is a *Delete*. The instruction in Figure 9–5 gives an example of such a delete operation.

FIGURE 9–5
ADMIN.EXE Import
Delete Data

```
Obj-Class,Mode,Directory Name,Alias Name,Display Name,E-mail Address
Remote,Delete,Jim White,WhiteJ,Jim White,SMTP:jwhite@pol.acme.com
```

Two other forms of import modes may also be used, the *Modify* operation and the *Update* operation. These functions may both be used to apply changes to existing custom recipient entries in the Directory, but they operate in very subtly different ways. For example, let's assume we performed an import operation with the following CSV file:

```
Obj-Class,Mode,Directory Name,Alias Name,Display Name,E-mail Address,Surname
Remote,Update,Jim White,WhiteJ,Jim White,SMTP:jwhite@pol.acme.com,White
```

In this case, any existing entry for Jim White already in the Directory is updated to reflect the new value for his surname. However, if the entry for Jim White doesn't exist at all, then the import operation creates a custom recipient entry for him. If we were to carry this operation out using a *Modify* command, e.g.:

```
Obj-Class,Mode,Directory Name,Alias Name,Display Name,E-mail Address,Surname
Remote,Modify,Jim White,WhiteJ,Jim White,SMTP:jwhite@pol.acme.com,White
```

the behavior is slightly different. An existing entry for Jim White found in the Directory will be updated with the new surname value, but if the entry didn't already exist, then an error would be generated and the entry would not be created. In this way, you might look upon an *Update* operation as containing an implicit *Create* action, if required.

Unlike the export operations, which require that each Exchange site has its own export instance, there's no such requirement for import operations. Simply loading information into a particular container within any site is sufficient to ensure that the data in that container will be distributed by means of Exchange's own directory replication mechanisms.

You can get a full list of the fields available either by looking at the Directory in Raw mode or by using the HEADER.EXE tool, which is available in the Exchange Server Resource Kit.

9.4   Using a Scripting Language

Crafting a synchronization environment that's free from administrator intervention means using a language of some description to perform various tasks. Compiled languages such as "C" are obviously feature rich, but they're complicated and sometimes awkward to use when all that you want to do is automate some system management tasks.

This area of programming lies firmly within the confines of the scripting language. Scripting languages should provide a simple means of sequencing and controlling ordinary operating system commands, but still have the capability to perform more complex operations that you normally wouldn't be able to do either at a command line or in front of a GUI.

In many of the examples later in this chapter, I've chosen to use Perl[*] as my language of choice for scripting and manipulating text and data files. Why Perl? Well, there are a number of reasons why Perl is useful for anyone involved in messaging integration and directory synchronization:

- Perl is a sophisticated scripting language that borrows many concepts from much more complex "proper" languages like "C" as well as concepts from other scripting languages like BAT files or shell programming.

- Perl is extensible so that it easily integrates with other operating system components.

- It is multiplatform, running on almost all UNIX platforms, Windows NT, OpenVMS, OS/2, Macintosh, DOS, etc. This multiplatform feature makes it exceptionally portable and appealing to integrators.

- There is already a large library of Perl scripts and modules freely available, so development times are significantly reduced.

But Perl isn't the only tool in the box. If it's not a scripting language that you're either familiar with or care to use then many different options are available. On Windows NT we're almost spoilt for choice, given that a variety of languages are available including Visual Basic, Visual Basic Script, JavaScript, or scripting using the Windows Scripting Host. However, it's likely that DOS BAT files won't provide enough functionality for any serious scripting work, but in some cases they are all that's required.

On UNIX platforms, there's just as much choice using shell scripting, which provides a rich environment for all sorts of command, file, and data manipulation. Combined with some of the specialized tools available on the UNIX platform, such as *sed* and *awk*, shell scripts can be used to accomplish everything that the integrator needs.

---

[*] Perl is an acronym for Practical Extraction and Report Language. You can get it, and much more information, from `http://www.perl.com/perl/`.

9.5 Modifying Existing Directory Entries

There are many times when you'll want to make some modifications to entries in the Directory, irrespective of whether those entries are native mailboxes or custom recipients. This is simple if you've just got modifications to make for one or two entries, but when hundreds or thousands of entries are involved, the process of using the Administrator program to select each entry individually and modify attributes isn't very appealing. In such circumstances we need to use an alternative means for dealing with bulk modifications.

9.5.1 Limitations of the Exchange Administrator

The major restriction imposed by the Administrator program is that there is no way to perform operations on many entries at the same time. If attributes on a mailbox or custom recipient entry need to be changed you must select the entry and make the modifications manually. This is true for almost any attribute, with the exception of some of the addressing properties.

Let's assume that you didn't want to take the out-of-the-box SMTP address structure that Exchange provides for you immediately after installation. The default value for the SMTP alias on a mailbox or custom recipient is the Exchange Alias, followed by an "@" sign, and then a derivation of the site name, followed by a ".com". But many organizations will want to change this to something more meaningful and friendly. It's easy to go to the Site Addressing property page and modify the template for the SMTP alias to be something else. For example, the following template:

```
%g.%s@bauby.com
```

would generate SMTP aliases of the form:

```
firstname.lastname@bauby.com
```

Having redefined the template, you can now have Exchange apply this new format to all mailbox and custom recipient entries within the site.

However, this represents the limit of what Exchange can do in a bulk mode. Imagine, for example, that you wanted to assign a secondary SMTP alias to each of mailboxes within your Exchange environment, so that the address format was:

```
firstname.lastname@ex.bauby.com
```

as well as the original (pretty) alias we described above. There's no mechanism available from the Administrator GUI that let's you assign secondary aliases in this way. Of course, it can be done, but it has to be implemented using the command line export and import features of the ADMIN.EXE program. In order to update all of the entries, you'd have to perform the following sequence of events:

```
Begin {

         Export all mailboxes from the Exchange container
         to a CSV file;

         Update the CSV file so that the secondary aliases are
         created for each entry;

         Import the CSV file data back into the Exchange
         container

} End
```

Once you've exported the information into the CSV file you've got many options for manipulating the data. You could easily open the file using Excel or Access and apply some macros that would apply the secondary aliases and modify each record so that it's now a *Modify* or *Update* operation.

However, even though this procedure is relatively quick and saves on a lot of unnecessary and tedious typing, it still requires manual intervention because you have to manually open the file in Excel or Access and apply the macros. In many circumstances, applying new address aliases or performing updates like this must be run regularly, and ideally we need some way of automating the process completely.

9.5.2 Using a Perl Script to Perform Directory Updates

Apart from adding extra aliases to mailboxes there are other occasions when you might need to make modifications to entries held in the Directory. It would be impossible to list all of them here since many factors specific to your own environment may dictate what needs to modified. For example, a large group of users may move from one building to another and you may need to change the Address data for all of those users. Similarly, the area code or prefix to telephone numbers may change and accordingly entries in the Directory will need to be updated to reflect the new number.

But even some of the directory synchronization tools that are part of Exchange can exhibit symptoms that require a helping hand from an external directory update program from time to time. Consider, for example, the behavior of the Microsoft Mail Connector and its directory synchronization process.

When the synchronization process runs, its main objective is to take naming and addressing information from the Microsoft Mail Address List and populate this into the Exchange GAL as custom recipient entries. Actually, it does this very well, but its effectiveness is dependent on the quality of the data in the source directory, in this case the Microsoft Mail Address List. In many customer environments that I've seen, the data isn't always that cleanly entered into the source environment. In fact it's common to see Display Name information entered like this:

```
Burrowes, Norma
```

but no values for given name and surname. While this is simply poor system management on the part of the Microsoft Mail environment administrators, it does have an effect on the entries that are synchronized into the Exchange GAL. As the synchronization process takes place, the Exchange custom recipient attributes for First name and Last name don't get populated.

Lacking this given name and surname information means that the appearance of the custom recipient entries isn't very pleasing to the eye, but there are more sinister problems as well. Firstly, searching the GAL using a surname or given name won't work because these attributes haven't been populated. And if your site addressing scheme is like that described in the Section 9.5.1, then generating SMTP addresses using given name and surname terms won't be possible.

What can we do? Unfortunately there's no magic spell that we can cast on the Microsoft Mail Connector to add this information during the synchronization process. However, as system integrators, we can put in place a mechanism to work around this deficiency—a simple instance of running a script to export the custom recipients, parse the Display Name information, generate First and Last name terms, and then import this new information back into the Exchange GAL.

Such a script should take care of all aspects of the procedure, including:

- Building the Exchange Admin command to export the information
- Building the Header line into the CSV export file

- Check for the presence of all required files

- Run the export

- Process the data

- Import the data back into the Exchange GAL

I've included a complete script to perform all of these functions in Appendix F. It's easily modified so that you can use it to perform any kind of Directory updates that you want.

9.6   Using LDAP to Access the Exchange Directory

Although the Administrator program, by way of its command line options, does provide a convenient and flexible method of accessing information in the Exchange Directory, it's not the only option for getting your hands on Directory data. Exchange Server also uses the LDAP[*] protocol to expose Directory information. Any software that supports the LDAP protocol is capable of making queries directly against an LDAP directory, and consequently to the Exchange Directory.

9.6.1   What Is LDAP?

Unless you've been living on another planet for this past few years, you'll hardly have failed to hear the term LDAP mentioned somewhere. Vendors have been talking about it for ages now and its been heralded as the great unifying savior for mixed directory environments.

In much the same way that SMTP has become the preferred messaging protocol, superseding X.400 as a possible leader, LDAP has its origins in the world of X.500. X.500 directories came equipped with their own protocols for facilitating directory access; in the X.500 world this protocol was aptly titled the Directory Access Protocol (DAP). However, DAP could well be described as a "heavyweight" protocol. It's certainly rich on functionality but it requires the use of an OSI stack (although it can run over TCP/IP using RFC1006) and uses the complicated ASN.1 syntax for encoding transmission data.

PC client mail systems, arguably the real users of directories, were ill-prepared for the heavy software requirements that DAP implied, and, not

---

[*]   LDAP is an acronym for the Lightweight Directory Access Protocol, defined in RFC-2251.

surprisingly, DAP failed to succeed as a mainstream directory access protocol for desktops.

But the requirements for an access protocol still remained, and after some early read-only implementations of the protocol from a number of vendors, the first LDAP specification was published in 1993 as RFC-1487. Since then the protocol has enjoyed significant revision, and in its current guise as LDAP V3 it supports both read and write operations.

Although rich in functionality, there's nothing too complicated about the LDAP protocol and it's been this ease of use that has contributed so successfully to its widespread acceptance. The protocol itself specifies a number of concepts covering naming and access to information stored in the directory through searches, add, delete, and modify operations.[*]

9.6.2 LDAP Client Access

For an Exchange environment, this form of access means two things. Firstly, it's possible for some clients to gain access directly to the Exchange Directory. This isn't very exciting news for Exchange clients like Outlook because it already has access to the Directory through its normal MAPI mode of operation. But for clients on other mail systems, it can be important.

Consider the environment shown in Figure 9–6. In such an environment we can significantly reduce the amount of directory synchronization that needs to take place. Instead of having to synchronize the Exchange Directory with the Netscape Directory *and* the Netscape Directory with the Exchange Directory, we can use LDAP so that we only need to do the Netscape to Exchange synchronization.

The architecture of this integration environment implies that Netscape users are loaded into the Exchange directory through some form of directory synchronization process. Since the Exchange Directory will now contain Exchange users (as mailboxes) and Netscape users (as customer recipients), the GAL contains a complete directory for all users in the mixed environment. As an alternative to extracting Exchange user details out of the Directory and subsequently importing that information into Netscape, you could have the Netscape clients point directly to the Exchange LDAP interface, where all of the directory information that they need can be found.

---

[*]   Within the scope of this text it is not possible to completely outline the LDAP specification. For further reading on this subject, I recommend *LDAP: Programming Directory-Enabled Applications with Lightweight Directory Access Protocol*, by Howes and Smith, 1997, and *Understanding and Deploying LDAP Directory Services*, by Howes, Smith, and Good, 1999.

Netscape clients can then lookup both Exchange users and their own Netscape client colleagues from one directory.

FIGURE 9–6
Netscape Users
Accessing Exchange
Directory via LDAP

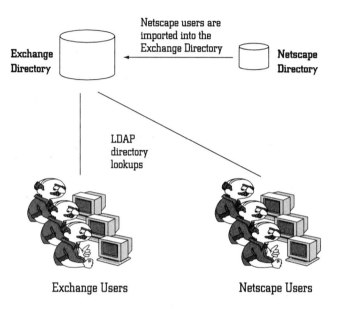

This concept of building a centralized directory is gaining popularity as more and more client environments begin to support LDAP as their protocol of choice for directory interrogation. However, some degree of directory synchronization still has to be performed in these cases because the central LDAP directory still has to be constructed from extracts of each of the subsidiary directories. And if your environment has a range of clients, some of which support LDAP and some of which don't, then this model may not be appropriate for you.

9.6.3 Using COMPAQ's LDSU Synchronizer

LDAP isn't just a protocol that's used by mail clients to perform directory lookups. Because LDAP provides searching facilities and read/write access to a directory it can be used by an application that's got a vested interest in directory information.

Although we've already met the Exchange ADMIN.EXE program and how it can be used to export and import information from and to the Exchange Directory, it should be obvious that LDAP can also be used for this purpose. Similarly, since many other messaging systems and directory products support LDAP nowadays, it appears that we've got a common means by which we can access their directories and manipulate the data held in them.

Writing a simple application to connect to a directory service over LDAP, export data from it, and then import that same data into another directory service over LDAP certainly goes part of the way to defining a complete directory synchronization solution. But such a tool is missing some components that are critical to an efficient synchronization, namely the ability to deduce what changes have occurred to a directory since the last synchronization run and functionality to allow data to be manipulated in-flight. All of these features, and more, can be found in the *LDAP Directory Synchronization Utility* (LDSU), which I've used as the foundation stone for many directory synchronization products.

LDSU Introduction

LDSU offers directory data synchronization between an LDAP directory and virtually any other directory or database that's capable of using text files to access data in their directories. Reflecting the heterogeneous nature of the messaging and directory environments, LDSU runs on most major operating system platforms including Windows NT, Digital UNIX, Solaris, and Linux.

Within the LDSU model, a number of different LDSU "runs" will be required to transfer data either into or out of a directory. Each LDSU run is known as an *instance*. In the simplest of environments, where perhaps we might be synchronizing between Exchange and Notes, four LDSU instances would be needed:

1.   An export of Exchange user data.

2.   An export of Notes user data.

3.   An import of Exchange user data into Notes.

4.   An import of Notes user data into Exchange.

LDSU Components
Each instance uses a number of components, as shown in Figure 9–7.

The components provide the following services:

- The **Layout File** contains a table of attributes in the LDAP directory used by LDSU. Each LDSU instance that uses the same type of LDAP directory may use the same Layout File. Each LDAP directory can have a separate layout file.

- The **Config File** contains a list of parameters for a given LDSU instance. These parameters determine the Mode (e.g., Import or Export), File Names, LDAP directory name, Unique Fields, etc.

- The **Record Description File (RDF)** contains a "mapping" of data in the Foreign Directory File to attributes in the LDAP directory (Layout File). LDSU also supports the LDAP Data Interchange Format (LDIF) as a built-in RDF type if the Foreign Directory File is in LDIF Content or Changes format.

- The **Foreign Directory File** is the Text file containing data to be imported into or exported from the LDAP Directory. This data may have been received from or is being sent to a Foreign (non-LDAP) Directory. It could also be from or destined for another LDAP directory. (If synching two LDAP directories.)

- The **LDAP directory** can be any LDAP compatible directory accessible to the machine where LDSU is running on the network via TCP/IP. It does not need to be on the same machine as the LDSU software. Each LDSU instance must involve an LDAP compatible directory.

FIGURE 9–7
LDSU
Components

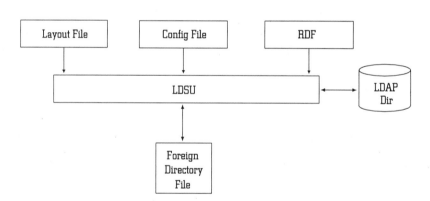

LDSU Modes of Operation

Each LDSU instance has a mode of operation, which determines the basic actions for the instance. The mode can be one of the following:

- IMPORT

- EXPORT

- TRANSACTION

- CHANGES

- UPDATE

When synchronizing two directory services which both support LDAP, the recommended mode of operation is an EXPORT/IMPORT pair, since this is the easiest mechanism to set up and the most reliable. With this operation mode a complete export from the source directory is taken and this export is used by the import instance. Although all the data from the source directory is used in the import instance, it is not merely just loaded into the target directory. LDSU compares the source data in the export file with the data that's already loaded into the target directory. In doing so, LDSU works out the changes that need to be applied and only these are loaded into the target directory.

While this is the simplest mode of operation, its drawback is that the data files which need to be exchanged between the directories can be rather large, in the region of about 30MB for 50,000 Exchange directory entries. This shouldn't cause you any real problems, but depending on the architecture of your environment you may not wish to move such files across your network. If that's the case, then there is an alternative.

The other approach that can be used is a pair of CHANGES/TRANSACTION instances. Using this model the changes that need to be applied to the target directory are calculated during the export at the source directory. In this way the least amount of directory data is transferred between the two instances and uses less resources on the target directory system since not all existing entries need to be extracted for comparison. However, using this slightly more complex transactional approach may allow the directories to become out of synch if the transactional import fails or other factors cause changes to the target directory.

Rather than describe all modes of operation, we'll cover just two: the EXPORT and IMPORT modes.

LDSU basic EXPORT mode extracts records from an LDAP directory, based on a search base and search filters, and writes the records to a formatted output file. Figure 9–8 shows these components in graphical form. This mode also allows many options, which are defined in the Config File:

- Allow the export of records belonging to Import Group IDs as specified by the Group ID. Multiple Group IDs can be included or excluded.

- Allow the export of only records matching the Synch ID.

- Allow the export of only records where a field matches a certain value. (The value can use wildcards as supported by the LDAP directory.)

- Allow the export of only records that meet the conditions specified by a custom LDAP filter that can be as complex as needed.

The Export RDF may allow the data in the output file to:

- Have header records that are copied from a specified header file.

- Contain data in fixed length fields or variable length fields.

- Contain constant strings interspersed with directory data that can be used to build command procedures or other formatted output.

- Consist of one or more lines per logical record.

- Be ignored if it meets certain user-defined criteria that could not be removed using the search filters.

- Be in the LDIF content format.

FIGURE 9–8
LDSU Export Mode
Operation

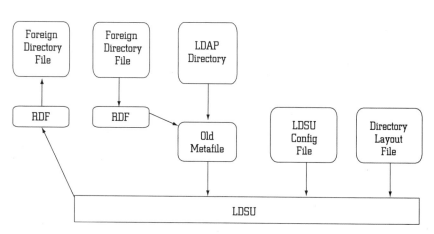

In addition, the RDF provides functions to process the data (substitute, substring, uppercase, etc.) and has hooks to call user-written procedures if needed.

LDSU IMPORT mode compares an input file against an LDAP directory and updates the LDAP directory as needed using Add, Modify, and Delete transactions. The input file is a Foreign Directory File that consists of all the entries to be contained in the LDAP directory (i.e., the input file is a Full Export of another Directory). This process is shown graphically in Figure 9–9.

FIGURE 9–9
LDSU Import Mode
Operation

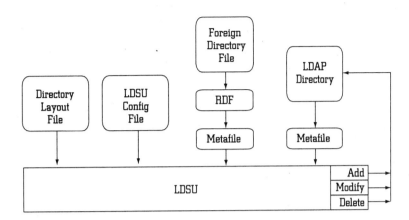

Each entry in the input file is assigned a *Group ID* to mark that these entries are "owned" by this foreign directory import. (The Group ID is a constant value given to any LDAP directory attribute.) LDSU compares all the entries in the input file (by creating a New Input Metafile by using the RDF) with all previously imported entries in the directory for this Group ID (by extracting the entries to an Old Output Metafile) and updates the LDAP Directory as needed using the Distinguished Name (DN) as the key:

- Any entries no longer in the input file are deleted from the LDAP directory.

- Any changed entries are modified in the LDAP directory (for those attributes that changed). Note: Any attributes in the LDAP directory for an entry that is not identified in the RDF are not modified.

- Any new entries are added to the LDAP directory with the Group ID.

LDSU Import mode also contains many options that are defined in the Config File:

- Creation of parent entries if needed on Add operations.

- A Synch ID, which marks all entries created by LDSU for all instances.

- Unique Field Checking, which can assure that LDAP attributes (or groups of attributes) are unique before adding or modifying an entry.

- Unique Field Generation, which can create a unique value for an attribute.

- A Case Checking switch, which can recognize or not recognize case changes to cause a change in the directory.

- Add-Only-Fields, which allow the import to set only the initial value of an attribute on an Add and never Modify it thereafter.

- Mark-for-Delete processing, which allows a record to be simply "marked" as deleted instead of physically removed from the directory.

- Threshold checking, which can invalidate an entire import if too many adds or deletes would have taken place (guards against partial files).

The Import RDF may allow the data in the input file to:

- Have header records that are skipped.

- Contain fixed length or variable length fields or a combination of both.

- If using variable length fields, contain a user specified separator character or string.

- Have an additional user specified "sub-field" separator to allow variable length fields within fields.

- Consist of one or more lines per logical record.

- Be ignored if it meets certain user-defined criteria (e.g., if a field marks a record to NOT be synched into the LDAP directory, which could be used for Admin or Test accounts for instance).

- Be in the LDIF content format.

In addition, the RDF provides functions to process the data (substitute, substring, uppercase, etc.) and has hooks to call user-written procedures if needed.

Example Directory Synchronization Environment

Writing about directory synchronization in abstract terms doesn't completely describe the processes that are involved in keeping two environments in synch. So rather than outline the processes and mechanisms for different forms of synchronization, I've chosen an example environment that illustrates many of the concepts that the average synchronization problem will exhibit.

Our example scenario consists of two mail systems: Exchange and Open-Mail. We'll use LDSU to perform the synchronization with LDAP access to Exchange, but in this environment, we'll access the OpenMail directory using its directory manipulation tools *omadddir*, *omdeldir*, and *omshowdir*.

OpenMail V5 does support LDAP access but older versions of the product don't and such restrictions are a common feature of many legacy mail systems. Because the target directory isn't using LDAP, we can't simply use LDSU in IMPORT mode to access the OpenMail directory, but instead we provide load files with additions and deletions that need to be made in the OpenMail directory. These additions and deletions need to be derived at the export from the Exchange Directory, so this LDSU instance needs to be a CHANGES export.

With a CHANGES export, the metafile that is produced as part of the directory export is compared with a metafile that is held over from the previous directory export. Thus, LDSU determines which modifications need to be made to the target directory at the point of export from the source directory.

Exporting Mailbox Entries from Exchange

The Exchange export instance configuration file, which controls the export operation is shown in Figure 9–10.

FIGURE 9–10
Exchange Export
Configuration File

```
! LDSU_CONFIG_CHANGES.DAT
!
! LDSU_CONFIG.DAT for CHANGES
!
! Modification History:
!
!   10-FEB-1999 KMC V1.0
!
!!!!!!!!!!!!!!!!!!!!!!!!!!!!!!!!!!!!!!!!!!!!!!!!!!!!!!!!!!!!!!!!!!!!!!!!
!!
!
synch_type = changes
synch_label = exch_export
!
layout_file = exch_export_layout.dat
bind_server = stiexc01.sti.com
bind_port = ! dflt: 389
bind_name = cn =ldsu
bind_password = "secret"
!
output_add_rdf = exch_add_export.rdf
output_add_file = exch_add_export.txt
output_del_rdf = exch_del_export.rdf
```

```
output_del_file = exch_del_export.txt
output_lines_per_record = ! dflt: 1
output_lines_per_record = ! dflt: 1
output_header_file =
output_field_separator = "^"
!
output_metafile = exch_export_new.mfl
input_metafile = exch_export_old.mfl
log_file = exch_export.log
verbose = Y
!
search_context = o=STI
synch_id_field =
synch_id_value =
gid_field = uid
gid_value = *
gid_exclude =
get_field =
get_value =
custom_filter  = (objectclass=organizationalPerson)
big_search_field = rfc822Mailbox
big_search_type = A
recognize_case_changes = N
```

Some points worthy of note in this configuration file are described below:

- The synch_type field indicates that this is a CHANGES export and determines some of the subsequent parameter settings for this export.

- The layout file maps LDAP and LDSU attribute definitions onto the Exchange schema.

- We identify the server from which we'll extract the Directory information using the bind_server and bind_port parameters.

- Although an authentication isn't strictly necessary for a simple export operation, some Exchange Directory attributes are not exposed on an anonymous LDAP bind. To overcome this, we explicitly quote a Windows NT username and password with which to be authenticated. You should create a special account·for this purpose and assign the appropriate Exchange permissions to it.

- Because this export produces changes we define separate RDF files for add and delete transactions. The structure of an add transaction to be executed on the OpenMail system is different from that for a delete and this is reflected in the RDFs.

- The `CHANGES` are determined by comparing the old metafile with the new metafile, so we explicitly quote the names for these files.

- We define the scope of the search as `o=STI` which means that we'll scan down through the complete Exchange organization to find mailboxes, not just a site. This is significantly different from the `ADMIN /E` export option that forces us to select a container name and thus we're only able to export recipients from within the scope of the site.

- The custom filter defines the type of objects that we're interested in searching for: in this case we're only taking Exchange mailboxes.

- The `big_search_field` and `big_search_type` parameters allow you to split the export into a number smaller searches. Rather than one big search which could potentially return many thousands of entries, the parameter values that I've chosen split the search into 26 (alphabetic) smaller searches based on the leading character in the `rfc822Mailbox` field.

As the mailbox entries are returned from the Exchange directory, and the comparison of the new metafile is made with the old metafile, LDSU will detect what modifications need to be made to the OpenMail directory and will use the RDF files to generate a sequence of transactions to be applied to the OpenMail directory.

For example, the RDF file for the ADD transactions looks like that shown in Figure 9–11.

FIGURE 9–11
Exchange EXPORT
ADD RDF File

```
! EXCH_ADD_EXPORT.RDF
!
! Export RDF for ADD Transactions
!
! Modification History:
!
!   10-FEB-1999 KMC V1.0
!
!!!!!!!!!!!!!!!!!!!!!!!!!!!!!!!!!!!!!!!!!!!!!!!!!!!!!!!!!!!!!!!!!!!!!
!!!!!
!
! Map the attributes into the transaction files
!
! Leading text
```

```
"omadddir -n '"=1.1.13

! (1-8) Given Name
givenName=1-*-#

! Space char
" "=1-*-#

! (1-7) Surname
sn=1-*-#

! Addr
"/stiexch ("=1-*-#
!
! (1-12) Target Email Address
rfc822Mailbox=1-*-#

! Close entry
")'"=1-*-#

! End of export.rdf
```

The result of processing data records through this file generates lines in a text file, which look like this:

```
omaddir —n 'Frank Brennan/stiexch (frank.brennan@exch.sti.com)'
```

When this command is executed on the OpenMail system, a foreign recipient entry for Frank Brennan is added to the OpenMail directory. If LDSU has detected a number of new entries that should be added to the OpenMail then a number of lines like this will appear in the data file.

The DEL transactions RDF file looks similar to the ADD RDF with the exception that instead of generating data lines with an omadddir command, the RDF generates omdeldir commands. Once again, a data file containing a sequence of DEL transactions can then be executed on the OpenMail system to delete entries from the directory.

Importing Exchange Entries into OpenMail

After generating the appropriate ADD and DEL transactions on the Windows NT system (where we ran the LDSU instance) the separate data files that contain the transactions are concatenated into one file and moved to the OpenMail system. (We'll see how this can be done later.) When the data file arrives on the OpenMail system it may look something like that shown in Figure 9–12, indicating two add transactions and one delete transaction.

FIGURE 9–12 OpenMail Import Data File (exch_export.txt)

```
omadddir -n 'Frank Brennan/stiexch (Frank.Brennan@exch.sti.com)'
omadddir -n 'Betty Caulfield/stiexch (Betty.Caulfield@exch.sti.com)'
omdeldir -n 'Joe Farrell/stiexch (Joe.Farrell@exch.sti.com)'
```

A UNIX shell script, like that shown in Figure 9–13, is then run to force the commands in the Import data file to be executed.

FIGURE 9–13
OpenMail
Import
Script

```
chmod 777 /users/dirsync/transfer/exch_export.txt
echo 'Importing Exchange Directory entries into Openmail...'
/users/dirsync/transfer/exch_export.txt
```

Exporting Mailboxes Entries from OpenMail

Importing Exchange user data into the OpenMail directory is easily achieved by using the omadddir and omdeldir commands. Similarly, an omshowdir command can be used to show the contents of the OpenMail Directory. The script, which is shown in Figure 9–14, exports the contents of the complete OpenMail directory to a text file.

FIGURE 9–14
OpenMail
Export Script

```
omshowdir -m all | grep -v stiexch > /users/dirsync/omusers.txt
awk -f process.awk /users/dirsync/omusers.txt >
    /users/dirsync/transfer/om_export.txt
rm /users/dirsync/omusers.txt
chmod 755 /users/dirsync/transfer/om_export.txt
```

This simple script will export all OpenMail users with the exception of entries that contain the text stiexch. This means that only *real* OpenMail user entries are exported will those entries that we imported into the Open-Mail directory to represent Exchange user get ignored. Your OpenMail configuration may be slightly more complex than this, but at least it illustrates the point.

The OpenMail users export may look similar to that format shown in Figure 9–15, and before we pass it over to the LDSU system, we have the option of performing some preprocessing on it.

FIGURE 9–15
OpenMail
Recipients
Export File
(omusers.txt)

```
alison groves /OMCENTRAL,Ireland
fedelmia regan /OMCENTRAL,Ireland
martin simpson /OMCENTRAL,UK
```

In this example we've used an awk script (Figure 9–16) to convert the OpenMail user data file into a format that we can pass to the LDSU system.

FIGURE 9–16
OpenMail
Preprocessing
Script

```
BEGIN {FS = "/"}
$0 != "" {
    sizeof = split($1,cn," ")
    sizeof = split($2,grp,",")
    gn=cn[1]
    cnt=sub(substr(gn,1,1), toupper(substr(gn,1,1)),gn)
    sn=cn[2]
    if (cn[2]!="") {
      sn=cn[2]
      cnt=sub(substr(sn,1,1), toupper(substr(sn,1,1)),sn)}
    if (sn=="") {
printf("%s^%s^%s^%s^%s/
    %s_%s@om.sti.com\n",gn,sn,grp[1],grp[2],gn,grp[1],grp[2])}
    else {
printf("%s^%s^%s^%s^%s_%s/
    %s_%s@om.sti.com\n",gn,sn,grp[1],grp[2],sn,gn,grp[1],grp[2])}}
```

This preprocessing script produces a data file, structured as:

`Alison^Groves^OMCENTRAL^Ireland^Groves_Alison/OMCENTRAL_Ireland@om.sti.com`

that includes naming information and a rather long addressing structure. The processed data file is then moved to a location to await transfer to the LDSU system.

Importing OpenMail Entries into Exchange

Once the processed OpenMail data has been received on the Windows NT LDSU system, it is processed through an LDSU import instance and loaded into the Exchange Directory. The LDSU configuration file that controls this import process is shown in Figure 9–17.

FIGURE 9–17

Exchange Import
Configuration File

```
! LDSU_CONFIG_IMPORT.DAT
!
! LDSU_CONFIG.DAT for IMPORT
!
! Modification History:
!
!   10-FEB-1999 KMC V1.0
!
!!!!!!!!!!!!!!!!!!!!!!!!!!!!!!!!!!!!!!!!!!!!!!!!!!!!!!!!!!!!!!!!!!!!!!!!
!!
!
synch_type = import
synch_label = om_import
!
layout_file = om_import_layout.dat
bind_server = stiexc01.sti.com
bind_port = ! dflt: 389
bind_name = cn=ldsu
bind_password = "secret"
!
input_rdf = import.rdf
input_file = om_export.txt
input_lines_per_record = ! dflt: 1
input_field_separator = "^"
input_num_header_lines =
input_metafile =
!
output_metafile = om_import_new.mfl
log_file = om_import.log
verbose = Y
!
max_transactions =
max_trans_file =
max_fail_transactions =
max_add_transactions =
max_delete_transactions =
!
dn_sequence = ! dflt: rdn order from ldsu_layout.dat
```

```
create_root =
search_context = cn=Openmail Recipients,ou=Central,o=STI
synch_object = person,Remote-Address
synch_id_field =
synch_id_value =
gid_field = Extension-Attribute-10
gid_value = om_import
!
unique_search_context = cn=Openmail Recipients,ou=Central,o=STI
unique_fields = Target-Address
make_unique_field =
make_unique_field_len =
make_unique_truncate =
make_unique_separator =
make_unique_program =
make_unique_params =
gen_profs_alias_fields =
gen_snads_alias_fields =
!
recognize_case_changes = Y
add_only_fields =
mark_for_delete_field =
mark_for_delete_value =
big_search_field =
big_search_type =
read_only_test =
```

This import configuration file instructs LDSU to take the data that's been provided from the OpenMail export operation, process it through an RDF file and upload the contents into the Exchange Directory in a recipients container called Openmail Recipients. Although we're taking all of the information from the OpenMail directory and using it for the import into Exchange, LDSU is smart enough to compare its load information with OpenMail information that's already in the Exchange Directory, so only changes get reflected in the Directory.

Of particular note in this configuration file are the settings for the unique_search_context and unique_search_fields. These settings defined here instruct LDSU to check that the SMTP address generated for each of the custom recipients is unique within the Openmail Recipients container, as well as providing a means of detecting changes that need to be applied to a target directory, LDSU can also check for duplicate addresses.

For completeness, I've included the RDF file that is used to map the OpenMail recipient data to Exchange Directory Attributes in Figure 9–18.

FIGURE 9–18

Exchange IMPORT
RDF File

```
! EXCH_IMPORT.RDF
!
! Import RDF for OpenMail Recipients
!
! Modification History:
!
!   10-FEB-1999 KMC V1.0
!
!!!!!!!!!!!!!!!!!!!!!!!!!!!!!!!!!!!!!!!!!!!!!!!!!!!!!!!!!!!!!!!!!!!!
!!!!!
!
cn = 1-2
cn_2 = "Openmail Recipients"
ou = "Central"
o = "STI"
!
uid = 1-2
cn_3 = 1-1
cn_3 = " "
cn_3 = 1-2
givenname = 1-1
sn = 1-2
physicalDeliveryOfficeName = 1-4
!
rfc822Mailbox = 1-5
textencodedoraddress = "c=us;a= ;p=sti;o=central;s="
textencodedoraddress = 1-2
textencodedoraddress = ";g="
textencodedoraddress = 1-1
textencodedoraddress = ";"
Target-Address = "SMTP:"
Target-Address = 1-5
mapi-recipient = "FALSE"
```

Merging Exchange Organizations

Merging different Exchange organizations together is really no different than any other directory synchronization problem. If anything, the solution is somewhat simpler because both participants in the directory synchronization have LDAP capabilities in their directories (so long as the appropriate software versions are available).

With both sides using LDAP, this means there's no need to produce and manipulate awkward load files and there's no compulsion to use the more troublesome CHANGES/TRANSACTIONS mode of operation for LDSU. Simply export the entire contents of one Exchange Directory and import this into the other Exchange Directory: LDSU works out all the changes that need to be applied so your workload is minimized.

Of course, it's not always just as simple or straightforward as this. In some circumstances you may find that there's some work that needs to be done to accurately represent data from one environment in the other, but LDSU helps out here.

Mapping Attributes

In most cases, that data that's stored in attributes in one environment can be mapped directly into the other environment. This is usually true for common attributes like Given Name or Surname, which have little variance between Exchange environments.

Switching Values. However, organizations often use other attributes in slightly different ways. The most common offenders in this case are the Office and Department attributes, as well as the Phone and Business Phone fields. For example, one Exchange implementation may store a value of Sales in their Office attribute, while the other Exchange implementation may store this data in the Department attribute. Similarly the use of internal extension numbers, direct dial numbers, and other contact numbers may not be used consistently across different organizations.

From a directory synchronization point of view, this presents no problem since the attribute values can be easily switched during the synchronization run. For example, if Office and Department are used inconsistently, then the data value that is contained in the Office attribute for the export can be used as the data value for the Department attribute during the import. It's a simple matter of subtle modification between the export and import RDF files.

Manipulating Values. Slightly more difficult to deal with is the problem of manipulating the information that's already held in a data field value. For instance, it's common to see the Display Name field being used differently across multiple Exchange environments. One Exchange implementation may adopt a structure that uses:

```
Lastname, Firstname
```

while another may adopt:

```
Firstname Lastname
```

This kind of mapping issue crops up time and time again, but fortunately LDSU has built-in functions that allow you to easily manipulate the data value. In this case, the simple sequence of RDF functions shown in Figure 9–19, would be sufficient to take a comma separated Display Name (referenced as cn_3 in Exchange LDAP terminology) stored in the first field in an import record and convert it into the other Firstname Lastname format.

FIGURE 9–19
RDF Functions to
Reformat
Display
Name

```
cn_3 = $INDEX (1-1,"2",",")
cn_3 = " "
cn_3 = $INDEX (1-1,"1",",")
```

Calling External Functions. Sometimes, mapping attribute values between Exchange organizations is even more complex. Rather than just manipulating the data that's already present in a field, there may be a requirement to use this data to derive a different value.

A simple example of this might be when two organizations use the *Location* attribute differently. Consider one organization that uses short form codes for the value, let's say SFO or SLC, while the other organization uses full name values, in this case San Francisco or Salt Lake City.

If you've just a few mappings to perform, then you can easily achieve this in the RDF file by using explicit mappings, e.g.,

```
? ("SFO" << 1-4) : location = "San Francisco"
```

that looks for the presence of the string "SFO" in the input file record and sets the Location attribute accordingly.

However, if you've many hundreds or thousands of such mappings to perform or the data changes frequently, you may need to adopt a different approach. An alternative is to make use of LDSU's ability to call an external function. For example, the following command:

```
location = $SYSTEM ("C:\LDSU\LOCMAP.EXE", 1-4)
```

will call an external program named LOCMAP.EXE and pass the short code data (e.g., SFO) as a parameter. The program could either use this parameter as an index into a lookup table, or perform a SQL query against a database. In any event, after processing the parameter value the result is returned to LDSU and assigned to the Location attribute.

Obviously, this is a simple example of referencing external functions, but it does open up a wide range of possibilities for mapping data values during a synchronization operation.

Dealing with Distribution Lists

We've already seen some example scripts for synchronizing Exchange mailboxes, and the model that we used could equally well be applied to custom recipients. However, when Exchange organizations are merged, there is often a need to synchronize Distribution List details as well.

Although synchronizing mailboxes and custom recipients is straightforward, synchronizing Distribution List information is slightly more complex. Three main options exist, the first two of which are relatively simple but offer reduced functionality, while the third option is richer in functionality but is considerably more complex to implement.

The simplest mechanism merely represents a Distribution List from one environment as a custom recipient in the other. Within Exchange, and from an LDAP perspective, Distribution Lists are defined as members of the object class groupOfNames. An export operation on the source Exchange Directory is carried out, looking only for this object class. Various attributes, including the Target Address (typically the rfc822Mailbox) and the Display Name should also be exported. Each Distribution List can then be represented in the other Exchange Directory as a custom recipient with a Target Address that points to the Distribution List on the source system. Users on the foreign Exchange environment can now simply send mail to this custom recipient, where the message is redirected to the proper Distribution List in the owning Exchange environment and expanded.

Although this is the simplest means of representing Distribution Lists, it is less aesthetically pleasing since the list is simply represented as a custom recipient in the other Exchange Directory. An alternative approach can be taken by importing the Distribution List into the target Exchange environment as an actual Distribution List, as well as creating a custom recipient for the list. When the Distribution List is created in the target environment, its membership list is updated so that the custom recipient that was created for it is seen to be the only member. To users in the target Exchange environment, they now see the Distribution List appear in their Exchange GAL as a Distribution List, not just a custom recipient.

However, both of these approaches suffer from one serious shortcoming: no meaningful list of members is maintained for the list, so it's impossible to tell which users are members of the list when it's synchronized into the target Directory. There is a way to circumvent this problem, that is, synchronize Distribution List information from one Exchange environment into another *and* maintain membership information. However, it's complicated to implement and is not particularly scalable. If you've got a small number of lists, and small number of members in each list, then this approach may be feasible in your environment. If, on the other hand, you have many hundreds of lists and thousands of members per list, then this approach may not be to your liking.

In your search against the source Exchange Directory for all objects within the class groupOfNames, the RDF for the export should also specify that the member attribute is extracted for each groupOfNames object. Unfortunately member is a multi-valued attribute and has one value for each mailbox or custom recipient that is a member of the Distribution List. LDSU doesn't provide any special handling for multi-valued attributes, so you have to specify each instance explicitly, with an instruction in the RDF file, which may look like this:

```
member = 1.*.#
member_2 = 2.*.#
member_3 = 3.*.#
member_4 = 4.*.#
...
```

You'll need to specify each member_*n* attributes explicitly, so if you've got up to a thousand entries in a list, you'll need a thousand lines up to member_1000. This exports the Distinguished Name for each member of the list and you can use it to rebuild the membership list when you create the Distribution List in the target Exchange environment. (Of course, in the target Exchange environment, the actual Distinguished Names will not be valid so you will have to manipulate them in the RDF import file so that the new member name coincides with the Distinguished Name of the custom recipient.)

This is clearly a complicated synchronization instance (there are some variations on it using LDSU reference syntax and specific import modes) but if you absolutely, positively must have Distribution List synchronization with membership information then it can be done. But maintaining list membership information across environments like this is very tricky for a number of reasons:

- As shown above, there's no iterating mechanism for dealing with the membership attributes so you end up manually compiling loop structures.

- There's a risk that zealous system administrators may be tempted into maintaining membership information for the lists in both environments. Bidirectional synchronization of structures like this is clearly to be avoided, so the only alternative is to use one list as the master and periodically overwrite any copies of it with definitive information. Clearly this could lead to administrative problems.

- Distribution Lists can have other Distribution Lists as members so the processing required would have to cater for complex, nested, and hopefully acyclic lists.

In summary, if you can, try to avoid synchronizing Distribution Lists with membership information. Adopting one of the other approaches provides a simple and easy way to maintain process, with the downside that the synchronized lists can't be edited, viewed for membership, or used for security or access control. It's all a tradeoff between function and complexity.

9.7   Building a Synchronization Infrastructure

Using LDSU to link two Exchange (or any other messaging) environments together can easily be achieved with just one directory synchronization system. For example, you could adopt an approach like that shown in Figure 9–20.

FIGURE 9–20
A Simple
Synchronization
Infrastructure

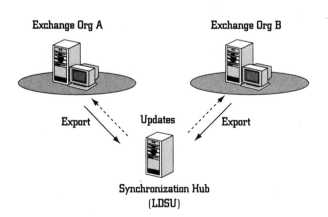

The architecture shown in Figure 9–20 is appealing because it's simple and inexpensive to implement, but it does suffer from some disadvantages. If you're merging two separate Exchange organizations it's likely that the link between them may involve a wide area connection. In our example, it's possible that the synchronization hub is colocated on the same LAN as one of the Exchange organizations, which means that wide area connections are only used for one half of the directory synch. But in any event, the wide area nature of the architecture may introduce performance problems and slow the synchronization process down. If possible, it's much better to adopt a more symmetrical approach like that shown in Figure 9–21.

FIGURE 9–21
Symmetric
Synchronization
Infrastructure

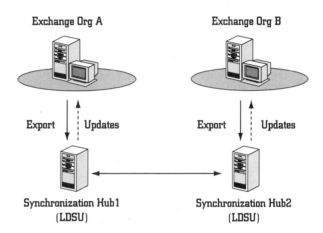

This architecture optimizes the connectivity between LDSU servers and the Exchange Directory Service so that exports and updates between Exchange and the LDSU system are as carried out across LAN connections. This significantly improves the efficiency of the synchronization model since LDAP operations are carried out quickly and only data files get transferred across the wide area connections.

Both of these architectures are peer-to-peer in nature and may be fine for synchronization between just two environments. However, if your synchronization requirements are more involved than this, a hierarchical synchronization architecture may be more appropriate.

The model shown in Figure 9–22 should be very appealing to any organization that wishes to put in place a synchronization topology that is flexible and scalable. The centralized directory can be used as a master repository for information from any data source, with all directory subsystems upload-

ing information to it. However, not all information needs to be synchronized back down to individual directory instances. Although all of the data
is maintained centrally, directory downloads can be modular in nature, and
only the information that a particular directory subsystem requires need be
downloaded. As new messaging systems are added to the environment, they
are easily included in the synchronization process.

FIGURE 9–22

A Hierarchical
Directory
Synchronization
Infrastructure

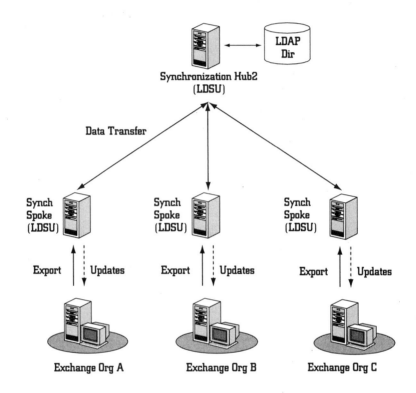

We've already discussed some of the merits of a central directory in
terms of naming and addressing structures, but a central directory like this
brings its own benefits. The LDSU synchronization approach used here can
also be used to synchronize Directory data with other sources, including
Human Resource systems and any other database environments, so the
concept of a global employee directory is easily realized.

If you do decide to implement a global directory architecture like this,
you may find that the Exchange LDAP directory is not sufficient. Although
the Exchange Directory does support many attributes, the schema exposed
by the LDAP interface isn't particularly customizable, so a more native

LDAP implementation may be required. Many such implementations are available from a variety of vendors including Netscape, Innosoft, and most X.500 vendors. Microsoft will also be offering a much richer directory service with the Active Directory due to debut with Windows 2000. The Active Directory will also provide its own replication mechanism, not dissimilar from the Exchange Directory replication mechanism, whereas as some other LDAP implementations don't provide great features in this respect. However, many other implementations do provide a replication capability based around X.500 shadowing mechanisms or directory synchronization procedures (perhaps using LDSU), so you won't be left with a single LDAP directory that can't be shadowed.

Building a solid directory synchronization topology should be partnered with a sensible approach to hardware sizing for synchronization systems. Whatever approach or means that you use to implement a synchronization environment, there'll be a number of characteristics which can be attributable to all of them.

For the best part, directory databases will be held on disk, and during synchronization activities you should expect to see considerable activity on the IO subsystem. Similarly, you can expect to see much of the differencing and sorting operations that any synchronization tools involve, exert high demands on CPU and memory resources. This can only mean one thing: don't skimp on the hardware that you put in place for your synchronization services. Buy the fastest disks and IO controllers that you can afford and implement a storage model based around RAID concepts, preferably with RAID0+1 configurations. And you should also use the fastest processors and reasonable amounts of memory that you can get your hands on. Dual CPU systems should be mandatory, and memory configurations of not less than 256MB should be configured.

These may seem like hefty configurations for systems that will only be used perhaps once or twice a day to perform synchronization runs, but the configuration that you decide on determines the length of time that the synchronization takes. Using sensible configurations means that nightly synchronization activities involving tens of thousands of entries can be completed in minutes. Cheaping out on hardware means your synchronization efforts are likely to take hours.

9.8   Driving the Synchronization Process

We've seen how a utility like LDSU can be used to make light work of the complex tasks that need to be carried out in a synchronization environment. But each of the separate synchronization instances need to be controlled and managed. Log files need to be maintained, and depending on the synchronization architecture data files need to be transferred from system to system.

For example, in the environment I've described in the section *An Example Directory Synchronization Environment* where we looked at synchronization between Exchange and OpenMail, each environment had two fundamental activities that needed to be performed: running the export and running the import.

Controlling the synchronization on the OpenMail system was easy because the data files that were used on that system inherently provided the commands to add and delete directory entries. The OpenMail export itself was a simple UNIX script (as shown in Figure 9–14). But what about the Exchange half of the synchronization process?

In many circumstances, it's possible to control this part of the process with the most straightforward of BAT scripts. Figure 9–23 shows a simple sequence of DOS commands that could be used to control the Exchange export instance.

FIGURE 9–23
Exchange Export
Control Script

```
cd \dirsync\ldsu\instances\sti\exch_export
echo "Running Exchange Export"
if exist exch-export.lg1 del exch-export.lg1
ren exch-export.log exch-export.lg1
f:\dirsync\ldsu\bin\ldsu.exe
if exist exch-export-sav.mfl del exch-export-sav.mfl
ren exch-export-old.mfl exch-export-sav.mfl
if exist exch-export-old.mfl del exch-export-old.mfl
ren exch-export-new.mfl exch-export-old.mfl
copy exch-del-export.txt+exch-add-export.txt exch-export.txt
echo "Transferring Exchange user data to OpenMail server"
ftp -s:transfer.ftp
cd f:\dirsync
```

This script performs all of the functions that's required to manage log files, manage LDSU metafiles (which are used to generate changes), export data from the Exchange Directory, build a single file containing Add and Delete transactions, and ultimately transfer that data to the target system (we'll look a little more at options for transferring data in the next section).

Similarly, another script can be used to control the import process, as shown in Figure 9–24.

FIGURE 9–24

Exchange Import
Control Script

```
cd \dirsync\ldsu\instances\sti\om_import
if exist om-export.old del om-export.old
if exist om-export.txt ren om-export.txt om-export.old
echo "Transferring OpenMail user data to Exchange server"
ftp -s:transfer.ftp
echo "Running OpenMail import into Exchange"
if exist om-import.lg1 del om-import.lg1
if exist om-import.log ren om-import.log om-import.lg1
f:\dirsync\ldsu\bin\ldsu.exe
cd f:\dirsync
```

These scripts don't need to be too complex, since most of the hard work for determining changes and selecting entries to be synchronized should be performed by the synchronization engine, in this case LDSU.

Depending on the operating system from which you run your synchronization processing, you may wish to mail log files to system administrators. On UNIX platforms you can simply use the *mail* command. On Windows NT the same functionality can be achieved using the Command Line Mail Sender that is part of the Exchange Resource Kit.

9.8.1   Transferring Synchronization Data

Arguably, the only complex scripting that needs to be done is that which controls how synchronization data is transferred between systems. If you're only using one LDSU system to perform synchronization across a range of directory environments then all the directory data can be maintained on that single system. Only LDAP transactions are carried out between the different directory systems and this requires no external intervention.

However, if you're using multiple LDSU systems or if your synchronization architecture produces more basic data files that need to be ferried to non-LDAP systems, you will need some vehicle for transferring these files.

The network environment within which you're confined can often determine how data is moved around. For example, LAN Manager shares can easily be used between different Windows NT systems, and in some cases between UNIX and other operating system environments. Alternatively, NFS mounts may be used to provide the same functionality.

For truly heterogeneous environments, it's likely that these facilities won't be available, but typically, one tool is almost always available across multiple platforms: FTP. FTP provides the most flexible approach to moving data between different systems, and its ability to be scripted and, thus, operate without user intervention makes it very suitable for a fully automated, unattended directory synchronization environment.

In our example Exchange and OpenMail environment, I've used a simple Windows NT mechanism for transferring directory data files between the Exchange system and the OpenMail system. The FTP process is engaged by using the following command:

```
ftp -s:transfer.ftp
```

This instructs the FTP client to operate in script mode, and the script itself, named `transfer.ftp` consists of a sequence of standard FTP directives:

```
OPEN omserver.sti.com
dirsync
secret
CD transfer
PUT exch_export.txt
BYE
```

The connection to the target OpenMail server is authenticated using a dedicated account (`dirsync`) whose only purpose in life is to provide a location for accepting data files. It makes sense to use a dedicated account since access controls and permissions can be tightly monitored, and you'll be free from any dependencies on password changes, which you might be subjected to if you used any other administrative account.

If your transfer requirements are more complex then simple DOS commands may not provide enough functionality for you. For example, if you need to check for the presence of lock files or perform more error checking, you'll probably want to use a more sophisticated scripting tool. The script extract in Figure 9–25 uses Perl to provide the FTP transfer service, but this could easily be implemented in Visual Basic or some other scripting language.

FIGURE 9–25
Perl FTP
Script
Sample

```
use Win32;
use Win32::Internet;

print "Opening FTP connection... \n";
$status=$INET->FTP($FTP, "omserver.sti.com", "dirsync",
  "secret");

print "Copy Exchange Data file from host...\n";

$FTP->Binary();
$FTP->Put("D:\ldsu\exch_export.txt",
  "\dirsync\exch_export.txt");

print "Data file copied successfully\n";

$FTP->Delete($LockFileMask)

print "Closing FTP connection... \n";
$status = $INET->Close ($FTP);
```

While this is a basic example, more complex scripts can be developed to cater for transactional processing where it's important that previous transaction files are processed by the foreign directory system before new ones are added. I've included a sample UNIX script to perform this function in Appendix G.

The sample UNIX script adopts a simplistic approach to dealing with transaction processing. Assuming that previous exports were correctly processed by the other partner in the directory synchronization relationship, the script writes the new export transaction to an FTP area and creates a lockfile which indicates that transactions are pending. After the transactions have been processed by the other system, the lockfile is deleted. If for some reason, the files haven't been processed by the time the next export synchronization events come around, the script detects the presence of the lockfile and abandons processing. In this way, there's no danger that pending transaction files will be overwritten by more recent ones.

More complex variations on this theme can be implemented, by using a sequence number associated with a set of transactions. The sequence number is maintained in an export sequence control file, let's call it seqnumexp.dat. When each directory export synchronization run takes place, the sequence number is read from the file and incremented. After export processing has completed, the export data file and a copy of the export sequence control file are moved to a transfer area, the data file named along the lines of the following structure:

```
TRANS<seqnumber>.DAT
```

Thus, a completed export run may generate a file called TRANS0007.DAT. When import processing takes place the files are copied from the transfer area and, amongst other things, the export sequence control file is read to determine the sequence number of the last export run. This value is compared with a value held in a local import sequence control file, and as result, the import process can determine how many sets of export transactions need to be processed to have the local directory in synch with the remote directory.

9.8.2 Scheduling Synchronization Activities

One more aspect of cross platform directory synchronization needs to be considered, that of scheduling.

In a hierarchically architected directory synchronization environment, all export operations from each directory subsystem should be completed first. These updates can then be loaded into the central directory, and when completed, exports from the central directory can be performed and the data used as update imports into each of the other directory subsystems. In a multiplatform environment, it's difficult for the central system to know when all of the directory subsystem exports have been completed, but a number of options exist.

For example, when each subsystem export is completed, the termination could be indicated by creating a signal file in a central transfer area to which all subsystem directories and the central directory have access. The central directory could poll this location periodically, checking that all signal files are in place before import processing is commenced. In fact, the presence of an export data file itself is enough to let the central directory know that an export has completed.

In more sophisticated environments, cross platform scheduling tools may be used to manage the process, with all export and import operations controlled from a single scheduling source. Scheduling products like this allow you to build complex rules and relationships between the synchronization entities so you can be sure that processing will take place in a particular order.

Of course, almost all operating systems provide their own mechanism for scheduling jobs and services. Windows NT provides basic functionality with the AT command scheduler, while UNIX and OpenVMS offer their own more sophisticated scheduling services via cron and batch queues. Providing you know that individual synchronization operations will complete within a certain time period, using basic scheduling functionality like this may be all that's required for your environment.

In such circumstances, directory subsystem export operations could be configured to run at 1.00 a.m., import operations to the central directory could be scheduled for 2.00 a.m., and exports of updated directory data scheduled for 3.00 a.m. This leaves a one-hour margin for each subsystem export or import to complete before you commence the next operation. In most environments this may be sufficient, but local factors, including frequency of synchronization activities, Exchange Directory replication cycles, and system management functions will determine how you schedule your own jobs. Remember, that the time to perform each activity is mostly governed by the speed of your synchronization hardware, so if you've built a sound hardware, scheduling should be the least of your worries.

Appendix A

X.400 Recommendations Currently in Force

MESSAGE HANDLING SYSTEMS

X.400 (1993)	[Rev.1] [80 pp.] [Publ.: Apr.93]	Message handling services: Message handling system and service overview Note - See F.400/X.400
X.402 (09/92)	[Rev.1] [84 pp.] [Publ.: Jul.93]	Message handling systems: Overall architecture
X.403 (1988)	[Blue Book Fasc. VIII.7] [Publ.: Dec.90]	Message handling systems: conformance testing
X.407 (1988)	[Blue Book Fasc. VIII.7] [Publ.: Dec.90]	Message handling systems: Abstract service definition conventions
X.408 (1988)	[Blue Book Fasc. VIII.7] [Publ.: Dec.90]	Message handling systems: Encoded information type conversion rules
X.411 (09/92)	[Rev.1] [174 pp.] [Publ.: Aug.93]	Message handling systems - Message transfer system: Abstract service definition and procedures
X.413 (04/95)	[Rev.2] [Publ. sched.: Jul.95]	Information technology— Message handling systems (MHS): Message store— Abstract service definition Note - C: 101/120/146
X.419 (09/92)	[Rev.1] [44 pp.] [Publ.: Jul.93]	Message handling systems— Protocol specifications
X.420 (09/92)	[Rev.1] [116 pp.] [Publ.: Oct.93]	Message handling systems: Interpersonal messaging system

MESSAGE HANDLING SYSTEMS (CONTINUED)

X.421 (07/94)	[New] [11 pp.] [Publ.: Feb.95]	Message handling systems: COMFAX use of MHS Note - C: 40/65/84
X.435 (03/91)	[New] [120 pp.] [Publ.: Sep.91]	Message handling systems: Electronic data interchange messaging system
X.440 (09/92)	[New] [113 pp.] [Publ.: Oct.93]	Message handling systems: Voice messaging system
X.445 (04/95)	[New] [Publ. sched.: Jul.95]	Asynchronous protocol specification—Provision of OSI connection mode network service over the telephone network Note - C: 101/120/146
X.460 (04/95)	[New] [Publ. sched.: Jul.95]	Information technology— Message Handling Systems (MHS) management: Model and architecture Note - C: 101/120/146
X.480 (09/92)	[New] [10 pp.] [Publ.: Jun.93]	Message handling systems and directory services - conformance testing
X.481 (09/92)	[New] [32 pp.] [Publ.: Jul.93]	P2 protocol: Protocol implementation conformance statement (PICS) proforma
X.482 (09/92)	[New] [40 pp.] [Publ.: Jul.93]	P1 Protocol—Protocol implementation conformance statement (PICS) proforma
X.483 (09/92)	[New] [36 pp.] [Publ.: Jul.93]	P3 Protocol—Protocol implementation conformance statement (PICS) proforma
X.484 (09/92)	[New] [42 pp.] [Publ.: Aug.93]	P7 protocol—Protocol implementation conformance statement (PICS) proforma
X.485 (09/92)	[New] [27 pp.] [Publ.: Aug.93]	Message handling systems: Voice messaging system protocol implementation conformance statement (PICS) proforma

Appendix B

IANA Registered MIME Types

RFC-1521 specifies that Content Types, Content Subtypes, Character Sets, Access Types, and Conversion values for MIME mail will be assigned and listed by the IANA.

Content Types and Subtypes

TYPE	SUBTYPE	DESCRIPTION	REFERENCE
text	plain		[RFC1521,Borenstein]
	richtext		[RFC1521,Borenstein]
	enriched		[RFC1896]
	tab-separated-values		[Paul Lindner]
	html		[RFC1866]
	sgml		[RFC1874]
	vnd.latex-z		[Lubos]
	vnd.fmi.flexstor		[Hurtta]
	uri-list		[Daniel]
	vnd.abc		[Allen]
	rfc822-headers		[RFC1892]
	vnd.in3d.3dml		[Powers]
	prs.lines.tag		[Lines]
	vnd.in3d.spot		[Powers]
	css		[RFC2318]
multipart	mixed		[RFC1521,Borenstein]
	alternative		[RFC1521,Borenstein]
	digest		[RFC1521,Borenstein]

TYPE	SUBTYPE	DESCRIPTION	REFERENCE
multipart (continued)	parallel		[RFC1521,Borenstein]
	appledouble		[MacMime,Patrik Faltstrom]
	header-set		[Dave Crocker]
	form-data		[RFC1867]
	related		[RFC2112]
	report		[RFC1892]
	voice-message		[RFC1911]
	signed		[RFC1847]
	encrypted		[RFC1847]
	byteranges		[RFC2068]
message	rfc822		[RFC1521,Borenstein]
	partial		[RFC1521,Borenstein]
	external-body		[RFC1521,Borenstein]
	news		[RFC 1036, Henry Spencer]
	http		[RFC2068]
	delivery-status		[RFC1894]
	disposition-notification		[RFC2298]
application	octet-stream		[RFC1521,Borenstein]
	postscript		[RFC1521,Borenstein]
	oda		[RFC1521,Borenstein]
	atomicmail		[atomicmail,Borenstein]
	andrew-inset		[andrew-inset,Borenstein]
	slate		[slate,Terry Crowley]
	wita		[Wang Info Transfer,Larry Campbell]
	dec-dx		[Digital Doc Trans, Larry Campbell]
	dca-rft		[IBM Doc Content Arch, Larry Campbell]
	activemessage		[Ehud Shapiro]
	rtf		[Paul Lindner]
	applefile		[MacMime,Patrik Faltstrom]

TYPE	SUBTYPE	DESCRIPTION	REFERENCE
application (continued)	mac-binhex40		[MacMime,Patrik Faltstrom]
	news-message-id		[RFC1036, Henry Spencer]
	news-transmission		[RFC1036, Henry Spencer]
	wordperfect5.1		[Paul Lindner]
	pdf		[Paul Lindner]
	zip		[Paul Lindner]
	macwriteii		[Paul Lindner]
	msword		[Paul Lindner]
	remote-printing		[RFC1486,Rose]
	mathematica		[Van Nostern]
	cybercash		[Eastlake]
	commonground		[Glazer]
	iges		[Parks]
	riscos		[Smith]
	eshop		[Katz]
	x400-bp		[RFC1494]
	sgml		[RFC1874]
	cals-1840		[RFC1895]
	pgp-encrypted		[RFC2015]
	pgp-signature		[RFC2015]
	pgp-keys		[RFC2015]
	vnd.framemaker		[Wexler]
	vnd.mif		[Wexler]
	vnd.ms-excel		[Gill]
	vnd.ms-powerpoint		[Gill]
	vnd.ms-project		[Gill]
	vnd.ms-works		[Gill]
	vnd.ms-tnef		[Gill]
	vnd.svd		[Becker]
	vnd.music-niff		[Butler]
	vnd.ms-artgalry		[Slawson]
	vnd.truedoc		[Chase]
	vnd.koan		[Cole]

TYPE	SUBTYPE	DESCRIPTION	REFERENCE
application (continued)	vnd.street-stream		[Levitt]
	vnd.fdf		[Zilles]
	set-payment-initiation		[Korver]
	set-payment		[Korver]
	set-registration-initiation		[Korver]
	set-registration		[Korver]
	vnd.seemail		[Webb]
	vnd.businessobjects		[Imoucha]
	vnd.meridian-slingshot		[Wedel]
	vnd.xara		[Matthewman]
	sgml-open-catalog		[Grosso]
	vnd.rapid		[Szekely]
	vnd.enliven		[Santinelli]
	vnd.japannet-registration-wakeup		[Fujii]
	vnd.japannet-verification-wakeup		[Fujii]
	vnd.japannet-payment-wakeup		[Fujii]
	vnd.japannet-directory-service		[Fujii]
	vnd.intertrust.digibox		[Tomasello]
	vnd.intertrust.nncp		[Tomasello]
	prs.alvestrand.titrax-sheet		[Alvestrand]
	vnd.noblenet-web		[Solomon]
	vnd.noblenet-sealer		[Solomon]
	vnd.noblenet-directory		[Solomon]
	prs.nprend		[Doggett]
	vnd.webturbo		[Rehem]
	hyperstudio		[Domino]
	vnd.shana.informed.formtemplate		[Selzler]
	vnd.shana.informed.formdata		[Selzler]
	vnd.shana.informed.package		[Selzler]
	vnd.shana.informed.interchange		[Selzler]
	vnd.$commerce_battelle		[Applebaum]
	vnd.osa.netdeploy		[Klos]
	vnd.ibm.MiniPay		[Herzberg]
	vnd.japannet-jpnstore-wakeup		[Yoshitake]

TYPE	SUBTYPE	DESCRIPTION	REFERENCE
application (continued)	vnd.japannet-setstore-wakeup		[Yoshitake]
	vnd.japannet-verification		[Yoshitake]
	vnd.japannet-registration		[Yoshitake]
	vnd.hp-HPGL		[Pentecost]
	vnd.hp-PCL		[Pentecost]
	vnd.hp-PCLXL		[Pentecost]
	vnd.musician		[Adams]
	vnd.FloGraphlt		[Floersch]
	vnd.intercon.formnet		[Gurak]
	vemmi		[RFC2122]
	vnd.ms-asf		[Fleischman]
	vnd.ecdis-update		[Buettgenbach]
	vnd.powerbuilder6		[Guy]
	vnd.powerbuilder6-s		[Guy]
	vnd.lotus-wordpro		[Wattenberger]
	vnd.lotus-approach		[Wattenberger]
	vnd.lotus-1-2-3		[Wattenberger]
	vnd.lotus-organizer		[Wattenberger]
	vnd.lotus-screencam		[Wattenberger]
	vnd.lotus-freelance		[Wattenberger]
	vnd.fujitsu.oasys		[Togashi]
	vnd.fujitsu.oasys2		[Togashi]
	vnd.swiftview-ics		[Widener]
	vnd.dna		[Searcy]
	prs.cww		[Rungchavalnont]
	vnd.wt.stf		[Wohler]
	vnd.dxr		[Duffy]
	vnd.mitsubishi.misty-guard.trustweb		[Tanaka]
	vnd.ibm.modcap		[Hohensee]
	vnd.acucobol		[Lubin]
	vnd.fujitsu.oasys3		[Okudaira]
	marc		[RFC2220]
	vnd.fujitsu.oasysprs		[Ogita]
	vnd.fujitsu.oasysgp		[Sugitomo]

TYPE	SUBTYPE	DESCRIPTION	REFERENCE
application (continued)	vnd.visio		[Sandal]
	vnd.netfpx		[Mutz]
	vnd.audiograph		[Slusanschi]
	vnd.epson.salt		[Nagatomo]
	vnd.3M.Post-it-Notes		[O'Brien]
	vnd.novadigm.EDX		[Swenson]
	vnd.novadigm.EXT		[Swenson]
	vnd.novadigm.EDM		[Swenson]
	vnd.claymore		[Simpson]
	vnd.comsocaller		[Dellutri]
	pkcs7-mime		[RFC2311]
	pkcs7-signature		[RFC2311]
	pkcs10		[RFC2311]
	vnd.yellowriver-custom-menu		[Olsson]
	vnd.ecowin.chart		[Olsson]
	vnd.ecowin.series		[Olsson]
	vnd.ecowin.filerequest		[Olsson]
	vnd.ecowin.fileupdate		[Olsson]
	vnd.ecowin.seriesrequest		[Olsson]
	vnd.ecowin.seriesupdate		[Olsson]
	EDIFACT		[RFC1767]
	EDI-X12		[RFC1767]
	EDI-Consent		[RFC1767]
	vnd.wrq-hp3000-labelled		[Bartram]
	vnd.minisoft-hp3000-save		[Bartram]
	vnd.ffsns		[Holstage]
image	jpeg		[RFC1521,Borenstein]
	gif		[RFC1521,Borenstein]
	ief	Image Exchange Format	[RFC1314]
	g3fax		[RFC1494]
	tiff	Tag Image File Format	[RFC2301]
	cgm	Computer Graphics Metafile	[Francis]
	naplps		[Ferber]
	vnd.dwg		[Moline]

Type	Subtype	Description	Reference
image (continued)	vnd.svf		[Moline]
	vnd.dxf		[Moline]
	png		[Randers-Pehrson]
	vnd.fpx		[Spencer]
	vnd.net-fpx		[Spencer]
	vnd.xiff		[Martin]
audio	basic		[RFC1521,Borenstein]
	32kadpcm		[RFC1911]
	vnd.qcelp		[Lundblade]
video	mpeg		[RFC1521,Borenstein]
	quicktime		[Paul Lindner]
	vnd.vivo		[Wolfe]
	vnd.motorola.video		[McGinty]
	vnd.motorola.videop		[McGinty]
model			[RFC2077]
	iges		[Parks]
	vrml		[RFC2077]
	mesh		[RFC2077]
	vnd.dwf		[Pratt]

The "media-types" directory contains a subdirectory for each content type and each of those directories contains a file for each content subtype.

```
                          |-application-
                          |-audio-------
                          |-image-------
           |-media-types- |-message-----
                          |-model-------
                          |-multipart---
                          |-text--------
                          |-video-------
```

Character Sets

All of the character sets listed the section on Character Sets are registered for use with MIME as MIME Character Sets. The correspondence between the few character sets listed in the MIME specification [RFC1521] and the list in that section are:

TYPE	DESCRIPTION	REFERENCE
US-ASCII	see ANSI_X3.4-1968 below	[RFC1521,Borenstein]
ISO-8859-1	see ISO_8859-1:1987 below	[RFC1521,Borenstein]
ISO-8859-2	see ISO_8859-2:1987 below	[RFC1521,Borenstein]
ISO-8859-3	see ISO_8859-3:1988 below	[RFC1521,Borenstein]
ISO-8859-4	see ISO_8859-4:1988 below	[RFC1521,Borenstein]
ISO-8859-5	see ISO_8859-5:1988 below	[RFC1521,Borenstein]
ISO-8859-6	see ISO_8859-6:1987 below	[RFC1521,Borenstein]
ISO-8859-7	see ISO_8859-7:1987 below	[RFC1521,Borenstein]
ISO-8859-8	see ISO_8859-8:1988 below	[RFC1521,Borenstein]
ISO-8859-9	see ISO_8859-9:1989 below	[RFC1521,Borenstein]

Access Types

TYPE	DESCRIPTION	REFERENCE
FTP		[RFC1521,Borenstein]
ANON-FTP		[RFC1521,Borenstein]
TFTP		[RFC1521,Borenstein]
AFS		[RFC1521,Borenstein]
LOCAL-FILE		[RFC1521,Borenstein]
MAIL-SERVER		[RFC1521,Borenstein]
content-id		[RFC1873]

Conversion Values

Conversion values or Content Transfer Encodings:

TYPE	DESCRIPTION	REFERENCE
7BIT		[RFC1521,Borenstein]
8BIT		[RFC1521,Borenstein]
base64		[RFC1521,Borenstein]
BINARY		[RFC1521,Borenstein]
QUOTED-PRINTABLE		[RFC1521,Borenstein]

MIME / X.400 Mapping Tables

MIME to X.400 Table

MIME CONTENT-TYPE	X.400 BODY PART	REFERENCE
text/plain		
charset=us-ascii	ia5-text	[RFC1494]
charset=iso-8859-x	EBP - GeneralText	[RFC1494]
text/richtext	no mapping defined	[RFC1494]
application/oda	EBP - ODA	[RFC1494]
application/octet-stream	bilaterally-defined	[RFC1494]
application/postscript	EBP - mime-postscript-body	[RFC1494]
image/g3fax	g3-facsimile	[RFC1494]
image/jpeg	EBP - mime-jpeg-body	[RFC1494]
image/gif	EBP - mime-gif-body	[RFC1494]
audio/basic	no mapping defined	[RFC1494]
video/mpeg	no mapping defined	[RFC1494]
Abbreviation: EBP - Extended Body Part		

X.400 to MIME Table—Basic Body Parts

X.400 BASIC BODY PART	MIME CONTENT-TYPE	REFERENCE
ia5-text	text/plain;charset=us-ascii	[RFC1494]
voice	No Mapping Defined	[RFC1494]
g3-facsimile	image/g3fax	[RFC1494]
g4-class1	no mapping defined	[RFC1494]
teletex	no mapping defined	[RFC1494]
videotex	no mapping defined	[RFC1494]
encrypted	no mapping defined	[RFC1494]
bilaterally-defined	application/octet-stream	[RFC1494]
nationally-defined	no mapping defined	[RFC1494]
externally-defined	See Extended Body Parts	[RFC1494]

X.400 to MIME Table—Extended Body Parts

X.400 EXTENDED BODY PART	MIME CONTENT-TYPE	REFERENCE
GeneralText	text/plain;charset=iso-8859- x	[RFC1494]
ODA	application/oda	[RFC1494]
mime-postscript-body	application/postscript	[RFC1494]
mime-jpeg-body	image/jpeg	[RFC1494]
mime-gif-body	image/gif	[RFC1494]

Appendix C

X.400 Content Definitions

The following tables define the content types, bodypart types, and converters which can be used by the MAILbus 400 MTA in a messaging interoperability environment.

Content Types

Content Type	Object Identifier	Description
Any content type	(1 3 12 2 1011 5 5 0 0)	Allows any content type to be delivered.
Unidentified	(1 3 12 2 1011 5 5 0 1 0)	Used by bilateral agreement between users of an MTS.
Electronic Data Interchange	(1 3 12 2 1011 5 5 0 1 35)	Used for documents of the EDI content type.
Interpersonal Messaging 1984	(1 3 12 2 1011 5 5 0 1 2)	IPMS content type as defined by the 1984 MHS Standards. This setting causes an X.400 MTA to downgrade 1992 interpersonal messages to 1984 IPMS format.
Interpersonal messaging 1992. Select one of:		
■ 1992 Externally Defined IPMS	(1 3 12 2 1011 5 5 0 1 22)	Use this content type for users who use applications such as ALL-IN-1™, Message Router Gateway. This setting represents the IPMs content type as defined by the 1992 MHS Standards and includes the interpersonal messaging 1984 content type setting. In this setting, File Transfer bodyparts (FTBPs) in 1992 interpersonal messages are translated to Externally Defined bodyparts. An example of an application generating File Transfer bodyparts is Microsoft® Exchange Server.

continued ▸

Content Type	Object Identifier	Description
▪ 1992 File Transfer	(1 3 12 2 1011 5 5 0 1 22 1)	Use this content type for users who use an application such as Microsoft Exchange Server. This setting represents the IPMs content type as defined by the 1992 MHS Standards and includes the interpersonal messaging 1984 content type setting. In this setting, Externally Defined bodyparts in 1992 interpersonal messages are translated to File Transfer bodyparts. Examples of applications that generate Externally Defined bodyparts are ALL-IN-1 and MailWorks.
▪ 1992 IPMS Passthrough	(1 3 12 2 1011 5 5 0 1 22 0)	Use this setting if you want Externally Defined bodyparts and File Transfer bodyparts in 1992 interpersonal messages to be passed through untranslated. This setting represents IPMS content type as defined by the 1992 MHS Standards and includes the interpersonal messaging 1984 content type setting.

Data Format/Bodypart

DATA FORMAT/BODYPART	EITs	DESCRIPTION
Any EIT	(1 3 12 2 10 11 5 5 1 0)	Allows delivery of any data format or bodypart.
ISO 6937[1]	(1 3 12 2 10 11 5 51 1 11)	Contains text created using the ISO 6937 character set.
ODIF[2] (any Document Application Profile (DAP)	Use the EITs for Externally Defined ODIF Q111, ODIF Q112 and ODIF Q121 specified further on in this table.	Bodypart in 1984 encoding that contains a documents in Open Documents Architecture (ODA). ODA documents can also occur in a 1992 Externally Defined encoding. See further on in this table.
USA Nationally Defined	(1 3 12 2 10 11 5 5 2 0 310)	Contains a bodypart defined by the Stable Implementation Agreements, and whose semantics and syntax are defined by registration within the USA.
IA5Text[3]	(2 6 3 4 2)	Contains text created using the IA5 international reference version (IRV) character set. IA5 text characters are similar to ASCII text characters.
Voice[3]	(2 6 3 4 2)	Contains digitized speech.
G3Fax[3]	(2 6 3 4 3)	Contains data in an encoding necessary for document transmission using Group 3 facsimile apparatus.
G4Class1[3]	(2 6 3 4 4)	Contains data in an encoding necessary for document transmission using Group 4 Class 1 facsimile apparatus.
Teletex[3]	(2 6 3 4 5)	Contains data suitable for transmission using teletex terminal equipment.
Videotex[3]	(2 6 3 4 6)	Contains videotex data.
Encrypted[3]	(1 3 12 2 10 11 5 5 2 0 8)	Contains another bodypart in encrypted form.
Message[3]	No EIT required, the MTA delivers on the basis of bodyparts contained in the forwarded message.	Bodypart that contains an IPM, enclosed in another, to represent forwarded messages.
Mixed-mode[3]	(2 6 3 4 9)	Contains a mixed mode document that contains characters and raster graphics.
Bilaterally Defined[3]	(1 3 12 2 10 11 5 5 2 0 7)	Contains data whose semantics and syntax are agreed on a national basis.

continued ▸

DATA FORMAT/BODYPART	EITS	DESCRIPTION
Externally Defined[3] can contain for example:		
▪ DDIF[4]	(1 3 12 1011 1 3 1)	Contains a document in Digital Document Interchange Format (DDIF), as used in Digital's compound document architecture, CDA.
▪ DECdx[4]	(1 3 12 1011 1 3 8)	Contains data in DECdx™ format, DECdx is an intermediate data format generated by Digital Gateways (such as the Message Router/P and Message Router/S Gateways) and User Agents.
▪ DEC MCS[4]	(1 3 12 2 1011 5 1 209)	Contains characters from the DEC Multi-national character set (MCS).
▪ DTIF[4]	(1 3 12 1011 1 3 3)	Contains a document in Digital Tabular Interchange Format (DTIF), as used in Digital's compound document architecture, CDA.
▪ DOTS[4]	(1 3 12 1011 1 3 2)	Contains a document in the Data Object Transport Syntax (DOTS) mail interchange format. DOTS is used to encapsulate data elements that have links between them, for example, a DDIF document and its references to external documents.
▪ Postscript[4]	(1 3 12 1011 1 3 6)	Contains a document in the PostScript® interchange and presentation format.
▪ ODIF Q111[5]	(2 8 1 0 1) (1 3 16 2 6 0 2)	Contains a document confirming to ODA. Document application profile (DAP) Q121.
▪ Message Router test[4]	(1 3 12 2 1011 5 1 210)	Assumed to contain characters from the DEC Multi-national character set (MCS).
▪ WPS-PLUS[4]	(1 3 12 1011 1 3 7)	Contains a document in WPS-PLUS™ format.
▪ SDK	(1 3 12 2 1011 5 1 184)	Super DEC Kanji Text bodypart.
▪ SJIS	(1 3 12 2 1011 5 1 185)	Shift JIS Text bodypart.
▪ jjpbody88	(1 2 3 9 2 6 1 4 0)	Bodypart defined by INTAP.[6]

continued ▸

DATA FORMAT/BODYPART	EITS	DESCRIPTION
General text[3]		Can carry any character set data registered in "International Register of ISO Coded Character Sets" published by ISO. Use the object identifiers stem (1 0 10021 7 1 0 n), where n is the integer defined for the appropriate character set(s) in above mentioned ISO publication.
Examples of General Text:		
■ ISO Latin 1	(1 0 10021 7 1 0 6) (1 0 10021 7 1 0 100) (1 0 10021 7 1 0 1) (1 0 10021 7 1 0 77)	Contains characters from the ISO Latin 1 character set.
■ T.61 Latin	(1 0 10021 7 1 0 102) (1 0 10021 7 1 0 103) (1 0 10021 7 1 0 106) (1 0 10021 7 1 0 107)	Contains characters from the T.61 Latin character set.
■ IA5	(1 0 10021 7 1 0 2) (1 0 10021 7 1 0 1)	Contains characters from the IA5 character set.
■ Jpbody84	(1 3 12 2 1011 5 5 2 0 440)	Bodypart defined by INTAP[7] as JPBodyParts. This bodypart is for IPMS content type Interpersonal Messaging 1984.

[1.] Bodypart defined in International Standard ISO DIS 9055 (the obsolete ISO standard corresponding to CCITT 1984 Recommendation X.420).

[2.] Bodypart defined in the Stable Implementation Agreements for Open Systems Interconnection Protocols, Version 7, Edition 1, December 1993, Chapter 7.

[3.] Bodypart defined in CCITT Recommendation X.420 and International Standard ISO/IEC 10021-7.

[4.] Bodypart defined by Digital Equipment Corporation.

[5.] Bodypart defined in International Standard ISO 8613 and related profiles Q111, Q112 or Q121.

[6.] INTAP is the Interoperability technology Association for Information Processing Japan.

[7.] The descriptive data in the bodypart is lost, but no message data in the bodypart is lost.

Converters

Converter Entity	Input (Source Bodypart Entity)	Output (Target Bodypart Entity)	Lossy
"ia5tolatin1"	"ia5text" (IA5 text)	"isolatin1" (ISO Latin 1)	False
"latin1to61"	"isolatin1" (ISO Latin 1)	"teletex" (Teletex)	False
"latin1togeneralia5"	"isolatin1" (ISO Latin 1)	"generaltextia5" (General Text containing IA5 characters)	True
"generaltoia5"	"generaltextia5" (Ge General Text containing IA5 characters)	"ia5text" (IA5 text)	False
"generalt61tolatin1"	"generaltextt61" (General Text containing T.61 Latin characters)	"isolatin1" (ISO Latin 1)	True
"t61togeneral"	"teletex" (Teletex)	"generaltextt61" (General Text containing T.61 Latin characters)	False
"generaltot61"	"generaltextt61" (General Text containing T.61 Latin characters)	"teletex" (Teletex)	False
"t61tolatin1"	"teletex" (Teletex)	"isolatin1" (ISO Latin 1)	True
"latin1toia5"	"isolatin 1" (ISO Latin 1)	"ia5text" (IA5 text)	True
"iso6937tolatin1"	"iso6937" (ISO 6937)	"isolatin1" (ISO Latin 1)	True
"latin1toiso6937"	"isolatin1" (ISO Latin1)	"iso6937 (ISO 6937)	False
"externaldeftobilatdef"	"externallydefined" (Externally Defined)	"bilaterallydefined" (Bilaterally Defined)	False[1]
"externaldeftoposte"	"externallydefined" (Externally Defined)	"bilaterallydefined" (Bilaterally Defined)	False
"decdxtolatin1"	"decdx" (DECdx)	"latin1" (ISO Latin 1)	True
"wpsplustolatin1"	"wpsplus" (WPS-PLUS)	"latin1" (ISO Latin 1)	True
"decmcstolatin1"	"decmcs" (DEC Multi-national character set)	"latin1" (ISO Latin 1)	True
"latin1todecmcs"	"isolatin1" (ISO Latin 1)	"decmcs" (DE Multinational character set)	True
"mrtexttolatin1"	"mrtext" (Message Router Text)	"isolatin1" (ISO Latin1)	True
"latin1tomrtext"	"isolatin1" (ISO Latin 1)	"mrtext" (Message Router Text)	True
"j84tosdk"	"jpbody84" (JPBody Part)	"sdk" (Super DEC Kanji)	False
"sdktoj84"	"sdk" (Super DEC Kanji)	"jpbody84" (JP BodyPart)	True
"j88tosdk"	"jpbody88" (Extended JP1)	"sdk" (Super DEC Kanji)	False
"sdktoj88"	"sdk" (Super DEC Kanji)	"JPBODY88" (Extended JP1)	True
"sjistosdk"	"sjis" (shift JIS)	"sdk" (Super DEC Kanji)	False
"sdktosjis"	"sdk" (Super DEC Kanji)	"sjis" (Shift JIS)	True

[1]. The descriptive data in the bodypart is lost, but no message data in the bodypart is lost.

Sample Script to Generate
Unique SMTP Addresses

This UNIX shell script searches a central LDAP directory for person entries that don't already have an SMTP address. For each entry that meets the search criteria, it will create a unique address.

Although this script is written in UNIX shell code, it could easily be modified to run under Perl or Visual Basic.

```sh
#!/bin/sh
#
# Filename: umail.sh
#
# Purpose:  To generate Internet mail addresses that are unique within
#           Zeitgeist.
#
# Define some script functions
#
im_givn () {
if [ ! "$GNREC" ]
then
   GNREC="$IRECORD"
   PREVFIELD="GN"
fi
}
#
im_surn () {
if [ ! "$SNREC" ]
then
   SNREC="$IRECORD"
   PREVFIELD="SN"
fi
}
#
```

```
im_init () {
if [ ! "$INREC" ]
then
    INREC="$IRECORD"
    PREVFIELD="IN"
fi
}
#
im_cont () {
IRECORD=`echo $IRECORD | sed 's/ //'`
case "$PREVFIELD" in
    DN)     DNREC=${DNREC}${IRECORD};;
    GN)     GNREC=${GNREC}${IRECORD};;
    SN)     SNREC=${SNREC}${IRECORD};;
    IN)     INREC=${INREC}${IRECORD};;
esac
}
#
IFILE=/pmdf/dirsync/atds/umail.ldif
TFILE=/pmdf/dirsync/atds/umail.tmp
LOGFILE=/pmdf/dirsync/atds/umail.log
IRECCORRUPT="FALSE"
RECINDEX=1
PREVFIELD=
#
# Define parameters for the LDAP utilities
#
LDAPHOST=ldapserver.zg.com
LDAPPORT=389
LDAPSCOPE="sub"
#
# Update the path to include the location of the LDAP utilities
#
LDAPUTILSDIR=/opt/IIIdds/bin
PATH=$LDAPUTILSDIR:$PATH; export PATH
#
if [ -f $LOGFILE ]
then
            echo "Saving old log file $LOGFILE to $LOGFILE.sav"
            mv $LOGFILE ${LOGFILE}.sav
fi
#
echo "umail.sh started at `date`" > $LOGFILE
#
```

```
# Create an LDIF file containing details of users without mail addresses
#
ldapsearch -L -h $LDAPHOST -p $LDAPPORT
"(&(objectclass=zeitgeistPerson)(!(mail=*)))" dn givenname initials sn > $IFILE
#
# Check for empty file
#
if [ -s $IFILE ]
then
#
# Add a blank line to the end of the file
#
   echo "" >> $IFILE
else
   echo "There are no entries without an Internet mail address" >> $LOGFILE
   exit 0
fi
#
# Open the LDIF file
#
exec 3<$IFILE
#
# Read each record in the LDAP extract file
#
OLDIFS=$IFS
IFS=
while read IRECORD 0<&3
do
#
# The first record in a block should be the dn: record
#
   if [ "$RECINDEX" = "1" ]
   then
           if echo $IRECORD | grep -i "dn:" > /dev/null
           then
                   DNREC=$IRECORD
                   PREVFIELD="DN"
                   RECINDEX=`expr $RECINDEX + 1`
                   continue
           else
                   IREC1=$IRECORD
                   IRECCORRUPT="TRUE"
                   break
           fi
```

```
    fi
#   echo "checkpoint 2"
#
# The second record in a block could be the givenname, initials or
# surname record
#
    if [ "$RECINDEX" = "2" ]
    then
            case "$IRECORD" in
                    *givenname:*)               GNREC=$IRECORD;;
                    *initials:*)                INREC=$IRECORD;;
                    *sn:*)                      SNREC=$IRECORD;;
                    " "*)               im_cont
                                        RECINDEX="1";;
                    *)                  IRECCORRUPT="TRUE"
                                        IREC2=$IRECORD
                                        break;;
            esac
            RECINDEX=`expr $RECINDEX + 1`
            continue
    fi
#
# The third, fourth, and fifth records in a block could be the givenname,
# initials or surname record or they could be blank records (indicating # the end
of a block)
#
    if [ "$RECINDEX" != "99" ]
    then
#
# Is this a blank record?
#
            if [ `expr "$IRECORD" : '.*'` != "0" ]
            then
                    case "$IRECORD" in
                            *givenname:*)               im_givn
                                                continue;;
                            *initials:*)            im_init
                                                continue;;
                            *sn:*)                      im_surn
                                                continue;;
                            " "*)               im_cont
                                                continue;;
                            *)                  IRECCORRUPT="TRUE"
                                                IREC4=$IRECORD
```

```
                                                  break;;
                          esac
               else
                          RECINDEX="99"
               fi
      fi
#
# Record Number 99 indicates the end of an entry block.
# The stored records are now processed to extract the givenname,
# initials, and surname values.
#
      if [ "$RECINDEX" = "99" ]
      then
               IFS=$OLDIFS
               GN=`echo $GNREC`
               IN=`echo $INREC`
               SN=`echo $SNREC`
               GN=`expr "$GN" : 'givenname: \(.*\)'`
               IN=`expr "$IN" : 'initials: \(.*\)'`
               SN=`expr "$SN" : 'sn: \(.*\)'`
#
# Keep everything to the right of a left bracket if present
#
               GN=`echo $GN | sed 's/ //g'`
               GN=`expr "$GN" : '\(.*\)(' \| $GN`
               SN=`echo $SN | sed 's/ //g'`
               SN=`expr "$SN" : '\(.*\)(' \| $SN`
#


# Remove invalid characters
#
               GN=`echo $GN | tr -c -d "[:alnum:]"`
               IN=`echo $IN | tr -c -d "[:alnum:]"`
               SN=`echo $SN | tr -c -d "[:alnum:]"`
#
# Generate the first attempt at a unique mail address
#
               if [ `expr "$GN" : '.*'` != "0" ]
               then
                       ADDR1=${GN}.${SN}
               else
                       ADDR1=$SN
               fi
               ADDR=${ADDR1}@zeitgeist.com
```

```
#
# Check for uniqueness by searching the LDAP directory for it
#
          RESULT=`ldapsearch -L -h $LDAPHOST -p $LDAPPORT —s
                $LDAPSCOPE "mail=$ADDR" dn | grep -c "dn:"`
#
# If the first attempt at uniqueness fails then use initials if they are present
#
          if [ "$RESULT" != "0" ] && [ `expr "$IN" : '.*'` != "0" ]
          then
                ADDR="$GN.$IN.$SN@zeitgist.com"
#               echo $ADDR
                RESULT=`ldapsearch -L -h $LDAPHOST -p $LDAPPORT —s
                      $LDAPSCOPE "mail=$ADDR" | grep -c "dn:"`
          fi
#
# If the address is still not unique then generate an address using
# givenname, surname, and a number suffix. Increment the number suffix
# until uniqueness is achieved
#
          INDEX=0
          until [ $RESULT -eq 0 ]
          do
                INDEX=`expr $INDEX + 1`
                ADDR="$ADDR1${INDEX}@zeitgeist.com"
                RESULT=`ldapsearch -L -h $LDAPHOST -p $LDAPPORT —s
                      $LDAPSCOPE "mail=$ADDR" | grep -c "dn:"`
          done
#
# Modify the entry in the LDAP directory with the unique mail address
# and write to a log file.
#
#         echo "Use ldapmodify to add mail address"
                ldapmodify -h $LDAPHOST -p $LDAPPORT -D "cn=manager"
                      -w mysecret <<- EOF
          $DNREC
          changetype: modify
          replace: mail
          mail: $ADDR

          EOF

          echo "" >> $LOGFILE
          echo "Distinguished Name:   " $DNREC >> $LOGFILE
```

```
                     echo "Internet Mail Address:" $ADDR >> $LOGFILE
#
# Reset variables
#
                RECINDEX="1"
                GNREC=""
                INREC=""
                SNREC=""
                IFS=
                PREVFIELD=
    fi
done
#
# Close LDIF file
#
exec 3<&-
#
# Check for corrupt data having occurred
    if [ "$IRECCORRUPT" = "TRUE" ]
    then
                echo "Input File appears to be corrupt" >> $LOGFILE
                echo "Record Buffers contain:" >> $LOGFILE
                echo "REC1:$IREC1" >> $LOGFILE
                echo "REC2:$IREC2" >> $LOGFILE
                echo "REC3:$IREC3" >> $LOGFILE
                echo "REC4:$IREC4" >> $LOGFILE
                exit 1
    fi
#
if [ -f $IFILE ]
then
        rm $IFILE
fi
#
if [ -f $TFILE ]
then
        rm $TFILE
fi
#
echo " " >> $LOGFILE
echo "umail.sh finished at `date`" >> $LOGFILE
#
#
exit 0
```

Appendix E

Sample Script to Generate PMDF Database Files

This UNIX shell script uses a central LDAP directory to build forward and reverse address translation files for PMDF. It is based on addressing structures used for the Zeitgeist environment and builds reverse entries for both Exchange and Notes destination environments.

Although this script is written in UNIX shell code, it could easily be modified to run under Perl or Visual Basic.

```sh
#!/bin/sh
#
# Filename: build_dir_table.sh
#
# Purpose:  To generate PMDF forward and reverse database files.
#
#
echo ""
echo "build_dir_table.sh is starting."
DATE=`date`
echo "Current time is $DATE."
echo   ""
#
# Define some string constants that we'll use for validation checking.
#
DNSTRING='dn:'
MAILSTRING='mail:'
IMASTRING='internalmailaddress:'
PPLCOUNT=0
ENTRYINDEX=1
PPLBFR01=''
PPLBFR02=''
PPLBFR03=''
```

```
PPLBFR04=''
PPLMAILBUFFER=''
PPLIMABUFFER=''
UNIQUENAME=''
EMA=''
IMA=''
PPLCORRUPT=FALSE
#
# Define some LDAP constants.
#
LDAPHOST=ldapserver.zg.com
LDAPPORT=389
LDAPBASE="o=Zeitgeist"
LDAPSCOPE="sub"
LDAPFILTER='(objectclass=zeitgeistPerson)'
LDAPATTRS='mail internalMailAddress'
#
echo "Using LDAP host $LDAPHOST."
echo "Using LDAP port $LDAPPORT."
echo "Using searchbase $LDAPBASE."
echo "Using search scope $LDAPSCOPE."
echo "Using LDAP filter $LDAPFILTER."
echo "Exporting LDAP attributes $LDAPATTRS."
echo ""
#
# Update the path to include the location of the LDAP tools.
#
LDAPTOOLSDIR=/opt/IIIdds/bin
PATH=$LDAPTOOLSDIR:$PATH; export PATH
#
# Set some working variables.
#
WORKDIR=/pmdf/dirsync
PPLFILE=/pmdf/dirsync/zeitgeist_people_dir.txt
OLDPPLFILE=/pmdf/dirsync/zeitgeist_people_dir.old
DIRFILE=/pmdf/dirsync/zeitgeist_directory.txt
OLDDIRFILE=/pmdf/dirsync/zeitgeist_directory.old
REVFILE=/pmdf/dirsync/zeitgeist_reverse.txt
OLDREVFILE=/pmdf/dirsync/zeitgeist_reverse.old
#
echo "Using work area $WORKDIR."
echo "Using PPLFILE $PPLFILE."
echo "Using DIRFILE $DIRFILE."
echo "Using REVFILE $REVFILE."
```

```
echo ""
#
# Check if there's an existing people export text file; if there is
# rename it.
#
if [ -f $PPLFILE ]; then
    echo "Found $PPLFILE; renaming to $OLDPPLFILE."
    echo ""
    mv $PPLFILE $OLDPPLFILE
fi
#
# Now export the zeitgeistPerson entries from the LDAP directory
#
echo "Starting export from LDAP directory."
DATE=`date`
echo "Current time is $DATE."
echo  ""
#
ldapsearch \
    -L \
    -h $LDAPHOST \
    -p $LDAPPORT \
    -b $LDAPBASE \
    -s $LDAPSCOPE \
    $LDAPFILTER \
    $LDAPATTRS \
    > $PPLFILE
#
echo "LDAP export written to $PPLFILE."
echo "Finished export from LDAP directory."
DATE=`date`
echo "Current time is $DATE."
echo  ""
#
# Now that we've got the people entries, let's start to build the raw
# directory file.
#
# Check if there's an existing people directory text file; if there is
# rename it.
#
if [ -f $DIRFILE ]; then
    echo "Found $DIRFILE; renaming to $OLDDIRFILE."
    echo ""
    mv $DIRFILE $OLDDIRFILE
```

```
fi
#
# Check if there's an existing people reverse text file; if there is
# rename it.
#
if [ -f $REVFILE ]; then
    echo "Found $REVFILE; renaming to $OLDREVFILE."
    echo ""
    mv $REVFILE $OLDREVFILE
fi
#
# Open the PPLFILE.
#
echo "Opening PPLFILE."
#
exec 3<$PPLFILE
#
# Now write some header info to the DIRFILE.
#
echo "!!!!!!!!!!!!!!!!!!!!!!!!!!!!!!!!!!!!!!!!!!!!!!!!!!!!!!!"   >$DIRFILE
echo "!"                                                        >>$DIRFILE
echo "! PMDF Directory Channel Database File"                   >>$DIRFILE
echo "! ----------------------------------"                     >>$DIRFILE
echo "!"                                                        >>$DIRFILE
echo "! This file was automatically generated by the"           >>$DIRFILE
echo "! build_dir_table.sh routine."                            >>$DIRFILE
echo "!"                                                        >>$DIRFILE
echo "! Generation time: $DATE"                                 >>$DIRFILE
echo "!"                                                        >>$DIRFILE
echo "!!!!!!!!!!!!!!!!!!!!!!!!!!!!!!!!!!!!!!!!!!!!!!!!!!!!!!!"   >>$DIRFILE
echo "!"                                                        >>$DIRFILE
#
# Now write some header info to the REVFILE.
#
echo "!!!!!!!!!!!!!!!!!!!!!!!!!!!!!!!!!!!!!!!!!!!!!!!!!!!!!!!"   >$REVFILE
echo "!"                                                        >>$REVFILE
echo "! PMDF Address Reversal Database File"                    >>$REVFILE
echo "! ----------------------------------"                     >>$REVFILE
echo "!"                                                        >>$REVFILE
echo "! This file was automatically generated by the"           >>$REVFILE
echo "! build_dir_table.sh routine."                            >>$REVFILE
echo "!"                                                        >>$REVFILE
echo "! Generation time: $DATE"                                 >>$REVFILE
echo "!"                                                        >>$REVFILE
```

```
echo "!!!!!!!!!!!!!!!!!!!!!!!!!!!!!!!!!!!!!!!!!!!!!!!!!!!!!"        >>$REVFILE
echo "!"                                                           >>$REVFILE
#
# Now start reading in data from the people file.
#
echo "Processing records from PPLFILE."
DATE=`date`
echo "Current time is $DATE."
echo  ""
#
while read PPLBUFFER 0<&3
do
    #
    # Only try to process line 1 if it's our turn.
    #
    if [ "$ENTRYINDEX" = "1" ]
    then
            #
            # The first line that we read should contain the dn attribute.
            # If not there's been some form of corruption; signal it and
            # exit.
            #
            if echo "$PPLBUFFER" | grep "$DNSTRING" > /dev/null
            then
                    #
                    # This line is valid, let's store the line in case we need
                    # it later.
                    #
                    PPLBFR01=$PPLBUFFER
            else
                    #
                    # The first line doesn't contain what it should. Signal an
                    # error.
                    #
                    PPLCORRUPT="TRUE"
                    #
            fi
    fi
    #
    # Only try to process line 2 if it's our turn.
    #
    if [ "$ENTRYINDEX" = "2" ]
    then
            #
```

```
        # Let's read the next line from the PPLFILE. It should contain
        # the mail or the internalmailaddress attribute. We can't be
        # sure of the order since the LDAP implementation may not be
        # consistent in how it returns attributes; so we need to check.
        #
        # Check for the mail or ima strings.
        #
        case "$PPLBUFFER" in
            *"$MAILSTRING"*)        PPLBFRO2=$PPLBUFFER
                                    PPLMAILBUFFER=$PPLBUFFER ;;
            *"$IMABUFFER"*)         PPLBFRO2=$PPLBUFFER
                                    PPLIMABUFFER=$PPLBUFFER ;;
             *)                     PPLCORRUPT="TRUE" ;;
        esac
fi
#
# Only try to process line 3 if it's our turn.
#
if [ "$ENTRYINDEX" = "3" ]
then
        #
        # Let's read the next line from the PPLFILE. It should contain
        # the mail or the internalmailaddress attribute. We can't be
        # sure of the order since the LDAP implementation may not be
        # consistent in how it returns attributes; so we need to check.
        #
        # Check for the mail or ima strings.
        #
        case "$PPLBUFFER" in
            *"$MAILSTRING"*)        PPLBFRO3=$PPLBUFFER
                                    PPLMAILBUFFER=$PPLBUFFER ;;
            *"$IMABUFFER"*)         PPLBFRO3=$PPLBUFFER
                                    PPLIMABUFFER=$PPLBUFFER ;;
             *)                     PPLCORRUPT="TRUE" ;;
        esac
fi
#
# Only try to process line 4 if it's our turn.
#
if ["$ENTRYINDEX" = "4" ]
then
        #
        # It looks like we've made it to line 4. Let's read the last
        # line.
```

```
                #
                # Check that it's a null line.
                #
                STRINGLENGTH=`expr "$PPLBUFFER" : '.*'`
                if [ "$STRINGLENGTH" = "0" ]
                then
                        PPLBFR04=DUMMY
                else
                        PPLCORRUPT="TRUE"
                fi
fi
#
# Check for an error along the way.
#
if [ "$PPLCORRUPT" = "TRUE" ]
then
        #
        # Something bad has happened. Looks like the PPLFILE is corrupt.
        # Print as much info as we have to help isolate the problem
        # and then exit with an error status.
        #
        echo "PPLFILE apears to be corrupt."
        echo "Processed $PPLCOUNT record(s) so far."
        echo "Dumping contents of the PPL buffers."
        echo "PPLBFR01, data:$PPLBFR01"
        echo "PPLBFR02, data:$PPLBFR02"
        echo "PPLBFR03, data:$PPLBFR03"
        echo "PPLBFR04, data:$PPLBFR04"
        echo "Exiting with error status."
        DATE=`date`
        echo "Current time is $DATE."
        echo  ""
        #
        exit 1
        #
fi
#
# We're really only interested in the first 3 lines of each entry.
# If the index counter says 3 then let's process the important
# stuff.
#
if [ "$ENTRYINDEX" = "3" ]
then
        #
```

```
# Let's deal with the PPLMAILBUFFER first. This should hold
# the complete external SMTP address of the person.
# Since we're only interested in addresses of @zeitgeist.com
# let's make sure that's what we've got.
#
if echo "$PPLMAILBUFFER" | grep "@zeitgeist.com" > /dev/null
then
        #
        # It's valid. Now let's clean it up and only take what we
        # need.
        #
        # First trim leading/trailing spaces and compress internal
        # space.
        #
        EMA=`echo $PPLMAILBUFFER`
        #
        # Now remove the 'mail: ' part at the start and the
        # '@zeitgeist.com' part at the end.
        #
        EMA=`expr "$EMA" : 'mail: \(.*\)'`
        UNIQUENAME=`expr "$EMA" : '\(.*\)@zeitgeist.com'`
        #
        # Now trim off the 'internalmailaddress: ' part at the start
        # of the IMA.
        #
        IMA=`echo $PPLIMABUFFER`
        IMA=`expr "$IMA" : 'internalmailaddress: \(.*\)'`
        #
        echo "$UNIQUENAME\t\t\t$IMA" >>$DIRFILE
        #
        # Now let's check to see what type of recipient we have
        #
        case "$IMA" in
            *@ex.zeitgeist.com)
                #
                # It's an Exchange address
                #
                echo "Exch|$EMA\t$IMA" >>$REVFILE
                echo "Notes|$IMA\t$EMA" >>$REVFILE
                echo "#" >>$REVFILE ;;
            *)
                #
                # It's a Notes address
                #
```

```
                               # We need to extract out the Notes native part
                               #
                               echo "Exch|$IMA\t$EMA" >>$REVFILE
                               echo "Notes|$EMA\t$IMA" >>$REVFILE
                               echo "#" >>$REVFILE ;;
                    esac
              else
                    #
                    # The external SMTP address for this entry doesn't end with
                    # @zeitgeist.com. We do not deal with these addresses.
                    # Log this and ignore the entry.
                    #
                    echo "Detected non-Zeitgeist address."
                    echo "Dumping contents of PPL DN buffer."
                    echo "PPLBFRO1, data:$PPLBFRO1"
              fi
    fi
    #
    # Update the index counter to show we've read another line.
    # Reset it back to one if we've done four already.
    #
    if [ "$ENTRYINDEX" = "4" ]
    then
        ENTRYINDEX=1
        PPLCOUNT=`expr $PPLCOUNT + 1`
    else
        ENTRYINDEX=`expr $ENTRYINDEX + 1`
    fi
    #
done
#
# We miss the last increment onto the PPLCOUNT when the last line gets
# read. Fix it up here, just before we print it.
#
PPLCOUNT=`expr $PPLCOUNT + 1`
echo "Processed $PPLCOUNT records from PPLFILE."
echo "Finished processing records from PPLFILE."
DATE=`date`
echo "Current time is $DATE."
echo ""
#
# Close the PPLFILE.
#
echo "%BLDDIRTBL-I-PPLCLOSE, closing PPLFILE."
```

```
#
exec 3<&-
#
# We're done.
#
echo "build_dir_table script is terminating."
DATE=`date`
echo "Current time is $DATE."
echo  ""
#
exit 0
```

Script to Update MS Mail Custom Recipients

This Perl script runs on Windows NT and exports custom recipients that are missing first name and last name attributes, but have a fully formed display name of the form (Lastname, Firstname). The display name attribute is parsed and the first name and last name attribute values are derived. The resulting CSV file is then imported back into the Exchange GAL.

The additional files, which this script references, are shown immediately after it. Although this script is written in Perl, it could easily be modified to run under Visual Basic.

```perl
# Filename:    MSUpdate.pl
#
# Purpose:     Updates First & Last attributes for MS Mail entries in
#              Exchange GAL.
#
#
use Win32;

# Some important definitions

$DirSyncPath="C:\\DirSync\\MsMailN";
$ExchSrvrBinPath="C:\\Exchsrvr\\Bin";
$InBufferSize=1;

{
     $status=Initialize();
     $status=ExportExchDir();
     $status=PrepImportFile();
     $status=ParseExportData();
     $status=ImportUpdatedData();
     $status=Terminate();
}
```

```perl
###
#
sub Initialize {
     print "Executing MS Mail Address Update at ";
     print (PrettyTime(), "\n");
     print (OperatingEnvironment(), "\n");
     print "\n"
     } #End of sub Initialize
###
#
sub PrettyTime {
     ($sec,$min,$hr,$mday,$mon,$year,$wday,$yday,$isdst)=gmtime(time);
     $PrettyD=join '/',$mday,$mon,$year;
     $PrettyT=join ':',sprintf("%2u",$hr),sprintf("%2u",$min),
          sprintf("%2u",$sec);
     $PrettyTime=join ' ',$PrettyD,$PrettyT;
     return $PrettyTime
     } #End sub PrettyTime
###
#
sub OperatingEnvironment {
     $PerlVer=Win32::PerlVersion();
     $OSVer=Win32::GetOSVersion();
     $Login=Win32::LoginName();
     $Domain=Win32::DomainName();
     $OEVersion=join ' ',"Perl",$PerlVer,"on NT Ver",$OSVer, "from
          user",$Login,"in domain",$Domain;
     return $OEVersion
     } #End sub OperatingEnvironment
###
#
sub ExportExchDir {

     #Check for existence of Exch Dir Export Options File

     $MsDirExpOptions=join '\\',$DirSyncPath,"msexp.opt";
     $PrintBuffer=join '',"Exchange Export Options file is: ",
          $MsDirExpOptions;
     print $PrintBuffer, "\n";
     open MsDirExpOptions or die "ABORT: Can't find Exchange ExportOptions
          file";
     close MsDirExpOptions;

     #Check for existence of Exch Dir Export Template File
```

```
$MsDirExpTemplate=join '\\',$DirSyncPath,"msexp.tpl";
$PrintBuffer=join '',"Exchange Export Template file is: ",
    $MsDirExpTemplate;
print $PrintBuffer, "\n";
open MsDirExpTemplate or die "ABORT: Can't find Exchange Export Template
    file";
close MsDirExpTemplate;

#Build file handle for Export Data File

$DateID=join '',$mday,$mon,$year;
$DataFile=join '',"msexp-",$DateID,".csv";
$MsDirExpData=join '\\',$DirSyncPath,$DataFile;
$PrintBuffer=join '',"Exchange Export Data file is: ", $MsDirExpData;
print $PrintBuffer, "\n";

#Copy Export Template File to Export Data file

$PrintBuffer=join '',"Copying: ",$MsDirExpTemplate," to: ",
    $MsDirExpData;
print $PrintBuffer, "\n";
$Command=join ' ',"COPY",$MsDirExpTemplate,$MsDirExpData;
system($Command);

#Build Exchange Admin command and export Ms Dir Entries to the
#Data File

$ExchSrvAdmin=join '\\',$ExchSrvrBinPath,"Admin.exe /E";
$Command=join '',$ExchSrvAdmin," ",$MsDirExpData," /N /O ",
    $MsDirExpOptions;

$PrintBuffer=join '',"Exporting MS Directory Entries to: ", $MsDirExpData;
print $PrintBuffer, "\n";
$PrintBuffer="This may take some time; please wait...";
print $PrintBuffer, "\n";

print $Command, "\n";
system($Command);
} #End sub ExportExchDir
###
#
```

```
sub PrepImportFile {

    #Check for existence of Exch Dir Import Header File

    $MsDirImpHeader=join '\\',$DirSyncPath,"msimp.hdr";
    $PrintBuffer=join '',"Exchange Import Header file is: ", $MsDirImpHeader;
    print $PrintBuffer, "\n";
    open MsDirImpHeader or die "ABORT: Can't find Exchange Import Header
        file";
    close MsDirImpHeader;

    #Build file handle for Import Data File

    $DateID=join '',$mday,$mon,$year;
    $DataFile=join '',"msimp-",$DateID,".csv";
    $MsDirImpData=join '\\',$DirSyncPath,$DataFile;
    $PrintBuffer=join '',"Exchange Import Data file is: ", $MsDirImpData;
    print $PrintBuffer, "\n";

    #Copy Import Header File to Import Data file

    $PrintBuffer=join '',"Copying: ",$MsDirImpHeader," to: ", $MsDirImpData;
    print $PrintBuffer, "\n";
    $Command=join ' ',"COPY",$MsDirImpHeader,$MsDirImpData;
    system($Command);

    } #End sub PrepImportFile
###
#
sub ParseExportData {

    $PrintBuffer="Processing Export Data & building Updates List...";
    print $PrintBuffer, "\n";

    #Open the newly exported data file, and write duplicates to disk

    open MsDirExpData or die "ABORT: Can't find Exchange Export Data file";
    $MsDirImpDataAppend=join '',">>",$MsDirImpData;
    open MsDirImpDataAppend or die "ABORT: Can't open $MsDirImpDataAppend";

    $RecCnt=0;

    ReadLn();
```

```
        while ($InBuffer ne "") {

                $status=ProcessBuffer();
                if ($OutputRequired eq "TRUE")
                        { print MsDirImpDataAppend $OutBuffer, "\n" };
                ReadLn()
                }
        close MsDirExpData;
        close MsDirImpDataAppend

        } #End sub ParseExportData
###
#
sub ReadLn {

        #Build a line from the Export Data file:

        $InBuffer="";
        $BR=read MsDirExpData,$Buf,$InBufferSize;
        while (($Buf ne "\n") && ($BR ne 0)){
                $InBuffer=join '',$InBuffer,$Buf;
                $BR=read MsDirExpData,$Buf,$InBufferSize;
                }
        $RecCnt++;
        if ($BR eq 0) { print "EOF detected. \n"}

        } #End sub ReadLn
###
#
sub ProcessBuffer {

        $OutputRequired="FALSE";

        #Split the fields from the input string

        ($obj,$dispn,$dirn,$emAddresses)=split /\t/,$InBuffer;

        #Only process valid data lines

        if ($obj ne "Obj-Class") {

                #Check first char of Display Name: if it's in /</
                #then ignore since this will be a DL of some description.
```

```
            if ((grep /</, (substr $dispn, 0, 1)) eq 0) {
                    $OutputRequired="TRUE";

                    #Process Records

                    $status=ProcessDisplayName();
                    $status=ProcessEMAddresses();

                    #Build the output data

                    $OutBuffer=join "\t",$obj,"Modify",$dirn,$fn,$ln,
                            $init,$emAddresses;
                    }

                }
        } #End sub ProcessBuffer
###
#
sub ProcessDisplayName {

    $fn="";
    $ln="";
    $init="";

    #Split the Display Name attribute to get the first last and
    #surname parts free

    #First take the Last Name out of the Display Name field. This is
    #always everything up to the first comma.

    ($ln,$spill)=split /,/, $dispn;

    #Now check to see if there's a SPACE immediately after the comma.
    #It's possible that the SPACE may have been left out at some
    #stage, so we'll check just to be sure and set the offset
    #accordingly for when we pluck the rest of the string.

    $firstSpillChar=substr $spill, 0, 1;

    if ($firstSpillChar eq " ") {
            $offset=1
            }
    else {
            $offset=0
            }
```

```
        #Take everything after the first space if it exists
        #Are you still paying attention?

        $spill=substr $spill, $offset;

        #Now take the Firstname out, and assume the rest is the initials

        ($fn,$spill)=split / /,$spill;

        #Check to see if there are any initials left, otherwise we've got
        #the lot. If we do find initials then take out the first SPACE if
        #it exists and use the rest as initials.

        if ($fn ne $spill) {
                $firstSpillChar=substr $spill, 0, 1;

                if ($firstSpillChar eq " ") {
                        $offset=1
                        }
                else {
                        $offset=0
                        }
                $init=substr $spill, $offset
                }
        } #End of sub ProcessDisplayName
###
#
sub ProcessEMAddresses {

        #Breakdown EMAddresses to give the SMTP address

        $status=DecomposeEMA();

        ($label,$rfc822)=split /:/,$smtp;

        ($lhs,$rhs)=split /@/,$rfc822;

        #Rebuild the SMTP address component of E-Mail Addresses with new
        #first and last name values we've just determined

        $lhs=join '.',$fn,$ln;
        $rfc822=join '@',$lhs,$rhs;
        $smtp=join ':',$label,$rfc822;
```

```
        $status=BuildEMA();

    } #End sub ProcessEMAddresses
###
#
sub DecomposeEMA {

        #The Exchange export may deliver address with variable
        #EMA attributes or in no fixed order, so we need to ID them here

        $msa="";
        $smtp="";
        $ms="";
        $ccmail="";
        $x400="";

        ($a1,$a2,$a3,$a4,$a5)=split /%/,$emAddresses;

        #This is dirty, but it works...

        if ((grep /MSA:/, $a1) ne 0) {$msa=$a1}
        if ((grep /SMTP:/, $a1) ne 0) {$smtp=$a1}
        if ((grep /MS:/, $a1) ne 0) {$ms=$a1}
        if ((grep /CCMAIL:/, $a1) ne 0) {$ccmail=$a1}
        if ((grep /X400:/, $a1) ne 0) {$x400=$a1}

        if ((grep /MSA:/, $a2) ne 0) {$msa=$a2}
        if ((grep /SMTP:/, $a2) ne 0) {$smtp=$a2}
        if ((grep /MS:/, $a2) ne 0) {$ms=$a2}
        if ((grep /CCMAIL:/, $a2) ne 0) {$ccmail=$a2}
        if ((grep /X400:/, $a2) ne 0) {$x400=$a2}

        if ((grep /MSA:/, $a3) ne 0) {$msa=$a3}
        if ((grep /SMTP:/, $a3) ne 0) {$smtp=$a3}
        if ((grep /MS:/, $a3) ne 0) {$ms=$a3}
        if ((grep /CCMAIL:/, $a3) ne 0) {$ccmail=$a3}
        if ((grep /X400:/, $a3) ne 0) {$x400=$a3}

        if ((grep /MSA:/, $a4) ne 0) {$msa=$a4}
        if ((grep /SMTP:/, $a4) ne 0) {$smtp=$a4}
        if ((grep /MS:/, $a4) ne 0) {$ms=$a4}
        if ((grep /CCMAIL:/, $a4) ne 0) {$ccmail=$a4}
        if ((grep /X400:/, $a4) ne 0) {$x400=$a4}
```

```
        if ((grep /MSA:/, $a5) ne 0) {$msa=$a5}
        if ((grep /SMTP:/, $a5) ne 0) {$smtp=$a5}
        if ((grep /MS:/, $a5) ne 0) {$ms=$a5}
        if ((grep /CCMAIL:/, $a5) ne 0) {$ccmail=$a5}
        if ((grep /X400:/, $a5) ne 0) {$x400=$a5}
} #End sub DecomposeEMA
###
#
sub BuildEMA {

        #We'll check for the presence of individual components before
        #building the EMAddresses string, since there's no guarantee
        #they'll all be there for an individual recipient

        $emAddresses="";

        if ($msa ne "") {$emAddresses=$msa}
        if ($smtp ne "") {$emAddresses=join '%', $emAddresses, $smtp}
        if ($ms ne "") {$emAddresses=join '%', $emAddresses, $ms}
        if ($ccmail ne "") $emAddresses=join '%', $emAddresses, $ccmail}
        if ($x400 ne "") $emAddresses=join '%', $emAddresses, $x400}
        } #End sub BuildEMA
###
#
sub ImportUpdatedData {

        #Check for existence of Exch Dir Import Data File

        open MsDirImpData or die "ABORT: Can't find Exchange Import Data file";
        close MsDirImpHeader;

        #Build Exchange Admin command and import updated Ms Entries

        $ExchSrvAdmin=join '\\',$ExchSrvrBinPath,"Admin.exe /I";
        $Command=join '',$ExchSrvAdmin," ",$MsDirImpData, " /O
           ",$MsDirImpOptions;

        $PrintBuffer=join '',"Importing updated MS Entries";
        print $PrintBuffer, "\n";
        $PrintBuffer="This may take some time; please wait...";
        print $PrintBuffer, "\n";

        print $Command, "\n";
```

```
     system($Command);

     } #End sub ImportUpdateddata
###
#
sub Terminate {
     print "\n";
     print "Finished MS Address Update at ";
     print (PrettyTime(), "\n")
     } #End sub Terminate
```

MSEXP.OPT

```
[Export]
ColumnSeparator=09
DirectoryService=ZUNIGA
Container="MS MAIL N"
ExportObject=Remote
InformationLevel=Full
Subcontainers=yes
```

MSEXP.TPL

```
Obj-Class      Display Name      Directory Name      E-Mail Addresses
```

MSIMP.HDR

```
Obj-Class      Mode      Directory Name      First Name      Last Name
          Initials      E-Mail Addresses
```

MSIMP.OPT

```
[Import]
ColumnSeparator=09
DirectoryService=ZUNIGA
Container="MS MAIL N"
InformationLevel=Full
```

Script to Transfer Directory Changes with Locking

This UNIX shell script performs a directory export operation and moves the resulting transactions file to a location that an FTP client can access to get the data.

Although this script is written as a UNIX shell script, it could easily be modified to run under Visual Basic.

```
#!/usr/bin/ksh
#
# /ldsu/sti_exchange_export/run_export
#
# -  Export run for STI Exchange dir information
#
################################################################
#
cd /ldsu/sti_exchange_export
#
# Save old log files
#
mv sti_exchange_export.lg sti_exchange_export.lg1
#
# Run ldsu export function
#
/usr/sbin/ldsu > sti_exchange_export.lg
#
# Now move the export file to the Exchange transfer area
#
# First check that the lock file isn't there...
#
if [ -f /filexfer/sti_exchange_import_pending.lock ] ; then
    #
```

```
        # Last CHANGES weren't imported to Exchange. Delete any new files
        # created and get back to the way we were before this run started,
        # thus abandoning this run.
        #
        echo "Lock File detected, processing abandoned..."
        rm /ldsu/sti_exchange_export/sti_exchange_export_del.dat
        rm /ldsu/sti_exchange_export/sti_exchange_export_add.dat
        rm /ldsu/sti_exchange_export/sti_exchange_export_mfl.new
        #
        # Now we exit and pretend this never happened.
        #
        exit 1
else
        #
        # There is no lock file so the last CHANGES run data has been imported
        # into Exchange.
        # First we'll build the new transaction files for Exchange
        #
        cat sti_exch_exp_hdr sti_exchange_export_del.dat >
                sti_exchange_export_del.csv
        cat sti_exchange_export_del.csv sti_exchange_export_add.dat >
                sti_exchange_export.csv
        cp sti_exchange_export.csv /ldsu/filexfer/sti_exchange_export.csv
        chown filexfer /filexfer/sti_exchange_export.csv
        #
        # Then we'll update the metafiles
        #
        mv sti_exchange_export_mfl.old sti_exchange_export_mfl.held
        mv sti_exchange_export_mfl.new sti_exchange_export_mfl.old
        #
        # Now signal that there's an export waiting
        #
        touch /filexfer/sti_exchange_import_pending.lock
        chown filexfer /filexfer/sti_exchange_import_pending.lock
        chmod 644 /filexfer/sti_exchange_import_pending.lock
        #
        # And we're done.
fi
#
```

Index

File name index

BF0.LOG 102
DBxxxxxx.DAT 93
DIR.EDB 6, 7
EMS_RID.DLL 65
EV0.LOG 101–2
GWART0.MTA 65, 67
GWART1.MTA 65
MTACHECK.EXE 94
MTACHECK.OUT 94
MTACHECK.TXT 94
PRIV.EDB 4
PUB.EDB 4
RPCRT4.DLL 20
WINMAIL.DAT 136

Main index

A

Abstract Syntax Notation One (ASN.1) 106–7
Activation
  schedule 73
  states 73
    and message rerouting 77–78
Active directory
  Windows 2000 and domain models 27
Address
  space
    and connector scope 85
    for the IMS connector 203

structure
  Distinguished Name (DN) 69
  Domain Defined Attribute (DDA) 69
  X.400 O/R (Originator/Recipient) 69
ADMIN.EXE (administrator program)
  directory
    export 292
    import 295
    viewing 292
  and domain relationships 38
  GWART status, checking 65
  home-server attribute 38
  location of 59
  raw mode, executing 59
  and RPCs 20
    domain relationships 38
ALL-IN-1 237, 243
Architecture
  Exchange implementation, factors affecting 16
Attachments
  IMS, control of 212
Authenticated RPC communication
  and NT infrastructure 35

B

Backbones (connecting to)—See *SMTP backbone* and *X.400 backbone*
Backup Domain Controllers (BDCs) 25
Base64 165
Bodypart types (X.400) 118
BP15 bodypart 155
  and MAILbus-400 241